METHODS FOR ASSE
OF FISH PRODUC
IN FRESH WATE

IBP HANDBOOK No. 3

Methods for Assessment of Fish Production in Fresh Waters

Edited by
TIMOTHY BAGENAL

THIRD EDITION

BLACKWELL SCIENTIFIC PUBLICATIONS

OXFORD LONDON EDINBURGH MELBOURNE

Published by Blackwell Scientific Publications Ltd.
Osney Mead, Oxford OX2 0EL
8 John Street, London WC1N 2ES
9 Forrest Road, Edinburgh EH1 2QH
P.O. Box 9, North Balwyn, Victoria, Australia

First published 1968
Reprinted 1970
Second edition 1971
Third edition 1978

British Library Cataloguing in Publication Data

Methods for assessment of fish production in
    fresh waters.—3rd ed.—(International
    Biological Programme.   Handbooks; no. 3).
    1. Fishes, Fresh-water   2. Freshwater
    productivity
    I. Bagenal, Timothy Bracegirdle   II. Series
    597′.05′2632   QL624

ISBN 0–632–00125–9

Distributed in the United States of America by
J.B. Lippincott Company, Philadelphia
and in Canada by
J.B. Lippincott Company of Canada Ltd, Toronto

Printed in Great Britain by
Western Printing Services Ltd, Bristol
Bound by Kemp Hall Bindery
Osney Mead, Oxford

Contents

Contributors

Timothy B. Bagenal Freshwater Biological Association, Windermere Laboratory, The Ferry House, Ambleside, Cumbria, England.

Gordon R. Bell Pacific Biological Station, P.O. Box 100, Nanaimo, B.C., V9R 5K6, Canada.

Stephen H. Bowen Department of Environmental, Population and Organismic Biology, University of Colorado, Boulder, Colorado 80309, U.S.A.

Erich Braum Institut für Hydrobiologie und Fischereiwissenschaft der Universität Hamburg, 2 Hamburg-Altona 1, Federal Republic of Germany.

Donald Wallace Chapman Cooperative Fishery Unit, College of Forestry, University of Idaho, Moscow, Idaho 83843, U.S.A.

John Alan Gulland Department of Fisheries, F.A.O. of United Nations, via delle Terme di Caracalla, 00100-Rome, Italy.

Karl Frank Lagler School of Natural Resources, University of Michigan, Ann Arbor, Michigan 48104, U.S.A.

Lindsay M. Laird* Unit of Aquatic Pathobiology, The University of Stirling, FK9 4LA, Scotland.

Rosemary H. Lowe-McConnell Streatwick, Streat, Via Hassocks, Sussex, England.

* Now at the Zoology Department, The University of Aberdeen, Scotland.

William E. Ricker   Pacific Biological Station, P.O. Box 100, Nanaimo, B.C., V9R 5K6, Canada.

Douglas S. Robson   Biometrics Unit, Warren Hall, Cornell University, Ithaca, New York 14850, U.S.A.

Brian Stott   Salmon and Freshwater Fisheries Laboratory, Ministry of Agriculture, Fisheries and Food, Whitehall Place, London, SW1, England.

Freidrich W. Tesch   Biologische Anstalt Helgoland, 2 Hamburg 50, Federal Republic of Germany.

John T. Windell   Department of Environmental, Population and Orgasmic Biology, University of Colorado, Boulder, Colorado 80309, U.S.A.

W.D. Youngs   Department of Natural Resources, Cornell University, Ithaca, New York 14853, U.S.A.

Contributors to supplementary material

Lloyd M. Dickie   Department of Oceanography, Dalhousie University, Halifax, Nova Scotia, Canada, B3H 3J5.

Thomas D. Iles   Biological Station, St Andrews, New Brunswick, Canada.

Robert G. Werner   Department of Forest Zoology, State University College of Forestry at Syracuse University, New York 13210, U.S.A.

Foreword to first edition

The International Biological Programme is a worldwide plan of research concerned with 'the biological basis of productivity and human welfare'. The handbook series of IBP is for volumes urgently needed by biologists around the world who are participating in the programme. Some volumes, such as No. 1 *Guide to the Human Adaptability Proposals*, deal with a whole section of I B P; others such as No. 2 *Primary Production of Forests*, deal with methods of research in a comparatively narrow branch of the programme. Some of these handbooks are brief, written by one scientist, who has been selected by the international section concerned and has consulted many specialists in the process of drafting. Other volumes, like this one, are larger, with chapters written by a number of different specialists under the guidance of a general editor.

This volume, dealing with fish production, is one of four which are concerned with methods of studying productivity in fresh waters. The others are on methods for assessing primary and secondary productivity and on chemical methods. Fish, being usually at the summit of the food-webs in water, should really follow the other three subjects. The fact that this is the first of the volumes to be published is to the credit of the editor and authors, for only twelve months elapsed between the technical meeting when this handbook was planned and the book going to press.

It must be emphasized that the methods described in this and other handbooks are *recommended* for the purposes of IBP, not *agreed*. To obtain universal agreement on any particular method, if it could be achieved at all, would take a long time. Moreover, it might retard rather than advance biology, because the methodology in a great many subjects within IBP is evolving rapidly. The methods described in these handbooks are recommended to scientists who themselves do not think they have better methods. They provide some guarantee that the results obtained by their use all over the world will be comparable.

A further point of importance is that all IBP handbooks are to some extent provisional. The methods recommended may need alteration as a result of practical experience by numerous workers in the field and the laboratory. Indeed, it is hoped that revised and more definitive editions of these books will be called for before the conclusion of IBP in 1972, and that they will be useful to biologists for many years thereafter.

Nineteen specialists, who bring experience from five different countries, all actively participating in IBP, have contributed to this volume. Its editor, W.E. Ricker received his degrees at the University of Toronto and then did salmon research for some eight years with the Fisheries Research Board of Canada. In 1939 he was appointed Professor of Zoology at Indiana University and in 1950 returned to the Fisheries Research Board of Canada where he is now Chief Scientist.

E.B. WORTHINGTON
Scientific Director
IBP Central Office
7 Marylebone Road
November 1967   London NW1

Preface to third edition

The exhaustion of the stocks of the second edition of this handbook has necessitated that a new edition should be prepared, and it is very sad that Dr W.E. Ricker felt that he did not wish to be involved with editing it yet again. The success of the first two editions is a tribute to his wise counselling, hard work and breadth of knowledge. Several of the original authors also felt that they did not wish to prepare another revision. In some cases a different author has produced a revised chapter based on the original version, and it seemed only reasonable in these cases for the work to be a joint effort. In other cases a completely new chapter has been written.

The advance in fish production methods and the number of papers stimulated by the first two editions are reflected in the increase in the reference list, which now serves also as an index to where the papers are cited. Much of the value of a handbook of this type should lie in its use as a lead in to the literature and I hope this new facility will prove helpful. Another change which will be noticed is the omission of the Table of Exponentials which used to form Appendix 4; the advent of the cheap pocket electronic calculator has reduced the value of this appendix. The general index has also been enlarged.

The Freshwater Biological Association,   T.B. Bagenal
Windermere Laboratory,
Ambleside, Cumbria, England.

Preface to first edition

In April 1965, when meeting in London, the International Committee of the PF Section (Production of Fresh Waters) of the IBP agreed to hold four technical meetings, one of which was to be devoted to freshwater fish production. Shelby D. Gerking was enlisted as organizing chairman for this meeting, and he in turn found enthusiastic support from E. David Le Cren (U.K.) as vice-chairman, K.H. Mann (U.K.) as local organizer, and other members of an organizing committee, namely—F.E.J. Fry (Canada), T. Lindström (Sweden) and T. Backiel (Poland). Initial plans were laid when some members of the committee were in Warsaw in August 1965, and an invitation from the University of Reading to hold the meeting there was gratefully accepted.

The primary object of the IBP/PF Technical Meetings is to prepare handbooks of methods for research for use in IBP/PF projects, but we considered that in the field of fish production it would be appropriate to enlarge our aims to include a review of the present status of research into freshwater fish production and what the perspectives of IBP projects in this field should be. Accordingly the meeting was divided into two parts. A symposium on various aspects of freshwater fish production was held on September 1–6, 1966. This consisted of twenty-one papers by invited contributors on (1) vital statistics of fish populations, (2) relationships between fish populations and their food, (3) competition and behaviour, and (4) predation and exploitation by Man; while a final paper forecast the contribution that freshwater fish might make to human nutrition over the next thirty years. This symposium was open to observers and 146 persons from nineteen countries attended, many of whom took part in the lively discussions. The Proceedings of this symposium, under the title 'The Biological Basis of Freshwater Fish Production', edited by Shelby D. Gerking, have been published in 1967.

For two days before and two days after this symposium a working party of nineteen assembled this handbook of methods. Each chapter was solicited from an expert in that particular aspect and most of these were available as drafts at the start of the working party sessions. Informal groups worked on revising and editing each chapter and integrating one with another. The whole working party met together to discuss general problems and especially symbols and terminology. It is a pleasure to record the good will and hard work shown by the members of the working party, many of whom prepared chapters at very short notice and then cheerfully put up with having them rewritten by their colleagues. W.E. Ricker kindly agreed to act as editor of the handbook and his experience, guidance and hard work have been of great value in bringing the project to a successful conclusion.

In our planning we had in mind the importance of making both the handbook and the symposium truly co-operative international ventures that would draw on a world wide experience of tropical as well as temperate fish populations. Although sponsored by the PF Section, we also invited some contributors from those whose work had been in the marine field; most of the basic problems in fish production are unaffected by the salt content of the water. In these aims we were greatly assisted by the wide range of experience, tropical and temperate, marine and freshwater, that was contributed by the total attendance at the meeting.

In organizing this project Shelby D. Gerking held prime responsibility, initiated the planning, invited the contributors to the symposium. David Le Cren enlisted the contributors to the handbook and acted as chairman during its sessions. Julian Rzóska, Scientific Co-ordinator of IBP/PF, was a constant help throughout the planning and the meeting itself. We are indebted to him, to the Special Committee for the IBP, to the United Kingdom National IBP Committee, to the Food and Agriculture Organization of the United Nations, and to the Fisheries Research Board of Canada for financial and other assistance, without which the meeting could not have been held, nor this handbook published. The Organizing Committee wishes to extend special thanks to the University of Reading for its hospitality and especially to the staff of Wessex Hall where the participants were housed and the working party met. We also wish to thank K.E. Marshall for the help given in checking the references.

This handbook is aimed at those younger biologists who, while having basic university training in zoology and some knowledge of ecology and freshwater biology, have no special experience in research on fish. It is hoped that with the aid of this handbook (and access to some of the literature cited in it) such biologists will be able to carry out worthwhile and rewarding researches in the field of fish production in any part of the world.

It is hoped that the handbook may be of use in training fishery biologists for work not only inside IBP but also in wider contexts such as the technical assistance programmes sponsored by FAO and other agencies. More advanced workers too may find parts of the handbook, and especially the references, helpful in indicating methods in aspects lying outside their normal experience. The book as a whole may also stimulate interest in this field of biology and serve to suggest to academic zoologists the breadth of problems existing in fish ecology and the intellectual challenges involved in tackling them.

The authors of any handbook are confronted with the dilemma of describing methods that will yield comparable data without dictating a rigid methodology which would discourage originality. A conscious effort has been made, therefore, to avoid presenting 'cookbook' techniques; and the reader will usually find more than one method described for accomplishing an objective together with the limitations and advantages of each. Terminology and mathematical symbols have received special attention and here the advantages of a consistent system have been considered to outweigh any disadvantages of dogma.

Over the next few years new methods will be perfected and the results of new researches continue to be published. IBP will therefore be grateful for suggestions for improvements in case a second edition is called for. Correspondence should be addressed to Dr J. Rzóska, Scientific Co-ordinator PF, IBP Central Office, 7 Marylebone Road, London NW1, England.

Department of Zoology,   Shelby D. Gerking
Arizona State University,
Tempe, Arizona, U.S.A.

Freshwater Biological Association,   E. David Le Cren
The River Laboratory,
Wareham, Dorset, U.K.

1

Introduction

W E RICKER

The production process

Organic materials are *produced* by biological activity, in natural or artificial environments. Some of them are *harvested* by man, to be used for his own biological or industrial needs. What is produced is the *production*, what man harvests is the *yield*. Either term must be applied to a clearly defined *product—* that is, a particular kind of group of organisms, or a particular kind or group of organic compounds.

Production in any major ecosystem begins with photosynthesis. It continues by way of a maze of food-chains whose most obvious products are successive stocks of organisms that typically increase in individual size as they decrease in total bulk. Equally important for the system as a whole are the micro-organisms that flourish on the dead plants and animals at every stage, and in turn serve as the platform for a new ascent up the food pyramid.

It is customary and convenient to divide the production process into several stages. *Primary production* is for practical purposes equivalent to photosynthesis. *Secondary production*, strictly speaking is production of organisms that feed on green plants, but it is difficult to separate these from feeders on detritus and bacteria; hence the general term *intermediate production*, usually applied to the production of invertebrates of all sorts, but especially to the smaller invertebrates.

Fish production, the subject of the present handbook, is defined with respect to a particular category of animals. The term *tertiary production* is sometimes used with the same meaning, but it is not very appropriate because the foods consumed by even a single species of fish may stand at one, two or several removes from the original green plants; or in some cases fish eat the plants themselves. The methods described here can also be applied to animals that are either 'higher' or 'lower' than fish in the usual classification.

Terminal production is a related concept, defined as the production of organisms directly used by man, such as whales, ducks, turtles, frogs or lobsters, in addition to fish.

In undertaking a study of production of a fish population it is first necessary to capture some fish. Chapter 2 tells how this may be done, and the precautions made necessary by the fact that practically all methods of fishing are selective. Next one must know what kind of fish one is dealing with. Chapter 3 reviews the present state of knowledge of fish faunas in different parts of the world, and gives references to aid in their identification. Having selected a population or stock of a particular fish species for study, the next step is to determine its distribution and its size. One popular technique for determining both of these is that of marking members of the population (Chapter 4), but other approaches are also possible (Chapter 6). The growth rate of the fish in this stock must then be determined (Chapter 5), and also mortality rates at successive life-history stages (Chapter 6). A stock gains new recruits from the reproductive activity of its mature members, which is usually accompanied by a high mortality rate among the very young individuals (Chapter 7).

With these data a calculation of production becomes possible (Chapter 8). The production in any stock depends directly upon the kinds and amounts of food that it consumes (Chapters 9 and 10). Finally, better understanding of factors controlling production will come from an examination of causes of natural mortality in the population (Chapter 11), and also of the effects of any fishery that may be in progress (Chapter 12).

While man's harvest is not the primary concern of this handbook, it is usually implied that yield statistics will be available. They may provide material for determining the production itself, and are needed in order to estimate the degree of man's utilization of the production of a fish population or of an ecosystem.

Definitions of concepts involved in production

The main symbols and concepts concerning biological production used in this handbook are listed below. They are taken, with a little adaptation to fit the particular organism, from the list of terms approved for use by the I B P. The order of presentation is more or less in the time sequence of the production process.

N *Population* (size)—a defined set (number) of individuals; also called *stock*.

w Weight of an individual.

w̄　Average weight of the individuals in a population.

B　*Biomass*—amount of substance in a population, expressed in material units such as living or 'wet' weight (=*Nw̄*), dry weight, ash-free weight, nitrogen content, etc; also called *standing crop*.

B　*Biocontent*—amount of substance in a population, expressed in energy units.

The following may be measured in terms of either matter or energy:

C　*Consumption* (=*P*+*R*+*F*+*U*)—total intake of food by a population of heterotrophic organisms during a specified time interval.

F　*Egesta*—that part of the total food intake which is not digested (or at any rate not absorbed), and leaves the alimentary canal. Also called *faeces*.

　　Absorption (=*C*−*F*)—that part of the food that is absorbed into the body through the wall of the alimentary canal.

U　*Excreta*—that part of the material absorbed which is passed from the body either in the urine or through the gills or skin (this does not include reproductive products).

　　Rejecta (=*F*+*U*)—egesta plus excreta.

A　*Assimilation* (=*R*+*P*=*C*−*F*−*U*)—the food absorbed less the excreta. Also called *physiologically useful energy* (or substance).

R　*Respiration*—that part of assimilation which is converted to heat or mechanical energy and is used up in life processes.

P　*Production* (1) (=*C*−*F*−*U*−*R*=*KC*)—increase in biomass (or biocontent); this includes any reproductive products released during the period concerned. (*K* is the utilization coefficient, or coefficient of growth.)

P　*Production* (2)—as above, except that released reproductive products are not included. Also called *growth*, particularly when a single individual is under consideration rather than a population.

Y　*Yield*—that portion of production which is used by man.

Notice that in estimating the above for a population during a stated interval of time Δ*t*, it is necessary to include the amount of *C*, *F*, *P*, etc. that occurred in the fish which died during Δ*t* as well as that in the fish surviving to the end of Δ*t*.

A more complete list of the symbols used in the handbook is given in Appendix I.

Productive relationships in an ecosystem

Fish production is of course only one aspect of the total production process in a body of water. Primary and intermediate production in fresh waters are the subject of separate IBP handbooks. But since fish production is often the end process from man's point of view, it is appropriate to say something here about production in the ecosystem as a whole.

A theoretical scheme developed by Bruevich (1939), Juday (1940), G.E. Hutchinson, Lindeman (1942), Ivlev (1945, 1966), Macfadyen (1948) and others pictures an ideal ecosystem with its organisms arranged in a series of *levels* corresponding to the steps in a food pyramid. When one organism consumes another, the latter's substance and energy is transferred (partly!) from level n to level $n + 1$. To trace the flow of matter or energy from primary photosynthesis up to a given fish product, it is necessary at each stage to determine the degree of utilization of organisms on one level by an organism on the next higher one—Ivlev's (1945) ecotrophic coefficient.* This (dynamic) ecotrophic coefficient ε_{n+1} is the fraction of the production of an organism on level n that is consumed by an organism on level $n + 1$ during a specified time interval Δt. Putting $n = 1$ for simplicity:

$$\varepsilon_2 = \frac{C_2}{P_1} \tag{1}$$

For this relationship to be meaningful it is necessary that Δt be a fairly long time interval, typically a year, so that short-term or seasonal fluctuations in production and consumption are evened out.

The simplest possible fish-producing ecosystem would perhaps be a pond containing vegetation (phytoplankton, filamentous algae or pondweeds) that is eaten by one species of edible fish. This provides a direct utilization of green plants, comparable to cattle cropping the grass on a range or pasture. As on the range, the severity of cropping by the fish may affect the size of the plant's biomass and amount of its production. The fish may also affect primary production indirectly if the waste products of their metabolism are used again by the plants, after intermediate bacterial activity. Presumably there is an optimum intermediate level of fish stock and hence of cropping

---

*The term ecotrophic coefficient was proposed by Ivlev and is applied by him to two related but distinct concepts. I have distinguished these as the 'static' and 'dynamic' ecotrophic coefficients (see Ivlev 1966, p. 1747, footnote). Only the dynamic ecotrophic coefficient is involved here.

at which plant production P_1 is fairly large and the ecotrophic coefficient ε_2 also fairly large, their product C_2 being a maximum. In any event the fish biomass produced is equal to P_1 multiplied by the ecotrophic coefficient ε and by the utilization coefficient K:

$$P_2 = C_2 K = P_1 \varepsilon_2 K \tag{2}$$

An approximation to such a simple system may exist in the pond culture of such species as milkfish, grass carp or silver carp, if the main food is provided by a single species (or group of similar species) of plant. If plants of different types are consumed, then a corresponding number of utilization efficiencies are involved. For example, the expression for fish production involving three plant foods is:

$$P_2 = K[P_1(1)\varepsilon_2(1) + P_1(2)\varepsilon_2(2) + P_1(3)\varepsilon_2(3)] \tag{3}$$

Plant-eating fishes are not particularly common. More typically, fish production involves at least two stages of consumption, each with its own values of ε and K. Consider a system with only one species on each level: say a fish which consumes a cladoceran which consumes a phytoplankter. In this case there are separate ecotrophic coefficients for each stage:

$$\varepsilon_2 = \frac{C_2}{P_1}; \quad \varepsilon_3 = \frac{C_3}{P_2} \tag{4}$$

The production of the fish, on level 3, becomes:

$$P_3 = P_1 \varepsilon_2 K_2 \varepsilon_3 K_3 \tag{5}$$

This is still an extremely simple system, and even in principle it is an unlikely one. For once a filter feeder (the cladoceran) is introduced, it opens the door for 'recycling'; that is, bacteria that live on dead plant and animal materials coming from any level are available as food for level 2. This immediately destroys the linearity of the system, and introduces a rather formidable complexity into a situation consisting of even a bare minimum of organisms. Nevertheless this complexity must be quantitatively analysed if we are to understand aquatic production.

The practical value of information on the productive process will be as a basis for redirecting production along lines that will produce more usable fish, or relatively more fish of superior flavour or nutritive value. As Ivlev (1945) has emphasized, investigators must be alert to recognize patterns and principles (*zakonomernosti*) that may be common to different stocks. Only in this way will the great complexity of the production processes leading to useful fishes be approximated by a limited number of reproducible quantitative relationships, which in turn will open the door for rational intervention and control.

2

Capture, Sampling and Examination of Fishes

KARL F LAGLER

Background

The key to the assessment of fish production is knowledge of the fish stock—its specific taxonomy, number of individuals, sex- and year-class composition, and the rates of growth, mortality, and recruitment. Such knowledge derives from the study of captured individuals. The investigator will either set out to catch the fish himself or he will use the landings of fishermen, often at fishery ports. In either event, as in most methods of capture*, the individuals taken comprise a sample that is usually very small in relation to the whole population; often it is only a fraction of one per cent of the total. Furthermore, samples from most environments are drawn blind with little or no study of the response of the fishes to sampling gears and without precisely replicable sampling methods.

All of the common problems of sampling error and bias must be faced by the fishery production biologist. They demand of him fullest possible understanding of habitats and habits of the fishes to be sampled, and of the construction, operation and selectivity of sampling gear.

Four truisms emerge: (1) most fish capture methods are selective, among other things, with respect to species and size of individual, often sex as well; (2) soundness of sampling procedure has too often been assumed and has too seldom been evaluated experimentally; (3) vast opportunities remain for discovering and developing new methods; (4) there is no substitute for operational experience in fish capture (reading this chapter will not suffice).

The sampling methods to be employed and the representativeness of the sample

*Capture is here used in the broad sense of meaning any intentional contact by the investigator with a fish that is useful for identification, the procurement of quantitative data, etc. Thus it embraces the gamut of contact methods from simple visual observation and those many and often cumbersome ones that put the fish in hand through sophisticated applications of remote sensing devices.

depend on the care and thoroughness with which the following six basic tenets are applied, and on the care with which the investigation plan has been made and its components scheduled.

Tenet 1. Know the hydrography (shape of the basin and characteristics of the water). Concentrate on the identification of all the possible habitats that may be sampled because this will largely determine the choice of gear. A good map of bottom contours is almost indispensable. Features to be considered include shoreline, depths, inlets, outlets, bottom type, cover, shelter, obstructions, chemical and thermal stratification, and any other factors that may affect distribution of fishes and operation of gear. Accurate location of fish-capture stations also requires a good hydrographic map and, in large bodies of water, classical or electronic (e.g. LORAN A-C) aids to navigation (Rustad *et al.* 1961).

Tenet 2. Know the fish. Make sure that taxonomic classification is as accurate and complete as possible (see Chapter 3). Centre attention at time of sampling on the probable distribution of the fishes by habitats and by life history stages. Use exploratory fishing to test assumptions concerning such distribution. If possible, couple the use of electronic fish finding apparatus with the selection of fishing gear and the positioning of effort. Modify and adjust methods in order to maximize gear efficiency relative to the habits of the fishes and their responses to fishing gear. Take advantage of movements, migrations, spawning and other behaviour which may concentrate a population and make adequate sampling easier, or use attractants, stimulants or anesthetics for the same purpose.

Tenet 3. Know fishing methods. In view of the great diversity of fish species and habitats in continental waters, the sampler of fish populations should know both old and new methods of fishing. Existing compendia of gear and methods* are of great value here, although they tend to be encyclopedic and usually lack comment on efficiency and limitations. An investigator should

*The most comprehensive recent work is the 3-volume *Modern Fishing Gear of the World*, Ed. Kristjonsson (Fishing News (Books) Ltd, London. Vol. 1, 1959; Vol. 2, 1964; Vol. 3, 1972). Some representative regional compendia on methods of fish capture are the following: California (Scofield 1951a); Caribbean (Whiteleather & Brown 1945); Europe (von Brandt 1964); Japan (Kask & Hiyama 1947); Korea (Park 1963); North Dakota (Corning 1957); Philippines (Umali 1950); United States (Goode *et al.* 1884–87); World (Nédélec 1975; Scharfe 1972).

also watch for unusual advantages that may be gained from advanced applications of remote sensing, from local variations in the construction or use of classical gear, or from fishing methods locally invented.

Too often a sampling programme must be or is undertaken fortuitously with 'available' gear, instead of being carefully planned to take advantage of the best possible fishing methods. This limited practice is to be avoided.

An important part of any method is that the gear be maintained in top working condition*; otherwise its inherent limitations of efficiency and selectivity may be magnified.

Tenet 4. Know the selectivity of the gear†. Since most fishing operations are selective, the catch is not representative of the population as a whole. Selectivity results from extrinsic factors (such as construction of the gear and the method of its operation), from intrinsic factors (such as behavioural differences among or within species according to sex, size, habits, time or season of fishing, etc.), or from the interaction of such factors.

To evaluate gear selectivity, the first step is to compare the length frequency distributions of the catches made by different kinds of gear fished in the same waters. One may compare, for example, the catches of trawls and gill nets, or of trawls with different mesh sizes in the cod end, or of gill nets of different materials and/or mesh sizes. When the length composition of the catch of the two gears differs, selection by at least one of the gears is manifest. It is also useful to compare catches by the same gear, made at different places or times, for selection is partly a function of the distribution and habits of the fish.

The size selectivity of a gear may be defined by a curve giving for each size of fish the proportion of the total population of that size which is caught and retained by a unit operation of the gear. For bag-type nets such as *trawls* and *seines*, an important part of selection is the escape of small fish through the meshes of the bag or cod end. The proportion of small fish escaping can be measured by putting a small-meshed cover over the cod end (details in Pope 1966). A typical curve thus obtained is shown in Fig. 2.1, where the ordinate is the percentage of each entering size group that is retained in the cod end. If the probability of a fish entering the net were the same for all sizes, this

---

*Useful references on the repair and construction of nets include: Ludgate (1948), U.S. Fish and Wildlife Service (1952), Carrothers (1957), Garner (1962), Gebhards (1960), Knake (1947), Knudsen (1966), and *Modern Fishing Gear of the World*, Ed. Kristjonsson, H.

†The essential guide for the detection and evaluation of selectivity of gear is Pope (1966). The material presented here is adapted from this source.

curve would be the selection curve of the gear: it would show the fraction of the fish of each size that is caught by the trawl, relative to the fraction of the biggest fish caught.

A typical selection curve for a *gill net* is shown in Fig. 2.2, where selectivity is expressed relative to the size of fish for which the gear is most effective. Methods of estimating the parameters of this curve by using mixed fleets (gangs) of gill nets have been developed (Baranov 1948; Art. 47, Holt 1957; Olsen 1959; McCombie & Fry 1960; Garrod 1959; Regier & Robson 1966). Most of these methods depend on the assumption that the selection curve is normal (Gaussian), although marked departures from normality have been observed for fish like lake trout that tangle easily by their teeth, or for fish of unusual shape (Gulland & Harding 1961). Other difficulties of interpretation occur when the spread (standard deviation) of the curve differs as between nets of different mesh sizes or of different materials. Particularly troublesome is the situation where nets of different mesh sizes differ in efficiency even at their 'best' fish size. For example, because of greater mobility a big fish may be more likely to encounter and be caught by a net with the most appropriate mesh than is a small fish to be caught by the most appropriate smaller mesh.

Estimates of selectivity obtained by comparison of catches of gears that differ only in mesh size (or hook size, etc.) will only give a partial estimate of selectivity. They measure only the component of selectivity due to characteristics of the gear and directly related fish behaviour, and not that due to differences in fish distribution. A qualitative indication of the latter can sometimes be obtained by comparing the length composition of catches from two completely different gears, or of the same gear set in different places or at different times, but there is no general procedure for obtaining quantitative estimates in this way.

Generally speaking, for a quantitative estimate of overall selectivity it is necessary to release marked fish into a population, covering the size range of all of the individuals naturally present and using different marks for successive length intervals. Provided there is no differential mortality or differential loss of marks by fish of different sizes, the differences in the proportions of different length groups recaptured by any particular gear provide a direct measure of its selectivity. Marking methods are discussed in Chapter 4.

When the selectivity of a gear has been estimated, the length composition of the population can be estimated from that of its catch, by dividing the number caught in each length group by the appropriate selectivity factor. This

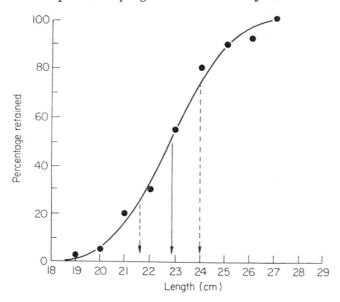

Figure 2.1. Trawl mesh selection curve for haddock, from Pope (1966, Fig. 1).

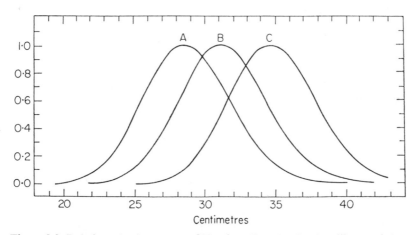

Figure 2.2. Relative selection curves of Newfoundland herring by gill nets of three sizes, after Olsen (1959, p. 336). A, 59·7 mm stretched mesh; B, 65·1 mm; C, 72·5 mm. *Ordinate*—capturing efficiency as a fraction of the maximum for each mesh. *Abscissa*—total length of the herring.

method widens the length range over which the catches of any one gear can be used to give acceptable information about the population. Care must be exercised near the ends of the selection curve, for here errors in estimates of selectivity tend to make population estimates quite uncertain.

Computations of this type can be reduced and accuracy improved by using combinations of sampling gear designed to make the combined selection curve more nearly flat. For instance, individual gill nets are highly selective, but a fleet of mixed gill nets with different mesh sizes at specified intervals will take much more nearly equal proportions of the fish of a wide range of sizes. Thus Ricker (1949) showed that a gang of gill nets of 11 different sizes from 38 to 127 mm stretched mesh captured whitefish of all sizes from 51 to 33 cm fork length equally well, but from 33 to 18 cm catchability declined gradually to about 30%. Mesh sizes in mixed gangs of gill nets have sometimes been chosen at equal arithmetic intervals, but because of this decline in vulnerability at small fish sizes it is usually better to use equal geometric intervals—for example, a gang of nets with meshes of 50, 65, 85, 110, 145, 190 mm, etc. (Regier & Robson 1967).

Selection is most often thought of in terms of length but may also be considered in relation to sex, age, maturity, etc. Some of these features are closely related to length. The problem of selection for different ages could be tackled directly, but it will usually be easier to stratify the sampling for age by length classes (Ketchen 1950). That is, the true length composition of the population is estimated, corrected for gear selection as well as possible, and samples from each length group are then taken to establish the relation between age and length. This procedure assumes that, for example, among fish of the same size, a 4-year-old is as likely to be captured as is a 5-year-old.

The above assumption need not always hold, for example if growth rate is correlated with fatness, so that the smaller fish of a given age tend to be slimmer than the larger ones or vice versa; for a gill net of a given size is more likely to retain the fatter individuals among the shorter fish it encounters, and the thinner individuals among the longer fish. This type of selection is particularly important when estimating the length–weight relationship (Chapter 5) or when determining the onset of maturity.

Where commercial or sporting catch records are to be used as indices of population structure and density, not only must the gear selectivity be known, but appropriate steps must be taken to adjust for it.

Tenet 5. Know how to sample a catch and maintain up-to-the-minute records

of sample composition. One aspect of representative sampling has been treated under gear selectivity above. An easier but by no means simple problem is that of taking samples from large catches of fish caught by commercial or sporting gear.

A very common characteristic of catches is 'clumping' of individuals by size. This may, of course, reflect gear selectivity. Such clumping can be discerned promptly in the field when a current size-frequency analysis is maintained for fish entering the sample. Clumping or skewness of the plot should immediately suggest that additional collection methods might be engaged to compensate for the selectivity of the original gear, and for efficiency, that the method yielding the clump be abandoned promptly when it has provided enough specimens for reliable analysis in its range of selection.

It is often impossible to take data on all of the specimens captured by experimental means or from commercial catches, whether on shipboard, or at landings, or elsewhere. Since the total mass of specimens at hand on a given day (say) is regarded as a sample, selection of smaller groups for examination is usually called subsampling. In subsampling, the objective is to obtain data free from any systematic bias due to the sampling procedure. Commonly, subsampling has been resorted to for data on length, weight, sex, scale or bone specimens for age determination, stage of sexual maturity, stomach contents, pathology, degree of deterioration, and other similar characteristics. Even the species composition of the catch may be estimated by subsampling, though this may present special problems. Acceptable procedures for subsampling are outlined by Gulland (1966), and what follows is largely drawn from that source.

The basic statistical concept of all sampling, including subsampling is randomness. Two practical means for securing a random sample from a large mass of fish specimens of one species are (1) to employ random numbers, or (2) to use a system of stratified sampling.

Tables of random numbers are included in many statistical texts (e.g. Fisher & Yates 1949; Snedecor & Cochran 1967). All of the individual specimens are considered in sequence, and those to be examined are determined from the table. For example, if a sample of 5 is to be taken from a population of 100, and the first five 2-digit random numbers in the table are 03, 43, 37, 73 and 00, the 3rd, 43rd, 37th, 73rd and 100th specimens would be used. On a wider scale, the times or places at which catches are to be examined may be selected using random numbers, as has been done in obtaining statistics of the coastal fisheries of India.

Stratified random sampling is particularly useful when the large sample is already separated into units (for example, catches taken in successive net hauls) that are known or suspected to differ in respect to the character being examined. Each of these units is then a stratum to be sampled independently by the system of random numbers. Estimates of mean values of length, for example, in each stratum can be combined (weighting each as the size of the stratum) to give the estimate for the whole population. An example is Ketchen's (1950) stratified estimate of age composition, mentioned earlier. Proportional stratified sampling (when variances within strata are equal) typically minimizes variability. It can also be used to provide adequate information about rare components without giving excessive attention to common types.

Optimization of sampling procedures is best achieved through previous detailed knowledge of characteristics of the population to which the procedures are to be applied. This can best be done if at the beginning considerable general information is obtained about the population, and if the sampling procedures that are to be applied are first evaluated statistically.

Tenet 6. Know how to handle records and specimens. Data on good samples become worthless when garbled with inconsistencies and omissions. Specimens are useless if improperly preserved. Uniformity, clarity, and precision are needed. Give well-considered reasons for, and good descriptions of, any techniques that depart from conventional ones well described in the literature (Laevastu 1965).

Compare likes with likes. For example, weights and other measurements on fresh specimens are seldom interchangeable with those on chemically embalmed or frozen specimens. To make differently-obtained data comparable may require extensive use of conversion factors.

The limits of precision in techniques and instruments used in measuring and counting must be established and recorded.

Data collected in field sampling for laboratory studies should be recorded and stored in a manner that maximizes the efficiency of subsequent tabulations and analyses. Electronic devices for sorting, tabulating, computing and collating can save years of human labour. Advance consultation with a machine programmer or statistician is desirable in order to design field sheets or books so that data can be transferred readily to punch cards or magnetic tapes.

Collecting and recording data in a manner adapted to machine processing is recommended wherever possible. There are available at computer centres many machine programs for data analysis, including analysis of covariance, regression analysis, population estimation, yield equations, and production estimation (Holt 1964). These programs can be readily adapted for many applications with minor effort by a machine programmer.

For small bodies of data or where no computer is available, an alternative to machine punch cards is the key-sort card. Field data from original sheets or forms are transferred to the key-sort card, preferably at the end of each day or other frequent intervals. Coded positions for data items are chosen and are punched on the cards. Cards punched in any given position will fall out when a needle is run through the stack of cards, then lifted and shaken.

The basic sample (e.g. a gill net catch) might require one card on which would be hand punched, in proper position and code, the date, location, orientation and depth of set, hours of set, bottom type, water temperature, light conditions, mesh size, number of each species taken, location in the net of each species, and other pertinent data. One card per fish can eventually carry a great deal of information.

The key-sort card method permits simple correlations of a number of samples by coded positions. Punching daily samples at the end of each field day also will help assure that data items are not forgotten, and also that omitted or illegible items will be salvaged. If suitably dimensioned cards are used (approximating playing cards), rapid sorting is possible even without recourse to any punch system.

Whether or not machine processing or hand key cards are used, much labour, and also possible errors or omissions, can be avoided by using a field or laboratory data form containing labelled blanks for all basic information to be collected. Several samples are shown in Lagler (1956). Careful design of the field form will minimize recording errors as well as ease the transfer of field data to punch cards. The form could be of pocket or notebook size, and should be on water-resistant paper or plastic. It may be designed so that certain data can be added after field work is completed. The data form must be revised as necessary to eliminate collection of data not needed and to assure that all important information is obtained.

Fatigue from routine data collection is one source of error. The use of carefully designed field or laboratory data forms will reduce this error.

To avoid loss of unusual information or supplementary data, users of field or laboratory blanks should always keep in mind the possible great value of data and observations not called for on the blanks, and should enter this under 'Remarks'. To prevent loss of routine data, a system of maintaining duplicates (by office copying machine, microfilm, etc.) is important.

Capture of fishes

The methods by which fish may be captured or otherwise sampled in production studies are legion (Table 2.1). They have evolved almost from the dawn of man, and innovations continue. Even today, on a worldwide basis, the use spectrum ranges from the most primitive to the very sophisticated. It

TABLE 2.1. Outline of general categories of methods of fish capture. (The methods currently most effective and widely used are preceded by an asterisk. See also Table 2.2)

Handling

Yielding fish alive	*Yielding fish dead*
Removal of water (as by *drawdown or pumping)	Removal of water
Anaesthesia	*Chemofishing
Hook-and-line fishing (angling, long-lining, trolling)	Hook-and-line fishing
Hand capture	Spearing, gaffing
Concussion (stunning effect)	Concussion (rupturing effect)
*Electrofishing	Electrocution
Active netting (dip nets, *seines, *trawls)	Active netting (*trawls)
Passive netting (gill nets or trammel nets when run continuously)	Passive netting (*gill nets, *trammel nets)
Impounding (*traps, weirs, set-back or swing nets)	

Sensing

Direct sensing (by fish watching, skin or free diving with or without snorkel, *SCUBA, or helmet, or by observing from aircraft or from submerged chambers or underwater craft)

Remote sensing (photography; television; radar; sonar; 'electric-eye'; infra-red)

Special methods for young fish

(see also Chapter 7)

*Plankton nets and other plankton samplers; fine-mesh handnets, seines and *trawls; weirs; fish stomachs

---

Figure 2.3. Back-pack shocker (a.c.) in use in a small, clear stream, and detail of shocker mounting. Courtesy Colorado Cooperative Fishery Unit.

Figure 2.4. Electrical shocker mounted on a boat for use in lakes or large quiet rivers. Courtesy Missouri Conservation Commission.

Figure 2.5. 'Electric seine' in use. Courtesy Missouri Conservation Commission.

Figure 2.6. Bag seine in operation in a small stream.

Figure 2.8. Surface trawl for capturing young fish, towed from two boats. Courtesy Fisheries Research Institute, University of Washington, Seattle.
Above: trawl extended on land; its mouth is about 3 metres square.
Below: trawl in use in the estuary of the Kvichak River.

Figure 2.10. Sockeye salmon caught in a gill net. Bristol Bay, Alaska. Courtesy
Fisheries Research Institute, University of Washington, Seattle.

Figure 2.11. Lifting a fyke net in Bull Shoals Reservoir, Missouri. Courtesy Missouri Conservation Commission.

Figure 2.13. Measuring, weighing, 'sexing', and taking scales and stomachs from a catch of sunfishes and largemouth bass. Photograph by Jack Van Coevering.

TABLE 2.2. Some principal methods of fish capture and their typical freshwater applications ('X' denotes major utility; 'm' denotes minor utility)

Habitat	Poisons	Electro-fishing	Shore seines	Offshore seines (surround nets)	Trawls Bottom	Trawls Midwater	Trawls Surface	Gill nets	Trammel nets	Hoop-fyke nets	Traps
Small streams	X	X	X	—	—	—	m	—	—	m	X
Large rivers	X[1*]	X	X	—	—	—	m	X	X	X	X
Lakes:											
Shoals	—	X	X	—	m	m	m	—	—	—	—
Surface	—	—	—	X	—	X	X	X	X	X	m
Midwater	—	—	—	—	X	—	—	X	X	—	—
Bottom	—	—	—	—	X	—	—	X	X	—	X

[1*]Generally applies to small bodies of water, up to about 500 ha, or to bays and arms of larger lakes.

B

would be impossible here to catalogue all fishing methods, even though this might bring about deeper understanding and hasten needed improvements. Rather, what follows is a guide to major categories of gear, methods of using them, and their known or suspected limitations, including selectivity. Methods of fish sampling that are widely usable are described below: the haul seine, certain trapping devices, purse seine, trawl, hook-and-line, gill net, and trammel net. These include the most important methods of commercial fishing.

In some procedures of population and production study, it is required that the fish be alive after capture. Table 2.1 is a list of categories of capture methods, partly given in two columns to show whether the method will *usually* yield live specimens or dead ones. When a method is listed in both columns, it may provide either dead *or* live specimens depending on the circumstances, or a mixture of both. The applications of the principal methods in common habitats are summarized in Table 2.2.

Direct sensing

Direct sensing of fishes by sight, literally fish watching, from above the water's surface, or beneath it, is useful for identification and in some situations can be used for counting or for estimating abundance. It is also useful for observing gear performance and fish behaviour in relation to fishing method. Fish watching can be improved by using polaroid eye-glasses or binocular field glasses above the water, and diving gear beneath it. Visual contacts from above the water may also be facilitated by the use of observation towers to extend the area of vision and to reduce daytime glare interference.

Turbidity in inland waters greatly limits many possible applications of direct observation. Generally least turbid are headwater streams and biologically young (oligotrophic) lakes. The tolerances of man also limit applications; as a result, knowledge gained by direct observation is meagre for night time, for uncomfortable climatic or weather conditions, and for waters containing vicious animals (such as crocodiles) or parasites (such as the trematodes causing schistosomiasis, including the dread bilharziasis).

Diving gear may be a simple face mask or goggles, or for prolonging observation periods, an air-breathing tube (snorkel) may be added. Further extension of underwater watching time derives from mechanical diving gear such as self-contained underwater breathing apparatus (scuba) or breathing helmets. Insulation of the body by wet- or dry-type diving suits extends the usefulness of diving methods into very cold water. Improved underwater lights have increased night-time observations; submersed floodlights aid direct observation from above the water in the darkness when the air is still.

Underwater observation chambers may provide maximum comfort and now range from simple, fixed tanks that may be entered directly from the surface, through stationary, self-contained, completely submersed laboratories, to self-propelled miniature submarines (several useful references are in volumes of *Geo-Marine Technology* and in *The Seahorse*, both from 1965 on). From some types of submersibles it is now possible to collect samples of both the living and non-living environment.

Remote sensing

Visual observations can be supplemented, augmented, or replaced by several methods of remote sensing (Cushing *et al.* 1952; Huebner 1975). Photography can be adapted to record visible contacts with fish, either when done by the observer or when done automatically or remotely. Television applications to date have included useful evaluations of performance of submersed fishing gear. Both underwater photography and television are, of course, limited by turbidity.

Methods of remote sensing of fish range from primitive taut-wire sensing (a practised hand on a fine heavily-weighted wire can recognize its contacts with fish as it moves slowly through a school) through echo sounding (vertical sound signals), echo ranging (direction variable—sonar and asdic), light beam interruption (electronic-eye), or light wave-length absorption (infrared sensing) to highly-sophisticated hydroacoustic data acquisition and digital data acquisition and digital data analysis for the assessment of fish stock abundance as evidenced by the work of the current FAO *ad hoc* Group of Experts on the Facilitation of Acoustic Research in Fisheries and such references as Moose & Ehrenberg (1971), and Nunnallee (1974). Although for most applications such sensing requires accompanying identification of the fish species involved (Smith & Ahlstrom 1948), it can also be used to determine the abundance of ecological groups of species: for example, fish concentrations at the surface or in the thermocline, middle zone, bottom, and littoral, as done by electronic fish finder or fathometer (Shiraishi & Furuta 1963). A grand-scale acoustic survey to estimate ichthyomass in a fresh-water body is that for Lake Tanganyika where the total standing crop was about 2·8 million tons (Bazigos 1975). Such an acoustic survey has been likened to traffic surveys, and the need remains for the development of 'quality check' surveys of the acoustic surveys.

It is even possible to locate fishes for capture on the basis of knowledge of their thermal preferences—the 'thermometric fish finding' of Dietrich *et al.* (1959)—and also possibly by their chemical exudates (pheromones). Recent refinements in the applications of acoustic telemetry to fish have enabled the extension of capabilities of tracking individuals within populations to the monitoring of physiological parameters including temperature and rate of heart beat (Kanwisher, Lawson & Sundnes 1974, Priede & Young 1977).

Removal of water

Removal of water by such means as drawdown or pumping may be used to strand fish or to concentrate them into an area or enclosure. From either of these situations, they can be recovered alive, if desired, by hand or with simple mechanical lifting devices. This method is the most precise of all for production studies, since it shows the total population (standing crop) at a particular time.

If the fish captured by drawdown are to be kept alive, a temporary holding enclosure is needed for them. Native materials have been used for such enclosures, as have many factory-made tanks, etc. Particularly useful have been fabric 'swimming pools' of plastic or canvas that are collapsible and can thus be readily removed from one drawdown site to another. In artificial drawdowns of dammed ponds, it is often advantageous rapidly to exhaust the volume of water through the control structure. If the drop of water through such a structure is as small as 0·5 metre, a Wolf-type trap (Wolf 1951) can be used to very great advantage. Sometimes the provision of a current in the water of a pond will be useful for concentrating the fish for capture.

Artificial drawdown is limited in its utility to small water areas. It is accomplished by gravity (either directly or by syphon), or by removing the water with a simple water lift (bucket; Archimedes screw) or with a pump (often diesel-powered). Generally the method is most successful when applied to fish-cultural ponds, or to stream pools that may be isolated by temporary damming or that have become isolated by natural drying.

Natural drawdown is the basis for final harvest in the extensive floodwater fisheries in seasonally inundated areas such as occur in many sluggish-water river basins of tropical South America, Asia and Africa. Fish are captured in the subsiding floodwaters by weirs, typically constructed of local materials such as bamboo stakes. In practice, these weirs are often large, elaborate structures with leads hundreds of metres in length. The typical site for the pot of such a weir is in the deepest drainage channel.

Anaesthetics and poisons

Anaesthetics. No large-scale use has been made of anaesthetics in fish production studies. Several chemicals are of known worth for the harmless quieting of fish (Bell 1967). They have often been used in operations related to population studies, such as transporting fish or marking them for future recognition. There is a real opportunity for discovery and/or development of relatively inexpensive anaesthetics or tranquilizers to facilitate capturing fishes in the field. Anaesthesia caused by electricity is described below, also that due to concussion.

Poisons. Although it is an age-old method of capturing fish in many lands, chemofishing (making the water poisonous to fish) has had extensive technical application only with the present generation of fishery scientists. The most commonly used chemical has been rotenone, produced naturally in plants of the genus *Derris*, among others. Other vegetable toxins have also been used successfully and, recently, a growing number of synthetic organic chemicals. Rotenone can also be used to stimulate fish so that they will dart out from crevices and become vulnerable to nets, etc. Prompt return to fresh water may revive a captured fish, depending on the toxin used, although once symptoms of distress are shown (as with rotenone) simple recovery by placing the fish in non-toxic water is not yet possible.

To both natural and artificial toxins have been added dilutants, dispersants (wetting agents), synergists, etc., to improve their efficiency. All toxicants require an even and complete dispersal in the environment, and they may advantageously be marked with dyes or other easily detectable substances to indicate their spread.

In production studies, chemofishing may be used to kill either part or all of a population. It may also be selective according to species, or to life history stages within a species, depending on differences in susceptibility or reaction time (Applegate *et al.* 1957; Lennon 1966).

Total poisoning can provide an estimate of the whole or some calculable part of the standing crop of fish in a lake, pond or stream. It is essential to know the volume of water to be treated and the minimum lethal concentration of the poison used. The latter must often be calculated specially for each application, because toxicity may depend on temperature and chemical content of the water. Concentrations are usually calculated in parts per million (ppm) of water. For example, for powdered *Derris* root containing 5 % of rotenone, a minimum lethal concentration for the powder in water is 0·5 ppm, but applications range as high as 2·0 ppm. In instances where it is hoped to recover all or known proportions of the individuals killed, control fishes (of all the species and sizes in question) should be marked for recognition on recovery and planted in known numbers in the water area prior to the poisoning. The percentage recovery of marked fish is divided into the total number recovered to obtain estimates of the total standing crop. This must be done for each species and size group separately, unless otherwise ascertained. It is difficult to recover dead fish that sink or that are obscured by turbid water on dense weed beds. For this and for predation on dead and dying fish (e.g. with rotenone the smallest fish are distressed first and larger predatory fishes often gorge on them) correction factors must be determined for population estimates.

In any use of toxicants, adequate attention should be given to unwanted and even unexpected side effects. In some countries, for example the United States, government licensing or approval must be obtained for each toxicant or anaesthetic that is to be used in water or on fish that may be consumed by man or his animals. Some poisons useful in fish capture (e.g. chlorinated hydrocarbons) are toxic also to other water organisms as well as to man. Furthermore, some poisons have residual effects that may destroy fish eggs and young of subsequent generations, and may even render a body of water incapable of supporting desired forms of aquatic life for many years. The use of toxicants in rivers is particularly fraught with danger because of the rapid downstream spread that is possible. Here special precautions are needed such as temporary damming, or the addition of detoxicants to the water. Potassium permanganate has been used successfully as a detoxicant for rotenone in such applications (Lawrence 1956).

Hook-and-line fishing

Line fishing gears and methods are extremely varied (Scofield 1951a; 'Sinker' 1952; Kolganov 1959; Shakespeare 1962). Though quite selective by species, and to a considerable extent by size, in some situations line fishing may be most productive. Also, in many of its forms, it can be conducted successfully by a single fisherman. It can produce excellent series of specimens from spawning or wintering concentrations of many fishes—concentrations that may be situated so that capture by other means is impracticable. Hook-and-line fishing reduced to catch-per-unit-of-effort (often number or weight of fish caught per hour) has been widely used as a measure of population status in recreational fisheries and in certain commercial fisheries. Conversely, for species in which the relationship of population size to angling yield has been established (Lagler & de Roth 1953), it is possible to estimate population numbers from yield data (within the size range of individuals susceptible to capture by angling).

Many methods of hook-and-line fishing may be practised, using either natural or artificial baits or lures. The most effective procedure is often best learned locally from guides or other experienced fishermen. Included among the basic methods of hook-and-line fishing are trolling (Beatty 1951; Tully 1954); casting bait, fly, or spinner (Kolganov 1959; Shakespeare 1962); still fishing; jigging or snagging; set lining, trot lining, and longlining; and jugging (Ludgate 1950; Starrett & Barnickol 1955). Among numerous less common methods I will mention only 'jugging': a baited hook is secured by a line to a float (often a stoppered jug) and set adrift; sudden movement or irregular bobbing of the float is a signal that a fish has been caught and is ready to be taken from the hook.

Ordinarily the size of fish caught is positively correlated both with the size of hook and with the size of lure used.

Among the factors affecting the efficiency and selectivity of hook-and-line fishing are differences in the attractiveness of baits, length of time that soft baits stay on the hook, seasonal and diurnal patterns of feeding behaviour, availability of natural food, density of fish (and of hooks in multiple-hook methods), incidental catch of secondary species, changes in hook condition with use, loss of fish through fracture of gear, and skill of the operators.

In inland waters, other than sport fisheries, hook-and-line fishing methods have generally not been used in fish population studies. However, many marine stocks, such as tuna, salmon and halibut, have been assessed on the basis of hook-and-line catches.

Capture by hand or with hand implements

A rather restricted method of catching fish is directly by hand, as in 'tickling' trout (Gudger 1950). Likewise suckers, lampreys, etc., may be taken in rapids by hand, or catfishes in crevices under overhanging banks. Of more general utility are dipnets, spears and gaffs, used mainly for fishes during upstream migration, or sometimes under the ice. Frogs, small alligators, crocodiles and turtles are also vulnerable to capture by hand or with hand-nets, spears or rakes.

Concussion

Fish collection by concussion (Schiemenz 1943) is a method of limited utility in production studies. Yet it does have application for some species and some habitats and it can be done by one person. In its simplest form it consists of striking ('tunking') a boulder that is partly emerged from the water with another boulder and then rolling the first boulder out of the way to recover the stunned fish beneath it, for example, sculpins. More widespread effects are obtained by the discharge of explosives under water. Dynamite sticks or hand grenades can be used, with proper caution of course. Explosives can sample fish from dense cover such as weed beds or from snag-ridden pockets of water, where other methods fail. Fish may be either killed or stunned, depending on the force of the explosion and their distance from it (Hubbs & Rechnitzer 1952).

Electrofishing

The use of electricity for capturing fish in production studies dates from the 1920's (Schiemenz & Schönfelder 1927). This method is one of the least selective of all active fishing methods (Boccardy & Cooper 1963; Libosvarsky & Lelek 1965). It involves creating an electrical field in the water by passing a current between two submersed electrodes, or between one electrode and the 'ground'. The apparatuses used vary from stationary to highly portable (Vibert 1967). An alternating current (a.c.) of proper strength stuns the fish in its field (electronarcosis); they temporarily lose equilibrium and may be dipped easily from the water. A direct current (d.c.) of adequate strength induces 'galvanotaxis' so that the fish move toward the anode, where again they may be dipped from the water (Schiemenz 1953; Blancheteau *et al.* 1961). Individual choice, habitat characteristics and availability of power source dictate the type of current to be used. Alternating-current generators are generally less bulky than direct, and give good results in clear, unobstructed waters. Direct current is particularly useful in turbid waters, or in thick weeds or brush, and whenever it is important not to damage the fish. Choice of current and its electronic modification from the power source, along with shape of electrodes is related to resistivity of the water; a partial guide is that of Lennon (1959).

Too strong an electrical current, prolonged exposure, or contact with electrodes can kill fish, or cause damage that later proves fatal. Low strength electrical fields, or fields with currents of experimentally determined configuration may be used to guide fishes into traps or to repel them from danger (Vibert 1967).

Electrofishing is potentially dangerous to the operators (Hösl 1959) and to any other warm-blooded animals that may enter the field in the water. Operators need to be well informed and accustomed to working in concert, hand-held electrodes need to be equipped with 'dead-man' automatic shut-off switches, and anyone in the water during electrofishing must have waterproof waders or boots.

It is fairly easy to construct an outfit for electrofishing, and there are about as many variants of this gear as there are centres of fishery research (see the articles in the *Canadian Fish Culturist* 1950, No. 9; Denzer 1956; Meyer-Waarden *et al.* 1960; Ming 1964; Meyer-Waarden *et al.* 1965; Vibert 1967). But it requires engineering expertise and biological experience to create a highly efficient unit. Some commercial sources of electrofishing apparatus are given by Meyer-Waarden *et al.* (1965). To this may be added Coffelt Electronics Co., Inc., 4090 W. Radcliff Ave., Boulder, Colorado, USA, 80236 who also issue useful descriptive brochures that are available on request.

Electrofishing has been done in streams (Harrison 1955) and in shallow-water habitats in lakes, ponds and impoundments (Sharpe 1964; Novotny & Priegel 1974).

For an a.c. operation a popular generator is of 500-watt capacity. Two workers, each holding the non-conductive handle of a submerged electrode, work upstream at distances up to 5 m apart in water up to a metre deep. Thus each operator has an electrode in one hand, and a dip net for recovering narcotized fish in the other. A third may follow with a tub or pail for the fish taken. Highly portable back-pack shockers with a small a.c. generator have also been developed (Fig. 2.3, following p. 16).

For a d.c. operation, a widely-used type of generator has a 2000-watt capacity and for back-pack use battery-powered devices have been constructed. One of the electrodes, the cathode (ground), is suspended in the water. The submersed anode plate is moved by its pole handle to lead fish to a hand-held dip net for recovery. Repeated electrofishing between stopnets in streams can yield good total population censuses, but for some species this can be a protracted process. It is possible to estimate quicker by computation from the rate of decrease in the catch of successive standard treatments (Ricker 1949; Elson 1962b), or by mark-and-recapture methods (Chapter 6).

Shockers for use in lakes are mounted in a motor boat using either a.c. or d.c. generator (Fig. 2.4, following p. 16). Electrodes may be of wire, chain or free-swinging metal rods, suspended from booms in front of the boat. The boat is driven slowly forward through the shallows or alongside weed-beds, and one or two workers stand near the bow to dip the stunned fishes from the the water. Direct current can be used very effectively for lake shocking, especially when fitted with an adjustable electronic interrupter or pulsator (Smith *et al.* 1959; Burnet 1961; Sharpe 1964; Meyer-Waarden *et al.* 1965; Novotny & Priegel 1974). Pulsed direct currents of high voltage can be unselective for size of fish. Efficiency of lake shockers has been enhanced by their use during hours of darkness (Loeb 1957), supplemented by an appropriate underwater light (the housing of which need not be watertight for use in ordinary fresh water).

Electrical seines (including the 'Hager'sche Kathodennetz', Meyer-Waarden *et al.* 1965) have been developed along two main designs, both of which have been limited in application to capture fish from the surface to the bottom in water usually less than 2 m deep. In one, the two electrodes of an a.c. source run respectively along the lead line and the float line of an actual seine. Suitable electrode material is bare, soft, braided copper wire. Electrification of the seine is said to increase its efficiency through a reduction in the avoidance reactions in fishes, such as diving under the lead line, leaping over the float line, or swimming out of the bag once in it. Some experiments have been carried out where trawl nets also have been similarly equipped with electrode lines.

The second type of electrical 'seine' is really not a seine at all. It may consist merely of two parallel exposed wires, a lower one dragged along the bottom (or previously laid zig-zag), and an upper one floated along the surface. Or it may be composed of a floated 2-wire, waterproof electrical cord with flexible drop electrodes alternately leaving each wire (Fig. 2.5, following p. 16). The droppers may be spaced at distances of 1 m or more, and are commonly a metre or more in length. The length of such an electrical seine, and the spacing and length of the electrodes are functions of the a.c. power supply and conductivity of the water. It operates by inducing electronarcosis, and requires a pick-up crew with dip nets to follow behind it to recover the fishes. The efficiency of this type of electrical seine may differ greatly for different species (Funk 1957, 1958).

Permanent installations of electrofishing apparatus, operated from line power, may be very useful in systematic fish sampling (Applegate & Moffett 1955) as well as in commercial harvest (Apostolski 1960).

In electrofishing with current of a single set of characteristics, there can be strong selectivity for size, fish of small sizes being caught least efficiently. This must be considered when population numbers and rates of mortality are calculated. For example, in order to calculate the total numbers of a species, separate calculations should be made for the several size groups, instead of using the massed data for all sizes (Cooper & Lagler 1956; Junge & Libosvarsky 1965).

Active netting

Active netting is defined as fishing with a fabricated mesh that is moved by man or machine to capture fish, as contrasted with netting where the mesh is set and left to fish by itself. Actively used nets include (1) dip nets—either hand, or levered (Nomura 1962); (2) fish wheels—a scoop net, based on aboriginal designs, rotated by the river current, used for salmon in western North America; (3) shallow-water push nets, haul seines and cast nets; (4) blanket nets (Radovich & Gibbs 1954); (5) deep, openwater encircling seines (roundhaul nets, lampara nets and purse seines); and (6) bottom, midwater, and surface trawls. Included among these are the most efficient and broadly applicable of all devices for fish sampling: shallow-water haul seines, openwater seines, and trawls. Only these three types will be described here.

Nets used actively have certain features of construction in common. All are typically made of thread or twine tied or woven into mesh. Until recently nets were made of such natural materials as cotton, linen and hemp, less often leather and silk (or even spider webs: Gudger 1924). Today however synthetic fibres such as nylon are used whenever possible, these being much more durable because of their greater strength and freedom from rotting. Prolonged exposure to direct sunlight, however, will weaken some synthetics.

Fine-mesh nets, suited for the capture of the planktonic young of fishes, are specified in numbers of meshes per inch or centimetre. Mesh sizes greater than about 2 mm are either given as the internal size of one side of the square (square-mesh, bar, or half-mesh measurement) or the internal length of the tight slit remaining when the square is pulled to bring two of its sides in contact with the other two sides (stretch-mesh or extension measurement). In some kinds of woven mesh the knots may slip and aperture size change during heavy pulling or by snagging. This can be avoided by using modern knotless mesh, or mesh with hard-tied or special knots.

There is lack of strict comparability of size records of quantities of fish taken in natural- and synthetic-fibre nets, because at any twine weight the synthetic is both stronger and more elastic than the natural, and usually more efficient.

Mesh size, twine weight and 'lay', and character of hanging, are features of all active fishing gear that must be specified to the manufacturer (US Fish and Wildlife Service 1956). Such gear, of course, depends in part for its effectiveness on its capacity to retain fish after they have been captured. Thus the mesh size must be chosen with due regard to the size-range of the fishes desired in any sample. It is false to reason that a mesh size smaller than required increases efficiency of capture. Small-mesh nets are harder to pull, hence will move more slowly through the water and increase the opportunities for some fishes to escape.

For active fishing loosely-hung nets are generally more effective than tightly-hung ones (see page 32). Thus a dip net, lift net, or haul seine that has a good bag or pocket when it is hauled is generally more efficient than one that is taut. Accentuation of the normal bag of an ordinary seine may be achieved by making it deeper near the middle; this may be accomplished by hanging it more loosely there, or by inserting additional specially-shaped pieces of netting. In one type of shallow-water seine (bag or pocket seine) the middle third contains an elongate bag resembling a trawl (Fort & Brayshaw 1961; Lagler 1956). A popular 8-m model has a bag that trails 4 m when the seine is pulled (Fig. 2.6, following p. 16). When there is much debris in the water or where the bottom is very soft, the bag may be a hindrance to effective fishing.

Fishing efficiency of haul seines and trawls of course differs by species (Threinen 1956; Paloumpis 1958; Funk 1957, 1958).

Efficiency is also affected by the kind of float line (head rope) and floats used at the top of the net, and by the lead line (foot rope) at the bottom. In haul seines, it is only by careful computation or testing that the best size, position and number of floats can be determined. The objective is to have sufficient flotation for all parts of the float line when the net is being hauled with maximum force. The particularly critical area is at the mid-region of the net, and here the number of floats per unit of length may be doubled. Similarly the lead line must be so weighted as to run on the bottom when the net is being pulled with maximum force and/or against maximum current. The tendency is for seines to be too lightly leaded to fish well on smooth, firm bottoms, and too heavily weighted for very soft or irregular bottoms.

Seining. *Haul seines* may be fished parallel to the shore or from offshore on-shore. Generally both types are most efficient when the net is equipped with a pole (bail or brail) at each end that is at least equal to the height of the net. Best results are obtained in water no deeper than 2/3 the height of the slack net. Additional efficiency may be achieved in some applications by adding an apron to the lead line to keep fish from moving out of the net at the bottom (Elson 1962a), by choosing habitat carefully (Threinen 1956), by seining after dark or by seining with the current in sluggish streams (Paloumpis 1958).

Seines tend to roll up and become ineffective when pulled over weeds. Such rolling can be overcome by tying short poles or 'scotch boards' to the netting at right angles to the lead line (Fort & Brayshaw 1961).

Offshore seining by nets such as the *lampara*, a round-haul seine, is facilitated by the use of two boats, advantageously with propellor and controls so located that the net can be paid out and/or taken in over the stern of either, or simultaneously by both (Garner 1962). For many inland lakes it is convenient to use wide skiffs about 6 m long, with flat bottom, a freeboard of 75 cm, and an outboard motor in a well near midships. A suitable lampara for some inland waters is about 200 m long, 20 m deep at its middle and 4 m deep at its ends. In use, some 20 m of line are passed from the slowly moving carrier boat to its stationary companion, then the attached net is paid out from the stern of the carrier in a semicircle, ending in a line attached to the carrier. Both boats are then moved toward each other to close the two ends of the net. The net is taken in until the fish are in a bag of net from which they can no longer sound (dive) to escape. The size of the bag is reduced by further uptake until the fish are concentrated and can be dip-netted (brailed) from it. Transfer of the net to one boat makes ready for the next set. Lamparas for commercial use may be as long as 315 m and as deep as 77 m, and mechanized gurdies are used to pull them (Phillips 1951).

A *purse seine* (ring net) is operated like a lampara for open-water surface seining, but the bottom of the bag is closed early in retrieval by means of a bottom pursing line that passes through rings (Fry 1931; Scofield 1951b). Commercial models of this gear are very effective in fishing for clupeids,

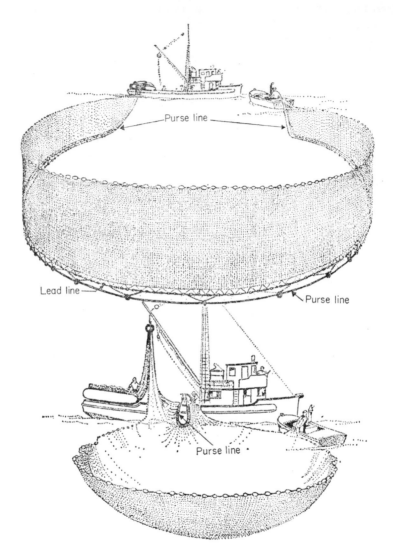

Figure 2.7. Diagram of a purse seine.

salmon, tuna, and other marine fishes (McNeely 1961). A fine-meshed purse seine has been used to capture young sockeye at lakes of British Columbia— specimens down to 3 or 4 cm long are readily captured at night (McDonald 1969). Many other freshwater surface-pelagic fishes can be taken in this manner, as practised, for example, in Lake Kariba on the Zambezi River (Balon & Coche 1974) and elsewhere in Africa and in Southeast Asia. A sardine purse seine in California (Fry 1931) may be 500 or more metres long, 62 m deep at the bag, with wings 70 m deep next to the bag and 48 m deep at their free ends. Bag mesh is 25 mm square, and that of the wings changes from 102 mm at the bag to 203 mm at the free ends (Fig. 2.7).

Trawling. Trawls are of two types. Beam trawls have a frame to keep the net open, whereas otter trawls do this by an appropriate combination of floats, planing-floats or hydrofoils on the top line, and weights, chains or rollers on the bottom line, plus the lateral pull from the two otter-boards. Either type may be used on the bottom, at the surface, or in mid-water. Proper size and engineering of the otter-boards in the otter-trawl is important in order to maintain the spread of the wings of the trawl with a minimum of drag— whether these run on the bottom or are in midwater. Designing the appropriate combination of materials and forces for a midwater otter-type trawl is particularly demanding (Barraclough & Johnson 1956, 1960).

Of marine origin, trawls have been successfully adapted to fresh waters (Garner 1962). Bottom trawls are ineffective on very soft or very rough substrates, and are not very useful in really shallow water. The otter trawl of marine commercial fisheries is typically large and requires mechanical aids for lifting (Knake 1956), so is adaptable to freshwater production studies only on large lakes. In smaller waters small otter trawls (such as the shrimp trynet) and beam trawls have both been used successfully. They can be handled by one or two men from a small, outboard-powered skiff. Although all trawls are to some extent selective, they are very valuable for sampling bottom fishes of limited mobility, including the young of many fishes that later become pelagic (Ferguson & Regier 1963; Moen 1958). The use of 'tickler chains' attached to a lightly-weighted foot rope may enhance fishing efficiency for off-bottom (demersal) fishes by permitting the net to ride up off the bottom and so reducing bottom drag.

Mid-water and surface trawls are adaptations of bottom trawls (Barraclough & Johnson 1960). In a midwater otter-type trawl, the net is held open and held submerged by modified otterboards (Kobayashi & Inoue 1960) or hydroplane floats (von Brandt 1962), or depressers, or some combination of these. The frame of a midwater beam trawl has a ventral flange to deflect it to the desired depth. The angle of the flange and the weight of the frame, along with speed and length of tow line, determine the fishing depth. A popular medium-sized high-speed model is the Isaacs-Kidd trawl.

Floating otter-type trawls are held open by floats and counterweights and by being towed by two vessels (Krason 1949). Surface beam-type trawls are held open by frames. In one type of 'high-speed' surface trawl, a circular, aluminium-tubing frame has been used. In a 'slow-speed' surface trawl, the frame is of plywood, rectangular, with exposed faces angled to form a rectangular funnel leading into the net.

Beam trawls used at the surface or in midwater grade insensibly into the tow nets used for larval fish and invertebrate plankton. A net 90 cm in diameter and 3 m long, towed at 11 km/hr, was very successful in capturing fingerling sockeye salmon in a lake at dusk (Johnson 1956). A larger square-mouthed model, used in Alaska, is shown in Fig. 2.8, following p. 16.

In general, the wider the mouth of a trawl is held open, the better the catch. The mesh at the cod end of a trawl largely determines selectivity (Nassif & Zaki 1960). Length of the net, along with the mesh size, determines ease of water passage and thus affects efficiency. The less the drag, the more rapidly the net can be moved per unit of available ship power. Veers in the course of a trawling vessel reduce efficiency (Lebedev 1959).

There are suggestions that efficiency of trawls can be improved, and selectivity reduced, by installing electrodes in advance of and/or at the mouth (Haskell *et al.* 1955; Loeb 1955). However, the mechanics of accomplishing this are sufficiently complex that the technique has not been widely adopted.

Passive netting

Passive netting is here construed as fish capture by entanglement in a fabric mesh that is not actively moved by man or machine after setting. Gill nets and trammel nets both capture by entanglement, and as ordinarily used they yield fish that are mostly dead when the net is run.

A *gill net* is a single wall of fabric, hung to a float line at the top and lead line at the bottom (Fig. 2.9). The hanging is typically somewhat 'loose', so that when the net is set in the water the mesh openings are of a vertically-elongate diamond shape rather than square. Variations in the looseness of hang affect fishing efficiency and the size range of fish caught (Bonde 1965).

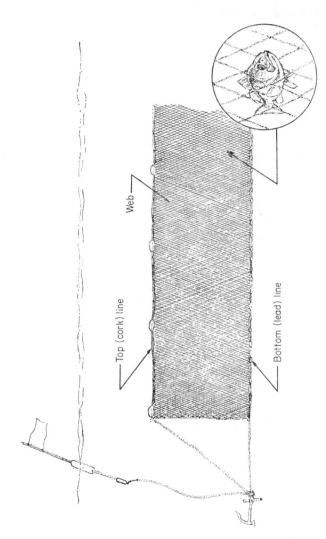

Figure 2.9. Diagram of a gill net when set. At right, a captured ('gilled') fish.

A *trammel net* (or 'tangle net') is made of three separate pieces of net suspended from the float line and extending to the lead line. The two outer ones are the same size, and are made of coarse twine and large mesh. The inner one is made of fine twine and small mesh. The coarse meshes are straight hung, 1/1, so that their apertures are square when the net is set; the fine mesh between them is diamond hung and very loose (taken up on the length on the half basis, 1/2). A commonly-used trammel net is 2 m deep and has stretchmesh sizes of 250 mm (10 in.) for the coarse mesh and 25 mm (1 in.) for the fine, with the latter made to hang 2/3 greater than the depth required.

Gill nets typically capture a fish by having it swim into and part way through the mesh to arrive at a position where it cannot disengage itself (Fig. 2.10, following p. 16). Trammel nets typically capture fish by having them swim into the net and carry the loose, fine mesh through adjacent coarse mesh. The fish thus becomes entrapped in a pouch of netting.

Regardless of mesh size, both gill and trammel nets tend to be more efficient in capturing fishes adorned with external roughnesses, teeth, etc. Furthermore, since the fishing success of passive nets depends on fish movement, their efficiency and selectivity may be subject to abrupt changes from shifts in barometric pressure, wind-driven currents, water level fluctuations, turbidity, and transmitted light (Berst 1961). In addition both fabric type and frequency of tending contribute to variations in the take. The classical natural net materials, linen and cotton, have been replaced by synthetics such as nylon to make greater the efficiency of both gill and trammel nets. In some fisheries, gill nets of nylon have been about three times as effective as those of cotton (McCombie & Fry 1960). Not only is the nylon less visible because lighter twines (often monofilament) do the job of heavier natural twine, but the synthetics may be manufactured in any permanent hue or camouflage-mixture of hues. In addition, of course, the synthetic meshes are more readily cleaned, need not be dried between intervals of use, hold fish better, are more durable, and are suspected of being less readily detected by the pressure senses of fishes than natural fabric nets. Monofilament synthetic twines are usually more efficient than multifilament, although a little more difficult to handle and repair.

Both gill nets and trammel nets are highly selective for size of fish, trammel nets somewhat less so than gill nets. To reduce selectivity, fleets or gangs of nets of different sizes are often used. Many different types of 'experimental' gangs have been used in quantitative (and qualitative) sampling (Ishida 1963, 1964). A common experimental type in North America is 2 m deep and has

8 m each of meshes 38, 51, 64, 76, 89, and 102 mm stretched measure (1·5, 2·0, 2·5, 3·0, 3·5, and 4·0 in.). This is approximately a fixed linear difference in size, instead of the fixed relative increase mentioned earlier. The twine weight, of course, becomes slightly heavier with increasing mesh size. The net is suspended by floats from its float or cork line and is held in a vertical position by weights spaced along the bottom or lead line. The ratio of floats to weights is adjusted to give a net that will fish either at the surface or at the bottom, as desired. To simplify handling for small-scale experimental work, brass rings of suitable weight, with diameter larger than the largest mesh, are sometimes substituted for conventional leads. An even better substitute is the braided integral foot rope with lead inside it. A similarly constructed integral float line eliminates the need for individual floats strung on the line.

Both gill nets and trammel nets may be set on the bottom (anchor or bottom sets) or at the surface (float or drift sets), the latter being either fixed or free-floating. Sets at intermediate depths may be made in two ways: a normally bottom-set net may be 'kited', that is, suspended by 'droplines' from large floats at the surface; or a normally floating net may be 'put on legs', that is, held below the surface by lines attached to weights on the bottom. Either system requires rather complex arrangements. A set may also be made vertically or on a diagonal between the surface and bottom (Horak & Tanner 1964). Sets may parallel the shore or be at an angle to it. In drift-net fishing, a surface set is used, without anchors.

Drift-sets usually require almost constant watching. Anchored sets also must be run frequently if live fish in good condition are required. Otherwise they may be left and tended only at intervals—often 'over-night', or for 24 hr if the water is not so warm as to cause rapid spoilage of the fish. When catch-per-unit-effort data are sought, some standard interval should be used; for doubling the 'soak' (length of time in the water) does not, in general, double the catch (Van Oosten 1936; Kennedy 1951). In large water areas the marking buoys may be flag-floats or beacons that are illuminated or emit coded radio signals. Needless to say, to set a gill net on trawling grounds is to invite disaster.

Local conditions determine the method of setting gill and trammel nets. Anchored sets should be made down wind or down current, with the net well stretched; they should be lifted upwind or up the current. These nets in general depend on active movement of the fish and it is sometimes possible to stimulate such movements. Methods available at present include 'Aqualin' (Harrison 1959); copper sulphate (Tompkins & Bridges 1958); light (Young

1950; Takayama 1956; Kawamoto 1956; Rasalan & Datingaling 1956; Kuroki *et al*. 1964); air screens (Igarashi 1963); electrical fields (see page 24); and noise (Lawler 1963a).

Time spent in removing many kinds of fishes from gill nets may be reduced by use of a short stick with a nail driven into the end, head cut off, and flattened. This resembles a miniature spatula or shoehorn, and is used as a substitute for the fingernail of the operator to slide the entrapping or gilling mesh off the body of the fish.

Catches by standardized sets of experimental gill nets and trammel nets tend to be very variable. For some species it is impractical to demonstrate a difference in catch at a probability level any greater than 80 % (Moyle 1950; Lawler 1963a). Therefore, such nets should not be used to compare abundances unless replicate trials are made to indicate the actual degree of variability and so permit a statistical test (Carlander 1953). Such tests are commonly based on the logarithms of catches obtained (or similar transformation), because of the skewed distribution of most catch series. Bagenal (1972b) suggests the number of gill nets required to obtain means of given accuracy when the nets are used for pike *Esox lucius*.

Impounding devices

A large variety of impounding devices has been developed to entrap fishes and other aquatic animals. Although stationary during operation, many kinds are portable. All conduct the animals by deflectors into an impounding enclosure or pot, escape from which is made difficult by baffles extending inward at the mouth. Usually the entrance to the pot is funnel-shaped or V-shaped and extends into the pot. The fishing zone of many impounding devices is greatly extended by wings that form an enlarged V leading to the small entrance V at the pot, and/or by leaders that extend directly outward from the pot.

Representatives of 'permanently' installed impounding gear are (1) the large, elaborate bamboo-stake traps used in the floodwater fisheries of southeastern Asia; (2) their webbed counterparts, the pound nets or 'pond' nets used in the Great Lakes and Atlantic coastal fisheries of North America (Reid 1955); (3) the fixed traps used for salmon and other species on the shores of the Pacific Ocean; (4) stone-winged eel weirs with wood-slat pots (used in many Atlantic coastal streams in Europe and North America); (5) pots for salmon (Britain); and (6) swing nets or set-back traps that strain fish from currents. A swing net is a stationary trawl bag attached at each of its sides to stakes driven into the bottom: the net swings, changing direction of capture, when the current reverses itself with the change of tide. Even a conventional otter trawl complete with otter boards and set with anchors has been used for sampling fish moving downstream.

Representative of portable impounding devices are framed nets (such as hoop or fyke nets) that may be bottom-set or floating (Burgner 1962), traps of mesh that are held open in fishing position largely through floats, and some kinds of weirs (MacKay 1950).

Investigators of fish production will seldom find themselves constructing large-scale permanent-type weirs and traps. Their permanent installations are most likely to be rather small, and are usually used for studies of migratory fish. Such are the two-way fish trap of Whalls *et al.* (1955), and the Wolf-type weirs (Wolf 1951; Hunter 1954). Often, however, an investigator will use data from the catch taken in large installations belonging to commercial operators or others. The kinds of portable impounding units that he will probably most often use in technical quantitative studies are framed nets and mesh traps.

Bagenal (1972a) investigated the variability between the catches of wire-netting traps set for perch *Perca fluviatilis*, and indicated the number of traps needed to give mean catches of given accuracy.

Hoop and fyke nets. A framed hoop net that is convenient to handle and transport (Fig. 2.11, following p. 16) has the following basic characteristics. The exterior netting is tied, in the shape of a cone, to the insides of 5 hoops often made of willow (*Salix* spp.). The diameter of the front hoop is 1·6 m, that of the last is 0·6 m and the second, third, and fourth are of appropriate, intermediate sizes. The hoops are equally spaced at about 1-m intervals to give a finished net that is 5 m long. Two funnel-shaped throats lead to the interior of the net; the first throat is attached peripherally to the front hoop and posteriorly to the third hoop. Comparable attachments for the second throat are the third and fifth hoops. The mesh at the pot or the cod end of the net is equipped with a drawstring that may be released for easy removal of the catch. Size of mesh depends on the needs of the investigation—particularly the size of fish to be caught. Larger or smaller hoop nets may be better in particular situations.

The effectiveness of such nets can be increased by adding two wings (each about 1·5 times the length of the net). If a leader is also used, usually about

5 times the length of the net, the combination may be termed a fyke net. Wings and leader will have a depth equal to the diameter of the first hoop. Both hoop and fyke nets are set taut by means of anchors and/or poles pushed into the bottom. The depth of set is typically in shallow water about equal to the diameter of the first hoop except when it carries bait inside, as for minnows, catfishes, etc. (Bernhardt 1960). A typical set is made for 24 hr, although there are great differences among species in rate of escape (Hansen 1944).

Hoop nets vary greatly in dimensions. The smallest are about the size of a 4-litre jug and have only one funnel. Similar nets can be made of materials other than twine, in which case wings and lead are usually absent. Cylindrical nets of wire mesh with a funnel at one or both ends, are usually called traps. They are very effective for sunfishes, perch and some minnows (Baker 1963). Split bamboo and wooden slats or sticks are also used, or even glass or clear plastic, as in the commercially available 'minnow traps' used by anglers to capture bait fishes. All such devices can be unexpectedly selective.

Hoop and fyke nets can be both strongly selective and differently efficient by species (Carter 1954; Harrison 1954; Cleary 1957; Funk 1957, 1958). A set made parallel to the shoreline can be either more or less efficient than one perpendicular to it, depending on the species, etc. (Bernhardt 1960). A study of escapement rate will give the information needed to establish the optimum length of time between lifts of these nets. For some fishes efficiency is improved by baiting. Catches are often larger during spawning seasons (Muncy 1957), and fish activators such as copper sulphate can be used to increase catches (Tompkins & Bridges 1958). Hoop and fyke nets have been useful for estimating populations of many species in shallow habitats (e.g. Lagler & Ricker 1943; Riethmiller MS 1948).

Underwater trap nets. In water deeper than the net itself, hoop nets are less useful than underwater traps (Fig. 2.12). These are held open laterally by anchors or stretcher rods, and vertically by floats (Crowe 1950). Modelled after the large deep-water commercial traps used in the Great Lakes of North America and elsewhere, a portable unit weighing about 100 pounds with anchors has the following characteristics: rectangular pot, 1·3 m deep, 2 m wide, and 2·6 m long of 3-cm stretched mesh; two wings leading to an outside heart of 100-mm stretched mesh and to an inside heart of 62-mm stretched mesh; both hearts covered top, bottom, and sides by similar netting; leader 30 m long by 1·3 m deep. Most efficient operation of a trap with

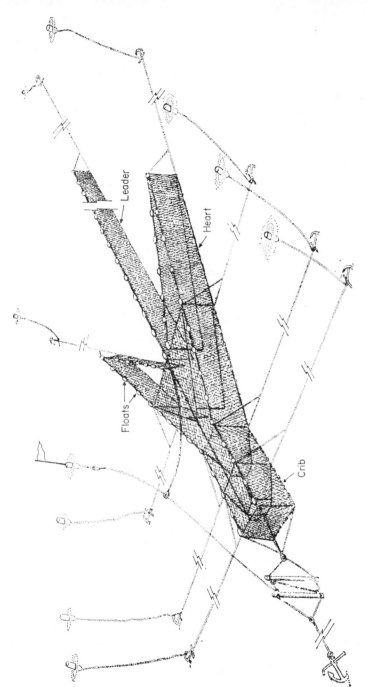

Figure 2.12. Diagram of a sunken trap net.

these dimensions is in water less than 12 m deep. In running the net, the line to the pot anchor is loosened and the line, and then the net, are under-run by the boat. To reset, the net is lowered into the water, stretched into position by the pot line, and the pot anchor replanted.

Trap nets of the foregoing character are selective by species (Crowe 1950; Latta 1959), and have been 'selective for the larger fish of a size class above the minimum size imposed by the physical dimensions of the net', probably due to differential behaviour of the fishes (Latta 1959). When used in studies of fish population size, unwanted effects of such selectivity can be overcome by estimating numbers by each size group of species. For mortality estimates, adjustment for net selectivity is also required.

Examination of fishes

The fish captured for productivity studies are usually enumerated, measured, and weighed. A sample is also taken of scales or some other hard structure from which age can be determined. Usually the sex, stage of maturity and condition of the gonads are recorded, also parasite infestation and any obvious disease or abnormalities (Chapter 11). Often it is useful to take a large sample for length data, and to subsample this for weight and other vital statistics. The digestive tracts of a subsample can be preserved for food analyses (Chapter 9). Frequently such data, along with those on time, place, and manner of collection, are recorded for each fish on a small envelope into which the scale or bone sample for age assessment is placed. Details of useful methods are given by Lagler (1956).

Length measurement. Length is best measured by using a measuring board (Fig. 2.13, following p. 16) in which the anterior extremity of the fish is put against a stop at the beginning of the measuring scale. One or more of three common fishery length measurements (described below) can then be read at the tail end of the fish. All are made as a straight line, not over the curve of the body, with the fish lying on its side and with the jaws closed in a normal position and not in any way extended.

Length measurements are made in either the metric or English scales, however the metric system is to be preferred for both length and weight, since it simplifies the mechanics of data processing. Fineness of measurement depends mainly on the size of the fish, and to some extent on the uses to which the data are to be put, also on the scale used. A common goal is a measurement precise to about 0·5 % of the overall length, but anything finer than the nearest millimetre is rarely attempted.

Although instruments such as dividers, simple calipers and dial-reading calipers are used in systematic studies, for fish production studies a measuring board is most efficient, potentially precise, and easy to make. Its length is determined by the size range of the fishes for which it is to be used. It can be made of a piece of 25 mm thick hardwood or of plastic, stainless steel, or aluminium. Onto this is attached an accurately graduated millimetre scale. At the zero end of the scale a suitable stop is placed, against which the front end of the fish will be placed.

Several refinements are possible. (1) The board may be machined into a broad V-shape to help hold the fish in position. (2) A collar may be added to help restrain a live fish. (3) To the side of the board may be attached a rod carrying a sliding right-angle arm that can be brought to rest at the measurement point on the fish; either the rod itself is graduated, or a scale is set beside it and length is indicated by a pointer attached to the arm, or the arm may be attached to a digit counter (in mm) by means of a heavy nylon thread under tension. (4) Special measuring scales may be prepared to give whole fish length in instances where, for example, only beheaded fish are available for measurement (Williams 1967). Substitute devices have included photography, and an assortment of mechanical contrivances that meet special needs.

For rapid recording of large masses of length data in the field the surface of a measuring board may be covered temporarily by a sheet of metal foil or polyethylene plastic. The length of each fish is then indicated with a pinprick or scratch on the sheet. The marks are readily converted to length-values at any later time; they also instantly provide a length-frequency polygon while they are being made, if appropriate dividing lines are marked on the sheet.

When otoliths are to be taken with length measurements, efficiency has been gained by marking a separate board with rows of holes in it. Each successive row of holes is assigned a length-group value, say by 1-cm intervals. When an otolith has been taken, it is placed in the board in a hole corresponding to the length of the fish. In some types of investigation no other record need be kept, and the filled holes become automatically a size-frequency analysis of the sample (Bückmann 1929).

Contributory to error or inconsistency in fish measurement are: (1) muscular tension among live fish, and its relaxation after death; (2) shrinkage of fish due to preservation, including freezing; (3) variations, at time of measurement, in the pressure applied to put the jaws into a normal closed position; (4) failure consistently to squeeze the tail fin so as to get the maximum total length (in fishes with forked caudal fins); (5) operator skill and consistency.

'Numeral bias' is a tendency to prefer the 'even' divisions of a scale (for example, whole centimetres rather than half), or to prefer scale divisions to interpolated length estimates. To overcome this, the divisions between length groups used in analysis should coincide with the marks on the measuring board. Best results are obtained by having measurers read the length to the nearest graduation of the scale above (or below) that actually observed; but if measurements to the nearest unit are desired, then the marks on the board must be offset by half a division.

Obviously, conversion factors can be created from empirical data to convert from any one kind of fish length measurement to any other, thus enabling the combined use of the different kinds. For any new species under investigation, it may prove advantageous to obtain all the different length measurements and to prepare conversion factors for all sizes of individuals. Such factors will facilitate comparisons with data of other workers.

The various length measurements in use have been described and discussed by Berg *et al.* (1949), Lagler (1956), and others.

Standard length in fishery usage, or *A D length*, is the greatest length of a fish from its most anterior extremity (mouth closed) to the hidden base of the median tail fin rays (where these meet the median hypural plate). This base, masked by overlying skin and musculature, is often identified by a crease when the tail is bent sharply from side to side. The measurement is to the midpoint of the crease in those fishes that exhibit it; in the few that don't a quick dissection may be done, or some other length may be used. 'Fishery' standard length can differ from the standard length used in systematic ichthyology, which is customarily measured backward from the tip of the snout (see Chapter 3), for in some fishes the tip of the snout is not the anteriormost extremity.

Fork length, median length, Schmidt's length or *A C length* is measured from the anteriormost extremity of the fish to the tip of the median rays of the tail. This measurement is the same as total length in species in which the tail fin is not notched or forked. Fork length is regarded by some as the most convenient length, and is particularly useful if specimens tend to abrade or otherwise lose a projecting extremity of the tail fin.

Total length, absolute length, or *A B length* is the greatest length of a fish from its anteriormost extremity to the end of the tail fin. In fishes having a forked tail, the two lobes are moved into the position which gives the maximum length measurement (the longer lobe is used, whichever it may be). This is the usual North American practice, and when necessary it can be distinguished as *extreme total length.* Most European investigators are accustomed to spreading the tail into a 'natural' position to measure total length, but this measurement is not usually repeatable with any great consistency, as between different observers. (NB: In the literature of 40 or more years ago the term 'total length' sometimes means fork length.)

There are of course special situations which call for special measurements. For example, salmon tend to lengthen their snouts as maturity approaches, and tails become frayed and shortened. Hence in Canada a 'hypural' length, or better 'orbit to hypural tip' length, has been developed. This is measured from the surface of the hind margin of the orbit of the eye to the hind margin of the median hypural plate of the tail, as determined from the crease which appears when the tail is flexed. A similar length used in western United States is measured from the estimated mid-point of the orbit.

For routine work only one measurement of length is necessary, and this should be accurate and repeatable. There is no consensus as to which is best (Royce 1942; Carlander & Smith 1945; Ricker & Merriman 1945; Hile 1948; Chugunova 1955, 1959, 1963), but either fork length or extreme total length are usually to be preferred. Where possible an agreed single method should be used by all workers on the same species or group of species; for example, all workers on tunas use fork length. Above all, in every publication the length used should be specified and defined, either by a complete description or by reference to a published account such as the above.

Weight measurement. Weight in fishes has been taken from specimens that are alive and lively, anaesthetized, freshly dead, or variously embalmed or frozen. Weights of fresh and preserved specimens are not comparable. Even for a single method of handling, great precision is not possible, sometimes no better than within several per cent, because of variations in stomach contents or in amount of water engulfed at capture. Both metric and English weight scales are in use, but the metric system is preferable.

Live weight is best taken in water by first weighing a container with enough water to satisfy the needs of the fish to be weighed, and then adding the fish. An attempt should be made to have the fish at a standard degree of wetness.

Specimens that are freshly dead, anaesthetized, or preserved in liquid preservatives must similarly be treated consistently in this respect.

From an adequate mass of paired measurements of length and weight, it is possible to derive conversion factors to obtain one of these measurements when the other is known (Lagler 1956). In the same way gutted or beheaded weights can be converted to live weights. These regressions should be prepared for as wide a size range as possible, and with more or less equal numbers of fish at successive equal size intervals. If the last precaution is not observed, least-squares regressions can give relationships that do not apply well even to the range of observations at hand. Obtaining a wide and representative set of paired values for length and weight usually requires that extra effort be made to sample the largest and smallest sizes of individuals in the population.

Determination of sex. The gonads are inspected to determine the sex of a fish. In adult females eggs are readily discernible in the ovaries. In adult males the testes are typically smooth, whitish and non-granular in appearance (care must be taken not to confuse testes with fat bodies). In adult fish the sex is readily determined by gross inspection (through a slit made on the right side of the body in case the specimen is to be used for taxonomic purposes, see Chapter 3). In immature specimens the shape of the gonad may be a guide to the sex (for example, testes have finger-like processes in many catfishes) but it will often be necessary to use a dissecting microscope to determine the sex of small immature fish. The beginning worker should open a series of specimens and establish his skill in sex determination from them before starting to make routine records. In some fish there is sexual dimorphism in colour, genitalia, or body proportions, particularly near spawning time. However, in general, there is no substitute for the actual examination of the gonads.

Determination of maturity stages. A record of the state of maturity of the fish examined is often required, since this bears on the condition factor and length–weight relation, and may explain what otherwise might appear to be anomalous data. It is also important to know the average size or age at first maturity. One should therefore determine whether each fish is sexually immature, mature, ripe or spent.

Lagler (1956) gives clear instructions on the practical procedures for fish living in temperate regions. During the breeding season the reproductive organs should be classified as immature, ripe or spent. Immature means that

TABLE 2.3. Two generalized classifications of maturity stages in fishes, with approximate correspondence between them

From Kesteven (1960)	From Nikolsky (1963a)
I. Virgin Very small sexual organs close under the vertebral column. Testes and ovaries transparent, colourless to grey. Eggs invisible to naked eye.	**I. Immature** Young individuals which have not yet engaged in reproduction; gonads of very small size.
II. Maturing virgin Testes and ovaries translucent, grey-red. Length half, or slightly more than half, the length of ventral cavity. Single eggs can be seen with magnifying glass.	**II. Resting stage** Sexual products have not yet begun to develop; gonads of very small size; eggs not distinguishable to the naked eye.
III. Developing Testes and ovaries opaque, reddish with blood capillaries. Occupy about half of ventral cavity. Eggs visible to the eye as whitish granular.	**III. Maturation** Eggs distinguishable to the naked eye; a very rapid increase in weight of the gonad is in progress; testes change from transparent to a pale rose colour.
IV. Developing Testes reddish-white. No milt-drops appear under pressure. Ovaries orange reddish. Eggs clearly discernible; opaque. Testes and ovaries occupy about two-thirds of ventral cavity.	
V. Gravid Sexual organs filling ventral cavity. Testes white, drops of milt fall with pressure. Eggs completely round, some already translucent and ripe.	**IV. Maturity** Sexual products ripe; gonads have achieved their maximum weight, but the sexual products are still not extruded when light pressure is applied.
VI. Spawning Roe and milt run with slight pressure. Most eggs translucent with few opaque eggs left in ovary.	**V. Reproduction** Sexual products are extruded in response to very light pressure on the belly; weight of the gonads decreases rapidly from the start of spawning to its completion.
VII. Spawning/spent Not yet fully empty. No opaque eggs left in ovary.	

TABLE 2.3—*continued.*

From Kesteven (1960)	From Nikolsky (1963a)
VIII. Spent Testes and ovaries empty, red. A few eggs in the state of reabsorption.	**VI. Spent condition** The sexual products have been discharged; genital aperture inflamed; gonads have the appearance of deflated sacs, the ovaries usually containing a few left-over eggs, and the testes some residual sperm.
II. Recovering/spent Testes and ovaries translucent, grey-red. Length half, or slightly more than half, the length of ventral cavity. Single eggs can be seen with magnifying glass.	**II. Resting stage** Sexual products have been discharged; inflammation around the genital aperture has subsided; gonads of very small size, eggs not distinguishable to the naked eye.

there are no easily visible eggs or milt. Ripe means that the gonads contain obvious eggs or sperms, and spent that the fish has spawned. The ovaries of recently-spawned (spent) fish are often flaccid and bloodshot. During the remainder of the year the fish should be classified as immature, with no eggs or milt obviously present, or mature when eggs or sperms are clearly apparent. At some times the use of a dissecting microscope is useful.

More complex maturity classifications have been suggested by Kesteven (1960) based on Bückmann (1929), and by Nikolsky (1963a, p. 170; 1963b, p. 160) and have value in special studies. Modifications of these classifications are presented in Table 2.3.

The maturity staging discussed above is only suitable for fish with a short distinct breeding season so that at any one moment the gametes are all at the same stage of development. Some tropical species spawn several times a year, and others more or less continuously throughout adult life. They may contain eggs in a wide range of development stages and it would be unrealistic to attach single unique maturity stages to these fish other than immature and adult (mature). Scott (1974) found that samples of *Mormyrus kannume* on a typical spawning ground in Lake Victoria contained ripe fish over a prolonged period of the year, but that this was made up of waves of ripe fish each having a 12-month cycle, but not in phase with each other. The maturity stages found in *Sarotherodon esculentus* in Lake Victoria are discussed by Lowe (1956).

Acknowledgments

I am grateful to several colleagues, including William C. Beckman, Sidney Holt, and Hilmer Kristjonsson, and especially to John Gulland, Henry Regier and E.D. Le Cren for helpful suggestions and contributions. Also gratefully acknowledged is the assistance of other members of the initial Working Party for this handbook, and particularly the editor of the first two editions, William E. Ricker and Tim Bagenal, editor of the third edition. Patient and competent technical assistance was given by Alice Bond, Lily Crane, and Jacqueline Howe, and, for the third edition, by Cindy Crean. Figures 2.8, 2.9 and 2.12 were prepared by A.A. Denbigh.

3

Identification of Freshwater Fishes

R H LOWE-MCCONNELL

The three principal tasks of the systematist are identification, classification, and the study of species formation and evolution (Mayr *et al.* 1953)*. Ecological and productivity studies may occasionally be able to by-pass problems of identification by thinking in terms of energy flow, but for most studies precise identification of the organisms is basic.

The problems encountered in identification by the field worker will differ according to whether he is in an area (Type A) where much taxonomic research remains to be done, or in an area (Type B) where the fauna is relatively well known.

Type A areas: In the tropics, for instance, fish faunas are very rich in species; often flocks of very similar species live together and many of the species are not yet described. Until recently, the scientific work in many of these areas was generally done by non-residents, or at least was published abroad, so that the resulting literature is widely scattered.

Type B areas: In the temperate zones the fish faunas tend to have fewer species and these are generally now fairly well known. Keys and descriptions exist for the identification of fishes for ecological studies. The emphasis in taxonomic work has here shifted to racial and population studies. These are generally areas (such as Europe and North America) with well-equipped laboratories where sophisticated modern techniques can be used, such as X-ray analyses, serology, chromosome studies, etc., and where results may be treated by computer when advantageous. Good library facilities are available and the work is generally done by residents, so publications are not so scattered.

As this handbook is most needed by those working in Type A areas, emphasis is here on identification of fishes under field conditions such as are encountered in much of Africa, South America and Asia. The field worker

*References for this chapter are at the end of the chapter, pages 64–83.

should, however, know of the modern techniques to which it may be possible to subject his collections later in a laboratory, and he may be asked to collect materials (such as blood samples for serology) for those engaged in relevant laboratory work.

Keys for identification are generally prepared from museum specimens, which are often few in number and of restricted size range. Therefore, field workers must be prepared to find specimens which may not fit existing keys, but which are not necessarily new species. Keys are only a guide and descriptions should always be consulted to obtain all the available information on the range of variation of various characters. On the other hand, a field worker must be prepared to encounter and distinguish undescribed species, and give them provisional designations.

Good reference collections should be kept, including specimens of all sizes and both sexes, related by a number system to full field notes (colours, ecology, behaviour, etc.) which will all help in the later laboratory work of identification. The preparation of a field key as the work proceeds is often helpful. The collection of names given to the fishes by local fishermen often draws attention to previously undescribed species. Co-operation with local fishermen, who often know a great deal about the natural history of the fishes, is greatly facilitated by learning the local names. Local fish markets often reveal species, or life history stages, not found in the collector's gear.

Procedure for identification

To identify a fish one first assembles the best available keys, checklists, and descriptions of the fishes of the region (see the world list of basic references, pages 63–83). One then proceeds to:
(1) Key the fish to its proper species designation.
(2) Verify identification by comparing fish with:
   (a) Pictures;
   (b) Detailed published descriptions;
   (c) Comparison with the known geographic range of the species;
   (d) Comparison with identified materials in museum collections or with specimens identified by a specialist.
(3) Confirm identifications by arranging for a specialist to see the fish and give an opinion on the name you have attached to it. Although you may have identified the fish correctly, animal taxonomy is an active science and for technical reasons the species represented by your specimen may be known

C

now by a different scientific name than that given in the reference materials you used. Indeed, you may yourself have found two or more names for the same specimens.

(4) If you think that you have a new species for a region, or a species new to science, use an arrangement like (3) above to make sure your fish is properly recorded. Type specimens, on which new species are described, need to be deposited in an established museum where they are available for study by subsequent workers.

In addition to identifications by the methods just given, in particular instances it may be necessary to take additional steps such as the following:

(1) Use skeletal preparations prepared by dissection, by dermestid beetles, ants or other organisms, or by clearing of tissues and subsequent staining of bone by alizarin;

(2) Use soft X-ray to disclose skeletal features without destroying the whole fish specimen;

(3) Use chromosome numbers and morphology for which careful histological preparations must be made, often of developing gonad cells;

(4) Employ differences in behaviour, which will demand quantification and careful analysis;

(5) Obtain accurate identification of parasites, for some of these are host-specific and thus may assist in identification of their hosts (when host-parasite relations and faunas are adequately known);

(6) Measure physiological differences among species and varieties, including those of a biochemical nature such as protein differences in tissues, tissue fluids, blood, etc. A widely used method of protein analysis is by electrophoresis.

X-ray and alizarin preparations can be made from formalin-preserved specimens. Chromosome studies usually require special treatment of fresh materials, as do parasite analyses. Biochemical differences also need fresh, even live, specimens. Sometimes sharp-frozen materials can be used, either as whole fish or frozen blocks of selected tissues such as whole blood. For sharp freezing dry ice and a suitable insulated container are useful in some field conditions.

Protein taxonomy

Regarding 'protein taxonomy' (Nyman 1965a) or 'biochemical systematics' (Tsuyuki & Roberts 1966), the following summary was prepared by T.D. Iles (Fisheries Research Station, St Andrews, New Brunswick):

A type of protein, such as haemoglobin, which in different species has the same function, may show specific differences in the rates at which it migrates through a gel medium under the influence of an electric current. These differences in electrophoretic mobility reflect differences in the fine structure of these proteins which have a genetic basis, and they may also be to a large extent independent of environmental factors. These characteristics, together with the fact that such differences can exist between species whose gross morphology may be very similar, emphasize the potential value of protein analysis in taxonomy.

In marine and freshwater fishes the proteins which have been most intensively studied include the haemoglobins (Sick 1961), serum and plasma proteins (Nyman 1965a, b), muscle myogens (Tsuyuki & Roberts 1965, 1966; Tsuyuki *et al.* 1965) and organ proteins (Nyman 1965b). The result of electrophoresis is the production of a pattern of bands that are revealed by staining with a suitable protein stain (usually Amido Black 10b). Each band represents one (at least) specific protein. The major features of the pattern of such bands on the gel medium have been shown to be species specific (Tsuyuki & Roberts 1966). It has also been possible to identify hybrid individuals between species of which the parent patterns are known, and to recognize distinct populations of the same species in different parts of its geographical range by minor differences in the patterns (Child *et al.* 1976; Brassington & Ferguson 1976; Child & Solomon 1977).

Individual variation in the band pattern is also well established. In a few instances the genetic mechanism determining the inheritance of different patterns in the same species has been determined (Sick 1961), allowing different populations of the same species to be characterized by the gene frequency of the various alleles which, usually by a co-dominant effect, are responsible for the differences in band pattern.

Although protein taxonomy requires facilities, techniques and some experience, there can be little doubt that it will become established as a valuable tool in the elucidation of taxonomic problems. (See bibliography by Hawkins & Mawdesley-Thomas (1972) and the papers by Ligny (1971), Avise (1974), Utter *et al.* (1974) and Markert (1975).)

Collection of fish for taxonomic work
(see also Chapter 2)

What to preserve. The days are gone when new species were often described from one specimen. At least 20 to 30 specimens should be collected from each locality. These samples are best selected at random (see Chapter 2). Avoid equally taking only what seem to be the most typical specimens, or concentrating on extremes of colour, form, etc. Both sexes are needed, and gonads should be left in the fish. As comprehensive a size range as possible is desirable. Extreme or aberrant specimens are of interest and should be collected, but they should be specially marked as atypical; often they will prove to belong to a different species.

To find young stages, it is often necessary to fish in different places, as fish often change their habits and habitats as they grow. It does not matter how the fish are caught, provided that they are not damaged; long-spined species often have their dangerous spines broken off by fishermen, destroying most of their value as specimens. Whole individuals should be kept whenever feasible.

Labelling and recording. It is essential to label individual fish or lots of fish immediately on collection. Serial numbers, written on a strip of good waterproof paper (high rag content) using a soft pencil or waterproof ink, can generally be fixed under the gill cover or in the mouth of individual specimens, or in the containers of lots of specimens, to correspond with the notes recorded at the time of collection in a field notebook. It is a good plan to give a serial number to each fishing operation, followed by a serial number denoted differently (say in a circle) for the specimen, together with the initials of the collector.

In the field notebook should be recorded date, time of day, place, fishing method, and as much about the ecological conditions, and colour and behaviour of the fish, as possible, together with data kept on its length, weight, sex, gonad state and stomach contents. Printed data sheets may be useful; Fig. 3.1 shows a format which has been used successfully in North America. Plenty of space should be allowed for supplementary information; when working in a new area it is difficult to foresee all the factors which it may prove desirable to record. Carbon copies may be advisable as there is a danger of losing field notes. Field notebooks tend to get very messy when handling fish, and it may be necessary to extract details from them into a more permanent log, and to keep a register of samples preserved each day. But wherever practicable a system should be devised to avoid excessive copying of notes, with its possibilities of introduced errors. In any event the original field notebooks should be retained, as the data accumulated in them often yield information about the life histories of the fishes which can only be appreciated later in the investigation when the overall picture is clearer. The use of cards for sorting data may also be helpful (see Chapters 2 and 5).

DEPARTMENT OF FISHERIES, UNIVERSITY OF MICHIGAN
FISH COLLECTION

Coll. No. ....

State or Country:.. Locality:..

....

County: .... Drainage:.................................

Water: ....

Vegetation:...

....

Bottom: .... Temp.: .... Air: ....

Shore:...Current:...........................

Distance from shore:...Tide: ....

Depth of capture:..Depth of water:..............

Method of capture:..

Collected by:...Date:...........................

Orig. preserv.:...Time:...........................

Figure 3.1. Suggested headings for field sheet to record fish collection notes.

How to preserve specimens. Formalin is generally a reliable preservative, after which they can be transferred to alcohol for lengthy preservation. Commercial formaldehyde (trade-name Formalin) is concentrated (about 40 %) and must be diluted before use, 1 part formalin to 9 parts water (approximately a 10 % solution of formalin) for most uses. Large fish need formalin of this strength or stronger (up to 20 %), but small fish can be fixed in a more dilute solution (down to 5 % formalin). The formalin bath can be reused but becomes diluted with use. Neutralized formalin is to be preferred, because ordinary formalin will soften the bones of fish after a time. It can be purchased ready neutralized or neutralized by adding about one level teaspoonful of household borax to each litre of preserving solution. The inconvenience of taking liquid formalin into remote field areas can be offset by carrying dry, powdered paraformaldehyde (e.g. Trioxymethylene, Fisher Scientific Co., USA). One litre of neutralized 10 % formalin is obtained by dissolving about 40 g of the paraformaldehyde, together with about 8 g of anhydrous sodium carbonate (Na_2CO_3) or other buffer and about a teaspoonful of ordinary powdered detergent (such as 'Tide') to aid in solution, with a litre of water, at room temperature. This mixture is then used as ordinary 10 % formalin.

Caution! Formaldehyde is a cumulative external poison. Different people vary greatly in susceptibility, but all become sensitized after repeated exposure. Avoid contact of formalin with the skin, for example by using rubber or plastic gloves.

Specimens more than a few inches in length should have a slit made along the belly, preferably to the right side of the mid-line, and care must be taken to see that the preservative really enters this slit. For large fish, it may be necessary to make deep incision(s) into the muscle mass on either side of the vertebral column (preferably operating from inside the body cavity) to ensure penetration. Fishes should remain in formalin for several days for fixation. 'Exercising' the fins by flexing them helps later flexibility. After about one week they may be wrapped, soaking the wrapping cloths in the preserving fluid, and sealed in plastic bags for transport. If desired to transfer to alcohol, the specimen should be soaked and washed thoroughly in water, then transferred to 50 % alcohol for a few days, before being put into 70 % alcohol for packing and storage. Alcohol is not a suitable preservative for very small larvae and eggs (which can be preserved in formalin). Specimens lose their colour less rapidly if kept in the dark. Ethyl alcohol is generally preferable to other alcohols.

Containers. Well-galvanized or heavily-tinned cans (such as milk churns) make good temporary storage for use in the field, as do large plastic containers. Wide-mouth jars, bottles and tubes of glass or polyethylene plastic are also required. Rolls of polythene tubing are particularly useful as lengths can be heat-sealed into bags (by folding about 25 mm of the tube back on itself across a table edge, placing a metal rule on top to expose about 3 mm of this fold and then running a match or candle along the fold, or by using the electrically heated sealer available through the tubing manufacturer). Very spiny fish will puncture polythene bags. Specimens in perforated polythene bags can be stored in tanks of spirit or formalin to obviate sealing. When dispatching fish through the post, use several bags of plastic one inside the other to ensure no leakage. Preserved specimens in plastic bags may be shipped moist in appropriate containers. All packages of specimens should carry appropriate collection data both inside and outside the container.

Summary list of equipment for fish preservation and handling. Containers; polythene (polyethylene) tubing; good-quality water-resistant paper of high rag content for labels; notebooks; soft pencils; good quality Indian ink and pen; sharp knife; forceps (for inserting labels); scissors; hand-lens (or watch-maker's glass); good quality stainless steel rule; callipers; binocular dissecting microscope with plenty of room below the objectives for large fish; dissecting instruments; waterproof gloves for handling formalin specimens (potassium permanganate will remove pain from fish spine wounds); good supply of cheese cloth or unbleached muslin; strong string.

Use of keys for identifying fish

Specialists vary slightly in their ways of taking certain measurements and counts. It is desirable to ascertain how these were made: this may be stated in the preamble to the key, or in the book where it is found. Learn, too, the sizes of specimens on which the key is based (the sizes of specimens available are often given in the species description), as the key may be based on fish of one size only and allometric growth changes will affect proportional measurements.

The topography of a typical spiny rayed fish is shown in Fig. 3.2, indicating how the various measurements are made. Fin ray counts, scale counts, morphometric measurements to define body shape, gill raker number, teeth, and colour patterns are characters commonly used for identifying fishes. Ordinarily counts and measurements needed for identification are made on the left side of the fish.

Fin ray counts. Fin ray formulae used in keys are typically given thus: D XIII 12, A III 7, P 6, V 7, C 9. (D = dorsal, A = anal, P = pectoral, V = ventral or pelvic, C = caudal.) Sometimes P_1 is substituted for P, and P_2 for V.

SPINES: True spines are single-shafted and of entire composition. They are designated by Roman numerals, no matter how rudimentary or how

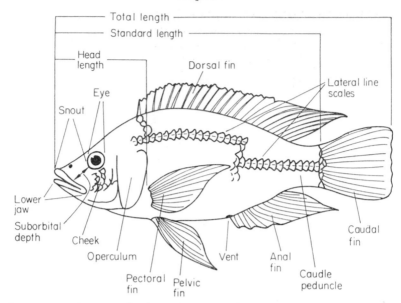

Figure 3.2. A spiny-rayed fish (*Sarotherodon mossambicus*, Cichlidae) showing topographical features and how certain measurements are made.

flexible they may be. Morphologically hardened soft rays (spiny in character) may be treated as spines, whether these be simple rays as in carp, or the consolidated product of branching, as in some catfishes (Ictaluridae).

SOFT RAYS: Soft-rays are bilaterally paired and segmented and are usually, though not always, branched or flexible. They are designated by Arabic numerals. In certain fishes (e.g. Cyprinidae and Catostomidae) the count is of the principal rays only, to accord with general practice and because the rudimentary rays are difficult to ascertain. In these families the principal rays generally include the branched rays plus one unbranched principal ray, since only one unbranched principal ray reaches to near the tip of the fin. In fishes such as Ictaluridae, Esocidae and Salmonidae, in which the rudimentary rays grade into fully developed ones, the total count is given. The last ray of the dorsal and anal fins is often divided to the base, making it difficult to decide whether it should be 1 or 2 (it is better to take it as 1, but record it as 1(+1) to see how it fits in with other people's keys).

CAUDAL FIN: Count the number of branched rays and add 2 (for the 2 principal unbranched rays, above and below).

PAIRED FINS: All rays are counted, including the smallest one at the lower or inner end of the fin base (good magnification is often needed). Sometimes a small ray (counted in pectoral but not pelvic) precedes the first well-developed ray (and may require dissection to be seen). In some fishes with reduced pelvics (e.g. Cottidae) the spine may be a mere bony splint bound into the investing membrane of the first soft ray.

Scale counts. The scales of most fishes have either a smooth exposed surface (cycloid scales) or a minutely denticulated surface (ctenoid scales) which is rough to the feel; the denticulations can be seen with a lens. In general the maximum possible scale count is stated (including small interpolated scales in the lateral line and scales of reduced size near the origins of vertical fins), but not including scales of fin bases or sheaths. Scale formulae are often written thus

$$29 \frac{3\frac{1}{2}}{4\frac{1}{2}},$$

indicating the lateral line count and the scales above and below it.

LATERAL LINE SCALE COUNT: This represents the number of pored scales in the lateral line or number of scales in the position which would normally be occupied by such scales. In some sciaenid fishes, in which the lateral line scales are greatly enlarged, or are obscured by overlapping smaller scales, the number of 'transverse' (i.e. oblique) rows along the side of the fish just above the lateral line is used, sometimes compared with number of scales with lateral line pores. The count is taken from the scale in contact with the shoulder girdle, to the structural caudal base (as determined without dissection by moving the caudal fin from side to side); the scales wholly on the caudal fin base are not included, even when they are well developed and pored.

In the Cichlidae, where the lateral line is in two parts, this count is generally now made to the end of the upper lateral line, then by sliding downward and forward (without counting), to the scale in front of the lower line, and continuing the count along the lower lateral line; this may give two extra scales over the mid-lateral count used by some earlier workers.

SCALES ABOVE LATERAL LINE: Unless otherwise stated, these are counted from the origin of the dorsal fin (first dorsal if two), including the small scales, and counting downward and backward to, but not including, the lateral line scale.

SCALES BELOW LATERAL LINE: These are counted similarly to those above but upward and forward from the origin of the anal fin (including the small scales). If, in continuing upward and forward, the series can with equal propriety be regarded as jogging backward or forward, the backward shift is accepted. Scales between pelvic fin and lateral line are used by some authors.

SCALES BEFORE DORSAL FIN: All those which wholly or partly intercept the straight midline from origin of dorsal to occiput (made in fishes in which the transverse occipital line very sharply separates the scaly nape from the scaleless head); the 'number of scales before the dorsal' (commonly fewer than the number of predorsal scales) is made to one side of the midline.

CHEEK SCALES: The number of scale rows crossing an imaginary line from eye to preopercular angle, or at the deepest point of the cheek in some cases.

CIRCUMFERENCE SCALE COUNT: Represents the number of scale rows crossing a line round the body immediately in front of the dorsal fin (particularly valuable in Cyprinidae).

CAUDAL PEDUNCLE SCALE COUNT: The circumference count around the narrowest part of the caudal peduncle (very useful in Mormyridae and Cyprinidae).

Morphometric measurements. Dividers or dial-reading callipers should be used, also a steel rule; the measuring boards commonly used in fishery investigations are generally not adaptable enough for systematic work.

The measurements aim at comparing the body shape in different species, and characters such as the position of the fins are important. Earlier works generally recorded measurements as proportions, e.g. head length $3\frac{1}{2}$ in standard length; but percentages are now more commonly used, e.g. head length as a percentage of body length. As there are changes in body shape and proportions with growth, comparisons must be made between fish of comparable size where possible. Certain features change with age; the eyes of small fishes are relatively much larger than in adults for example. Others change with sexual maturity or breeding condition, such as the lower jaw elongation found in certain male salmonids and in male tilapia of the *S. mossambicus* group, and dimorphic structures such as warts developed on the snouts of some breeding cyprinids, and the adipose nape hump developed by certain male cichlids when in breeding condition, or the snout tentacles of some loricariid catfishes.

It is better to use bony rather than flesh measurements where possible (e.g. from the bony rather than from the fleshy edge of the orbit), as museum keys have generally been prepared on preserved specimens in which there is less soft padding of flesh than in fresh fish.

TOTAL LENGTH AND FORK LENGTH: These are not commonly used in systematic work (see definitions in Chapter 2).

STANDARD LENGTH: In systematic work this is typically taken as the distance from the anterior part of the snout or upper lip (whichever extends farthest forward) to the caudal base (junction of hypural bone and caudal fin rays) in a straight line (not over body curve). Notice that the 'fishery' standard length is measured to the end of the fish with the jaw closed—hence often begins at the tip of the *lower* jaw.

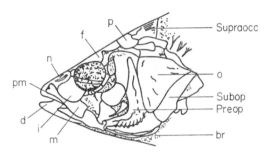

Figure 3.3. Superficial head bones of a spiny-rayed fish to show nomenclature of headbones most commonly used in identifications.
br = branchiostegals;   d = dentary;   f = frontal;   i = first infraorbital;
m = maxillary; n = nasal; o = opercular; p = parietal; pm = premaxillary;
preop = preopercular;   subop = subopercular;   supraocc = supraoccipital.

RELATIONSHIP BETWEEN TOTAL AND STANDARD LENGTHS: To relate fisheries data and systematic data it is often necessary to know the relationship of these measurements in a particular species. Therefore, both should be recorded in early samples, over the whole size range, to enable a curve to be constructed for conversion of one to the other in later work.

BODY DEPTH: This is taken at the deepest point, exclusive of fleshy or scaly structure at fin bases.

HEAD LENGTH: This is measured, with the mouth closed, from the tip of the snout or upper lip (whichever extends farthest forward) to the posterior edge of the opercular bone or to the extremity of the membrane margining the bone (depending on the author), but excluding the opercular spines if these are present.

HEAD WIDTH: This is the greatest dimension, with gill covers closed in normal position.

SNOUT LENGTH: This is taken with dividers from the most anterior point on the snout or upper lip (whichever extends farthest forward) to the front margin of the orbit.

POSTORBITAL LENGTH OF HEAD: This is the greatest distance between the hind margin of the orbit and the bony opercular margin (some authors use the membranous opercular margin as the posterior extremity of measurement).

INFRAORBITAL DEPTH: Generally taken from the bony edge of the orbit to the margin of the first infraorbital bone (preorbital = lachrymal) at its deepest point; sometimes taken as the 'least' measurement from orbit to infraorbital ring margin; usage varies with group of fish and author.

INTERORBITAL WIDTH: Unless specified as least fleshy width, this is the least bony width, from orbit to orbit.

EYE DIAMETER: This is generally taken as length of orbit, the greatest distance between the free orbital rims, and is often oblique.

UPPER JAW: Upper jaw length is taken from the anteriormost point of the premaxillary to posterior point of the maxillary.

LOWER JAW: Lower jaw length is the length of the mandible, taken with one tip of the dividers inserted in the posterior mandibular joint to give the maximum possible dimension.

GAPE WIDTH: This is the greatest transverse distance across the mouth opening, with the mouth closed.

Other characters. GILL RAKERS: Unless otherwise stated, the count is that of the first arch, and often of the lower limb only, or of the two limbs separately. The junction of the two limbs can be felt with a divider point, and if a gill raker straddles the angle of the arch, this is generally included in the lower-limb count, as are all rudimentary gill rakers at the anterior end.

TEETH: The numbers and kinds of *jaw teeth*, number of tooth rows, and (as in siluroids) the relative widths and shapes of *vomerine* and *palatine* tooth bands may be useful characters.

LOWER PHARYNGEAL BONES: These represent the modified fifth gill arches. The bones may be more or less C-shaped and paired (as in Cyprinidae), but the two are sometimes united into a triangular median plate (as in Cichlidae). Their shape, toothed area, and the type and density of teeth on them, are very important characters for the identification of fish of these two families, among others. To remove the bone in cichlids, lift the left gill cover, continue forward with scissors the slit between the fourth gill arch and the blade of the lower pharyngeal bone; then cut the membrane along the side of the bone and the muscles joining its hind corner to the shoulder girdle. Do the same on the other side, being careful not to cut the anterior blade. Cut the bone clean away from the oesophagus and from the tissues beneath it; remove bone, clean off soft tissues and let it dry. The teeth can then be examined with a lens, and the bone replaced if the specimen is to be kept (if not, a more drastic method of removal can be used).

PHARYNGEAL (THROAT) TEETH: These often have to be counted among cyprinids, for precision in identification. For this the pharyngeal bones have to be temporarily removed (with great care) and cleaned. Each bone bears 1 to 3 rows of teeth. Teeth in each row are counted and given a formula in order from left to right; thus '2,5–4,2' indicates that the left pharyngeal has 2 teeth in an outer row and 5 in an inner one, whereas the right has 4 in

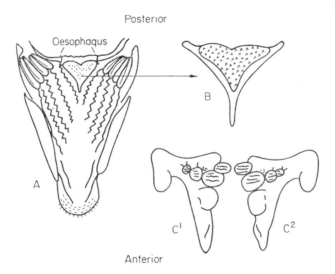

Fig. 3.4. Pharyngeal bones and teeth.
A. Horizontal section through head of *Tilapia*, dorsal view to show position of lower pharyngeal bone.
B. Lower pharyngeal bone of *Tilapia*, showing toothed area.
C. Lower pharyngeal bones of carp, with tooth formula 1,1,3:3,1,1. (Shown in comparable position with A and B, so c^1 is the bone from right side of fish, c^2 from the left side, dorsal view.)

the inner and 2 in the outer row; the formula 4–4 discloses that teeth are present in one row only.

BRANCHIOSTEGAL RAYS, PYLORIC CAECA, AND VERTEBRAE: These and certain other taxonomic characters may be used for fish identification, but are less commonly used under field conditions. Methods of making these counts are given by Hubbs & Lagler (1947).

BARBELS: The numbers and relative lengths of barbels ('whiskers') are important in such fishes as the catfishes, as is their branching in Mochokidae. Tiny barbels are sometimes well hidden in grooves at the sides of the head in some cyprinids. Similarly the dorsal filaments present in some gymnotoids are well hidden in the congealed mucous cover of preserved specimens, necessitating probing them out before they can be seen.

COLOUR: Fish colours may change diurnally, according to habitat, with emotional displays, and on death; also breeding colours, often brightest in the male, may be assumed over a prolonged breeding period. Although bright colours fade, basic colour patterns, such as dark stripes or spots, remain in preserved fishes and are important characters in some groups (e.g. Cichlidae, Characidae). Differences in breeding colours may also give important clues to species. For example, in Lake Nyasa (now Malawi) two species of tilapia are practically indistinguishable except by the colour of the breeding male and differences in time of year and depth of spawning. Such cases stress the importance of non-morphological characters and the need to relate field and ecological data to the specimens kept for museum examination.

Statistical analysis. Since taxonomic conclusions are reached on the basis of samples from large populations, it is incumbent upon a classifier of fishes to be knowledgeable regarding the statistical treatment of data. He should also, as far as possible, be careful to avoid bias, and should evaluate statistically the conclusions that he reaches. For example, often available samples of two kinds of fish will differ in respect to the mean value of some count or measurement; in that event the degree of confidence in the reality of this difference must be established statistically, as well as the variation (standard deviation) of the count in both species, and degree of overlap. Taxonomic hypotheses formulated in terms of quantitative characteristics may be tested by means of the chi-square test, Student's t-test, analysis of variance, multiple range or non-parametric tests (Steel & Torrie 1960). The t-test has some-times been misapplied in taxonomy; Rothschild (1963) discusses this problem and suggests proper procedures. Multivariate analysis may be useful when it is necessary to combine information on several characters to obtain the best possible discrimination between two groups (Sokal & Sneath 1963; Royce 1954).

Taxonomic references for different parts of the world

Only the main works can be listed here, those with keys where available, otherwise check lists, or papers with good bibliographies of the numerous short papers on the region concerned. Where no recent synoptic treatments exist, it is wise to consult a specialist about the literature. Contact a local museum, or see the list of taxonomists working on Pisces, pp. 79–85 in the Directory of Zoological Taxonomists of the World (compiled by Blackwelder, R.E. and R.M., 1961, for the Society of Zoology, Southern Illinois University Press, Carbondale, Illinois); this gives the specialities and addresses of fish taxonomists. The Smithsonian Information Exchange, Washington, D.C., may also be able to help with such information.

As the literature is growing rapidly, the Pisces Section of the Zoological Record should be consulted to keep up to date. The Zoological Record (Section 15, Pisces) is available, singly or by annual subscription, from the Publications Officer, Zoological Society of London, Regent's Park, London, NW1. Many back issues are still available. Abstracting journals are another source of information especially Biological Abstracts (Philadelphia) and Referativnyi Zhurnal (Moscow).

Comprehensive works and special topics

General

ATZ J. (ed.) (1971; 1973). *Dean bibliography of fishes*. Am. Mus. nat. Hist. New York. (For 1968; 1969.)

BERG L.S. (1955). Sistema ryboobraznykh i ryb, nyne zhivushchikh i iskopaemykh (new edition). *Trudy Zool. Inst. Akad. Nauk SSSR* **20**, 1–286.
English text of 1940 edn *Classification of fishes, both recent and fossil*. Dover Publs, Ann Arbor, Michigan, 1947; reprinted ASRCT Bangkok, Thailand, 1965, 304 p.

BERG L.S. (1958). *System der rezenten und fossilen Fischartigen und Fische*. Berlin, 311 p.

CHERFAS B.I. (ed.) (1969). *Genetika, selektisiya i gibridizatsiya ryb*. Isdatelstvo Nauk, Moskva. *Genetics, selection and hybridization of fish*. Israel Program Scientific Translations, 1972, Jerusalem, 269 p.

GREENWOOD P.H. (1975). Classification, p. 330–396, in J.R. Norman, *A history of fishes*, 3rd edn, E. Benn, London.

GREENWOOD P.H., MILES R.S. & PATTERSON C. (eds.) (1973). *Interrelationships of fishes*. Zool. J. Linn. Soc. 53, Suppl. No. 1, 1–536. Academic Press.

GREENWOOD P.H., ROSEN D.E., WEITZMAN S.H. & MYERS G.S. (1966). Phyletic studies of teleostean fishes, with a provisional classification of living forms. *Bull. Am. Mus. nat. Hist.* **131**(4), 339–455. (Outline drawings for each family.)

LINDBERG G.U. (1971). *Opredelitel i kharakteristika semistrv ryb morovoi fauny*. Izdatelstvo Nauka Leningrad. *Fishes of the world a key to families and a checklist*. Trans. H. Hardin, Israel Prog. Sci. Trans., Jerusalem, 1974. Wiley & Sons, New York, 472 p.

LOWE-McCONNELL R.H. (1975). *Fish communities in tropical freshwaters*. Longman, 337 p.

NIKOLSKY G.V. (1971). *Chastnaya Ikhtiologiya*. Moskva. *Special Ichthyology*, Israel Prog. Sci. Trans., Jerusalem, 1961. (Trans. of 1954 edn.)

STERBA G. (1970). *Süsswasserfische aus aller Welt*. 2 vols. Neumann-Neudamm, Melsungen, 688 p. *Freshwater fishes of the world*, translation of 1959 edn revised by D.W. Tucker, Vista Books, London, 878 p.

THINÈS G. (1969). *L'évolution régressive des poissons cavernicoles et abyssaux*. Masson et Cie, Paris, 394 p. (Blind cave fish.)

Protein taxonomy

HAWKINS R.I. & MAWDESLEY-THOMAS L.E. (1972). Fish haematology—a bibliography. *J. Fish Biol.* **4**, 193–232.

JOHNSON M.S. (1975). Biochemical systematics of the Atherinid genus *Menidia*. *Copeia* **4**, 662–691.

LOVE R.M. (1970). *The chemical biology of fishes with a key to the chemical literature*. Academic Press, 547 p.

NYMAN L. (1965a). Species specific proteins in freshwater fishes and their suitability for a 'protein taxonomy'. *Hereditas*, **53**, 117–126.

NYMAN L. (1965b). Inter- and intraspecific variations of proteins in fishes. *K. svenska VetenskAkad. Arsb.*, **9**, 1–18.

SICK K. (1961). Haemoglobin polymorphism in fishes. *Nature, Lond.*, **192**, 894–896.

TSUYUKI H. & ROBERTS E. (1965). Zone electrophoretic comparison of muscle myogens and blood proteins of artificial hybrids of Salmonidae with their parental species. *J. Fish. Res. Bd. Can.* **22**(3), 767–773.

TSUYUKI H., ROBERTS E. & VANSTONE W.E. (1965). Comparative zone electrophoresis of muscle myogens and blood haemoglobins of marine and freshwater vertebrates and their applications to biochemical systematics. *J. Fish. Res. Bd. Can.* **22**(1), 203–213.

TSUYUKI H. & ROBERTS E. (1966). Inter-specific relationships within the genus *Oncorhynchus* based on biochemical systematics. *J. Fish. Res. Bd. Can.* **23**(1), 101–107.

Statistical procedures and numerical taxonomy

PARKER E. (1973). *Introductory statistics for biology*. Studies in biology No. 43, E. Arnold, London, 122 p.

ROTHSCHILD B.J. (1963). Graphic comparisons of meristic data. *Copeia* **4**, 601–603.

ROYCE W.F. (1954). Preliminary report on a comparison of the stocks of yellowfin tuna. *Proc. Indo-Pacif. Fish. Counc.* **4**(3), 130–145.

SOKAL R.R. & SNEATH P.H.A. (1963). *Principles of numerical taxonomy*. W.H. Freeman, San Francisco & London, 359 p.

STEEL R.G.D. & TORRIE J.H. (1960). *Principles and procedures of statistics*. McGraw-Hill, New York, 481 p.

Chromosome numbers

BLAXHALL P.C. (1975). Fish chromosomes—a review of selected literature. *J. Fish. Biol.* **7**, 315–320.

GYLDENHOLM A.O. & SCHEEL J.J. (1971). Chromosome numbers of fishes. I. *J. Fish. Biol.* **13**, 479–486.

HUBBS C. *et al.* (14 authors) (1970). Symposium on fish cytogenetics. *Trans. Am. Fish. Soc.* **99**(1), 98–248.

SCHEEL J.J. (1966). Taxonomic studies of African and Asian tooth-carps (Rivulinae) based on chromosome numbers, haemoglobin patterns, some morphological traits and crossing experiments. *Vidensk. Meddr dansk naturh. Foren.*, **129**, 123–148.

SCHEEL J.J. (1974). Rivuline studies. Taxonomic studies of revuline cyprinodonts from tropical Atlantic Africa. *Annls Mus. r. Afr. cent.*, 8°, *Sci. Zool.* No. 211, 1–150.

WEBB C.J. (1974). Fish chromosomes: a display by scanning electronmicroscopy. *J. Fish Biol.* **6**, 99–100.

Africa

General

BANISTER K.E. (1973). A revision of the large *Barbus* (Pisces, Cyprinidae) of East and Central Africa. *Bull. Br. Mus. nat. Hist.* (Zool.), **26** (1), 1–148.

BOULENGER G.A. (1909–1916). *Catalogue of the freshwater fishes of Africa in the British Museum (Natural History)*, 1 (1909), 373 p.; 2 (1911), 525 p.; 3 (1915), 526 p.; 4 (1916), 392 p. London (Reprinted 1964 in 2 vols. Wheldon & Wesley and J. Cramer.) (Keys.)

HARRY R.R. (1953). A contribution to the classification of the African catfishes of the family Amphiliidae, with description of collections from Cameroon. *Revue Zool. Bot. afr.* **47**, 177–232.

MATTHES H. (1973). *A bibliography of African freshwater fish.* FAO, Rome, 299 p.

POLL M. (1957). Les genres des poissons d'eau douce de l'Afrique. *Annls Mus. r. Congo Belge. Sci. Zool.* **54**, 191 p.

POLL M. (1967). Revision des Characidae nains Africains. *Annls Mus. r. Afr. cent. Ser.* 8°, *Sci. Zool.* **162**, 1–158. (Keys.)

POLL M. (1971). Revision des *Synodontis* africains (family Mochocidae). *Annls Mus. r. Afr. cent., Sci. Zool.* **191**, 1–497.

POLL M. (1973). Nombre et distribution géographique des poissons d'eau douce africains. *Bull. Mus. natn. Hist. nat. Paris*, 3e ser., No. 150, *Ecol. Gen.* **6**, 113–128.

POLL M. (1974). Synopsis et distribution géographique des Clupeidae d'eau douce africains. *Bull. Acad. roy. Belg.* (*Cl. Sci.*), **60** (2), 141–161. (Key.)

ROBERTS T.R. (1975). Geographical distribution of African freshwater fishes. *Zool. J. Linn. Soc.* **57**, 249–319.

TAVERNE L. (1972). Ostéologie des genres . . . considérations générales sur la systématique des poissons de l'ordre Mormyriformes. *Annls Mus. r. Afr. cent., Sci. Zool.*, No. 200, 1–194. (Key to genera; references to other mormyrid papers.)

TREWAVAS E. (1965). *Tilapia aurea* (Stdr) and the status of *T. nilotica exul, T. monodi* and *T. lemassoni* (Cichlidae). *Israel J. Zool.* **14**, 258–276.

TREWAVAS E. (1973). On the cichlid fishes of the genus *Pelmatochromis*, the relationship between *Pelmatochromis* and *Tilapia* and the recognition of *Sarotherodon* as a distinct genus. *Bull. Br. Mus. nat. Hist.* (Zool.) **25**, 1–26.

North Africa and the Nile

ALMAÇA C. (1965). Sur la systématique des barbeaux marocains (Pisces, Cyprinidae, *Barbus*). *Archos Mus. Bocage* (2e ser.) **1**, 111–121.

AMIRTHALINGAM C. & KHALIFA M. EL Y. (1965). *A guide to the common commercial fishes of the Sudan.* (In Arabic and English.) Game & Fish. Dept., Rep. of Sudan, 197 p.

BOULENGER G.A. (1907). *The fishes of the Nile.* (Zoology of Egypt, vol. 2.) Hugh Rees, London, 578 p. (Reprinted 1965.)

PELLEGRIN J. (1921). Les poissons des eaux douces de l'Afrique du Nord française. *Mém. Soc. Sci. nat. Phys. Maroc* **1**(2), 216 p.

SANDON H. (1950). An illustrated guide to the freshwater fishes of the Sudan. *Sudan Notes Rec.*, 61 p.

Lake Chad

BLACHE J. (avec collaboration de MITON F., STAUCH A., ILTIS A., LOUBENS G.) (1964). *Les poissons du bassin du Tchad et du bassin adjacent du Mayo Kebbi.* O.R.S.T.O.M., Paris, 483 p. (Keys.)

West Africa

BOESEMAN M. (1963). An annotated list of fishes from the Niger delta. *Zool. Verh. Leiden*, No. 61, 1–48.

DAGET J. (1954). Les poissons du Niger supérieur. *Mém. Inst. fr. Afr. noire*, **36**, 391 p. (Keys.) (Daget has written numerous papers, e.g. 1961, *Ibid* **62**, 325–362 Niokolo-Koba Park fish; 1962, *Ibid* **65**, 1–210 Fouta Dialon and Basse Guinée fish; 1963, *Ibid* **66**,

573–600 Mont Nimba reserve fish, and many others which for reasons of space it is impossible to cite here.)

DAGET J. (1962). Le genre *Citharinus* (Characiformes). *Revue Zool. Bot. afr.* **66** (1–2), 81–106.

DAGET J. (1965). Les genres *Nannaethiops* et *Neolebias* (Characiformes). *Revue Zool. Bot. afr.* **72**(1–2), 1–23.

DAGET J. (1966). Abondance relative des poissons dans les plains inondées par la Bénoué à hauteur de Garoua (Cameroun). *Bull. Inst. fr. Afr. noire* **28**(1), 247–258. (Lists species.)

DAGET J. & ILTIS A. (1965). Poissons de Côte Ivoire (eaux douces et saumâtres). *Mém. Inst. fr. Afr. noire* **74**, 385 p.

DAGET J. & STAUCH A. (1963). Poissons de la partie Camerounaise du bassin de la Bénoué. *Mém. Inst. fr. Afr. noire* **68**, 85–107.

GERY J. (1965). Poissons du bassin de l'Ivindo. *Biologica Gabonica* **1**(4), 375–393. (Bibliography Gabon freshwater fish.)

HOLDEN M. & REED W. (1972). *West African freshwater fish.* Longman, 68 p.

HOPSON A.J. & J. (1965). *Barbus* (Cyprinidae) of the Volta region. *Bull. Br. Mus. nat. Hist.* (Zool.) **13**(4), 101–149.

JOHNELS A.G. (1954). Notes on fishes from the Gambia River. *Ark. Zool.* Ser. 2 **6**(17), 327–411.

LEWIS D.S.C. (1974). *An illustrated key to the fishes of L. Kainji.* Overseas Devt Admin., London, 105 p.

LOWE-MCCONNELL R.H. (1972). *Freshwater fishes of the Volta and Kanji lakes.* (Keys, illustrated by A.A. Wuddah.) Ghana University Press.

ROMAN B. (1966). Les poissons des Hautes-bassins de la Volta. *Annls Mus. r. Afr. cent.* 8°, *Sci. Zool.*, No. 150, 1–191 (Keys).

ROMAN B. (1971). *Peces de Rio Muni, Guinea ecuatorial. (Aguas dulces y salobres.)* Fund. La Salle Cienc. Nat. Venezuela, 295 p.

STAUCH A. (1966). Le bassin Camerounais de la Bénoué et sa pêche. Mém. O.R.S.T.O.M., Paris, 152 p.

THYS VAN DEN AUDENAERDE D.F.E. (1967). The freshwater fishes of Fernando Poo. *Verh. K. Vlaamse Acad. Wet. Lett. sch. Kunst. Belge* **29** (100), 167. (Keys.)

TREWAVAS E. (1974). The freshwater fishes of the rivers in West Cameroon. *Bull. Br. Mus. nat. Hist.* (Zool.) **26**(5), 331–419.

TREWAVAS E., GREEN J. & CORBET S.A. (1972). Ecological studies on crater lakes in West Cameroon: fishes of Barombi Mbo. *J. Zool., Lond.* **167**, 41–95.

TREWAVAS E. & IRVINE F.R. (1947). Freshwater fishes, pp. 221–282 in *The fish and fisheries of the Gold Coast* by F.R. Irvine, Crown Agents, London, 352 p.

Zaïre Region

DAGET J. (1963). Poissons de la rive droite du Moyen-Congo. Mission A. Stauch (1961). *Bull. Inst. Rech. scient. Congo* **2**, 41–48.

GOSSE J-P. (1963). Le milieu aquatique et l'écologie des poissons dans la région de Yangambi. *Annls Mus. r. Afr. cent.* 8°, *Sci. Zool.* No. 116, 113–270.

GOSSE J-P. (1968). Les poissons du bassin de l'Ubangi. *Documn zool. Mus. r. Afr. cent.* No. 13, 1–56.

MATTHES H. (1964). Les poissons du Lac Tumba et de la région d'Ikela, étude systématique et écologique. *Annls Mus. r. Afr. cent.* 8°, *Sci. Zool.* No. 126, 1–204.

POLL M. (1932). Contributions à la faune des Cichlidae du Lac Kivu (Congo Belge). *Revue Zool. Bot. afr.* **23**(1), 29–35.

POLL M. (1959). Recherches sur la fauna ichthyologique de la région du Stanley Pool. *Annls Mus. r. Congo belge*, 8°, *Sci. Zool.* **71**, 75–174.

POLL M. (1961). Revision systématique et raciation géographique des Protopteridae de l'Afrique centrale. *Annls Mus. r. Afr. cent.*, *Sci. Zool.* **103**, 1–50.

POLL M. (1965). Contribution a l'étude des Kneriidae. *Mem. Acad. r. Belg. Cl. Sci.* **36**(4), 1–28. (Also other Poll papers too numerous to list here.)

POLL M. (1976). Poissons. *Exploration du Parc National de l'Upemba*, **73**, 1–127. Fondation Favoriser Recherches Scient. Afrique, Brussels.

POLL M. & GOSSE J-P. (1963). Revision des genres *Nannaethiops* Gthr 1871 et *Neolebias* Stdr 1894 (Citharinidae). *Annls Mus. r. Afr. cent.*, 8°, *Sci. Zool.* **116**, 7–40.

POLL M. & LAMBERT J.G. (1965). Contribution à l'étude systématique et zoogéographique des Procatopodinae de l'Afrique Centrale (Cyprinodontidae). *Bull. Séanc. Acad. r. Sci. outre-Mer*, 1965(2), 615–631.O

ROBERTS T.R. & STEWART D.J. (1976). An ecological and systematic survey of fishes in the rapids of the lower Zaïre or Congo River. *Bull. Mus. comp. Zool. Harv.* **147**(6), 239–317.

THYS VAN DEN AUDENAERDE D.F.E. (1964). Révision systématique des espèces congolaise du genre *Tilapia* (Cichlidae). *Annls Mus. r. Afr. cent. Sci. Zool.* **124**, 155 p.

Angola

POLL M. (1967). Contribution à la fauna ichthyologique de l'Angola. *Compan. Diamant. Angola, Publ. Cult.* No. 75, 381 p.

East Africa

BAILEY R.G. (1968). Fishes of the genus *Tilapia* (Cichlidae) in Tanzania, with a key for their identification. *E. Afr. agric. For. J.* **34**(2), 194–202.

BAILEY R.G. (1969). The non-cichlid fishes of the eastward flowing rivers of Tanzania, E. Africa. *Revue Zool. Bot. afr.* **80**(1–2), 170–199.

GREENWOOD P.H. (1954). On two cichlid fishes from the Malagarazi River (Tanganyika) with notes on the pharyngeal apophysis in species of the *Haplochromis* group. *Ann. Mag. nat. Hist., Ser.* 12 **7**, 401–414.

GREENWOOD P.H. (1956; 1959). The monotypic genera of cichlid fishes in L. Victoria. Pt. I, 1956, *Bull. Br. Mus. nat. Hist.* (Zool.) **3**(7), 295–333; Pt. II, 1959, *Ibid* **5**(7), 163–177.

GREENWOOD P.H. (1956–69). A revision of the L. Victoria *Haplochromis* species (Pisces, Cichlidae). 1956, Pt. I, *Bull. Br. Mus. nat. Hist.* (Zool.) **4**(5), 223–244; 1957, Pt II, *Ibid* **5**(4), 76–97; 1959, Pt III, *Ibid* **5**(7), 178–218; 1960, Pt IV, *Ibid* **6**(4), 227–281;1962, Pt V, *Ibid* **9**(4), 139–214; 1967, Pt VI, *Ibid* **15**(2), 29–119; 1969, Pt VII (with GEE J.M.), *Ibid* **18**(1), 1–65.

GREENWOOD P.H. (1963). A collection of fishes from the Aswa River drainage system, Uganda. *Proc. Zool. Soc. Lond.* **140**, 61–74.

GREENWOOD P.H. (1965). The cichlid fishes of L. Nabugabo, Uganda. *Bull. Br. Mus. nat. Hist.* (Zool.) **12**(9), 313–357.

GREENWOOD P.H. (1973). A revision of the *Haplochromis* and related species (Pisces, Cichlidae) from L. George, Uganda. *Bull. Br. Mus. nat. Hist.* (Zool.) **25**, 139–242.

GREENWOOD P.H. (1974). *The cichlid fishes of L. Victoria: the biology and evolution of a species flock.* Bull. Br. Mus. nat. Hist. (Zool.), Supplt 6, 1–134.

GREENWOOD P.H. (1974). Review of the Cenozoic freshwater fish faunas in Africa. *Ann. Geol. Survey Egypt* **4**, 211–232.

LOWE R.H. (1959). Breeding behaviour patterns and ecological differences between *Tilapia* species and their significance for evolution within the genus *Tilapia. Proc. zool. Soc. Lond.* **132**(1), 1–30.

POLL M. & DE WITTE G.F. (1939). Poissons. *Explor. Parc. nat. Albert* (1933–35) **24**, 1–81.

POLL M. & DAMAS H. (1939). Poissons. *Explor. Parc. nat. Albert* (1935–36) **6**, 1–73.

POLL M. (1953). Poissons non Cichlidae. *Explor. hydrobiol. L. Tanganyika* (1946–47) **3**(5A), 251 p.

POLL M. (1956). Poissons Cichlidae, *Ibid* 5B, 619 p.

TREWAVAS E. (1966). A preliminary review of the genus *Tilapia* in the eastward-flowing rivers of Africa, with proposals of two new specific names. *Revue Zool. Bot. afr.* **74**(3–4), 394–424.

WELCOMME R.L. (1964). Diagnoses and key to the juveniles of *Tilapia* in L. Victoria. *E. Afr. agric. For. J.* **30**(2), 129–136.

WORTHINGTON E.B. & RICARDO C.K. (1936). Scientific results of the Cambridge expedition to the E. African lakes, 1930–31, No. 15. The fish of L. Rudolf and L. Baringo. *J. Linn. Soc. Zool.* **39**, 353–389.

Central Africa

BALON E.K. & COCHE A.G. (eds.) (1974). L. Kariba: a man-made tropical ecosystem in Central Africa. *Monographiae biol.* **24**, Junk, The Hague, 767 p.

BELL-CROSS G. (1965). Additions and amendments to the check list of the fishes of Zambia. *Puku*, No. 3, 29–43.

BELL-CROSS G. (1973). The fish fauna of the Buzi River system in Rhodesia and Mozambique. *Arnoldia (Rhodesia)* **6** (No. 8), 1–14. (Checklist.)

BELL-CROSS G. (1976). *The fishes of Rhodesia.* Trustees National Museums and monuments of Rhodesia, Salisbury. 256 p.

FRYER G. (1959). The trophic interrelationships and ecology of some littoral communities of L. Nyasa with especial reference to the fishes, and a discussion of the evolution of a group of rock-frequenting Ciclidae. *Proc. zool. Soc. Lond.* **132**(2), 153–281.

FRYER G. & ILES T.D. (1972). *The cichlid fishes of the Great Lakes of Africa.* Oliver & Boyd, Edinburgh, 641 p.

JACKSON P.B.N. (1959). Revision of the clariid catfishes of Nyasaland, with a description of a new genus and seven new species. *Proc. zool. Soc. Lond.* **132**(1), 109–128.

JACKSON P.B.N. (1961). Checklist of the fishes of Nyasaland. *Occ. Pap. natn. Mus. S. Rhod.* **25**B, 535–621.

JACKSON P.B.N. (1961). *The fishes of Northern Rhodesia.* Govt. Printer, Lusaka, 140 p.

JACKSON P.B.N., ILES T.D., HARDING D. & FRYER G. (1963). *Report of the survey of northern Nyasa* 1954–55. Govt. Printer, Zomba, 171 p. (Annotated species list.)

JUBB R.A. (1961). *An illustrated guide to the freshwater fishes of the Zambezi River, L. Kariba, Pungwe, Sabi, Lundi and Limpopo Rivers.* Stuart Manning, Bulawayo, 171 p.

JUBB R.A. & GAIGHER I.G. (1971). Check list of the fishes of Botswana. *Arnoldia (Rhodesia)* **5** (No. 7), 1–22.

KIMPE P. DE (1964). Contribution à l'étude hydrobiologique du Luapula-Moero. *Annls Mus. r. Afr. ent.*, 8°, *Sci. Zool.* **128**, 1–238.

RICARDO C.K. (1930). The fishes of L. Rukwa. *J. Linn. Soc. Zool.* **40**, 625–657.

TREWAVAS E. (1964). A revision of the genus *Serranochromis* Regan (Pisces, Cichlidae). *Annls Mus. r. Afr. cent. Zool.*, No. 125, 1–58.

TREWAVAS E. (1966). Fishes of the genus *Tilapia* with four anal spines in Malawi, Rhodesia, Mozambique and Southern Tanzania. *Revue Zool. Bot. afr.* **74**(1–2), 50–62.

Southern Africa

JUBB R.A. (1967). *Freshwater fishes of southern Africa.* A.A. Balkema, Cape Town/Amsterdam, 248 p.

Madagascar and neighbouring islands

KIENER A. & MAUGE M. (1966), Contributions à l'étude systématique et écologique des poissons Cichlidae endémiques de Madagascar. *Mém. Mus. natn. Hist. nat., Paris, N.S., Ser. A, Zool.* **40**(2), 51–99. (Keys.)

KIENER A. & RICHARD-VINDARD G. (1972). Fishes of the continental waters of Madagascar, p. 477–499, in Biogeography and ecology in Madagascar, eds. R. Battistini & G. Richard-Vindard, *Monographiae biolog.* **21**, Junk, The Hague, 765 p.

PELLEGRIN J. (1933). Les poissons des eaux douces de Madagascar et des îles voisines (Comores, Seychelles, Mascareignes). *Mém. Acad. malagache* **14**, 1–222.

Eurasia

Europe (except USSR)

ALMAÇA A. (1965). Contribution à la connaisance des poissons des eaux intérieures du Portugal. *Archos. Mus. Bocage* (2ᵉ ser.) **1**(2), 9–39.

BAGENAL T.B. (1973). *Identification of British fishes.* Hulton Educat. Publs Ltd, 199 p.

BALON E.K. (1966). *Ryby Slovenska.* Obzor, Bratislava.

BANARESCU P. (1964). Pisces-Osteichthyes. *Fauna Republicii Romine* **13**, 1–959, Bucuresti. (In Romanian with extensive bibliography.)

BLANC M. *et al.* (1971). *European inland water fish: a multilingual catalogue.* Fishing News (Books) Ltd, London (for FAO, Rome).

DRENSKI P. (1951). Ribitje v Balgariya. *Fauna na Bulgariya* No. 2, 270 p. Bulg. Akad. Nauk, Zool. Inst. i. Mus., Sofia.

DUNKER G. (completed by LADIGES W.) (1960). Die Fische der Nordmark. *Abh. Verh. naturh. Ver. Hamburg, N.F.* 3, Suppl. 432 p.

GAŞOWSKA M. (1962). Kraglouste i ryby (Cyclostomi et Pisces). *Klucze do Oznaczania kegowcow Polski,* Pt. I, PWN, Warsara-Krakow, 240 p.

HOLCIK J. & HENSEL K. (1971). *Ichtyologiká prírička.* Obzor, Brazislava, 215 p.

LADIGES W. & VOGT D. (1965). *Die Süsswasserfische Europas.* Paul Parey, Hamburg & Berlin.

LOZANO Y REY L. (1952). Los peces fluviales de España. Madrid: Ministerio de Agricultura, 251 p.

MAITLAND P.S. (1972). Key to the British freshwater fishes with notes on their distribution and ecology. *Scient. Publs Freshwat. Biol. Ass.* No. 27, 139 p.

MUUS B.J. & DAHLSTRØM P. (1967). *Europas Ferskvandsfisk.* Copenhagen: G.E.C. Gads Forlag. English edn. Ed. A. Wheeler as *Collins guide to freshwater fishes of Britain and Europe,* Collins, London, 1971, 220 p. (German edn. see Terofal, 1967.)

OLIVA O., HRABĚ S. & LÁC J. (1968). *Stovovce Slovenska.* I. Ryby, objživelniky a plazy. Slovenkej Akadémie Vied, Bratizlava, 389 p.

SCHINDLER O. (1953). *Unsere Süsswasserfische.* Franckh'sche Stuttgart, 222 p. Trans. and Ed. P.A. Orkin as *Freshwater fishes,* Thames & Hudson, London 1957, 243 p.

SOLJAN C.J. (1948). *Ribe Jadrana* (Fishes of the Adriatic Sea) (Key). Split.

SPILLMANN C.J. (1961). *Poissons d'eau douce.* Fauna de France, No. 65, Lechevalier, Paris, 303 p.

STAFF F.R. (1950). *Ryby slodkowodne Polski i krajów ościennych.* Traska, Evert, Michalski, Warzawa, 286 p.

STEINMANN P. (1948). *Schweizerische Fischkunde.* H.R. Sauerlander & Co., Aarau, 222 p.

TALER Z. (1953). *Glavnik Muzeja Srpske Zemlje,* Ser. B, Biol. nauk, vol. 5–6, Beograd. (List of freshwater fishes of Yugoslavia.) (In Serbian.)

TEROFAL F. (1967). *BVL Bestimmungsbuch Süsswasserfische Europas.*(Muus & Dahlstrøm übersetzt und bearbeitet.) BVL München, Basel, Wien, 224 p.

VUKOVIC T. & IVANOVIC B. (1971). *Slatkovodne ribe Jugoslavije.* Zemaljski Muzej Bosne i Hercogovine u Sarajevom Posebno, Izdanje, 268 p.

Asia Minor

AKŞIRAY F. (1948). Türkische Cyprinodontidae I. *Istanb. Univ. Fen. Fac. Mecm, Ser. B,* **13**(2), 97–138. (Many short papers by C. Kosswig and co-workers on Turkish fishes are to be found in *Istanb. Univ. Fen. Fac. Mecm, Ser. B,* 1940 onwards.)

BECKMAN W.C. (1962). The freshwater fishes of Syria and their general biology and management. *FAO Fish. Biol. tech. Pap.* No. 8, 297 p.

KHALAF K.T. (1961). *The marine and freshwater fishes of Iraq.* Baghdad, 164 p.

LADIGES W. (1960). Süsswasserfische der Turkei I. Teil Cyprinidae. *Mitt. hamb. zool. Mus. Inst.* **58,** 105–150. II. Teil Cobitidae, *Ibid* **58,** 159–201. (1964) III. Teil Restliche Gruppen, *Ibid* **61,** 203–220.

MAHDI N. (1961). *Fishes of Iraq.* Baghdad, 82 p.

SLASTENENKO E. (1955–56). *Karadeniz havzasi Baliklari.* [The fishes of the Black Sea basin.] Translation of Russian text into Turkish by H. Alten, Istanbuhl, 711 p.

STEINITZ H. (1953). The freshwater fishes of Palestine. An annotated list. *Bull. Res. Coun. Israel* **3**(3), 209–227.

Ceylon, India and Pakistan

DAY F. (1889). *The fauna of British India including Ceylon and Burma. Fishes.* 2 vols., Taylor & Francis, London, 548, 509 p.

HORA S.L. (1920–50). A whole series of papers, many in *Rec. Indian Mus.* (See 1951, Bibliography of the publications of S.L. Hora, Calcutta.)

HORA S.L. (1937–41). The game fishes of India. Series of papers in *J. Bombay nat. Hist. Soc.* (e.g. 1941 **42**(2), 305–319).

HORA S.L. (1941). Homalopterid fishes from Peninsular India. *Rec. Indian Mus.* **43**(2), 221–232.(Keys.)

HORA S.L. (1941). Siluroid fishes of India, Burma and Ceylon. *Rec. Indian Mus.* **43**(2), 97–115. (Keys.)

HORA S.L. & LAW N.C. (1941). The freshwater fish of Travancore. *Rec. Indian Mus.* **43**(2), 233–256.

HORA S.L. & SILAS E.G. (1952). Revision of the glyptosternoid fishes of the family Sisoridae, with descriptions of new genera and species. *Rec. Indian Mus.* **49**(1), 5–30. (Keys.)

JAYARAM K.C. (1974). Ecology and distribution of freshwater fishes, p. 517–584, in Ecology and biogeography in India, ed. M.S. Mani, *Monographiae biol.* **23**, Junk, The Hague, 733 p.

JAYARAM K.C. (1976). Index Horana: an index to the scientific fish names occurring in all the publications of the late Dr Sunder Lal Hora. *Records Zool. Surv. India, Occasional Paper*, No. 1, 190 pp.

MENDIS A.S. & FERNANDO C.H. (1962). *A guide to the freshwater fauna of Ceylon.* Fish. Res. Sta., Dept Fish. Ceylon, 160 p.

MIZRA M.R. (1974). Freshwater fishes and ichthyogeography of Baluchistan and adjoining areas of the Indus Plain, Pakistan. *Biologia (Lahore)* **20**(1), 67–82.

MUNRO I.S.R. (1955). *The marine and freshwater fishes of Ceylon*, Dept Ext. Affairs, Canberra, Australia, 351 p.

PRASHAD B. & MUKERJI D.D. (1929). The fish of the Indawgyi Lakes and streams of the Myitkyina district (Upper Burma). *Rec. Indian Mus.* **31**(3), 161–224.

QURESHI M.R. (1965). *Common freshwater fishes of Pakistan.* Government of Pakistan Press, Karachi, 61 p. (Keys.)

SHAW G.E. & SHEBBEARE E.O. (1938). The fishes of Northern Bengal. *Jl R. Asiat. Soc. Beng., Science* **3**, 1–137. (Keys.)

SRIVASTAVA G.J. (1968). *Fishes of Eastern Uttar Pradesh.* Vishwavidyalaya Prakashau, Varanasi, India, 163 p.

TRIPATHI S.D., CHAKRABORTI P.K. & KHAN R.R. (Compilers) (1962–). *Bibliography of Indian fisheries and allied subjects.* Govt. India, Central Inland Fisheries Research Inst., Barrackpore, W. Bengal.

WITT H.H. DE (1960). A contribution to the ichthyology of Nepal. *Stanford ichthyol. Bull.* **7**(4), 64–88. (Check list, no keys.)

Southeastern Asia

ALFRED E.R. (1966). The freshwater fishes of Singapore. *Zool. Verh., Leiden* **78**, 1–68.

AUBENTON F. DE (1965). Compte-rendu summaire d'une mission ichthyologique au Cambodia. *Bull. Mus. Hist. nat. Paris* **37**(1), 128–138. (Lists species.)

BISHOP J.E. (1973). Limnology of a small Malayan River Sungai Gombak. *Monographiae biol.*, **22**, Junk, The Hague.

BLACHE J. & GOOSSENS J. (1954). Monographie piscicole d'une zone de pêche au Cambodge, *Cybium* **8**, 1–49.

BRITTAN M.R. (1954). A revision of the Indo-Malayan freshwater fish genus *Rasbora*. *Mongr. Inst. Sci. Tech. Manila* **3**, 1–224.

CANTOR T. (1850). Catalogue of Malayan fishes. *J. Asiatic Soc. Bengal* **18**(2), 983–1443. (Reprinted A. Asher & Co., Amsterdam, 1966.)

CHEVEY P. & LE POULAIN LE F. (1940). La pêche dans les eaux douces du Cambodge. *Mem. Inst. oceanogr. Indoch.* **5**, 1–193.

HERRE A.W.C.T. & MYERS G.S. (1937). A contribution to the ichthyology of the Malay peninsula. *Bull. Raffles Mus., Singapore*, No. 13, 5–75.

HORA S.L. (1941). Notes on Malayan fishes in the collection of the Raffles Museum, Singapore. Pts 2 and 3. Loaches of the families Cobitidae and Homalopteridae. *Bull. Raffles Mus.* **17**, 44–64. (Keys.)

HORA S.L. & GUPTA J.C. (1941). Notes on Malayan fishes in the collection of the Raffles Museum, Singapore. I. Catfishes of the families Siluridae, Bagridae, Amblycepidae, Akysidae, Sisoridae, Chacidae, Schilbeidae and Clariidae. *Bull. Raffles Mus.* **17**, 12–43. (Keys.)

KAWAMOTO N., TRUONG N.V. & TUY-HOA T.T. (1972). Illustrations of some freshwater fishes of the Mekong delta, Vietnam. *Contrib. Fac. Agric. Univ. Cantho*, No. 1, 1–49.

LINDSEY C.C. (1963). *Guide to families of Malaysian fishes.* Guides to fauna of the Malayan region No. 1, 60 p. (Mimeo). Dept. Zool. Univ. Singapore.

SMITH H.M. (1945). *Freshwater fishes of Siam or Thailand.* Bull. U.S. natn Mus., Washington **188**, 1–622.

SUVATTI CHOTE (1965). *Fish fauna of Thailand.* Thai Fish. Dept, Min. Agric., Bangkok.

TAKI Y. *et al.* (1974). *Fishes of the Lao Mekong basin.* U.S. Agency for Int. Devt, Mission to Laos, Agric. Divn, 232 p.

THIEMMEDH JINDA (1966). Fishes of Thailand: their English, scientific and Thai names. *Kasetsart Univ. Fish. Res. Bull.* **4**, 15 plus 212 p., 160 text figs.

TWEEDIE M.W.F. (1952). Notes on Malayan freshwater fishes. *Bull. Raffles Mus.* **24**, 63–95. (Includes No. 3. The Anabantoid fishes, and No. 5. List of Malay names; these are part of a series of short papers on Malayan freshwater fishes in *Bull. Raffles Mus.*)

China and Korea

BERG L.S. (1932). A review of the freshwater cottoid fishes of the Pacific slope of Asia. *Copeia* **1**.

CHANG HSIAO-WEI (1944). Notes on the fishes of Western Szechwan and Eastern Sikiang. *Sinesia, Shanghai* **15**(1–6).

CHEN J.F.T. (1951–53). Check list of the species of fishes known from Taiwan (Formosa). (Mainly marine.) *Q. Jl Taiwan Mus.* **4**(3–4), 181–210; **5**(4), 305–341; **6**(2), 102–140.

CHU Y.T. (1931). Index piscium sinensium. *Biol. Bull. St John's Univ. Shanghai*, No. 1, 290 p.

CHU Y.T. (1935). Comparative studies of the scales and on the pharyngeals and their teeth in Chinese cyprinids, with particular reference to taxonomy and evolution. *Biol. Bull. St John's Univ., Shanghai*, No. 2, 225 p.

CHU Y-T., LO Y-L. & WU H-L. (1963). [A study of the classification of the Sciaenoid fishes of China.] (In Chinese + 94 figs.) Shanghai Fisheries College, 100 p. (Reprinted 1972, Antiquariat Junk, The Hague.)

FOWLER H.W. (1930–1962). A synopsis of the fishes of China (10 parts). *Q. Jl Taiwan Mus.* (Pt. 19, 1962, is vol. 15 No. 1 and 2, 77 p.)

MIYADI D. (1940). (Freshwater fishes of Manchoukuo) p. 22–28 in *Report of the limno-biological survey of Kwantung and Manchoukuo*, 573 p. Public Bureau, Kwantung Agency, Kyoto. (In Japanese.)

MORI T.A. (1934). The freshwater fishes of Jehol. Rept First Sci. Expedn Manchoukuo. *J. Chosen nat. Hist. Soc.* **19.**

MORI T.A. (1936). *Studies on the geographical distribution of freshwater fishes in Eastern Asia.* Keijo Imperial Univ., Chosen, Japan, 88 p. (Good bibliogr. freshwater fishes of eastern Asia, p. 67–88.)

MORI T.A. (1952). Check list of the fishes of Korea. *Mem. Hyoga Univ. Agric.* **1**(3), 1–228.

MORI T.A. & UCHIDA K.A. (1934). A revised catalogue of the fishes of Korea. *J. Chosen nat. Hist. Soc.* **19.**

NICHOLS J.T. (1943). The freshwater fishes of China. *Am. Mus. nat. Hist., Nat. Hist. Cent. Asia* **9**, 322 p.

TCHANG T.L. (1933). The study of Chinese cyprinoid fishes Pt I. *Zoologia Sinica* **2**(1), 1–247.

UCHIDA K. (1939a). [Fish fauna of Korea and Manchuria.] Tokyo, 458 p. (In Japanese.)

WU HSIEN-WEN *et al.* (1964). [The cyprinid fishes of China.] Shanghai, 228 p. (In Chinese.)

Japan

AOYAGI HYOZI (1957). [*The general description of the freshwater fish fauna of the Japanese Islands.*] Taishyakan, Tokyo, 272 p. (In Japanese.)

MATSUBARA KIYOMATSU (1955). [*Morphology and classification of fishes*, Pts 1, 2, 3.] Iskizaki Co. Ltd, Tokyo, 1605 p. (In Japanese.)

MIYADI D., KAWANABE H. & MIZUNO N. (1963). [Coloured illustrations of freshwater fishes of Japan.] 259 p. Hoikusha Co., Tokyo. (In Japanese.) (Recommended for general descriptions.)

NAKAMURA MORIZUMI (1963). [Keys to the freshwater fishes of Japan, fully illustrated in colour.] Hokurykan, Tokyo, 258 p. (In Japanese.)

NAKAMURA MORIZUMI (1969). Cyprinid fishes of Japan—studies on the life history. *Res. Inst. Nat. Res., Tokyo*, Spec. Publs No. 4, 1–449 p. (In Japanese.)

OKADA Y. (1959–60). Studies on the freshwater fishes of Japan. Pt I. General; Pts 2 & 3 Systematic studies. *J. Fac. Fish. pref. Univ. Mie-Tsu* **4**(1), 1–265; **4**(2), 267–588; **4**(3), 589–860.

OKADA Y. & MATSUBARA K. (1953). *Bibliography of fishes in Japan* (1612–1950). Fac. Fish. pref. Univ. Mie-Tsu, Japan. (Mainly in Japanese.)

WATANABE MASAO (1960). *Fauna Japonica, Cottidae (Pisces).* Tokyo News Service Ltd, Tokyo, 218 p.

USSR

BERG L.S. (1948–49) (4th edn). *Ryby presnykh vod SSSR i sopredel'nykh stran.* Opredeliteli Fauny SSSR, 27, 3 vols: 504, 496, 510 p. Akad. Nauk, SSSR. *Fishes of the USSR and adjacent countries*, English translation, Israel Prog. Sci. Trans, Jerusalem, 1962–65.

BERG L.S., BOGDANOV A.S., KOZHIN N.I. & RASS T.C. (ed.) (1949). Promyslovye ryby SSSR. [Commercial fishes of the USSR.] Pishchepromizdat. Text 783 p., Atlas 230 p.

LADIGES W. & VOGT D. (1965). *Die Süsswasserfische Europas bis zum Ural und Kaspischen Meer.* Paul Parey, Hamburg and Berlin, 250 p.

LEBEDEV V.D., SPANOVSKAYA V.D., SAVVAITOVA K.A., SOKOLOV L.I. & TSEPKIN E.A. (1969). *Ryby SSSR.* [Fishes of the USSR.] Mysl Press, Moscow, 446 p.

NIKOLSKY G.V. (1938) *Ryby Tadzhikistana.* [Fishes of Tadzhikistan.] Akad. Nauk, SSSR.

NIKOLSKY G.V. (1940). *Ryby Aral'skogo morya.* [Fishes of the Aral Sea.] Moskovskoe Obshchestvo Ispytatelei Prirody.

NIKOLSKY G.V. (1956). *Ryby basseina Amura.* [Fishes of the Amur River basin.] Akad. Nauk, SSSR, 557 p.

NIKOLSKY G.V., GOMCHEVSKAYA N.A., MOROZOVA G.I. & PIKULEVA V.A. (1947). *Ryby basseina verkhnei Pechory.* [Fishes of the basin of upper Pechora River.] Moscow.

SVETOVIDOV A.N. (1963). *Clupeidae. Fauna of USSR Fishes* 2(1), 1–428. Zool. Inst. Acad. Sci. USSR N.S. No. 48, 1952, translated Israel Prog. Sci. Trans. Jerusalem, 1963.

TALIEV P.N. (1955). *Bychki-Podkamenshchiki Baïkala (Cottoidei).* [The Cottoidei of L. Baikal.] Isdatelstvo Akad. Nauk, SSSR, Moskva, 603 p.

TARANETS A.YA. (1936). Presnovodnye ryby basseina severozapadnoi chasti Yaponskogo morya. [Freshwater fishes of the basin of the northwestern part of the Sea of Japan.] *Tr. Zool. Inst. AN SSSR,* 4.

Australasia and Oceania
Indopacific Islands

BERRA T.M., MOORE R. & REYNOLDS L.F. (1975). The freshwater fishes of the Laloki River system of New Guinea. *Copeia* 2, 316–326.

GOSLINE W.A. & BROCK V.E. (1960). *Handbook of Hawaiian fishes.* Univ. Hawaii Press, Honolulu, 372 p. (Mainly marine.)

HERRE A.W.C.T. (1924). Distribution of the true freshwater fishes in the Philippines. I. The Philippine Cyprinidae. *Philippine J. Sci.* 24, 249–306; II. The Philippine Labyrinthici, Clariidae and Siluridae. *Philippine J. Sci.* 24, 683–707.

HERRE A.W.C.T. (1926). A summary of the Philippine catfishes, order Nematognathi. *Philippine J. Sci.* 31, 385–411.
(*Note:* Papers on fishes in *Philippine J. Sci.* have recently been reprinted by the Smithsonian Institution, Tfh fund.)

HERRE A.W.C.T. (1953). The eleotrid gobies of the Philippines and adjacent regions. *Philippine J. Sci.* 82, 345–373. (Keys.)

HERRE A.W.C.T. (1953). Check list of Philippine fishes. *Res. Rep. U.S. Fish Wildl. Serv.,* No. 20, 977 p. (Mainly marine.)

INGER R.F. & KONG C.P. (1962). The freshwater fishes of North Borneo. *Fieldiana: Zool.* 45, 268 p. (Keys.)

SCHUSTER W.H. & DJAJADIEDJA R.R. (1952). *Local common names of Indonesian fishes.* Bandeng.

WEBER M.G. & DE BEAUFORT L.F. et al. (1911–62). *Fishes of the Indo-Australian archipelago.* 12 vols. Leiden.

Australia

ANDREWS A.P. (1976). A revision of the family Galaxiidae (Pisces) in Tasmania. *Aust. J. mar. Freshwat. Res.* 27, 297–349.

LAKE J.S. (1959). The freshwater fishes of New South Wales. *Res. Bull. St. Fish. N.S.W.* 5, 19 p., 7 pl.

LAKE J.S. (1967). Freshwater fish of the Murray–Darling River system—the native and introduced species. *Res. Bull. St. Fish. N.S.W.* **7**, 1–48.
LAKE J.S. (1971). *Freshwater fishes and rivers of Australia.* Nelson, 61 p.
MUNRO I.S.R. (1956–59). Handbook of Australian fishes. Nos. 1–36. Series in *Fish. Newsl. Australia*, vols. 15–19.
SCOTT E.O.G. (1966). The genera of Galaxiidae. *Austr. Zool.* **13**(3), 244–258.
SCOTT T.D. (1962). *The marine and freshwater fishes of South Australia.* Govt. Printer, Adelaide, 332 p.
TAYLOR W.R. (1964). *Fishes of Arnhem Land.* Records American–Australian Scientific Expedition to Arnhem Land. Smithsonian Instn, Washington D.C., 307 p.
WHITLEY G.P. (1964). *Native freshwater fishes of Australia.* Revd edn, Jacaranda Press, Brisbane, 127 p.
WHITLEY G.P. (1964). Presidential address—a survey of Australian ichthyology. *Proc. Linn. Soc. N.S.W.* **89**, 11–127. (Bibliography.)

New Zealand

McDOWALL R.M. (1964). A bibliography of the indigenous freshwater fishes of New Zealand. *Trans. R. Soc. N.Z. (Zool.)* **5**(1), 1–38.
McDOWALL R.M. (1966). A guide to the identification of New Zealand freshwater fishes. *Tuatara* **14**(2), 89–104. (Keys.).
STOKELL G. (1955). *Freshwater fishes of New Zealand.* Smith & Williams, Christchurch, 145 p.
WOODS C.S. (1963). *Native and introduced fishes.* Nature in New Zealand, A.H. & A. Reed, Wellington–Aukland, 64 p.

Pacific Islands

GOSLINE W.A. & BROCK V.E. (1960). *Handbook of Hawaiian fishes.* Univ. Hawaii Press, Honolulu, 372 p. (Mainly marine fishes.)
HERRE A.W. (1953). Check list of Philippine fishes. *Res. Rep. U.S. Fish. Wildl. Serv.*, No. 20, 977 p. (Mainly marine.)

North America
General

BAILEY R.M. (Ed.) with LACHNER E.A., LINDSEY C.C., ROBINS C.R., ROEDEL P.M., SCOTT W.B. & WOODS L.P. (1960). A list of common and scientific names of fishes from the United States and Canada (2nd edn). *Spec. Publs Am. Fish. Soc.* No. 2, 102 p.
GUNTHER G. (1942). A list of the fishes of the mainland of North and Middle America recorded from both freshwater and seawater. *Am. Midl. Nat.* **28**(2), 305–326.
HUBBS C.L. & LAGLER K.F. (1947). Fishes of the Great Lakes region. *Bull. Cranbrook Inst. Sci.* **26**, 186 p.
HUBBS C.L., MILLER R.R. & HUBBS L.C. (1974). Hydrographic history and relict fishes of the North-Central Great Basin. *Mem. Calif. Acad. Sci.* **7**, 1–259.
HUVER, C.W. (1973). *A bibliography of the genus* Fundulus. G.K. Hall & Co., Boston, Mass., 138 p.

JORDAN D.S. & EVERMANN B.W. (1896–1900). *The fishes of Middle and North America.* 4 vols., 3313 p.

JORDAN D.S. & EVERMANN B.W. (1923). *American food and game fishes.* Rev. edn Double-day, Page & Co. (Reprinted 1969, Dover Publications Inc., New York.)

JORDAN D.S., EVERMANN B.W. & CLARK H.W. (1930). Check list of the fishes and fishlike vertebrates of North and Middle America north of the northern boundary of Venezuela and Columbia. *Rep. U.S. Commer. Fish.* 1928, Pt 2, 674 p.

LA MONTE F. (1945). *North American game fishes.* Doubleday, Doran & Co. Ltd, New York, 202 p.

Canada and Alaska

CARL G.C. & CLEMENS W.A. (1953). The freshwater fishes of British Columbia. 2nd edn. *Handbk Br. Columb. prov. Mus.* **5**, 136 p.

FEDORUK A.N. (1971). *Freshwater fishes of Manitoba: checklist and keys.* Manitoba: Dept Mines & Natural Resources, 130 p.

LEGENDRE V. (1954). *Clef des poissons de pêche sportive et commerciale de la province de Québec.* (2nd edn.) Société Canadienne d'Écologie, Montreal, 180 p. (Also English edn 1954.)

McPHAIL J.D. & LINDSEY C.C. (1970). Freshwater fishes of northwestern Canada and Alaska. *Bull. Fish. Res. Bd Can.* **173**, 381 p.

PAETZ M.J. & NELSON J.S. (1970). *The fishes of Alberta.* Govt Alberta, 282 p.

SCOTT W.B. (1967). *Freshwater fishes of Eastern Canada.* (2nd edn.) Univ. Toronto Press, Toronto, 128 p.

SCOTT W.B. & CROSSMAN E.J. (1973). Freshwater fishes of Canada. *Bull. Fish. Res. Bd Can.* **184**, 966 p.

WALTERS VLADIMIR (1955). Fishes of western arctic America and eastern arctic Siberia. Taxonomy and zoogeography. *Bull. Am. Mus. nat. Hist.* **106**(5), 275–368.

WILIMOVSKY N.J. (1958). *Provisional keys to the fishes of Alaska.* Fish. Res. Lab., U.S. Fish. Wildl. Serv., Juneau, Alaska, 113 p.

United States (contiguous states)

BAILEY R.M. & ALLUM M.O. (1962). Fishes of South Dakota. *Misc. Publ. Mus. Zool. Univ. Mich.* No. 119, 131 p. (Keys.)

BROWN C.J.D. (1971). *Fishes of Montana.* Montana State Univ., Bozeman, Montana, 1–207 p.

BUCHANAN T.M. (1973). *Key to the fishes of Arkansas.* Arkansas Game and Fish Commission, 68 p., 198 maps.

CLAY W.M. (1975). *The fishes of Kentucky.* Kentucky Dept. Fish Wildlife Resources Frank-fort, Kentucky, 416 p.

CROSS F.B. & COLLINS J.T. (1975). *Fishes in Kansas.* Univ. Kansas Mus. nat. Hist., Publ. Education Ser. No. 3, 1–189.

DOUGLAS N.H. (1974). *Freshwater fishes of Louisiana.* Louisiana Wildlife and Fish. Commission, Claitor's Pub. Divn, Baton Rouge, La, 443 p.

EVERHART W.H. & SEAMAN W.R. (1971). *Fishes of Colorado.* Colorado Game Fish. & Parks Divn, 75 p.

LA RIVERS I. (1962). *Fishes and fisheries of Nevada.* Nevada Fish & Game Comm., 782 p.
MOYLE P.B. (1976). *Inland fishes of California.* University of California Press, 405 p.
NELSON J.S. & GERKING S.D. (1968). *Annotated key to the fishes of Indiana.* Aquatic Res. Unit, Indiana Univ., Bloomington, 84 p. (Keys.) Multigraphed.
PFLIEGER W.L. (1975). *The fishes of Missouri.* Missouri Dept of Conservation, 342 p.
SMITH-VANIZ W.F. (1968). *Freshwater fishes of Alabama.* Agric. Exp. Stn, Auburn Univ., Alabama, 211. (Keys.)
TRAUTMAN M.B. (1957). *The fishes of Ohio, with illustrated keys.* Ohio State Univ. Press, 683 p.

Mexico

ALVAREZ DEL VILLAR J. (1970). Peces mexicanos (claves). *Serie Invest. Pesq. Mexico,* No. **1,** 1–166.
DARNELL R.M. (1962). Fishes of the Rio Tamesi and related coastal lagoons in east-central Mexico. *Publs Inst. mar. Sci. Univ. Texas* **8,** 299–365.
HUBBS C.L. (1936). Fishes of the Yukatan Peninsula. *Publs Carnegie Instn* **457,** 157–287.
ROBINSON D.T. (1959). The ichthofauna of the lower Rio Grande, Texas and Mexico. *Copeia* **3,** 253–256.

Central America

ASTORQUI I. (1976). Peces de la cuenca de los grandes lagos de Nicaragua. In *Investigations of the ichthyofauna of Nicaraguan lakes.* (Ed. T.B. Thorson.) University of Nebraska, Lincoln. (Reprinted from *Rev. biol. Trop.,* 19, 7–57, 1971.)
BUSSING W.A. (1967). New species and new records of Costa Rican freshwater fishes with a tentative list of species. *Revta Biol. trop.* **14**(2), 205–249.
BUSSING W.A. (1976). Geographic distribution of the San Juan ichthyofauna of Central America with remarks on its origin and ecology. In *Investigations of the ichthyofauna of Nicaraguan lakes,* pp. 157–175 (Ed. T.B. Thorson). University of Nebraska Press, Lincoln.
CARR A.F. Jr & GIOVANNOLI L. (1950). The fishes of the Cloluteca drainage of southern Honduras. *Occ. Pap. Mus. Zool. Univ. Mich.* No. 523, 38 p. (Key.)
FINK W.L. & WEITZMAN S.H. (1974). The so-called Cheirodontin fishes of Central America with descriptions of two new species (Pisces, Characidae). *Smithson. Contr. Zool.* No. 172, 1–46.
HILDEBRAND S.F. (1925). Fishes of the Republic of El Salvador. *Bull. U.S. Bur. Fish.* **41,** 238–287. (Keys.)
HILDEBRAND S.F. (1938). A new catalogue of the freshwater fishes of Panama. *Publs Field Mus. nat. Hist., Zool. Ser.* **22**(4), 219–359. (Some keys, good bibliography.)
HUBBS C.L. (1935). Freshwater fishes collected in British Honduras and Guatemala. *Misc. Publ. Mus. Zool., Univ. Mich.* **28,** 22 p.
HUBBS C.L. (1936). Fishes of the Yukatan Peninsula. *Publs Carnegie Instn* **457,** 157–287.
MEEK S.E. (1907). Synopsis of the fishes of the Great Lakes of Nicaragua. *Field Colombian Mus. Pub.* (*Zool.*) 7(5), 97–132. (Keys.)
MILLER R.R. (1966). Geographical distribution of Central American freshwater fishes. *Copeia* **4,** 773–802. [Reprinted with Addendum in Thorson, 1976.]

REGAN C.T.L. (1906–1908). *Biologia Centrali-Americana. Pisces.* 203 p.

ROSEN D.E. & BAILEY R.M. (1963). The poeciliid fishes (Cyprinodontiformes), their structure, zoogeography and systematics. *Bull. Am. Mus. nat. Hist.* **126**(1), 1–176.

THORSON T.B. (1976) (ed.). *Investigations of the ichthyofauna of Nicaraguan lakes.* University of Nebraska, Lincoln, 663 p.

South America

Note: The freshwater fish fauna is very rich, literature abundant and widely scattered. Check lists exist but synoptic surveys are only available for a few groups and areas. Gery (1972; *Zool. Verh. Leiden* No. 122) gives the most extensive recent bibliography (52 pp. references) for characoid and associated fishes, with keys to characoid groups to tribes; Gosline (1954) for nematognaths (9 pp. refs.); Fowler (1954) for Brazilian freshwater fishes; Godhino & Britski (1964) an annotated bibliography for Brazilian freshwater fishes; Eigenmann (1910) catalogued all the then-known freshwater fishes. Authors producing series of papers include: characoids—Bohlke, Gery, Travassos, Weitzman; and Surinam catfishes—Boeseman, Njissen; for Myers' papers, see Myers (1970). References given here are to papers most readily available and those with good bibliographies. Small species are often first described in aquarium literature.

General

EIGENMANN C.H. (1910). Catalogue of the freshwater fishes of tropical and south temperate America. *Rep. Princeton Exped. Patagonia 1896–1899* **3**(4), 375–511.

EIGENMANN C.H. (1917, 1918, 1921, 1927). The American Characidae. Parts 1–4. *Mem. Mus. comp. Zool. Harv.* **43**(1, 2, 3, 4), 1–428.

EIGENMANN C.H. (1918). The Pygidiidae, a family of South American catfishes. *Mem. Carneg. Mus.* **7**(5), 259–398.

ELLIS M.M. (1913). The gymnotid eels of tropical America. *Mem. Carneg. Mus.* **6**(3), 109–195.

GERY J. (1964). A review of the Chilodinae, with a key to the species (Characoid fish study No. 36). *Trop. Fish. Hobby,* May 1964, p. 5–10, 63–67.

GERY J. (1969). The freshwater fishes of S. America. Pages 828–848 in E.J. Fittkau *et al.* (ed.) Biogeography and ecology in S. America. *Monographiae biol.,* vol. 2, No. **19**, 449–946. Junk, Hague. The (Annotated list of fish families.)

GERY J. (1972). Corrected and supplemented descriptions of certain characoid fishes described by Henry W. Fowler, with revisions of several genera. *Stud. neotrop. Fauna* **7**, 1–35.

GERY J. (1977). *Characoids of the world.* T.F.H. Publications Inc., Neptune, New Jersey, U.S.A., 672 p. (Keys, numerous coloured photographs.)

GOSLINE W.A. (1945). Catalogo dos nematognathos de agua-doce da America do Sul e Central. *Bolm. Mus. nac. Rio de J., Zoologia* **33**, 1–138.

GOSLINE W.A. (1947). Contributions to the classification of the loricariid catfishes. *Archos Mus. nac. Rio de J.* **41**, 79–144.

GOSSE J-P. (1976). Revision du genre *Geophagus* (Pisces Cichlidae). *Mém. Acad. r. Sci. Outre-Mer Cl. Sci. nat. med.,* 8°, *N.S.* **19**(3), 1–172, 5 pl., 35 figs.

MENEZES N.A. (1969). Systematics and evolution of the tribe Acestrorhynchini (Pisces, Characidae). *Archos. Zool. Est. S. Paulo* **18**(1–2), 1–159. (Keys.)

MYERS G.S. (1970). Annotated chronological bibliography of the publications of G.S. Myers (to end of 1969). *Proc. Calif. Acad. Sci.*, 4th ser. **38**(2), 19–52.

MYERS G.S. (1972). *The Piranha Book.* Trop Fish. Hobby Publs Inc.

REGAN C.T. (1905). A revision of the fishes of the S. American cichlid genera *Acara, Nannacara, Acaropsis* and *Astronotus. Ann. Mag. nat. Hist.*, Ser. 7, **15**, 329–347. (Key.)

REGAN C.T. (1905). A revision of the fishes of the American cichlid genus *Cichlosoma* and of allied genera. *Ann. Mag. nat. Hist.*, Ser. 7, **16**, 60–77, 225–243, 316–340. (Key.)

REGAN C.T. (1906). A revision of the fishes of the South American cichlid genera *Cichla, Chaetobranchus* and *Chaetobranchopsis*, with notes on the genera of American Cichlidae. *Ann. Mag. nat. Hist.*, Ser. 7, **17**, 230–239. (Key.)

REGAN C.T. (1913). A synopsis of the cichlid fishes of the genus *Crenicichla. Ann. Mag. nat. Hist.*, Ser. 8, **11**, 498–504. (Key.)

ROBERTS T.R. (1973). Osteology and relationships of the Prochilodontidae, a S. American family of characoid fishes. *Bull. Mus. comp. Zool. Harv.* **145**, 213–235.

WEITZMAN S.H. (1960). Further notes on the relationships and classification of South American characid fishes of the subfamily Gasteropelecinae. *Stanford ichthyol. Bull.* **7**(4), 217–239. (Key.)

WEITZMAN S.H. & COBB J.S. (1975). A revision of the S. American fishes of the genus *Nannostomus* Günther (Family Lebiasinidae). *Smithson. Contr. Zool.* No. 186, 1–36.

Brazil

Extensive bibliographies of the numerous papers on Brazilian fishes appear in Fowler (1954), Godinho & Britski (1964) and Travassos (1951, 1952).

FOWLER H.W. (1948, 1950, 1951, 1954). Os peixes de agua doce do Brasil. I, 1948, 1–204; 1950, 205–404; 1951, 405–628. *Archos. Zool. Est. S. Paulo* **6**, 1–628. II, 1954, 1–400. *Archos. Zool. Est. S. Paulo* **9**, 1–400. Bibliography is in vol. 2, p. 353–383. (No keys.)

GERY J. (1964). Poissons characoides nouveaux ou non signalés de l'Ilha do Bahanal, Bresil. *Vie Milieu Suppl.* 17 (Vol. Jubilaire dédié à G. Petit), 447–471.

GERY J. (1965). Poissons characoides sud-américains du Senkenberg Museum. II. Characidae et Crenuchidae de l'Igarapé Préto (Haute Amazonie). *Senkenberg biol.* **46**(1), 11–45.

GODINHO H.M. & BRITSKI H.A. (1964). Peixes de agua doce. Pages 317–342 in P.E. Vanzolini (ed.), *Historia natural de organismos aquaticos do Brasil, Bibliografia comentada.* Publição Custeada pela Fundação de Amparo à Pesquisa do Estado de São Paulo. (Annotated bibliography.)

GODOY M.P. DE (1975) *Piexes do Brasil. Suborde Characoidei, Bacio do Rio Mogi Guassu.* Editora Franciscana for M seu de Histo'na Natural, Pirassununga, S. Paulo, 4 vols, 847 p.

MENEZES R.S. DE (1955). Listas dos nomes vulgares de peixes de aguas doces e salobras da zona sêcado nordeste e léste do Brasil. *Archos. Mus. nac. Rio de J.* **42**(1), 343–388.

RIBEIRO P. DE MIRANDA (1954–1962). (Parts I–XI.) Catalogo dos peixes do Museu Nacional. *Publ. avuls. Mus. nac., Rio de J.*

TRAVASSOS H. (1951, 1952). Catalogo dos generos e subgeneros de subordem Characaoidei

(Actinopterygii, Cypriniformes). *Dusenia* **1**, 1–158 (Bibliography p. 143–158). *Dusenia*, **2**, 1951, 205–224, 273–292, 341–360, 419–434. *Dusenia* **3**, 1952, 141–180, 225–250 313–328.

TRAVASSOS H. (1960a). Catalogo dos peixes do vale do Rio São Francisco. *Bolm. Soc. cearense Agron.* **1**, 1–66.

TRAVASSOS H. (1960b). Ictiofauna de Pirassununga IV. Subordem Gymnotoidei Berg, 1940 (Actinopterygii, Cypriniformes). *Bolm. Mus. nac. Rio de J. Zoologia*, **217**, 1–34.

Guianas

BOESEMAN M. (1956). On recent accessions of Surinam fishes. *Zool. Meded. Leiden* **34**(12), 183–199.

BOESEMAN M. (1968). The genus *Hypostomus* Lacépède, 1803, and its Surinam representatives (Siluriformes, Loricariidae). *Zool. Verh. Leiden* No. **99**, 1–89, 18 pl.

BOESEMAN M. (1971). The 'comb-toothed' Loricariinae of Surinam, with reflections on the phylogenetic tendencies within the family Loricariidae (Siluriformes, Siluroidei). *Zool. Verh. Leiden*, No. **116**, 1–56.

EIGENMANN C.H. (1912). The freshwater fishes of British Guiana, including a study of the ecological grouping of species and the relation of the fauna of the plateau to that of the lowlands. *Mem. Carneg. Mus.* **5**, 1–578. (Keys.)

GERY J. (1972). Poissons characoides des Guyanes. I. Généralités. II. Famille des Serrasalmonidae. *Zool. Verh. Leiden* No. **122**, 1–250. (Keys to families, subfamilies and tribes, p. 53–71. Large bibliography, p. 82–133.)

HOEDEMAN J.J. (1952). Notes on the ichthyology of Surinam. The catfish genera *Hoplosternum* and *Callichthys* with key to the genera and groups of the family Callichthyidae. *Beaufortia* **12**, 1–12.

HOEDEMAN J.J. (1961). Notes on the ichthyology of Surinam and other Guianas. 6. Additional records of Cyprinodontiform fishes. *Bull. aquat. Biol.* **2**(17), 61–64.

LOWE (MCCONNELL) R.H. (1964). The fishes of the Rupununi savanna district of British Guiana. *J. Linn. Soc. Zool.* **45**(304), 103–144. (Species list.)

LOWE (MCCONNELL) R.H. (1969). The cichlid fishes of Guyana, S. America, with notes on their ecology and breeding behaviour. *Zool. J. Linn. Soc.* **48**, 255–302. (Keys.)

MEES G.F. (1974). The Auchenipteridae and Pimelodidae of Suriname (Pisces, Nematognathi). *Zool. Verh. Leiden* No. **132**, 1–256.

NIJSSEN H. (1970). Revision of the Surinam catfishes of the genus *Corydoras* Lacépède, 1803 (Pisces, Siluriformes, Callichthyidae). *Beaufortia* **18** (No. 230), 1–75.

PUYO J. (1949). *Poissons de la Guyana française*. Fauna Empire Française, No. 12, Off. Recherche Sci. Outre-Mer, Paris, 280 p.

WHITEHEAD P.J.P. (1973). The clupeoid fishes of the Guianas. *Bull. Br. Mus. nat. Hist.* (Zool.) Supplt 5, 1–227.

Trinidad, Venezuela and Colombia

BEAUFORT L.F. DE (1940). Freshwater fishes from the Leeward group, Venezuela and Eastern Colombia. *Studies Fauna Curaçao, Aruba, Bonaire and the Venezuelan Islands* **2**, 109–114.

D

BOESEMAN M. (1960). The freshwater fishes of the island of Trinidad. *Stud. Fauna Curaçao* **10** (No. 48), 72–153.

BOESEMAN M. (1964). The freshwater fishes of the Island of Trinidad: Addenda, errata et corrigenda. *Stud. Fauna Curaçao* **20** (No. 82), 20, 52–57.

DAHL G. (1971). *Los peces del norte de Colombia.* Inderena, Bogata, Colombia, 391 p. (Keys.)

DIAZ E.L. (1965). Bibliographic material of the fishes of Colombia and north-western S. America. *FAO Fish. tech. Pap.* **53,** 70 p. (Principal source.)

FERNÁNDEZ YÉPEZ A. (1968). Contribucion conocimiento de la familia Doradidae en Venezuela. *Boln. Inst. oceanogr., Cumana* **7**(1), 7–72.

GERY J. (1972). Contribution à l'étude des poissons characoïdes de l'Equateur avec une revision du genre *Pseudochalceus* et la description d'un nouveau genre endemique du Rio Cauca en Colombie. *Acta humboldt, Ser. Geol. Palaentol. Biol.* No. **2,** 1–110.

LUENGO J.A. (1963). La fauna ictiologica del Lago de Valencia (Venezuela) y algunas consideraciones sôbre las demas hoyas del pais y Trinidad. *Acta biol. Venez.* **3**(22), 319–339.

LUENGO J.A. (1970). Notas sôbre los cichlidos de Venezuela (Pisces). *Lagena* Nos. 25–26, 27–36.

MAGO F.M.L. (1970). *Lista de los peces de Venezuela incluyendo un estudio preliminar sôbre la ictiogeografia del pais.* Min. Agric. y Cria-Oficina Nat. de Pesca, Caracas, Venezuela, 283 p.

MAGO F.M.L. (1972). Consideraciones sôbre la sistematica de la famille Prochilodontidae con una sinopsis de las especies de Venezuela. *Acta biol. Venez.* **8,** 35–96.

MILES C.B. (1947). *Los peces del Rio Magdalena.* Min. Econ. nac., seccion Piscicultura, Pesce y caza, Bogata, 214 p.

MILES C.W. (1973). Estudio económico y ecológico de los peces de agua dulce del Valle del Cauca. *Cespedesia (Biol. cient. Dept Valle del Cauca) Colombia* **2**(5), 9–63. (Reprint of 1943 paper, pub. Dept Valle del Cauca, but 1973 reprint lacks Appendix I: species list.)

PRICE J.L. (1955). A survey of the freshwater fishes of the Island of Trinidad. *J. agric. Soc. Trin. Soc. Pap.* No. 863, 1–28.

SCHULTZ L.P. (1944). The catfishes of Venezuela, with descriptions of 38 new forms. *Proc. U.S. natn Mus.* **94**(3172), 173–338. (Keys.)

SCHULTZ L.P. (1944). The fishes of the family Characinidae from Venezuela with descriptions of 17 new forms. *Proc. U.S. natn. Mus.* **95**(3181), 235–267. (Keys.)

SCHULTZ L.P. (1949). A further contribution to the ichthyology of Venezuela. *Proc. U.S. natn. Mus.* **99**(3235), 1–211. (Keys.)

TREWAVAS E. (1948). Cyprinodont fishes of San Domingo, Island of Haiti. *Proc. zool. Soc. Lond.* **118**(2), 408–415.

WEITZMAN S.H. & WOURMS J.P. (1967). S. American cyprinodont fishes allied to *Cynolebias* with a description of *Austrofundulus* from Venezuela. *Copeia* **1,** 89–100.

Western South America

BÖHLKE J. (1958). Studies on fishes of the family Characidae No. 14. A report on several extensive recent collections from Ecuador. *Proc. Acad. nat. Sci. Philad.* **110,** 1–121. (No key but bibliography.)

CHIRICHIGNO F. NORMA (1963). Estudio de la fauna ictiologica de los esteros y parte bajo de los rios del Departamento de Tumbes (Peru). *Divulgs. Cient. Serv. Pesq. Peru* **22**, 1–87.

EIGENMANN C.H. (1922). The fishes of western S. America. Pt I. The fishes of north-western S. America. *Mem. Carneg. Mus.* **9**, 1–346. (Colombia, Panama and Pacific slopes of Ecuador and Peru.)

EIGENMANN C.H. & ALLEN W.R. (1942). *Fishes of western S. America. I. The intercordilleran and Amazonian lowlands of Peru. II. The high pampas of Peru, Bolivia, and northern Chile, with a revision of the Peruvian Gymnotidae and of the genus* Orestias. Univ. Kentucky, Lexington, 494 p.

GERY J. (1964). Poissons characoides de l'Amazonie peruvienne. *Beit. neotrop. Fauna* **1**(1), 1–44. (Characoid fishes study No. 37.)

GILBERT R.J. & ROBERTS T.R. (1972). *A preliminary survey of the freshwater food fishes of Ecuador.* Survey Rept Project: AID/csd-2780, Alabama Agric. Exp. Sta., 49 p.

MANN G.F. (1950). *Peces de Chile, clave de determinacion de las especies importantes.* Min. Agric. Santiago.

MANN F.G. (1954). Vida de los peces en aguas Chilenas. Min. agric., Univ. Chile, 342 p.

MANN F.G. (1954). *Vida de los peces en aguas Chilenas.* Min. agric., Univ. Chile, 342 p.

OVCHYNNYK M.M. (1968). Annotated list of the freshwater fishes of Ecuador. *Zool. Anz.* **181**, 237–268.

Argentina, Paraguay and Uruguay

CARTER G.S. & BEADLE L.C. (1931). The fauna of the swamps of the Paraguayan Chaco in relation to its environment. II. Respiratory adaptations in the fishes. *J. Linn. Soc. Zool.* **37**(252), 327–368. (Species list.)

EIGENMANN C.H. (1909). The freshwater fishes of Patagonia. *Rept Princeton Univ. Expedn to Patagonia, 1869–1899, Zool.* **3**, 225–374.

FOWLER H.W. (1943). Notes and descriptions of new or little known fishes from Uruguay. *Proc. Acad. nat. Sci. Philad.* **95**, 311–334.

LUENGO J.A. (1971). La familia Cichlidae en el Uruguay. *Mems Soc. Cienc. nat. La Salle* **31** (No. 90), 279–298.

RINGUELET R.A., ARAMBURU R.H. & ALONSO DE ARAMBURU A. (1967). *Los peces Argentinos de agua dulce.* Comisión de Investigación Cientifica, B.A., La Plata, 602 p. (Keys.)

TERRAZAS URQUIDI W. (1970). Lista de peces Bolivianos. *Publnes Acad. nac. Cienc. Bolivia* No. **24**, 1–65. (Checklist, bibliography, photographs.)

4

Marking and Tagging

LINDSAY M LAIRD and BRIAN STOTT

Introduction

A mark is defined as any factor which makes a fish identifiable either as an individual or as a member of a batch. Marks may be artificial, e.g. mutilation of fins or addition of tags, or natural, e.g. genetic markers or parasites.

The objectives of marking fish are to enable their numbers to be estimated indirectly or to follow the fate of labelled individuals. Their main uses are for studies on:

(a) Population parameters—
   (1) Densities;
   (2) Mortality rates;
   (3) Rates of exploitation;
   (4) Rates of recruitment.
(b) Movements and migration.
(c) Growth and age determinations.
(d) Behaviour work and other studies where the recognition of individuals is involved.
(e) Telemetry of physiological parameters in free swimming fish or aquarium dwellers.

The ideal marking method would make any fish permanently and unmistakably recognizable individually to anyone examining it. It would be inexpensive, easy to apply in field conditions and have no effect on the fishes' growth, mortality, behaviour, liability to capture by predators or fishing gear, or its commercial value. Unfortunately no such technique has been developed and indeed the objective is probably illusory. Nevertheless an investigator can select a method which complies as far as possible with the above requirements in his particular circumstances.

Group marking techniques

Methods dealt with under this heading do not involve tagging. They are most commonly used as batch marks although in some circumstances they may be used to identify individual fish.

Fin clipping

This widely used technique has the advantages of being simple and quick to operate and requiring a minimal amount of equipment. Where the fin is completely removed regeneration is uncommon, or not sufficient to preclude recognition. Regeneration tends to be more rapid and more complete among young fish than old, among spiny-rayed fish than soft-rayed and for median fins compared with paired fins. Even fairly complete regeneration does not preclude the use of fin-clips where fish are to be examined by trained personnel or when recoveries are to be made before regeneration has made much progress. In such circumstances, partial amputation may be preferable to complete fin removal since less damage is done to the fish. This also makes the marking of large fish much more easy. Stuart (1958) working with brown trout was able to use three successive clips on pelvic fins at yearly intervals (Fig. 4.1).

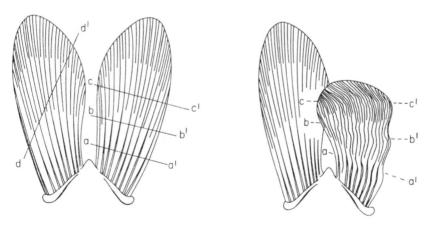

Figure 4.1. Patterns of regeneration resulting from clipping the pelvic fins of brown trout at yearly intervals. A cut along *d–d'* gives rise to maximum regeneration and least distortion. Redrawn from Stuart (1958) and reproduced by permission of Her Majesty's Stationery Office.

Damaging fins by partial clips or amputation may affect mobility, and any fins which have a well-defined behavioural role, such as the dorsal and anal fin of salmonids are best left alone unless it is quite clear that the mutilation will not prejudice the investigation. Much evidence suggests that fish readily adapt to the loss of a fin (Armstrong 1947; Churchill 1963; Horak 1969). In salmonids removal of the adipose fin seems to have least effect on growth and survival (Phinney 1974). Coble (1967) showed that for yellow perch, survival was reduced by clipping the anal fin, but unaffected by clipping of the left pectoral, right ventral or both ventrals. Growth was, however, reduced by a pectoral clip. He suggested that in general, fin clipping reduces survival in fry, may affect survival and growth of fingerlings and has little or no effect on larger fish. Removal of part of the maxillary bone has also been used to mark fish but has been shown to increase mortality (Weber & Wahle 1969; Phinney 1974). There is some evidence that clipping during the spawning season may cause increased mortality rates (Stott, unpublished).

Extra caution may be necessary when marking tropical fish by fin clipping. Van Someren & Whitehead (1959) found that *Tilapia* regenerated pelvic fins in as little as 30 days, although even so it was possible to recognize the marked fish since regenerated fin rays showed an altered pattern of branching.

Fish are sometimes caught that have natural fin deformities but they are not common, and it is usually possible to distinguish between these and true clipped fins. Natural deformities are a cause for concern only if a few recoveries are being sought among many thousands, or even millions of specimens. Here a 'blank' recovery trial is desirable before marking begins.

Where possible blunt nose scissors should be used to clip fins, although sharp-pointed scissors may be needed for small fish. Fish with protruding spines in their dorsal fin can be marked individually using a binary coding system of spine clipping (Rinne 1976).

Opercular and fin punches

Circular, triangular, etc., punches can be made by adapting small pliers to punch holes in opercula or fins. It is possible to distinguish quite a number of batches of individuals, particularly when used in conjunction with other group marking techniques. Not all fish can be marked this way; those with brittle or fleshy opercula are unsuitable. This method was used by Petersen (1896) on plaice in some of the first marking experiments. Le Cren & Kipling (1963) have applied the method to char. In both studies regeneration was rapid, and while regenerated holes could usually be detected on close examination, the method is suitable for short-term experiments only.

Branding

Methods of branding, using heated or cooled metal brands, have been used with varying degrees of success. The method offers the possibility of recognition of individuals without tagging. Brands heated by boiling water were used by Groves & Novotney (1965) and Fujihara & Nakatani (1967). Electrically heated nichrome wire brands produced marks in steelhead trout lasting up to five months (Johnson & Fields 1959) and wood burning pencils have also produced marks (Buss 1953). Cold branding, using a mixture of ethanol and dry ice gave marks lasting up to six weeks in chinook salmon and steelheads (Everest & Edmundson 1967). However, the most consistent branding method used seems to be cold branding using liquid nitrogen as the coolant. Mighell (1969) and Piggins (1972) found that 94% of returning grilse, marked as smolts bore legible marks. Brauhn & Hogan (1972) produced marks lasting up to at least ten months in Channel catfish and Coutant (1972) successfully marked centrarchids. Best results have been obtained on fish with fairly small scales. Carp have successfully been branded on the head (Fujihara & Nakatani 1967). Branding with liquid nitrogen appears to cause little tissue damage (Laird *et al*. 1975). Turner *et al*. (1974) who devised a marking table for field use found mortality associated with marking to be mainly the result of handling and anaesthetizing fish. The brands they applied to brown trout lasted for 2 years. Champion & Hill (1974) have shown a higher survival rate of branded smolts than tagged ones.

The success of branding depends on the temperature of the brand, its size and shape, and the time for which the brand is applied to the fish (Raymond 1974). Branding apparatus is cheap, easy to construct and convenient to use under field conditions. The main disadvantage of the method is that marks are not immediately obvious and can easily be overlooked.

A recent innovation in fish marking technology involves the use of laser beaming to produce branded individual numbers on fish without handling (Anon. 1971). Raymond (1974) states that results from this technique are variable, small fluctuations in voltage can damage fish severely; equipment is also expensive. A highly successful new technique for marking channel catfish uses a silver nitrate pencil (readily available from veterinary suppliers) and gives long lasting marks (Thomas 1975).

Tattooing

Several workers have tamped pigments beneath the skin to produce numbers, letters or code spots, using needles operated by hand or electric vibrators. By hand the method is slow and may thus stress the fish. A machine developed by Dunstan & Bostick (1956) speeds up the process. This has been used with a variety of dyes and insoluble pigments, some of the latter remaining visible for three months. Using India ink and trypan blue in titanium dioxide, Chapman (1957b) was able to mark rainbow trout for 5 months.

Providing tattooing is done with care, marking mortality can be low and it is said behaviour is not affected. The method is not successful on fish with large scales and is essentially a short-term mark.

Subcutaneous injection

Dyes. A wide range of substances have been used for this technique but few have lasted long enough to be of value. Lotrich & Meredith (1974) used acrylic colours and found 9 out of the 15 tested produced discernible marks for 4 months or longer. Lampreys marked with carbon and mercuric sulphide retained marks for at least 18 months (Wigley 1952). Kelly (1967a, b) screened and tested over 150 dyes and found that National Fast Blue 8 GXM and hydrated chromium oxide lasted for 2 and 1 years respectively provided that size increase in the fish was not excessive. He also suggested the use of a jet inoculator, a technique taken up by Hart & Pitcher (1969) who used Alcian Blue 8GX (similar to National Fast Blue 8GXM) in a modified dental tool. This produced marks visible for a year in field tests. Jaw injections have been found to give good results and when used together with other sites a coding system can be used to increase the information obtained.

Injection with liquid latex. Since Davis (1955) first used liquid latex the method has been tried by several workers. Reports are varied: Gerking (1958, 1962) found no difference in survival compared with fin clipping in red-ear sunfish when injected alongside the dorsal fin. However, recoveries from fish injected in the occiput region were few. Green & Northcote (1968) marking catostomids found that colour spots were readily visible for 3 years afterwards. Their best results came from marking fish over 25 cm, although Riley (1966) found latex suitable for marking small plaice. Chapman (1957a) found the method unsuitable for rainbow trout. European perch retained a mark near the dorsal fin for at least 9 months in laboratory tests (Stott, unpublished).

For such marking methods, a syringe is necessary and one with a Luer lock is much better than a push-on fitting, particularly if liquid latex is being used. The syringe need not be a large one; quite a number of fish can be marked subcutaneously with a dye from one of 5-ml capacity. Liquid latex tends to clog, so the plunger of its syringe should be lubricated with silicone stop-cock grease (Riley 1966).

Vital stains

Vital staining, either by immersion or incorporation of a dye into food, is one of the few methods available for marking very small fish. Bouchard & Mattson (1961) found that a 1:300,000 concentration of Neutral Red gave the best results for salmon fry, colour being retained for up to 7 days. However, other workers (Ward & Verhoeven 1963; Jessop 1973) have found Neutral Red to be toxic, and have obtained best results with Bismarck Brown. Deacon (1961) succeeded in marking several species of warm water fish with Bismarck Brown. Zuromska (1966) marked roach fry with this stain, the colour lasting about 4 days. Mathews (1970) marked coarse fish for 14 days using Acridine Orange (1:100,000). Morgan (1973) used a variety of stains to mark eggs but most of these failed to permit embryonic development.

Eipper & Forney (1965) combined the use of fin clipping and vital stains by applying a concentrated solution of Sudan Black to the cut ends of fins. This produced a coloured line after regeneration. Arnold (1966) in a review of fish marking with dyes concludes that immersion staining is of value only for short-term experiments.

Incorporation of dyes into food has been used to mark small fish (Loeb 1966). Bagenal (1967) fed maturing female brown trout (*Salmo trutta*) with pelleted food mixed dry with powdered Sudan Black. The resulting eggs were darkly stained and the colour remained in the fry for 6 weeks after they started to feed themselves.

Fluorescent materials

Fluorescent dyes have been introduced under the skin by means of a tattooing machine (Duncan & Donaldson 1968) giving a retention time of up to 19 months, and by using compressed air and a sand-blasting gun (Phinney *et al.* 1967) which gave a mark lasting up to eighteen weeks. Phinney & Matthews (1969, 1973) have reported improved retention time, 2 years in coho salmon marked with a fluorescent dye in melamine sulphonamide formaldehyde resin. Marking is rapid and does not affect survival under hatchery conditions. Andrews (1971) marked fat-head minnows in this way; all fish retained marks on the operculum and fin bases for the 600-day duration of the experiment. Matson & Bailey (1969) described a frame for holding fish to ensure even marking.

The fluorescent properties of tetracycline and oxytetracycline drugs have been exploited (Weber & Ridgeway 1962, 1967; Weber & Wahle 1969; Scidmore & Olson 1969). Injecting and feeding fish with, or immersing them in, tetracycline results in the drug being deposited at sites of calcification at the time of administering. Treatment neither hinders nor favours survival and mark retention of $3\frac{1}{2}$ years has been reported (Weber & Ridgeway 1967). Trojnar (1973) fed tetracycline hydrochloride to rainbow trout fry and found that although 100 % initial mark was not achieved, successfully-marked fish were all recognizable a year later. Bones stored in 10 % formalin or 40 % isopropyl alcohol retained their fluorescent properties for 4 days.

Mark retention was not demonstrated in fry stocked into the wild; it is known that sunlight can deactivate tetracyclines although the filtering effect of the water may prevent this.

Tetracycline is used in the treatment of bacterial diseases and the use of this antibiotic to mark fish may increase the occurrence of bacteria resistant to the drug. Resistant strains of *Aeromonas salmonicida*, the causative organism of furunculosis, have already been isolated (Aoki *et al.* 1971). There is also the problem that many hatchery fish may become marked following therapeutic administration of the drug.

The detection of fluorescent marks necessitates a source of ultraviolet light, which may cause some difficulty in the field, as may access to the sites of ossification.

Deep injection techniques

Hasler & Faber (1941) appear to have been the first to produce a lasting mark by this method. They injected trout fingerlings interperitoneally with a slightly radioactive suspension of thorium dioxide in a carbohydrate carrier. The material should be retained quantitatively throughout life. Detection requires X-ray equipment, making field use impractical.

Dunn & Coker (1951) report little success with trials of a variety of other substances. Injections of lead acetate have been successful in producing a 'time mark' on fish scales (Hiyama & Ichikawa 1953; Ichikawa & Hiyama 1954) and the method has been modified by Fry *et al.* (1960) who used lead disodium versenate. An injection at a dosage of 50 mg/kg body weight results in lead being deposited within a day or so. Mortality and growth do not appear to be affected.

Individual marking techniques (tagging)

The great advantage of tags is that they can be serially numbered, thus enabling individual fish to be identified. A wide variety of tags have been used by fishery workers. Jakobson (1970) and Jones (1977) give extensive reviews of tags and their use. The following section includes many of the types now in common use. The principal ones are illustrated in Fig. 4.2 with the usual attachment sites indicated. The larger types may carry a message requesting information from the finder and details of where to send it.

Internal tags

These are plastic or metal plates. Because of the difficulty of recovery they are usually used on fish which are handled at commercial cleaning stations, and are often brightly coloured to make them conspicuous. Metal tags may be recovered by magnets or themselves be magnetic (Kroger *et al.* 1974). Tags may also be located by induction detectors or X-rays (Lindroth 1955). Wilomovsky (1963) used a radioactive metal tag on herring.

Subcutaneous tags

This method was first used by Le Cren (1954) on char (*Salvelinus willughbii*)—which had proved difficult to tag by other methods—in conjunction with a clipped fin and a metal detector (Moore & Mortimer 1954). This tag was, however, unsuccessful when applied to trout. Jefferts *et al.* (1963) developed a colour-coded magnetic subcutaneous tag for use in Pacific salmon. Hatchery pond studies were encouraging but subsequent field trials showed severe tag loss. Bergman *et al.* (1968) experimented with this tag and found that it did not affect the growth of salmon fingerlings over a period of a year. Leary & Murphy (1975) successfully tagged Hawaiian anchovies with a magnetized colour-coded wire implanted into the head cartilage or intramuscularly. After 30 days the tag loss was 14·7% and survival was 80·5%. Ebel (1974) describes a system for the automatic detection and separation of adults tagged as juveniles with binary- and colour-coded wire tags. A method for recovery of magnetized wire tags from cartilage was described by Hager (1975).

External tags—wired on

A widely-used technique is to fasten tags, made of various materials, to fish by means of a loop of wire. Silver, stainless steel, nickel, titanium,

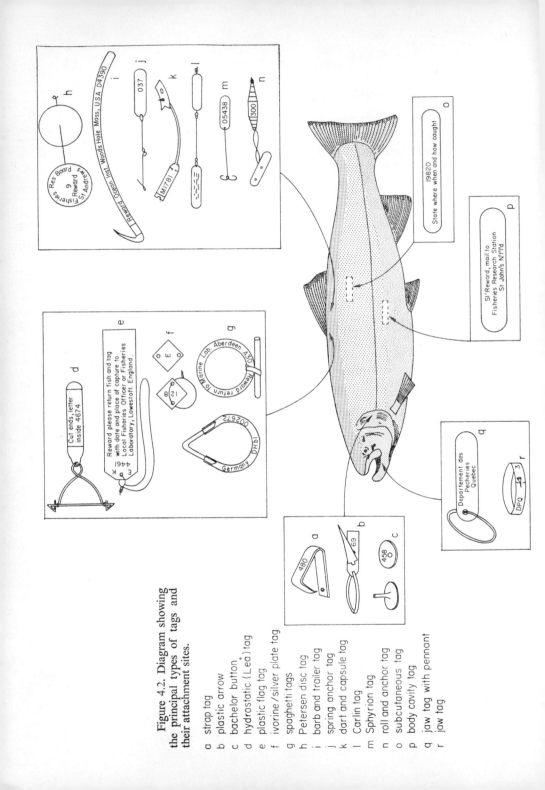

Figure 4.2. Diagram showing the principal types of tags and their attachment sites.

a strap tag
b plastic arrow
c bachelor button
d hydrostatic (Lea) tag
e plastic flag tag
f ivorine/silver plate tag
g spaghetti tags
h Petersen disc tag
i barb and trailer tag
j spring anchor tag
k dart and capsule tag
l Carlin tag
m Sphyrion tag
n roll and anchor tag
o subcutaneous tag
p body cavity tag
q jaw tag with pennant
r jaw tag

tantalum and monel wire have been used as have nylon, terylene or poly-ethylene either braided or monofilamentous. Thorpe (1975) found that in experiments with brown trout in Loch Leven, monel wire was at least as suitable as silver and only 1/30th of the cost. Polyethylene attachment has been found to chafe less than stainless steel but the stainless steel gave higher recapture rates (Saunders 1968).

Wire and plate tags. These are usually attached by means of a wire loop to which is fastened a small numbered plate of metal or plastic. A common modification is the flag tag where a strip of flexible polyvinyl chloride (PVC) numbered with waterproof ink replaces the plate. A simple and quickly applied staple tag suitable for short-term work has been developed by Jordan & Smith (1968).

The hydrostatic tag (Lea tag). This tag may be attached with a wire, as above, or by means of a bridle. It consists of a transparent plastic cylinder, plugged at either end and containing paper bearing the number and message. The tag is usually made to be neutrally buoyant in sea water. A range of sizes is available and the tag has proved highly successful on adult salmonids. A modification is the inclusion of a magnet inside the cylinder to enable tagged fish to be detected as they ascend fish passes.

The Petersen tag. One of the earliest tags, this consists of two metal or plastic discs connected by a wire or filament passing through the body of the fish, often under the dorsal fin. The tag has also been used on fins or operculum, but with much less success (Koshinsky 1972). A modification, the batchelor button, where a connecting rod replaces the wire, has been frequently used as an operculum tag, but it tends to be lost rapidly.

The double attachment trailer tag. This tag has given good returns on sal-monids (Carlin 1955). It consists of articulated stainless steel fastened to a strip of cardboard in celluloid and bears a message. It is attached by two wires passing through the interneural bones under the dorsal fin. A similar, but simple and cheaper tag uses a polyethylene monofilament for attachment (Saunders 1968) and is now extensively used on Atlantic salmon smolts. Carlin tags of this type have been shown to be less susceptible to tag loss than the wire and plate type (Swain 1974).

External tags with an internal anchor

These tags are in two parts; the anchor, which is inserted so as to lodge between the interneurals or behind the body wall, and a trailing portion which remains outside the fish and bears a number and a message. The best-known patterns are the Sphyrion tag (Scarratt & Elson 1965), the spring anchor (Lawler 1963b), the bark-type plastic (Everhart & Rupp 1960) and the Danish roll and anchor. A nylon or nylon/PVC internal anchor tag has been developed together with a magazine loading applicator (Thorsen 1967; Dell 1968). Pletcher (1968) described the grow-through tag which relies on fish tissue growing through holes in the head of the tag to anchor it in place.

Spaghetti tags

Experiments on albacore in water tunnels carried out by Alverson & Chenowith (1951) led to the development of the Spaghetti tag by Wilson (1953). This tag is made from 0·25 to 2·5-mm diameter plastic tubing with a printed message which is passed through the musculature in front of or under the dorsal fin. The two ends may either be tied or fastened together by a wire or nylon plug. Similar thin tubing may also be attached to an internal anchor; the tubing trails backwards below the dorsal fin.

Strap tags

These are flat, metal or plastic strips with a point at one end which is passed through a hole in the other end and bent over. They are usually attached to the operculum or around the mandible; attachments to fins were formerly used but are much less permanent.

Opercular tags. These have given variable results which seem to depend on whether the opercular bone is hard enough to prevent the tag wearing through and falling out. European perch have been successfully marked by fastening a strap tag round the pre-opercular bone (Bardach & Le Cren 1948 as have bream (Goldspink & Banks 1971). Lockard (1968) reported good results with a nylon-reinforced plastic material used on rainbow trout and largemouth bass.

Jaw tags. These tags are used for larger fish (above 200 mm) which have a robust mandible. They are easily applied using a pair of long-nosed pliers and are well suited for recognition by anglers. However, they have been shown to affect growth, possibly by interfering with feeding (Schuck 1942; Warner 1971).

Sonic tags

A sonic tag is a transmitter which emits an inaudible untrasound signal detectable by hydrophones. The individual fishes' positions can be determined to within a few metres without disturbing its normal activity. Trefethen (1956) and Poddubnyi *et al.* (1966) were among the first to report the use of this method. Stasko (1975) gives a comprehensive bibliography and edits a newsletter keeping workers informed of new developments in the field.

Tags are powered by small dry cells which make up a large part of the weight; the larger the battery the more powerful the signal and the longer the life of the tag. In practice the tag weighs between 2 and 20 g, the underwater weight should not exceed 1–2 % of the fish wet weight in air. High frequency tags are smaller but have a shorter range for a given power. Typical signal frequencies used for tags are from 3 to 300 kHz and the life of tags can be from 1 day to 2 months with ranges from 100 m to 1 km. Mitson & Young (1975) discuss the effect of different design constraints. It is doubtful if satisfactory tags can be made for fish of less than 75 g. Tags may be attached externally but insertion into the stomach is commonly used for macrophagous species. External tags increase the drag on the fish (McCleave & Stred 1975) but internal ones could affect feeding behaviour.

A pulsed output signal increases battery life and tags of different pulse repetition frequency rates may be used to distinguish several fish being tracked simultaneously.

The simplest receiving system is a hand-held directional hydrophone, a pair of which can give triangulation fixes on the fish. Static hydrophone arrays have also been used (Young *et al.* 1972; Hawkins *et al.* 1974).

Range as well as bearing determination with a single receiver is possible with transponding tags (Mitson & Storeton-West 1975). Vertical movements can be monitored with special receivers (Greer Walker *et al.* 1971; Gardella & Stasko 1974), or with a pressure transducer in the tag which modulates the pulse repetition rate (Luke *et al.* 1973). Temperature can be similarly telemetered and fish movements through thermoclines monitored particularly effectively (Nyman 1975). Telemetry can be extended to the study of heart rate (Priede & Young 1976). Radio transmitters may be used for telemetry (Frank 1968; Nomura *et al.* 1972) but position fixing is not so precise as with sonic tags.

Biological marks

While biological or natural marks are not strictly marking methods they are mentioned here because certain naturally occurring characteristics may be used to distinguish fish stocks. Different growth rates may help to confirm that adjacent, or even mixed populations are in fact distinct. Frost (1963) found that the two components of the Windermere char population, which were separable according to their place and time of spawning also had different growth rates after the second year of life. Meristic characteristics can be used for the same purposes, in the above example the populations were also separable by their differing numbers of gill rakers. Fish from different stocks of sockeye and chum salmon may be distinguished, though usually incompletely, by the number of circuli on the scales in different years of life, or by the average distance between them. Spring and autumn spawning stocks of herring in the southern Gulf of St Lawrence can be distinguished by the shape of their otoliths (Messieh 1972).

The incidence of parasitic infections has also been used to separate stocks (Sindermann 1961; Margolis 1963; Templeman & Fleming 1963). The technique requires much preliminary work to identify suitable parasites, ascertain their natural range, seasonal incidence and year-to-year variability in numbers. Kabata (1963) suggested five criteria for the use of parasites as stock indicators. These are:

(a) High rate of stock infestation in certain areas and absence in others.

(b) Simplicity of life history (no other hosts).

(c) Infection of reasonably long duration.

(d) Stability—no seasonal or annual fluctuations.

(e) Wide environmental tolerance.

Blood groups and serological characters can be used in separating fish stocks (Sick 1961; Marr & Sprague 1963; Calaprice & Cushing 1967). Payne *et al.* (1971) and Child *et al.* (1976) give evidence to support the presence of two races of Atlantic salmon in British waters, based on analysis of transferrin polymorphism.

Choice of a marking method

This is inevitably a compromise decision for which no strict rules can be laid down since the weight placed on the contributory factors will vary with the situation. However, there are several considerations to be borne in mind:

(a) The objectives of the marking experiment.

(b) The duration of the experiment.

(c) The methods available to recover marked fish.

(d) The type (i.e. species, size, stage of life cycle) and numbers of fish involved.

(e) The personnel, finance and equipment available for marking.

The objectives of the experiment should be the most important considerations in arriving at a decision as to whether or not it is necessary to use tags to mark the fish. Much information can be obtained through group marking methods which are quicker to apply than tags, may have a less traumatic effect and are cheaper. Thus it may be possible to mark greater numbers of fish by group marks and so increase the chances of recapturing significant numbers of marked fish.

Many of the merits of different marking methods have already been discussed. Of the group marks, fin-clipping and cold-branding (in salmonids and small-scaled fish) are perhaps the best long-term marks, but the use of the jet inoculator seems quite satisfactory for work lasting up to 18 months. Immersion in certain vital stains provides a method for marking fry but marks seldom last longer than a few days. Latex and dye injection marks may be slower to apply than branding but are more useful on large-scaled fish or on fish with no scales where branding is unsuccessful. Fluorescent dyes and deep injections have the disadvantage of requiring sophisticated detection equipment.

If more than a single batch mark is required, different brand symbols or colour spots at different positions can be used.

The choice of a tag is a much more difficult decision to make in the absence of prior knowledge. The return rates of the different tag types may differ appreciably. Tag losses differ between different types of tags. Koshinsky (1972) found that pike retained 92% of barb-anchored strap tags for two years but only 13% of monofilament attached preopercular discs. A 90% loss of anchor tags in 12 weeks by channel catfish was thought to be caused by the lack of solid attachment where there was not enough filament for the barb to open out behind the interneurals (Greenland & Bryan 1974). Keller (1971) improved the retention of flag tags by brook trout by altering the attachment sites.

Tag returns will also be affected where the tag used alters the fishes' vulnerability to recapture. Adult salmon tagged with Spaghetti tags were recaptured in gill nets at twice the rate of those tagged with discs (Hartt 1963). Jaw and opercular tags may also tangle with gill nets and jaw tags may affect the rate of recapture by angling. The colour of tags can also affect the recapture rate. McCracken (1963) showed that fishermen tended to recover more red, white and yellow tags than monel metal from cod, but Swain (1974) showed returns from conspicuously coloured tags to be less than returns from silver on salmon. In general the choice of colours is a compromise; bright colours are easily seen at recapture but may also be conspicuous to predators. However, some colours which are conspicuous out of the water may be less so when submerged (Lythgoe 1975). In inshore and freshwater red is clearly visible, while yellow is less so (red colours in many freshwater fish intensify during the mating season). In clear marine water red is absorbed but yellow shows up clearly.

Mortality rates of fish tagged in different ways may also vary and affect return rates. Saunders and Allen (1967) found indications of a reduced survival of salmon tagged as smolts with Carlin-type tags compared with unmarked fish. Koshinsky *loc. cit.* reported a higher mortality among dart-tagged pike than among pike tagged with preopercular discs attached with monofilament, but over a 2-yr period the higher mortality rate was only 12%. The rate of tag returns may also be affected by the water temperature at the time of marking (Aslanova 1963; Morgan & Roberts 1976).

Field organization of marking experiments

As with the choice of marking method it is impossible to lay down rules for the field organization of marking experiments; everything depends on the objectives of the study, the site and the labour available. Even so, there are factors common to all situations.

Catching and holding fish for marking

Methods of capturing fish are discussed in Chapter 2. If there is a choice of method available the one selected should be that which damages the fish least. Electric fishing can produce fish in good condition, although delayed mortality from severe shock has been reported. Traps may provide fish in good condition if they are emptied at frequent intervals. Gill nets are usually less satisfactory, but some gilled fish are useable, especially if the mesh holding them is cut to release them. The results from seining are variable. It is satisfactory if skilfully carried out and if the fish are robust enough to tolerate the loss of scales which inevitably occurs to some degree; small fish are often badly damaged. Beverton & Bedford (1963) and Kotthaus (1963) have shown that the appearance and level of activity of the fish at the time of tagging were significantly related to their subsequent recapture rates.

If it is necessary to keep the fish for some time after they are caught and before they are marked it is worthwhile doing all that the field conditions allow to minimize the effect on the fish. Keep-nets or pens should be as large as possible to prevent overcrowding, and should be situated in shade where the fish will not be disturbed continuously. In warm weather nets or pens need aerating, but generally a slow water flow through them is sufficient to prevent deoxygenation. Knotless netting is preferable to knotted for keep-net construction as it causes less damage to fish by scale removal.

Marking the fish

Most of the points under this heading will have been determined with the selection of the marking method. It is often worthwhile to use an anaesthetic when tagging, branding or using injection techniques. A range of anaesthetics used for fish is discussed by Bell (1967). MS 222 has been used on a wide variety of species. However, it has been shown that anaesthesia by unbuffered MS 222 can result in a marked stress effect (Wedermeyer 1970) who suggested benzocaine, a closely related compound to MS 222, as an alternative. Benzocaine, a relatively inexpensive chemical, has been used successfully by McErlain & Kennedy (1968), and Laird & Oswald (1975) who give details of working concentrations.

The layout of the marking site should consist of a reception (and anaesthetizing where appropriate) area, an area for measuring, marking and possibly removing scales, and a system for releasing marked fish. It is important to have sufficient labour to keep the marking personnel at full stretch. Marking is most efficiently carried out when a table and protection from the weather can be provided but this may be impractical under field conditions. The recorder should be supplied with some means of keeping satisfactory data in the wet; pressure sensitive paper under polythene sheets can be used or figures may be recorded on roughened plastic sheets.

Fish should be released as near as possible to their place of original capture, with shoaling species released in large batches. A note should be made of any fish not in good condition.

Recapture of marked fish

The arrangements for the recapturing and recording of recaptures will have been considered when determining the method of marking to be used in the experiment. If recaptures are to be made during sampling the problem is simplified, but the desirability of using more than one catching method to avoid bias should be borne in mind. If anglers or commercial fishermen are expected to recapture marked fish, the problem is more complicated. In such situations the experiment must be widely publicized and over an area larger than that from which recaptures might be expected. Frequent reminders are necessary to maintain interest. Rewards may be given for the return of tags together with the required information, or for the whole fish with the tag attached to it. If, as sometimes happens, incomplete information is given about a recapture, the fisherman should be contacted as soon as possible. Most fishermen take an intelligent interest in their quarry and are often as interested in the information resulting from their recapture as in the reward itself. It is obviously important to encourage this attitude by providing as many details as possible of the recapture (e.g. age, growth, time at liberty and movements) and by explaining the purpose of the experiment.

5

Age and Growth

T B Bagenal and F W Tesch

The ability to determine the age of fish is an important tool in fishery biology. Work on this topic started some 250 years ago; its history has been described many times, for example by Dahl (1909), Suvorov (1948, 1959), Heder-ström (1959) and Ricker (1975, p. 203). Age data in conjunction with length and weight measurements, can give information on stock composition, age at maturity, life span, mortality and production.

Whereas reasonably precise methods for determining age are known for many fishes (e.g. Mohr 1927, 1930, 1934; Graham 1929), there is still need to develop better methods for tropical species. Workers should proceed with caution, with both temperate and tropical fishes. General accounts of metho-dology are to be found in books by Bückmann (1929), Rounsefell & Everhart (1953), Lagler (1956) and Parrish (1956). Chugunova's indispensable hand-book, available in Russian (1959) and in English (1963), gives details con-cerning most of the procedures in use and illustrates the apparatus required.

Introduction

The steps to be taken in age and growth studies are:

1 Procure a random sample of fish from the population large enough to include representatives of all sizes and ages present and take from it a strati-fied sub-sample so that very large numbers of the early dominant age-classes do not have to be aged. It is essential that particular attention is paid to any source of bias inherent in the sampling gear. For example a net which allows the smaller members of an age group to escape will not be suitable in growth studies (see Chapter 2).

2 Record for each specimen the date, place and manner of collection.

3 Determine and record sex, stage of maturity of the gonads, length and weight of each individual (see Chapters 2 and 7).

4   Take from each specimen the structure(s) that will be used for age determination, making sure that such structures are cross-referenced to the data
in 2 and 3 above.
5   Assign an age to each individual, using more than one method wherever
possible; if only one method is used, make comparisons between readings
made by different people. It is important *not* to know the length of the fish
before examining the ageing structure. If the fish length is known, and a
probable age has been considered, one is tempted unconsciously to make the
visible ring structure fit that age. The length may be an indicator of likely
age, but is not necessarily a function of age. Either rings observed on the age
structure conform to a regular recognizable and validated time scale, or they
do not. The use of knowledge of the length when ageing fish for growth
studies is highly likely to lead to a fallacious circular argument.
6   Calculate growth in relation to age for each sex separately; combine the
two sexes if they are not significantly different.
7   Determine the length–weight relationship for each sex separately, and
combine them if appropriate.
8   Calculate the condition of the fish in the population and determine its
changes with age, sex, season, etc., when applicable.
    The information on age, growth and condition may now be applied to
questions of recruitment, mortality and other aspects of population dynamics
(Chapters 6, 8, 12 and 13).
9   Calculate Instantaneous Growth Rates in length and weight.

Age and growth studies

The most frequently used method of age determination is the interpretation
and counting of growth zones or growth *checks* which appear on the hard
parts of fishes. Those that are considered to be formed annually are called
year marks, annual marks, annual rings or annuli. These are formed during
alternate periods of faster and slower growth (or no growth at all), and
reflect various environmental or internal influences (see Simkiss 1974; Bilton
1974). In temperate regions the period of little or no growth usually occurs
between the beginning of winter and early summer. In general the greater
the seasonal temperature differences, the clearer are the annual marks. For
this reason they are most distinct in northern and southern parts of the world
with a continental climate.

Another commonly-used method is known as the *Petersen method*. When fish spawn annually and the progeny grow at roughly uniform rates, a size frequency distribution for the whole population exhibits a mode for each age group. This method requires individual lengths of a large number of fish in the population and little overlap in the sizes of fish in adjacent age groups. Usually these requirements are only met in the younger age groups of a population.

Age and growth may also be estimated from marking and tagging fish, whether specifically for this purpose or in other studies. However it is absolutely essential to determine that marking or tagging does not affect the growth rate; without this information the data must be treated with very great caution.

In tropical regions the determination of age is often particularly difficult (Menon 1950, 1953; De Bont 1967; Fagade 1974). The rings on scales and hard parts are not necessarily annual, and may be associated with external factors such as a dry season (Daget 1952; Johnels 1952; Lowe-McConnell 1964), changes in food supply, stock density, and so on; and these may not occur annually. The rings may also be associated with spawning (Hopson 1965), or associated loss of condition (Holden 1955; Garrod 1959). Age determinations made from these rings must be checked by other methods, and unfortunately the Petersen method cannot be used because the fish spawn throughout much of the year and the life cycles are often short. Further from the equator, where spawning occurs during annual rainy seasons length frequency analysis can be used (Lowe 1952). Mathews (1974) has illustrated the use of probability paper and a computer program NORMSEP in ageing tropical marine fish. Direct observations on growth rates in ponds may sometimes be helpful, but for many species growth in ponds varies greatly with the prevailing conditions and hence offers little guidance to growth in nature.

The choice of age determination methods

Great care must be taken with any species for which no established ageing method is available. The first step is to examine the scales and otoliths, and to prepare dried bones, particularly flat ones such as the operculum, but including vertebrae and cross-sections of spines and fin rays, from three or four individuals. The aim is to find a structure that satisfies two criteria:

1 A recognizable pattern must be visible either by direct viewing or after some form of preparation.

2   A regular time scale must be allocated to the visible pattern. This is the essential part of validating the structure for age determination.

Particular attention must be paid to ensure that the time scale starts early in the life history. In this respect otoliths and bones are more satisfactory than scales (Williams & Bedford 1974; Gulland 1958) since they are formed earlier in life, even as early as 14 days before hatching from the egg (McKern, Horton & Koski 1974). The position where the earliest scales are formed may be found by staining larval fish at the beginning of metamorphosis with alizarin. Scales should be taken from the region where they are found to be first formed. Ideally at the start of a study, the fish should be aged by more than one method since it has been found that two methods do not always agree (Messieh & Tibbo (1970). In this case the disagreement should if possible be explained, or a third method tried.

Whichever method of age determination is chosen, good photographic records of some of the structures used should be kept (Blacker 1964, 1974; Mina 1965; Banks & Irvine 1969).

Validation of the chosen method

It is essential that whatever method of age determination is chosen, the time scale must be validated. Graham (1929) lists five criteria for validation as follows:

1   Agreement with Petersen's method. Care must be taken that the modes represent age groups and not only particularly strong year classes.

2   The seasonal record of the edge of the ageing structure. If it is reliable, the supposed annulus will appear at the edge of the scale, otolith or bone only during a relatively short period of the year. This method requires large samples collected regularly throughout the year.

3   The observation of year classes over a period of years. Recognizably strong and weak year classes should appear as successively older age groups each year.

4   Marking experiments. Fish marked or tagged and later recaptured should show the number of annuli corresponding to the period of liberty. It is not necessary for the fish to be of known age.

5   Tank or pond experiments. Fish reared in ponds or aquaria and of known age, should have annuli corresponding with this age.

Even if a year class is not easily recognizable, each mode in a size frequency distribution should progress through the year to the position previously occupied by the next older age group. Sometimes an otolith or scale may have a recognizable feature, or pattern of growth (e.g. good-poor-poor-good). This feature or pattern should be exhibited by older age groups each year.

An additional, and extremely useful, validation method uses tetracycline antibiotic. If this is injected (Kobayashi *et al.* 1964; Holden & Vince 1973) or added to food (Weber & Ridgeway 1962) it is taken up where bone, otolith and scale growth is active, and fluoresces under ultraviolet light. After treatment the fish may be kept in ponds or tagged and released. When re-examined after a period, the known time interval since the tetracycline administration should agree with the age determination time scale from the fluorescent band to the bone, otolith and scale edge. However the use of tetracycline for this purpose is not allowed in all countries.

Agreement with age readings from other skeletal structures may be suggestive of a valid time scale, but is not strictly applicable as evidence unless the other structures have themselves been validated by one of the methods already mentioned. For example, scale readings may be validated by comparison with those from otoliths if the otolith readings have already been shown to be valid. However if one structure suggests a wrong age, it is likely that the other structures from the same fish will do so too.

The procedures used in age determination
Definition and designation of age. The term 'age-group' expresses age in years, while 'year class' refers to the fish produced in a given year. A consistent system for designating age is necessary, regardless of the method by which the age is determined. Unfortunately there is not yet complete agreement on age designation or terminology.

However by common usage the age of a fish is usually designated by reference to the annual marks on its hard parts, and to some extent the season of the year, rather than according to its exact length of life (which in any event is usually not precisely known). A fish in its first growing season belongs to the age-group 0, and its successive stages may be called a larva (fry or sac fry), alevin (advanced fry), and fingerling (young-of-the-year or under-yearling). A fish in its second growing season is said to be a member of the age-group 1, or simply age 1, and may be called a yearling. In the third growing season the fish is age 2 and is called a 2-year-old, and so on.

A yearling will typically have one annual mark on its hard parts. However, in some species the time when the annual mark appears may vary over as much as two or three months in different individuals, while in centrachids may be formed as late as July. Much confusion would arise if fish of the same brood, all taken at the same time, were classified in different age-groups. To avoid this Hile (1950) and others have proposed that January 1 be regarded as the date on which the age designation changes (in the Northern Hemisphere), whether or not an annual mark is yet recognizable on the hard parts; for the Southern Hemisphere July 1 would be the corresponding date. However some species may need different treatment depending on when they spawn, but it is important that some birth-date be designated and ages assessed accordingly. Care must be taken if occasionally annuli are formed after the designated birth-date.

An alternative designation is age 1+ for yearlings, 2+ for 2-year-olds, etc. The plus sign refers to growth beyond the annual mark, which is appropriate enough but not necessary. Chugunova (1959) equates '1+' to the Russian *dvukhletka*, German *zweisommerige*, and suggests that it is used for age 1 fish in late summer and autumn. However, the English combination *two-summer* is rarely used and its adoption would only lead to confusion.

Roman numerals have sometimes been used to designate age, but arabic numerals are to be preferred because of the awkwardness of the Roman system.

Fish that migrate between fresh and salt water have special designations to show the time spent in either environment. Although several systems are in use, the European system of age designation (Koo 1962) is widely used with salmonids. In this, age 1.3 indicates 1 year of freshwater life and 3 years of sea life.

The determination of age from scales
Techniques for collecting, cleaning and mounting scales. In general there is no difficulty in taking scales from fishes. For many fishes a useful instrument is a pair of pointed tweezers. When the scales are small (trout, eels), or embedded or heavily coated in mucus (tench, spawning salmon), scales may be scraped from, or dug out of, the fish with a sharp knife.

The most generally used area for scale sampling is the middle region of the side of the body. The most useful scales for age assessment are usually large and symmetrical. For comparability, the scales in any one study series should be taken from the same location on all the fish, which may differ according to species (Figs. 5.1–5.3). In special studies of growth it may be desirable to use a *key scale*—that is, a scale taken from the same scale row and at the same point, on each fish, because this gives the least variation in scale size for the fish of any given length.

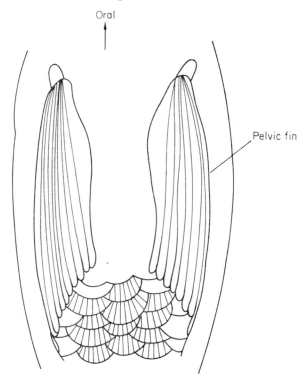

Figure 5.1. Position of Einsele's standard scales (shaded), after Einsele (1943).

To identify year marks, and measure distances between them, several scales may be required because there are differences in size and morphology. That is, an annulus that appears doubtful on one scale may be clear on others. In addition, some species have many regenerated (replacement) scales, for example up to 73 % (Tesch 1956b) or even 100 % (Le Cren, unpublished) of the scales of brown trout may be regenerated. In species with primarily normal scales, a sample of six scales may be enough to get five that are useful for age assessment and measurement, but with other species, e.g. brown trout, at least 20 scales may be needed.

Annuli on scales of many species can be identified without any special treatment of the scales provided they are preserved, as is most often done, in paper envelopes. These should not be adhesive or leave traces of material on

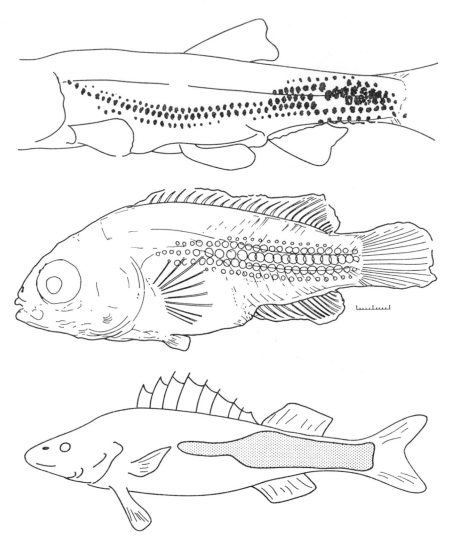

Figure 5.2. Location of the first scales on the body of three fishes.
Above: roach 18·5 mm long.
Middle: Rio Grande perch 10·5 mm long, from Balon (1955, 1959).
Below: zander 34 mm long, from Priegel (1964).

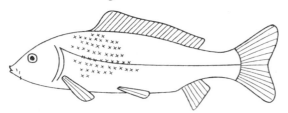

Figure 5.3. Position of normally-shaped scales on carp, from Dürr (1957).

the scales; a cellophane insert may be useful. When cleaning is necessary, it may be done with warm water or with 5 % caustic potash or similar solution, which is then washed off.

Clean scales can sometimes be examined dry and unmounted, but they tend to curl. It is simplest, and usually satisfactory, to mount them dry and bound tightly between two slides with sellotape (Scotch tape).

Another satisfactory technique is to prepare an impression of the outer surface of the scale (Nesbit 1934; Smith 1954; Redkozubov 1966). This is done by placing the scale, sculptured outer side down, on a slide of clear cellulose acetate about 1 mm thick. The slide with the scale is placed between two more acetate slides and is run through a roller press, using enough pressure to make a distinct *and complete* impression. If large numbers of fish are being handled, scales from many specimens can be mounted on large slides, and a heated vertical press is used to make the impressions (Clutter & Whitesel 1956). The use of scale impressions saves time, material and storage space and affords permanency.

Scales or impressions can be examined through a microscope, but for any large number it is more satisfactory to use a microprojector that will throw an image of 10- to 30-cm diameter. This requires somewhere between 10- and 100-diameters magnification. In general, scales of spiny-rayed fishes require greater magnification because their annuli tend to be closer together. Many models of projector are available or can be constructed (e.g. Van Oosten *et al.* 1934; Tester 1941). Projection also facilitates discussion with one's colleagues and making measurements of the image. If a microscope is used, an ocular micrometer is required for making measurements.

Age determination from scales. The structure and appearance of scales of bony fish differ in different species. Nitsche *et al.* (1932), Lagler (1947, 1956) and Galkin (1958) have published excellent photographs of various fish scale types. Among higher bony fishes most of the upper surface of the scale is covered by *ridges* or *circuli*. These are usually but not always nearly concentric, surrounding a central spot or *focus*. In many species the ridges are interrupted by *radii* that extend from the focus to the margin and branch occasionally. The *oral* or *anterior field* of the scale is usually the more useful one for identifying annual marks.

Ctenoid scales usually have posterior short conical teeth, which may interrupt the ridges and make them unrecognizable, though these may be reduced or even missing. Fish with ctenoid scales usually have spiny rays and thoracic pelvic fin, whereas those with cycloid scales generally have soft rays and abdominal pelvic fins.

The following scale features have been useful, in various combinations, for identifying annual marks in different fishes:

1 A zone of closely-spaced ridges is followed by a zone of widely-spaced ridges (Fig. 5.4); the annulus is usually considered to be at the outer border

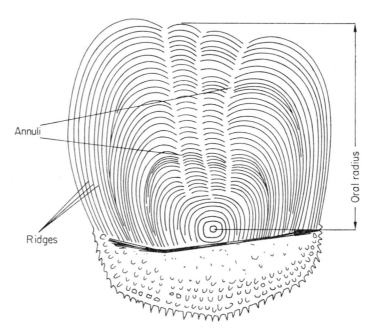

Figure 5.4. Scale of a percid fish with two annual marks, somewhat diagrammatic, after Tesch (1955).

of the closely-spaced ridges (Fig. 5.5*), but sometimes in the central part or at the inner margin of such ridges (Fig. 5.6). Tesch (1955) showed that times of rapid growth correspond to the formation of widely-spaced ridges, but the spacing of ridges on young goldfish scales is not directly temperature dependent (Van Coillie 1967; Ouchi 1969). Bilton (1974) found that the formation, but not the spacing, of circuli was associated with periods of feeding and starvation.

2　A clear zone, devoid of ridges (perhaps with ridges absorbed), occurs between a zone of closely-spaced ridges and a zone of widely-spaced ridges (Fig. 5.7).

3　Ridges become markedly discontinuous.

4　'Cutting over' occurs, where one or two ridges appear to cut across several others (Figs. 5.4 and 5.8). This is usually discernible on the dorso-lateral and ventro-lateral parts of the scale. Lieder (1959) and Muzinić (1964) discuss possible causes of this.

5　In clupeidae, where the ridges form two broad arcs across the anterior field of the scale, the annual mark is indicated by a slight bend or waviness in the ridges.

6　In some scales, especially ctenoid ones, the radii end or bend at the annual (Larreñeta 1964).

Checks are quite often found which are not annuli (Fig. 5.9), but which nevertheless exhibit one or more of the above criteria. For this reason a comparison with the age structures of bones or otoliths is useful. Burnet (1969) showed that fin sections of brown trout sometimes gave better results, especially with the first year's growth. In temperate latitudes annuli are sometimes not formed or are not certainly recognizable during a summer of slow growth, or they may fail to appear in age 0 fish that overwinter at small sizes (Regier 1962; Buchholz & Carlander 1963). In the latter case the size frequency distribution will usually indicate the error.

A special danger with Atlantic and Pacific salmon, and sea-run trout and char is the resorption of scale material at spawning time (Crichton 1935; Bilton & Jenkinson 1968; Grande 1965).

Sych (1970, 1974) has discussed at length the criteria for annulus definition. The appearance of scales may sometimes be improved by treatment with cobalt nitrate and ammonium sulphate (Wallin 1957; Keeton 1965), or by staining the ridges with Alizarin Red-S. However such treatments are usually unnecessary.

* Figs. 5.5–5.9 and 5.13 follow p. 112.

Figure 5.10. Vertical section of the head of a flatfish, for obtaining otoliths.

The determination of age from otoliths

Techniques for collecting and preserving otoliths. To obtain otoliths, a *dissection of the head* is necessary. Different cuts have to be made to find the otoliths in different species, as described by Bückmann (1929) (Figs 5.10–12). A cut suitable for finding salmonid otoliths is illustrated in Figs 5.10 and 5.11. Of the three otoliths on each side, only the largest, the sagitta, is used. These should be removed with fine tweezers to prevent breakage, and can be preserved dry in paper envelopes or suitable vials after being rubbed between the fingers to remove mucus, etc. Although some workers have used a liquid preservative (Brigham & Jensen 1964; Rounsefell & Everhart 1953), this is unnecessary.

Age determination from otoliths. Illustrations of various types of otoliths are given by Adams (1940) and Schmidt (1968). In most teleosts from the Northern Hemisphere, the otoliths consist of opaque material laid down mainly in late spring, summer and early autumn, and hyaline material laid down mainly during the winter. However the seasonal appearance of the two zones varies

Figure 5.5. Scale of a chum salmon with nearly three seasons of ocean life (freshwater life exhibits no whole season and no wintering). The annual mark (A) is in the usual position at the outer margin of the closely-spaced ridges (R), after LaLanne & Safsten (1969).

Figure 5.6. Scale of a chum salmon similar to that of Figure 5.5., but with the annual mark (A) at the inner margin of the closely-spaced ridges (R), after LaLanne & Safsten (1969).

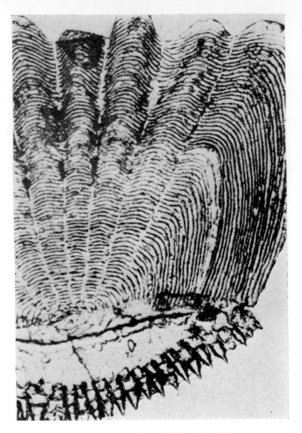

Figure 5.7. Scale of a perch 115 mm in total length, with one annual mark, taken January, after Tesch (1955).

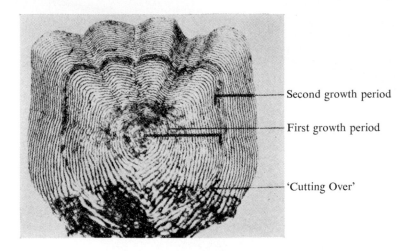

Figure 5.8. Scale of a hybrid between carp and crucian carp, with one annual mark at the end of the second summer, after Lieder (1959).

Figure 5.9. Scale of a coregonoid fish reared in tanks, with four annual marks (A1–A4) and accessory marks (ac). Taken in April; total length of fish 404 mm, after Hogman (1968).

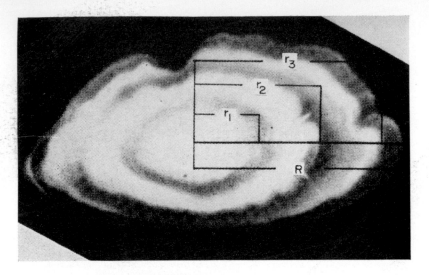

Figure 5.13. Otolith of a Japanese dab with three annual marks. R = radius from the centrum to the posterior margin of the otolith; r_1–r_3 are the distances from the centrum to the anterior margin of each 'resting zone', which begins to form in May, after Suzuki (1967).

Figure 5.11. Horizontal section of the head of a cod, for obtaining otoliths.

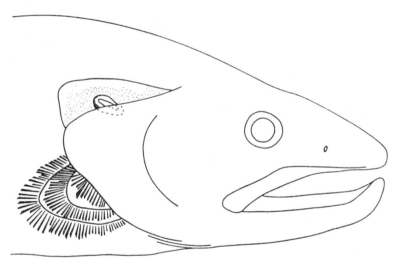

Figure 5.12. Lateral dissection to remove otolith without great injury to the fish specimen.

from one species to another. Pannella (1974), Brothers *et al.* (1976) and Struhsaker & Uchiyama (1976) illustrate daily growth rings in otoliths.

Most otoliths from freshwater fish can be viewed adequately if placed in water in a black dish and illuminated at an angle from above (i.e. by reflected

E

light). Against the dark background, the opaque zones appear as white or light-coloured rings, and the hyaline zones as dark rings (Fig. 5.13, facing p. 113). To accentuate the appearance of the growth rings, glycerine, xylol, cedar wood oil or cresol may be used (Bückmann 1929; Schott 1965; Sinha & Jones 1967; Peñáz & Tesch 1970).

However if transmitted light is shone through a thin otolith, the opaque zones appear as dark shadowy rings, and the hyaline zones as bright light rings. The fact that the same zones appear as light or dark depending on the illumination can lead to considerable confusion. For this reason the terms opaque and hyaline must always be used, and never the terms light and dark.

Some workers grind flat one surface of large, old or compact otoliths to make the growth marks more apparent (Tåning 1938; Bedford 1964) or make thin cross-sections (Rauck 1975, 1976; Deelder 1976). An alternative is to break the otolith between the thumbs or with a cutting tool. Any section must of course be through the nucleus. The half otolith is mounted in a piece of plasticine with the broken surface uppermost and horizontal. It is then illuminated from the side in such a way that the surface is kept in shadow. The effect is that the opaque zones appear as dark shadowy rings, and the hyaline zones as clear light rings.

Otoliths of some species (i.e. sole, crucian carp, zander and eel) are much clearer after burning on a low gas or spirit flame (Christensen 1964). The degree and rate of charring can quickly be found by experience. Albrechtsen (1968) and Benech (1975) advocate staining otoliths.

Yet another method for identifying annual rings in otoliths is to use photo-electric measurements by which the different transparencies are registered automatically on a recorder, and the annuli become visible as peaks on a graph (Schulz 1965; van Utrecht & Schenkkan 1972; Deelder 1976).

Complete accounts of the use of otoliths for age determination have been given by Williams & Bedford (1974) and Blacker (1974). See also Moriarty (1973) and Benech (1975). It must however be remembered that fish pre-served in non-neutralized formalin for any length of time do not yield otoliths useful for age assessment, because of decalcification.

The determination of age from bones

Techniques for collecting, cleaning and storing bones. The removal of bones, except fin rays and spines, means killing the specimen. The most frequently used bones are the operculum, vertebrae, the cleithrum, fin spines or spiny rays and soft rays.

After dissection, bones have to be cleaned of skin, flesh and fat, and then dried. Opercula can be removed quite quickly, using a scalpel to cut round the posterior edge (without damaging the bone) and then twisting with the fingers. They should then be cleaned by soaking in hot, but not boiling, water; fragments of flesh remaining can be removed by a cloth or paper tissue between the fingers and thumb. The rings appear on drying and become clearer after storage, usually in paper envelopes. Thick parts of opercula can be carefully filed or scraped to reveal inner layers and rings. Thin ground sections of bones and fin spines may be prepared (Bückmann 1929), and special sectioning and polishing machines have been developed by Chugunov (1926)—see Chugunova (1963) and Schoffman (1954) for large spines, while comparable apparatus for soft rays is described by Boiko (1951). If grinding really is necessary, a sheet of carborundum paper or wet carborundum powder on a piece of glass is usually sufficient.

Age determination from opercula and other bones. On the opercula of temperate fish, broad opaque zones correspond to the more rapid summer growth, and fade into narrow transparent winter bands which usually end abruptly with the start of the next summer zone. The bands show most clearly when viewed by reflected light against a matt black background which makes the summer zones appear white and the winter zones black. The bands, particularly the first, are often made more apparent by immersion in xylol, or wetting with cedar wood oil.

With transmitted light the summer zones appear dark and shadowy and the winter zones appear clear and bright. It may be helpful to use polarized light by rotating the bone between two 'crossed' polaroid discs, or in front of one piece while wearing polaroid glasses (Le Cren 1947; Frost & Kipling 1959; Menon 1950).

Techniques of age determination from vertebrae are described by Freidenfelt (1922), Aikawa (1937) and Appelget & Smith (1951). Casselman (1974) has described the use of the cleithrum, and Deelder & Willemse (1973) describe a simple method for the preparation and illumination of fin rays. The cross-section of the ray, cut close to the body of the fish, is polished on a smooth hone and mounted upright in plasticine on a microscope slide. A horizontal light beam is arranged so that the cut surface is in shadow under the microscope objective. Winter growth zones appear as light rings and summer growth as wider darker rings.

Age determination from length frequency distributions (Petersen method)

The length composition of a population will often exhibit modes among the smaller fish, which correspond to the youngest age groups. These modes will be most pronounced in fish with a short spawning season and rapid and uniform growth, in which event the mean (or at least the modal) length of the first few age groups can easily be determined (Fig. 5.14). Even when age determination is possible from scales, etc., using the length composition may make it possible to reduce greatly the amount of age determination needed. Close to the modes, all, or nearly all of the fish may be expected to be of one age group; age determination can then be concentrated on those that lie between the modes, and on the bigger fish whose length distributions overlap.

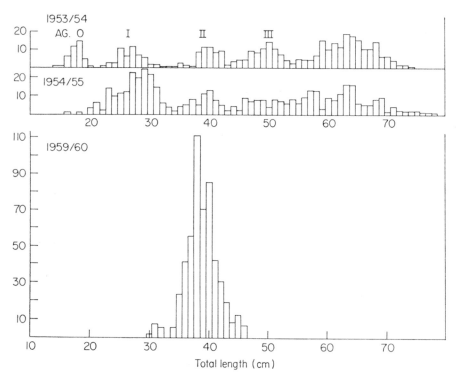

Figure 5.14. Length-frequency of zander, after Tesch (1956a, 1962).

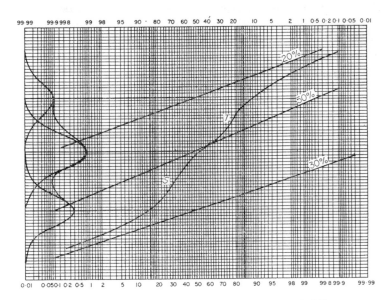

Figure 5.15. Transformation of size frequency curves using probability paper.

If it can reasonably be assumed that the distribution of length within an age group is normal (Gaussian), the position of the modes may be made clearer by fitting a normal curve to the left-hand side of the youngest age group (say 2-year-old fish), and subtracting the resulting estimate from the population. This leaves the length distribution of fish 3 years old and older, from which the length distribution of 3-year-old fish may be estimated. This can be done by a direct graphical method, or by transformation and the use of probability paper (Fig. 5.15) on which the normal curve becomes a straight line (Harding 1949; Cassie 1954). Another graphical method is to plot frequency polygons on semi-logarithmic paper, which transforms the normal distribution to a parabola (Tanaka 1962).

Care must be taken when using the Petersen method that the modes do in fact belong to successive age groups, and not dominant year classes, separated by one or more scarce broods.

Mathews (1974) used probability paper ('Cassie curves') and also a computer program NORMSEP to analyse length frequency distributions of tropical marine fish for which the otolith data were poor.

If, over a period of years, growth rate does not vary much but there is variation in year class strength, the sensitivity of the Petersen method can be improved by using the deviation of the percentage length composition in a particular year from the mean length composition over a long period. The modal lengths of strong and weak year classes then appear as peaks and troughs respectively (Rollefsen 1954).

The Petersen method can also be applied to other frequency measurements, for example the weight of eye lens (Carlton & Jackson 1968) or the weight of otoliths (Müller 1953).

Age determination errors

No one can claim that his age determinations are infallibly accurate. Errors most often arise either by missing the first annulus (which can be corrected from length frequency analysis) or with the older fish with very closely-spaced annuli. The possibility of errors must always be borne in mind, and a very useful discussion of the various sources and methods of overcoming errors has been given by Carlander (1974). Blacker (1974) describes the ICNAF cod otolith exchange scheme designed to eliminate errors, and Brander (1974) discusses the effects of age reading errors on the reliability of marine fishery modelling. Le Cren (1974) points out that age determinations are not required for some methods of production estimation, particularly that based on the Allen curve. He emphasizes that the accuracy of production estimates is more likely to depend on the precision of the biomass and population estimates than on ageing errors.

Methods of studying growth

Introduction

Once validated age determinations have been made on fish obtained by the chosen sampling gear (Chapter 2), the study of growth appears superficially to be simple. In practice there are numerous difficulties. Every kind of gear seems to have some degree of size selectivity. Many fish swim in shoals that are size determined so catching samples representative of the habitat is difficult even with efficient gear. Furthermore most fishing and natural mortality is size selective so that the population's growth rate will differ from an individual's. In addition immigration and emigration are likely to alter the size distribution in the population.

The estimation of growth

We will start by considering growth in length. Some methods, such as 1 and 6 below, yield growth rates of individual fish (=True Growth Rates). Others, such as 3, 4 and 5, give the rate of growth as shown by the population affected by mortality, migration, etc. (=Population Growth Rates). Both are valid estimates, but of different things, and the worker must realize this difference and decide for what purpose he is studying growth.

Fish growth may be studied by:

1   Experiments in tanks, ponds, etc. starting with fish of known size.

These experiments rarely yield information relevant to the natural situation unless the conditions are carefully controlled.

2   Tagging and marking. When tagging is used to study growth, the data must be evaluated with extreme care. Only marking techniques which do not affect health, behaviour and mobility, yield unqualified data. Internal tags, colouring with dyes, and marking by fin clipping are methods which cause little or no retardation of growth (Hazzard 1947; Churchill 1963; Saunders & Allen 1967; Stauffer & Hensen 1969; Fagerström *et al.* 1969). The undesirable effects of external tags have been shown many times, e.g. DeRoche (1963) (Fig. 5.16), Møller-Christensen (1961), Eschmeyer (1959) and Shetter (1967). Little or no effect of various kinds of tags was found on the growth of cod (Kohler 1963; Jensen 1967). It is essential to show in every study that the tags do not affect growth before the data may be used for growth estimation.

3   From age–length data. The age of each fish in a random sample, caught with a gear with the least bias, and used to sample the habitat thoroughly, is determined. Then the mean length, with confidence limits, is calculated for each age group. Properly carried out, this is the most satisfactory method.

4   From Petersen's method of age determination. The modal length of each age group is obtained from the size frequency distribution. The same provisos apply to growth rate determinations by the size frequency method, as apply to age determinations. The standard deviation of the average lengths can be obtained most easily from a plot on probability paper (Cassie curve) (Cassie 1954), and the confidence limits calculated from these.

5   By cohort analysis. Modal lengths of a particular age group (usually of a specially strong year class) are estimated at yearly intervals. Difficulties arise

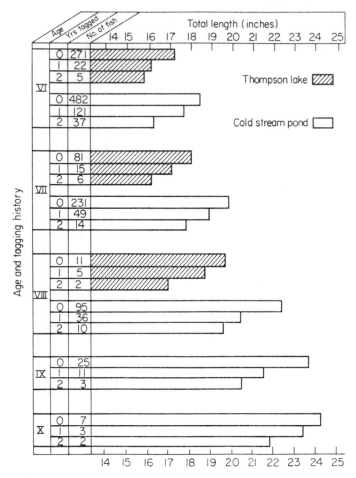

Figure 5.16. Growth of tagged and untagged lake trout in two Maine lakes, from DeRoche (1963).

if the growth is density dependent. With this method, and size frequency distribution analysis, the growth rate can be indicated without actually knowing the age of the fish, though knowing the age is more satisfactory.

6   By back calculation. For simplicity most emphasis in this discussion will be in terms of scale measurements, however otoliths and bones may also be used (Zamachaev 1941; Le Cren 1947; Koops 1959; Peňáz & Tesch 1970; Reay 1972; Tesch 1977) and the same methods of analysis usually apply. From the body length scale radius relationship and measurements of annuli radii, the body lengths for each age represented by an annulus are calculated. This is accomplished by:

1   From the mounted scales or impressions for each fish select at random a readable scale, or, if possible, use only 'key' scales.

2   With a microscope and ocular micrometer, or preferably a micro-projector, measure a radius from the nucleus mid point to the scale margin, usually the anterior median margin.

3   Measure along the same line as 2 the radius to each annulus. It is important that the same lines are used. With a microprojector many workers lay a strip of card along the chosen radius and mark each annulus and the scale margin, and write on the fish's serial number and length.

4   Continue for each fish, Use the same magnification, otherwise an adjustment must be made later.

5   Plot a graph of fish length (Y axis) against each scale radius (X axis). From this scatter diagram decide whether the relationship is (1a) linear and passing through the origin, (1b) linear but not passing through the origin; (2) curved (slope increasing); (3) S-shaped (Bryuzgin 1963; Hile 1970); or (4) a combination of different linear or curved relationships (Woolland & Jones 1975). The procedures to be used in the different cases are given below:

METHOD 1   When the body:scale relationship is linear and passes through the origin, the scale growth is directly proportional to body growth (isometric). The fish length corresponding to any scale annulus radius is given by Lea's (1910) formula (illustrated in Fig. 5.17):

$$l_n = \frac{S_n}{S} l \qquad (1)$$

where l_n = length of fish when annulus 'n' was formed,
   l = length of fish when scale sample was obtained,
   S_n = radius of annulus 'n' (at fish length l_n'),
   S = total scale radius.

Example: Suppose $l = 500$ mm, $S = 10$ mm, $S_1 = 2$ mm, then the length of the fish when the first annulus was formed was:

$$l_1 = 500 \times 2/10 = 100 \text{ mm}.$$

METHOD 2   The body:scale relationship is linear, but the line does not pass through the origin, as in Fig. 5.18. The line should be fitted by least

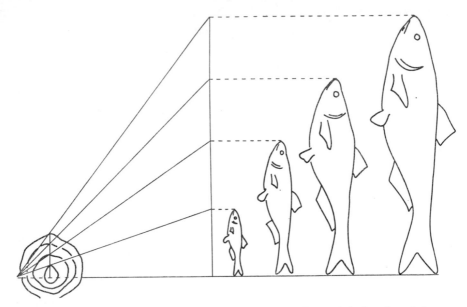

Figure 5.17. Direct proportionality between the rate of growth in length and that of the scale.

squares using the standard regression procedures (Bailey 1959; Snedecor & Cochran 1967), or the method of Schindowski & Tesch (1957). Since the regression equation is to estimate fish lengths from scale radii it is preferable to compute the regression of length on radius:

$$l = a + b \times S$$

where a is the intercept on the length axis and b is the regression coefficient (slope of the line). Ricker (1973, 1975) recommends using a G.M. regression, but its use has not been generally accepted by fishery statisticians.

The relationship of the regression line can also be represented by a modification of the direct proportion formula (Fraser 1916; Lee 1920):

$$l_n - a = \frac{S_n}{S}(1 - a). \tag{2}$$

Example: Suppose l, S, and S_n are as in the previous example and $a = 20$ mm; hence $l - a = 480$ mm, then

$$l_1 - 20 = 480 \times 2/10 = 96; \qquad l_1 = 116 \text{ mm.}$$

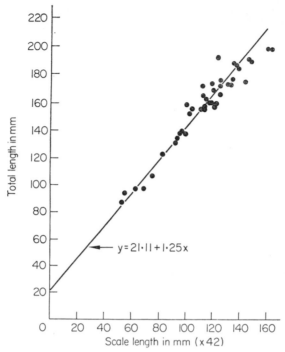

Figure 5.18. Body:scale relationship for Lake Michigan alewives, after Norden 1967).

METHOD 3 When the body:scale relationship is non-linear an empirical method can be used. A line may be drawn on the graph by eye, or with the aid of some smoothing device such as running averages.

In the method of Ricker & Lagler (1942), the fish lengths were read from the smoothed curve that corresponded to successive average scale sizes. If any scale happened to be of exactly the average size for that length, the fish sizes could be read directly from the graph. Usually this was not the case, so the following was used:

$$\bar{S}_n = \frac{\bar{S} S_n}{S} \tag{3}$$

where $\bar{S}_n$ = adjusted distance to the nth annulus,
$\bar{S}$ = average scale radius for a fish of the observed length.

Having $\bar{S}_n$, l_n was obtained from the graph. When many scales are to be processed, it is convenient to prepare a table of average values from the graph. *Example:* Suppose as before $l = 500$ mm, $S = 10$ mm and $S_1 = 2$ mm; and $\bar{S}$ for a fish of 500 mm $= 12$ mm, then

$$\bar{S}_1 = 12 \times 2/10 = 2\cdot4 \text{ mm}.$$

The figure 2.4 is entered on the graph and the corresponding fish length read from the empirical curve.

Another, more complex, method was used by Segerstråle (1933), Zuromska (1961) and Nagięć (1961).

METHOD 4   A simple curved body:scale relationship can sometimes be converted to a straight line by a transformation, usually a logarithmic transformation (Monastyrsky 1930; Hile 1941), then:

$$\log l = \log a + b \, (\log S). \tag{4}$$

This line should be calculated by the method of least squares. The length at each age adjusted for allometry then becomes:

$$\log l_n = \log l + b \, (\log S_n - \log S). \tag{5}$$

Fry (1943) subtracted a constant c (determined by trial and error) from the fish lengths before taking logarithms:

$$\log (l - c) = \log a + b \log S \tag{6}$$

This sometimes gives a straight line where the simple log transformation fails to do so.

Instead of using a transformation, a curved line may be fitted directly using the power series or polynomial (Thompson 1923). A second degree parabola of the form

$$l = a + bS + cS^2 \tag{7}$$

will probably give a good fit in most cases of simple curvature (Mann 1973, 1974).

COMBINATIONS OF METHODS.   Some authors have used different methods for fish of different sizes (Hile & Jobes 1941; El-Zarka 1959; Latta 1963).

Reay (1972) found that in sand eels, 50 % of the body growth increment was reached 3–4 weeks earlier than that of the otoliths. This was shown by regular variations in the body length: otolith ratio, and the amplitude of these variations was believed to decrease with age. A series of equations (1) and (2) were used as appropriate for different months.

6   Once the form of the relationship has been determined, use the appropriate equation to calculate the lengths for each age (l_n) from each annulus radius (S_n). For each age group calculate the mean back-calculated lengths for each age, and their confidence limits, and enter in a table.

Calculation aids. When the calculations are by direct proportion (Method 1 above) and strips of card, as recommended above, are used, they can be laid on a piece of graph paper which has the expected range of fish lengths marked on the ordinate (Y-axis). With the zero of the scale measurements at the origin, the strip is rotated until the scale edge mark is opposite the observed length fish. The back-calculated lengths corresponding to each annulus can then be read directly from the Y-axis.

Other devices of varying complexity have been described by Huntsman (1919, Monastyrsky (1934), Hile (1941), Fry (1943), Le Cren (1947), Bryuzgin (1955), Vovk (1956), Chugunova (1959) and others. These are rarely worthwhile unless the data are very extensive.

Much time can be saved if only *average* values for age groups are required rather than for individual fish. Then average fish lengths and scale measurements of all fish of a given age can be used by the appropriate method to give average back-calculated lengths. The loss of information is negligible (Van Oosten 1953).

Lee's phenomenon. Back-calculated lengths for a given age group are frequently smaller the older the fish from which they are calculated. This is Rosa Lee's phenomenon and has often been studied (Bryuzgin 1961, 1963; Graham 1929; Hile 1936; Jones 1958, 1960; Kuznetsov 1957; Lapin 1969; Ricker 1969; Smith 1956; Taylor 1958; Thompson 1923; Van Oosten 1929; Vovk 1956).

Four possible causes have been suggested:

1   Incorrect back-calculation procedure, for example if method 1 above is used when method 2 is actually appropriate.
2   Non-random sampling of the stock, for example, if the sampling tends to select the larger members of the younger ages.
3   Selective natural mortality, favouring greater survival of the smaller fish of a given age group.
4   Selective fishing mortality, similarly biased.

To ascertain which causes are involved requires intimate knowledge of the fish population and the sampling procedure. Lee's phenomenon is not always present in back-calculated lengths, and occasionally the reverse effect has been observed. The latter could arise from size selective mortality that bears most heavily on the smaller fish of an age group.

The dimensions of growth

Growth may be measured in any dimension, including weight, and the above methods may be applied. However it is usual, and easiest, to measure length and then convert to weight.

The length–weight relationship. In fishes the length–weight relationship can usually, or always, be represented by

$$w = al^b \qquad (8)$$

where b is an exponent usually between 2 and 4. A logarithmic transformation gives the straight line relationship

$$\log w = \log a + b \log l. \qquad (9)$$

First plot log weight against log length and then calculate the regression line by the method of least squares. The regression coefficient is b, and $\log a$ is the intercept of the line on the Y-axis.

These coefficients differ not only between species but sometimes also between stock of the same species. During development fish typically pass through several stages or *stanzas* (Vasnetsov 1953a), each of which may have its own length–weight relationship (Fig. 5.19). There may also be differences in the relationship due to sex, maturity, season, and even time of day (because of changes in stomach fullness). Hence it may be necessary to calculate a number of regressions, one for each group of fish, and by analysis of co-variance test for significant differences before pooling (Le Cren 1951). Within any stanza, the coefficient b will often be nearly constant throughout the year, or a series of different environments (but see Bagenal 1957). The value of a will often vary seasonally, with time of day, and between habitats. Changes in b often occur between stanzas, at metamorphosis, at first maturity and with major environmental changes. However within a stanza it is usual to calculate some average relationships that can be used in growth, production and other studies.

Another approach which may save computation time is to use the mean lengths ($\bar{l}$) and weights ($\bar{w}$) for each age group and calculate

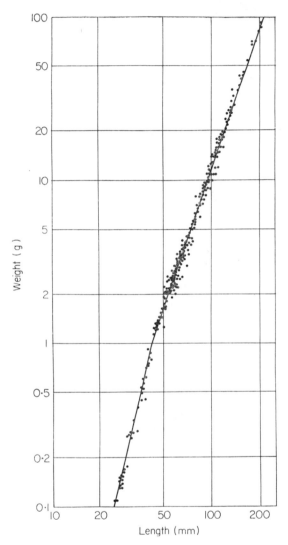

Figure 5.19. A 'dot diagram' of weight against length, plotted on double logarithmic axes. Two lines are drawn by eye, to represent the length–weight relationship below and above a length of 42 mm. Data are from a population of brown trout, supplied by E.D. Le Cren.

$$\log \bar{w} = \log a' + b'(\log \bar{l}) \qquad (10)$$

by the least squares method, either weighted by the number of each fish in each age group or not as seems appropriate. The values of a' or b' (or both) will exceed a and b of equation (9) (Ricker 1975, section 9.3.6).

Ricker (1973, 1975) recommends the G.M. functional regression equation which minimizes the products of the distances on the x and y axes of a point from the line, rather than the standard predictive regression based on the least squares on the x axis. Ricker claims that the G.M. regression is more formally correct, but this has not yet been generally accepted by statisticians.

Estimation of instantaneous growth rate. This is the natural logarithm of the ratio of final weight to initial weight of a fish in unit time, usually a year,

$$G = \frac{\log_e \bar{w}_2 - \log_e \bar{w}_1}{\Delta t}. \qquad (11)$$

As with length, the True Instantaneous Growth Rate (G) for individuals may differ from the Population Instantaneous Growth Rate (G_x). To calculate G_x proceed as follows:

1   Determine by one or more of the above methods the mean initial and final lengths for each age separately.

2   Calculate b' from equation (10) using mean lengths and weights derived from representatively sampled range of ages.

3   Substract the natural logarithms of the initial lengths (1 above) from the natural logarithms of the final lengths for each age group. This gives the instantaneous rate of length increase at each age.

4   Convert for each age to weights (G_x) by multiplying by b'. This product is the instantaneous increase in weight at each age.

To calculate the mean True Instantaneous Growth Rate ($\bar{G}$):

(a)   Calculate the regression coefficient b from lengths the and weights from a representative sample.

(b)   Obtain the back-calculated lengths for the fish and convert these to natural logarithms. Subtract the initial from the final for each year's growth. This gives for each fish the instantaneous rate of length increase for each year.

(c)   Average the instantaneous rates of increase in length for each age group and multiply by b to give the mean instantaneous rate of increase in weight, $\bar{G}$, at each age.

Isometric and allometric growth. When the regression coefficient $b = 3$ the growth is isometric, that is growth with unchanging body proportions and specific gravity. However in most fish the different dimensions change with growth. Then b is greater or less than 3 and the growth is allometric.

Condition factors. These are used to compare the 'condition', 'fatness' or 'well being' of fish, and are based on the hypothesis that the heavier fish of a given length are in better condition.

Fulton's Condition Factor (K) is calculated from:

$$K = \frac{100w}{l^3} \tag{12}$$

where w and l are the observed total weight and total length of a fish. With growth that is nearly isometric, Fulton's Condition Factor is satisfactory and may be used to compare differences related to sex, season or place. Even with allometric growth and whatever the value of b in equation (9), Fulton's condition factor may be used if the fish are approximately the same length. However, if the length range is large, equation (13) should be used:

$$K' = \frac{100w}{l^b}. \tag{13}$$

Alternatively the expected weight ($\hat{w}$) for a given length (which from equation (9) will be the expected geometric mean weight) is used in:

$$K'' = \frac{w}{\hat{w}}. \tag{14}$$

The effects of a large length range is illustrated by a group of 36 perch *Perca fluviatilis* for which equation (9) was found to be log $w = 3.460$ log $l - 2.577$. The 95 % confidence limits of b were from 3·296 to 3·625. If we consider three fish of 10, 20 and 30 cm whose weights are 7·6, 84·1 and 341·8 g, which happen to fall exactly on the line described by the equation. The condition factors calculated from equations (12), (13) and (14) are shown for these fish below:

Length	K	K'	K''
10	0·76	0·264	1·0
20	1·05	0·265	1·0
30	1·27	0·265	1·0

These figures clearly show that the combination of regression coefficient significantly greater than 3 and a large length range make Fulton's condition factor give misleading results.

Clark's condition factor is used less often than those described above and consists of the gutted weight divided by the fork length.

Methods for adequate analysis of condition are given, described and discussed by Le Cren (1951), Weatherly (1972), and Ricker (1975).

Addendum: Mathematical models of Growth

L. M. DICKIE

Because of sampling errors, data on sizes or instantaneous growth rates at age may yield the most useful information when they are combined into growth curves or models. Such growth models are constructed for two main purposes: generalized description of the pattern of growth, or the study of factors controlling growth.

The most important practical application of growth studies is generalized description, free from the minor variations in the original observations. Such description facilitates comparisons of growth among species or of species at various times and places. Furthermore, parameters derived in curve-fitting of the data may be directly usable in fishery assessments (see Chapter 12). For this purpose descriptive growth models should contain as few parameters and initial conditions as is consistent with accuracy.

A number of mathematical growth curves have been published, together with methods for fitting them statistically. Examples in the literature include the Gompertz (Winsor 1932a; Weymouth & McMillan 1931; Silliman 1969), the logistic (Winsor 1932b; Hjort *et al.* 1933), the von Bertalanffy (von Bertalanffy 1938; Beverton & Holt 1957) and various straight line approximations (Baranov 1918; Knight 1969), or exponential curves (Brody 1945; Parker & Larkin 1959). The results of these studies have revealed a remarkable stability and small range of pattern in the fitted observations, whether they come from successive growth observations on individual fish or from population sampling.

The best-known growth model used in fisheries assessments is that of von Bertalanffy, who based his formulation on physiological considerations. A least-squares method of fitting observations to this model if a computer is available has been described by Allen (1966). However more general graphical fittings often provide fully satisfactory estimates of the parameters. Various methods are described in some detail by Ricker (1975), who should be consulted for further details or alternatives to the methods outlined here.

Because of seasonal changes in condition factors, growth may initially be better studied in terms of length than weight. The von Bertalanffy expression for length (l_t) at age t as a function of t is usually written as:

$$l_t = L_\infty\{1 - \exp[-K(t - t_0)]\} \tag{15}$$

where: L_∞ = the mathematical asymptote of the curve (often referred to as the 'final' or 'maximum' size).

K = a measure of the rate at which the growth curve approaches the asymptote.

t_0 = a time scaler equivalent to the (hypothetical) starting time at which the fish would have been zero-sized if they had always grown according to expression (15).

That is, data on length at age are required to fit the three parameters L_∞, K, and t_0.

Several graphical fittings may be used. For example by re-arranging equation (15) and taking logarithms we have:

$$\log_e(L_\infty - l_t) = (\log_e L_\infty + Kt_0) - Kt \tag{16}$$

according to this equation if we have an estimate of L_∞, a plot of $\log(L_\infty - l_t)$ against t in natural logarithmic units yields a straight line with a slope of $-K$ and an intercept 'a', on the ordinate, equal to ($\log L_\infty + Kt_0$). The scaling factor t_0 may then be calculated from the relation $(a - \log L_\infty)/K = t_0$. A plotted example in Fig. 5.20 is discussed later.

As indicated by Brody (1945), a value of L_∞ can be found by making successive guesses until that one is obtained which gives the best straight line fit to the array of data points. Incorrect estimates of L_∞ will result in upward or downward curvature. In practice a satisfactory estimate of the asymptote can usually be obtained from the 'Walford' plot of l_{t+1} on l_t. That is, if growth rate is regularly decreasing, the line fitted to plots of length at successive time intervals will approach the diagonal of the graph, at which point l_{t+1} is the same as l_t and length has reached its asymptotic value, L_∞. The slope of this line is equal to e^{-K}. An example of such a plot is given in the lower part of Fig. 5.21, based on the data of Table 5.1.

It has been pointed out by Gulland (1964a) that equation (15) can also be written for equal time intervals in the form

$$l_{t+1} - l_t = L_\infty[1 - e^{-K}] - [1 - e^{-K}]l_t. \tag{17}$$

That is, growth in a given period $(l_{t+1} - l_t)$ plotted against beginning size for the period (l_t) is also a straight line with slope $-[1 - e^{-K}]$. In this plot the intercept on the abscissa, that is, where $l_{t+1} - l_t = 0$ is equal to L_∞.

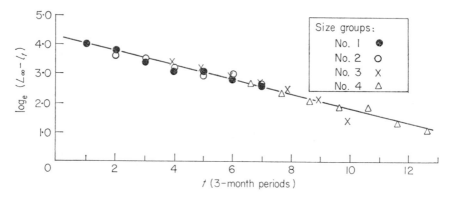

Figure 5.20. The logarithmic plot of asymptotic growth rate on relative age (see equation (16)) as suggested by Brody (1945), where L_∞ is estimated asymptotic length, l_t is length at relative age, t. (Data from Table 5.1.)

TABLE 5.1. Growth data for the common edible mussel (*Mytilis edulis*) collected from Halifax Harbour, Nova Scotia, in early 1971 and held in cages for an 18-month period. The animals were initially sorted into 4 size-groups of 25 animals each. Data are given for total number of survivors (n), average length of all animals living on the date of observation (l_t), and average length of those animals which survived throughout the experiments (l_{ts}). (Data from Freeman 1974)

| Date | \multicolumn{12}{c}{*Size-group*} |
| | \multicolumn{3}{c}{1} | \multicolumn{3}{c}{2} | \multicolumn{3}{c}{3} | \multicolumn{3}{c}{4} |
	n	l_t	l_{ts}	n	l_t	l_{ts}	n	l_t	l_{ts}	n	l_t	l_{ts}
Mar. 15	25	17·4	18·1	25	28·5	27·5	25	41·6	42·7	25	57·9	58·5
June 15	23	27·3	27·8	24	38·6	37·6	23	48·6	50·8	23	62·4	62·8
Sept. 15	22	41·5	42·5	23	48·2	48·4	19	54·1	57·1	14	64·6	65·7
Dec. 15	21	48·6	48·8	19	52·5	51·6	17	57·8	60·6	12	65·7	67·6
Mar. 15	20	49·7	49·9	18	53·1	52·8	16	59·5	62·0	12	66·0	68·0
June 15	19	55·7	56·2	15	57·5	57·4	16	63·7	66·8	11	68·5	70·5
Sept. 15	13	58·3	58·3	8	58·8	58·8	9	67·9	67·9	8	71·6	71·6

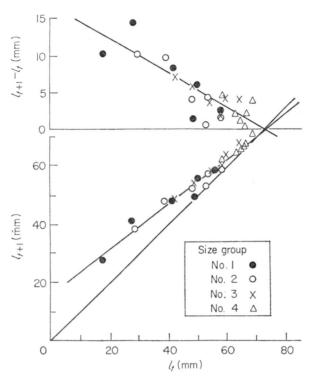

Figure 5.21. Plots of length at age data, suitable for estimating parameters of the von Bertalanffy growth equation.
Below: the 'Walford' plot. Above: plot of equation (17).

The data of Table 5.1 are plotted this way in the upper part of Fig. 5.21 with the descending line intersecting the estimate of L_∞ on the Walford plot to emphasize the identity.

The data used to illustrate this analysis are given in Table 5.1 and were taken from experiments of Freeman (1974) who made observations on the growth of the common marine mussel, *Mytilis edulis*. While the data are for a bivalve mollusc rather than a fish, they exhibit many features found in fish data. Freeman collected mussels from the wild and separated them into 4 size categories, thus their initial ages are unknown. They were held under specified conditions and periodic growth and mortality observations made on them. In the table we present growth and survivorship data at 3-month intervals over an 18-month period. Analysis would appropriately start by plotting size at successive time periods for all four size groups as is shown in either the lower or upper panel of Fig. 5.21. The plots reveal no reason to differentiate between the size groups so the data may be combined for a best common estimate of L_∞. Because the points for larger animals may become crowded in the Walford plot, the upper form may sometimes be preferred. Best graphical estimate of L_∞ in Fig. 5.21 is about 72.5 mm.

In the case of the mussel data it then appears appropriate to proceed with construction of a plot of equation (15), this is, of growth on relative age as in Fig. 5.20. In this case, the common plot established in Fig. 5.21, provides a basis for expecting a common L_∞ and K for all size groups. Therefore the data for size group 1 may be used to establish the position of a line for all groups. Data points for the larger size groups are positioned along the time axis so that they fall evenly about this line. The resulting combined plot yields an index of their mean relative ages. In Fig. 5.20, for example, it appears that the mussels of size-group 4 were of the order of $1\frac{1}{2}$ years older than those of size-group 1. The estimate of t_0 derived from the data places the hypothetical time at 0- size in late December for size-group 1, a season which is later than mussel larvae are found in north-west Atlantic waters. It is frequently the case that estimates of t_0 will be somewhat later in time than true birth date in this way since, as pointed out by Brody (1945), there is frequently an early but short exponential phase of growth in length, prior to the 'die-away' phase which is described by the Bertalanffy growth curve. One would thus infer that size-group 1 animals resulted from late larval settlement of the year prior to collection. The largest size group must then have settled early in the previous year. That is the size-group 1 animals were initially about 6 months old while size-group 4 animals were about $1\frac{3}{4}$ years old.

If these growth parameters are to be used in fishery assessment work it is necessary to convert from length to weight. That is, the parameter L_∞ must be converted to an equivalent value for W_∞. If the conventional Beverton & Holt (1957) model is used it is usual to assume in the conversion $W = aL^b$ that $b = 3$; that is, that growth is isometric. A value of 'a' may then be derived as a 'condition index' from a set of data on length and weight as indicated in the preceding sections of this chapter. However, if the empirical value of b is significantly different from 3, the calculation may need to be more complicated (Allen 1969; Ricker 1975).

The other growth parameters, t_0 and K, apply to growth curves in both length and weight.

The problem of relating the growth parameters of any mathematical curve to the factors controlling growth is of continuing biological interest. The von Bertalanffy curve was originally adopted by Beverton & Holt for fisheries assessment because of its supposed physiological foundation in relation to food absorbing surface area and metabolic volume. However, this interpretation has been rejected by some workers (Ricker 1975; Richards 1959; Hemmingsen 1960). In any case the physiological variables on which it is based cannot be measured unequivocally. As has been pointed out frequently (Gray 1929; Kavanagh & Richards 1934; Medawar 1945) repeated instances of satisfactory statistical fittings of observational data to a model do not provide a critical test of the hypotheses underlying that model. Questions of the theoretical basis for of any such model are unlikely to be resolved without direct experimental and field study of the mechanisms postulated. Such questions led Paloheimo & Dickie (1965, 1966a, b) to attempt formulation of growth equations explicitly in terms of such observed variables as rations intake, or total metabolic expenditure per unit time. Subsequent observations have indicated that growth rates may have a high degree of predictability from a general knowledge of metabolic levels and food particle sizes (Kerr 1971b, c). The formulations for such curves are subjects of active experimental research and will probably undergo successive modifications, particularly as computer models permit the incorporation of refinements in the time-dependent variables (Jones & Johnston, in press). However, there seems little doubt that formulations of this type are important for the study of factors underlying growth. They are also likely to be of increasing importance to fishery assessments as fisheries become more intense and it becomes necessary to use food-chain models in the prediction and management of fisheries yields.

In their study of the generalized form-of-growth curves Parker & Larkin (1959) found that in certain salmonids a Bertalanffy growth curve provided a satisfactory fit to average size at age data derived from population sampling, but that growth data for individuals sampled throughout their life-times was described by a different expression, such as an exponential curve. Such findings serve to emphasize the fact, long recognized by students of population dynamics, that there may be significant correlation between the growth rates and mortality rates. The general nature of correlations between growth and mortality rates between species was emphasized by Beverton & Holt (1959) who expressed it in the form of relations between natural mortality and the K of the growth curves. The likelihood of correlations within species was recognized by Jones (1958) and Taylor (1958) and has recently been more fully considered by Ricker (1969), Jones (1973) and Ware (1975b). It is a common experience that the faster growing members of a cohort may exhibit higher mortality. If so, the growth data may exhibit Lee's phenomenon, that is a decrease in estimated average size at age as it is back-calculated from older and older animals. For this reason in Table 5.1 we have calculated average size at age using data from only those mussels which lived throughout Freeman's experiments. Estimates of l_{ts} for size-group 2 survivors show Lee's phenomenon compared with the population l_t. However, group 3 and 4 animals show the reverse, i.e. the survivors consisted of the faster growing individuals. It appears that with small numbers one must be wary of effects which may arise only from the chance sampling or selection of faster or slower growing animals.

As Ricker (1969) points out, fishery assessment calculations ought properly to be carried out with growth data on individuals, rather than population growth data. If significant Lee's phenomenon is present uncritical use of population growth rates, since they already incorporate the effects of selective natural or fishing mortality, may lead to underestimates of the productive capacity of the stocks by as much as 25 %.

Considerations such as these suggest that information about both the growth and mortality rates of fish stocks and their sensitivity to environmental factors may be obtained from careful treatment of growth data. For such purposes, care with sampling to ensure representative collections, as well as efforts to derive data on size at age among successive cohorts should be rewarded with important information on potential yields.

6

Estimation of Population Number and Mortality Rates

W D YOUNGS and D S ROBSON

Introduction

Rational management of a fishery necessitates some knowledge of the dynamics of the fish population being managed. The change in number of fish with time is a basic consideration in determining the absolute, as opposed to relative, level of production. A number of factors, as for example inaccessibility and lack of personnel or money, preclude direct enumeration of fish in most populations thus requiring sampling and statistical inference methods different in many respects from the census work done with human populations.

Since the first edition of this handbook there have been several textbooks, manuals and handbooks dealing with fish population analysis and management. Among these publications are Cushing (1968), Cormack (1968), Royce (1972), Seber (1973), Gulland (1974), Ricker (1975), Everhart et al. (1975) and Jones (1977). The book by Seber (1973) provides excellent coverage on statistical methodology of population number and mortality estimation. Ricker (1975) has provided us a revised version of his previous handbook (Ricker 1958) which included yield and production estimation in addition to population number and mortality methods. In this chapter we have attempted to present the more commonly used methods along with the basic assumptions and comments on the consequences of violation of these assumptions. An attempt has been made to present guidelines for the practical interpretation of underlying statistical concepts. Elementary accounts of some population estimation methods have been given by Parr, Gaskell & George (1968) and by Cross (1972).

Estimation of population number

A variety of techniques for estimating population number are available. There is a rich literature describing both theory and applications to a wide range of species and habitats; the general references cited above provided an excellent introduction to this literature. The method chosen for a given study will in large part be determined by consideration of the biology of the species, objective of the study, characteristics of the habitat, and resources available. It is difficult to overemphasize the importance of planning and using prior knowledge before a study is undertaken. All too frequently resources are allocated or expended which are inadequate *a priori* to accomplish the stated objective. At best most estimation problems concerning fish populations are difficult in the sense of meeting underlying assumptions and in the necessity for using all information available, including the advice of experienced researchers, before planning a study. This seems obvious but is all too frequently overlooked.

Designing a study such that more than one method of estimation can be used for analysis may provide insights concerning assumptions of the methods if estimation results from the different methods are not in agreement. Meeting the assumptions of the methods should provide results which vary only by random error associated with the sampling. One would expect when sample size is large only a small proportion of sample estimates, 5%, to fall more than two standard error units away from the estimation target if only random error from sampling is involved. Therefore one would expect such intervals from two different methods to overlap if only random error was present. This range is called a confidence interval, or the end points of the range are called confidence limits. Formulae for calculating standard error for the estimate will be given along with the formulae for calculation of the estimate. It is important to note that if assumptions or method of obtaining a sample are violated, then the estimate and its standard error are no longer valid. This is particularly important when considering the standard error. It is not always possible to determine an exact variance for an estimate, in which case approximate variances may be given. The problem of obtaining variance estimates when the method cannot be assumed to be nearly correct has been discussed by Regier & Robson (1967).

There are three general approaches to population estimation: ratio methods, catch-effort methods and direct enumeration. The ratio methods seem the broadest class including the mark-recapture, correlated population and change-in-ratio subclasses. The mark-recapture methods have been extensively used for both estimation of population number and estimation of mortality (survival) rates. The use of serially numbered tags as a mark (see Chapter 4) has led to the recent development of a number of techniques for estimating survival and harvest rates. Change-in-ratio estimators have been discussed in detail by Paulik & Robson (1969). There seem to be no new developments in methods for estimation of population number.

Ratio methods

Mark-recapture. Estimation of population number by mark-recapture experiment is based on the assumption that the proportion of marked fish in a random sample is the same as the proportion of a known number of marked fish in the population. The estimation formula is:

$$\hat{N} = \frac{mc}{r}$$

where $\hat{N}$ = number of fish in population
m = number of marked fish in population
c = number of fish in a sample
r = number of marked fish in c.

An estimation experiment is conducted by securing a sample from amongst the unknown population, N, identifying the sample by marking or tagging, and returning the fish to the population. A second sample of c fish is secured from the population and the number of marked fish counted are designated r. This method is referred to as the Petersen method.

The manner in which the recapture sample, i.e. the second sample, is taken determines the variance of the estimated population number, $\hat{N}$. Sampling as described above where a sample of size c is preselected and drawn without replacement leads to the following variance for $\hat{N}$:

$$V(\hat{N}) = \frac{\hat{N}^2(\hat{N} - m)(\hat{N} - c)}{mc(\hat{N} - 1)}.$$

Other sampling procedures would lead to other variances for $\hat{N}$. For example if the recapture sample of size c were taken by removing one fish at a time, examining for marks and then returning to the water, the variance of $\hat{N}$ would be:

$$V(\hat{N}) = \frac{m^2c(c - r)}{r^3}.$$

The estimated population number, $\hat{N}$, will on the average be smaller than the actual population number N even if all of the assumptions of the method are met. This negative statistical bias is approximately equal to $100 \exp(-mc/M)\%$. This bias becomes negligible as mc/N becomes greater than 4, e.g. $mc/N = 3$ bias is approximately 5%; $mc/N = 4$ bias is approximately 2%.

Robson & Regier (1964) outline methods for determining sample size for variance and cost restraints in conducting population estimation by the Petersen method. They provide graphs for determining sample size in terms of m and c in order that the estimate $\hat{N}$ is within a given percentage of the true population N at a stated level of confidence, e.g. within 25% of the true population with 95% confidence. These graphs are similar to the one shown in Fig. 6.1 which is 10% of true population with 95% probability and is the level recommended for research. The high level of accuracy is considered necessary in order to maintain a reasonable variance for product or ratios using population number, as for example in biomass or survival determinations. These charts are based upon hypergeometric sampling; i.e. selection of the sample of size c without replacement.

In addition to the statistical bias cited above, and of greater consequence, is experimental bias resulting from failure to meet assumptions of the method. These assumptions are: (1) the population is closed to recruitment and immigration, (2) marked fish are in every way the same as unmarked fish, i.e. same mortality, behaviour to gear, etc., (3) marked fish do not lose their mark, (4) all marked fish are reported upon recapture, and (5) either marking or recapture sample is random, or there is random mixing of marked and unmarked fish. Loss of marks, increased mortality of marked fish and reduced catchability of marked fish all cause the estimate $\hat{N}$ to be greater than the actual population number N. Factors, such as baiting traps and territorial behaviour, may cause marked fish to be more vulnerable to the gear in which case population number will be underestimated. Detailed discussions of the effects of violating these assumptions may be found in Robson & Regier (1968), Seber (1973) and Ricker (1975).

Two conditions, however, deserve particular emphasis and should be examined in any Petersen estimation experiment. These are size (age) selectivity of the sampling gear and recruitment into the population. If different size classes of fish have different vulnerability to the sampling gear, the estimate of population number based on all size classes combined is not valid. Assuming a short-time lapse between marking and recovery such that growth is negligible, and a separate mark for each size category (numbered tags would better serve this purpose), it is possible to construct a selectivity curve

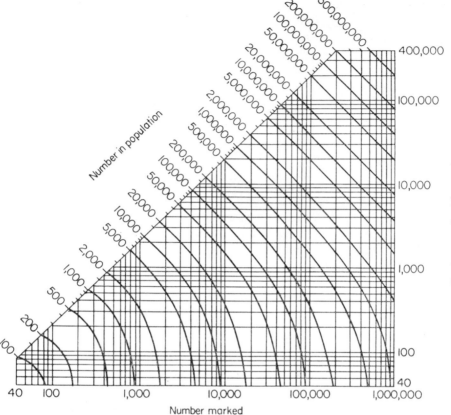

Figure 6.1. Combinations of sample sizes for Petersen mark-recapture experiments with error of 10% of the true value when chance of an error this large or larger is less than 1 in 20.
The usual conditions for valid ratio estimates are assumed to be fulfilled:
(1) Marked members are distributed at random and/or sample is at random.
(2) Mark or marking procedure does not influence probability of recapture.
(3) Marked members are randomly distributed.

and to test the recaptured to marked ratio in each size class. Table 6.1 details the data necessary. The selectivity curve may be constructed by plotting r/m for each size class against the size class. A chi-square contingency test on the data in Table 6.1 provides a test for a common ratio. Population estimates should be conducted separately for those classes having statistically different r/m ratios.

TABLE 6.1. Data summary for constructing a selectivity curve or for testing equality of catchability for size classes of marked fish

| | Size-class of marked fish at time of release | | | | | |
	1	2	3	...	k	Total
Recaptured	r_1	r_2	r_3	...	r_k	r
Not recaptured	m_1-r_1	m_2-r_2	m_3-r_3	...	m_k-r_k	$m-r$
Number released	m_1	m_2	m_3	...	m_k	m

A similar test for recruitment into the population may be conducted by a contingency chi-square statistic using information summarized as in Table 6.2. Recruitment would normally result from young fish growing into the catchable size between the time of mark release and time of recapture. This results in an excess of unmarked fish in these classes and an overall effect of overestimating population number.

TABLE 6.2. Data summary for testing for recruitment in a mark–recapture experiment

| | Size-class in recapture sample | | | | |
	1	2	...	k	Total
Marked	r_1	r_2	...	r_k	r
Unmarked	c_1-r_1	c_2-r_2	...	c_k-r_k	$c-r$
Total	c_1	c_2	...	c_3	c

Multiple mark-recapture. The number of marks released or recaptured in the single mark-recapture experiment are often insufficient to estimate population number to the desired level of precision and accuracy. Continued sampling with marking of unmarked fish and release of newly-marked and recaptured-marked fish result in an increasing proportion of marked fish in the population. Assumptions of the Petersen or single mark-recapture experiment are also necessary for the first method discussed below and in addition it is assumed that mortality is negligible during the time necessary to conduct the estimate. A number of models have been proposed for the situation (Schnabel 1938; Chapman 1952; Darroch 1958) and for this situation in which an accounting of known marking mortality may be made (Robson & Regier 1968). We present first the model of Darroch (1958) in which no mortality takes place. The reader is referred to the cited publications or to Seber (1973) for detailed rationale and worked example. The estimate of population number under this procedure is taken as the iterative solution to the equation:

$$1 - \frac{u}{\hat{N}} = \left(1 - \frac{c_1}{\hat{N}}\right)\left(1 - \frac{c_2}{\hat{N}}\right) \dots \left(1 - \frac{c_k}{\hat{N}}\right)$$

where c_i is the catch of the ith sample and u refers to the total number of unmarked fish captured in k samples. Computational aids for the solution of $\hat{N}$ are given by Robson & Regier (1968) as follows: Start with an initial guess for N called N_0 and let the right-hand side of the above equation evaluated at N_0 be called P_{N_0}. The next trial value N_1 is taken as

$$N_1 = N_0 + \frac{N_0 P_0 - (N_0 - u)}{\Delta_{N_0}}$$

where P_{N_0-1} is the right-hand side evaluated at $N_0 - 1$ and

$$\Delta_{N_0} = 1 + (N_0 - 1)P_{N_0-1} - N_0 P_{N_0}.$$

Iteration continues until two estimates say $\hat{N}_i$ and $\hat{N}_{i+1}$ are essentially equal. The variance of $\hat{N}$ may be estimated by

$$\hat{V}(\hat{N}) = \frac{\hat{N} - u}{\Delta_{\hat{N}}}$$

where $\Delta_{\hat{N}}$ is from the last iteration in estimating $\hat{N}$, or alternatively by the approximation:

$$\hat{V}(\hat{N}) = \left[\frac{1}{\hat{N} - u} + \frac{k - 1}{\hat{N}} - \sum_{i=1}^{k} \frac{1}{\hat{N} - c_i}\right]^{-1}.$$

The question of gear selectivity may be addressed by a chi-square test of uniformity of capture probabilities in different size classes of marked fish as discussed previously for the 2-sample mark-recapture experiment. A contingency chi-square may be calculated for each of the samples 2 through k. These $k - 1$ chi-squares are independent and may be added to provide a total chi-square.

Robson & Regier (1968) show that the situation of known mortality occurring for example at the time of marking may be accommodated by the above procedure if the joint probability of not being captured, i.e. the right-hand side of the estimation formula, is adjusted by subtracting the known mortality. For example suppose that $c_1 = 60$, $c_2 = 43$ and $c_3 = 49$, and that 4, 2, and 0 fish were dead or died from samples c_1, c_2 and c_3 respectively. The right-hand side of the estimation formula would then be:

$$\text{rhs} = \left(\frac{N - 60}{N}\right)\left(\frac{N - 4 - 43}{N - 4}\right)\left(\frac{N - 4 - 2 - 49}{N - 4 - 2}\right)$$

$$= \left(\frac{N - 60}{N}\right)\left(\frac{N - 47}{N - 4}\right)\left(\frac{N - 55}{N - 6}\right).$$

Solution proceeds as outlined above with the variance being computed using $\Delta_{\hat{N}}$. The chi-square contingency test is appropriate for size-class selectivity as stated above.

Example. The following data are from Robson & Regier (1968) and represent result of a simulation experiment.

Sample	Catch	Recaptures	Number dead on capture	Number of mark released	Unmarked catch
1	60	0	4	56	60
2	43	8	2	41	35
3	49	7	0	49	42
					137

The population number is estimated iteratively from the equation:

$$1 - \frac{137}{\hat{N}} = \left(1 - \frac{60}{\hat{N}}\right)\left(1 - \frac{43}{\hat{N} - 4}\right)\left(1 - \frac{49}{\hat{N} - 4 - 2}\right)$$

or

$$\frac{\hat{N} - 137}{\hat{N}} = \left(\frac{\hat{N} - 60}{\hat{N}}\right)\left(\frac{\hat{N} - 47}{\hat{N} - 4}\right)\left(\frac{\hat{N} - 55}{\hat{N} - 6}\right).$$

Starting with a trial value of 305 for N_0 gives the following for

$$N_0 P_{N_0} = 305 \times \left(\frac{305 - 60}{305}\right)\left(\frac{305 - 47}{305 - 4}\right)\left(\frac{305 - 55}{305 - 6}\right) = 175 \cdot 585284$$

$$(N_0 - 1)P_{N_0-1} = 304 \times \left(\frac{304 - 60}{304}\right)\left(\frac{304 - 47}{304 - 4}\right)\left(\frac{304 - 55}{304 - 6}\right) = 174 \cdot 656509.$$

Therefore

$$\Delta_{N_0} = 1 + (N_0 - 1)P_{N_0-1} - N_0 P_{N_0}$$
$$= 1 + 174 \cdot 656509 - 175 \cdot 585284$$
$$= 0 \cdot 071225$$

giving the next trial value as

$$N_1 = 305 + \frac{175 \cdot 585284 - 168}{0 \cdot 071225} = 412.$$

Repeating the process with 412 as a trial guess results in a N_2 of 460, repeating again with 460 results in $N_3 = 466$ and since $N_3 = N_4$ the process stops.

The variance of $\hat{N}$ may be estimated from

$$\hat{V}(\hat{N}) = \frac{\hat{N} - u}{\Delta_{\hat{N}}}$$

which for this example is

$$\hat{V}(\hat{N}) = \frac{466 - 137}{0 \cdot 031401} = 10477 \cdot 3733.$$

Assuming normal theory to be approximately correct, the 95% confidence interval is given by

$$P(265 \leqslant N \leqslant 667) = 0 \cdot 95.$$

The methods of open population, i.e. immigration and permanent emigration in addition to mortality are covered in detail with worked examples given by Darroch (1959), Jolly (1965), Seber (1965) and Seber (1973). For populations in which recruitment does not occur the method given in the next section of multiple mark and recapture with numbered tags permits estimation

F

of population number over an extended period of time during which mortality may occur.

Multiple mark-recapture, allowing unknown mortality. The prior multiple mark-recapture method was for populations closed except to known mortality at the time of marking. The method proposed here assumes that the population is closed to recruitment but does allow for unknown mortality between sample periods. The assumption of no recruitment to the population provides estimates of population number having smaller variance than the Jolly–Seber method. This assumption seems reasonable for certain situations such as populations generated through stocking programmes where released stock may be batch identified, for example by fin clip (Chapter 4) or where age or size may serve to delineate the population under study.

The general procedure for this method is to secure a random sample from the population and tag all fish with a serially numbered tag recording tag number with respect to date of release. Subsequent random samples are taken with untagged fish being tagged, tag numbers of recaptured fish recorded and all fish released.

Let N_i represent the population number at time t_i, m_i represent a sample of fish from N_i at t_i, and r_i the number of subsequent recaptures of fish from the release of m_i tagged fish. Further let c_i represent the number of distinct fish captured *after* the ith sample. With the assumptions of no recruitment into the population, each sample being a random sample, no loss of tags, and capture, tag and release do not affect survival, we have the following estimate of population number:

$$\hat{N}_i = \frac{m_i c_i}{r_i}.$$

This estimate is biased with the bias in $\hat{N}$ being approximately equal to

$$100 \exp\left(-\frac{m_i + 1}{r_i}\right)\%.$$

Adjustment for bias results in the following estimator of population number:

$$\tilde{N}_i = \frac{(m_i + 1)(c_i + 1)}{r_{i+1}} - 1.$$

The estimated variance of $\tilde{N}$ is:

$$\hat{V}(\tilde{N}_i) = (\tilde{N}_i + 1)(\tilde{N}_i + 2) - \frac{(m_i + 1)(m_i + 2)(c_i + 1)(c_i + 2)}{(r_i + 1)(r_i + 2)}.$$

If $m_i + c_i \geqslant N_i$, this estimated variance is unbiased.

The survival rate may be estimated by the ratio $\tilde{N}_{i+1}/\hat{N}_i$. This is dealt with in the section on mortality rate.

Example. A small pond is stocked with fish of a particular year class and all are marked by fin clip such that the group may be identified. For the purpose of this example this serves to eliminate the problem of recruitment by dealing only with fin-clipped fish. The pond is sampled by trap net at yearly intervals with fish taken in the trap net being tagged with numbered tags thus enabling the identification of a recaptured tagged fish as to the date of release. Notice that a tag recapture also becomes one of the marked fish released for that particular date but that in counting recaptures only distinct recaptures for a given release are counted.

Data for estimation of population number by this method may be conveniently summarized as follows:

Time of sampling	Sample size	Number of fish subsequently recaptured	c
t_1	m_1	r_1	c_1
t_2	m_2	r_2	c_2
.	.	.	.
.	.	.	.
.	.	.	.
t_k	m_k	$r_k = 0$	$c_k = 0$

The $c_i = (m_{i+1} - r_{i+1}) + (m_{i+2} - r_{i+2}) + \ldots + (m_k - r_k)$. In our specific example the numbers are:

Time of sampling	Sample size	Number of fish subsequently recaptured	c
1971	200	30	163
1972	100	15	78
1973	50	7	35
1974	25	3	13

Population number for 1971 using the unbiased estimator, $\tilde{N}$, becomes

$$\tilde{N}_{71} = \frac{(m_{71} + 1)(c_{71} + 1)}{r_{71} + 1} - 1$$

$$= \frac{(200 + 1)(163 + 1)}{(30 + 1)} - 1$$

$$= 1062.$$

The estimated variance for this estimate is given as:

$$\hat{V}(\tilde{N}_{71}) = (1062 + 1)(1062 + 2)$$

$$- \frac{(200 + 1)(200 + 2)(163 + 1)(163 + 2)}{(30 + 1)(30 + 2)} = 23481{\cdot}47.$$

Using normal theory approximation, the confidence interval from the above estimate will be:

$$P(762 \leqslant N \leqslant 1362) = 0{\cdot}95.$$

Change-in-ratio methods. The mark-recapture methods required equal vulnerability of the marked and unmarked fish. Where two groups of fish are known to be differentially vulnerable to the sampling gear another type of ratio estimator makes use of this property. This type of estimate is referred to as the change-in-ratio method and has been discussed in detail by Paulik & Robson (1969). This method is also known as the survey-removal, dichotomy or change in composition method.

This method assumes (1) two classes of fish present which are distinguishable and have different vulnerability to the sampling gear, (2) the population is closed, i.e. during the time of the experiment there is no recruitment or migration, and (3) that the only mortality, removal, or addition is exactly known. The classes may be sex of fish, different species of fish, different size groups, or native and stocked fish for example. Let the number in two classes at time t_i be X_i and Y_i respectively with $N_i = X_i + Y_i$ being the population number; define $p_i = X_i/N_i$, $C_x = X_1 - X_2$ and $C_y = Y_1 - Y_2$. The general procedure is to estimate p_1 by a sample before any harvest (or addition) is made in the population and let $\hat{p}_1 = x_1/n_1$ where x_1 is the number of X class fish in a sample of n fish from the population. The population is then subjected to harvest (or addition) resulting in a catch (or addition) of C_x and C_y fish with $C = C_x + C_y$. This is then followed by a second estimate of the fraction of class X in the population, $\hat{p}_2 = x_2/n_2$ with obvious notation.

The population N_1 at time t_1 is estimated by the formula:

$$\hat{N}_1 = \frac{C_x - \hat{p}_2 C}{\hat{p}_1 - \hat{p}_2}.$$

The number in class X_1 is just $p_1 N_1$ and is estimated by

$$\hat{X}_1 = \frac{\hat{p}_1(C_x - \hat{p}_2 C)}{\hat{p}_1 - \hat{p}_2} = \hat{p}_1 \hat{N}_1.$$

Variance estimates are given approximately as:

$$\hat{V}(\hat{N}_1) \doteq [\hat{N}_1{}^2 \hat{V}(\hat{p}_1) + \hat{N}_2{}^2 \hat{V}(\hat{p}_2)]/(\hat{p}_1 - \hat{p}_2)^2$$

and

$$\hat{V}(\hat{X}_1) \doteq [\hat{N}_1{}^2 \hat{p}_2{}^2 \hat{V}(\hat{p}_1) + \hat{N}_2{}^2 \hat{p}_1{}^2 \hat{V}(\hat{p}_2)]/(\hat{p}_1 - \hat{p}_2)^2$$

where $\hat{N}_2 = \hat{N}_1 - C$. The estimated variance of $\hat{p}_i$, $\hat{V}(\hat{p}_i)$, will depend upon the manner in which the p_i's are estimated. Generally these estimates will be by one of two procedures: with replacement (binomially) or without replacement (hypergeometrically). Sampling with replacement may occur when fish are just observed as for example by a SCUBA diver and the variance is estimated as:

$$\hat{V}(\hat{p}_i) = \frac{\hat{p}_i(1 - \hat{p}_i)}{n_i}.$$

If sampling to estimate p_i is without replacement as for example by a trap-net, then the variance of p_i is estimated as

$$\hat{V}(\hat{p}_i) = \frac{\hat{N}_i - n_i}{\hat{N}_i} \frac{\hat{p}_i(1 - \hat{p}_i)}{n_i - 1}.$$

Worked examples and methods for obtaining confidence intervals are given in Paulik & Robson (1969) and Seber (1973) along with discussion of assumptions of the method.

EXAMPLE. Paulik & Robson (1969) provide the following hypothetical data for a lake containing brook trout (*Salvelinus fontinalis*) and cisco (*Coregonus artedii*). Gill nets set before the fishing season catch 150 brook trout and 50 cisco. A total of 700 brook trout are caught during the first 3 weeks of the season and a second gill net set at that time resulted in a catch of 30 brook trout and 30 cisco. Let the number of brook trout be represented by X and cisco by Y. The estimate of p_1 is given by $\hat{p}_1 = 150/200 = 0.75$; p_2 is estimated by $\hat{p}_2 = 30/60 = 0.50$. Since no cisco was removed by angling, the population number of brook trout at the start of fishing was:

$$\hat{X}_1 = \frac{\hat{p}_1(C_x - \hat{p}_2 C)}{\hat{p}_1 - \hat{p}_2}$$

$$= \frac{0.75(700 - 0.50 \times 700)}{0.75 - 0.50}$$

$$= 1050.$$

The population number for both species before fishing was therefore

$$\hat{N}_1 = \hat{X}_1/\hat{p}_1 = 1050/0.75 = 1400.$$

The number of cisco being then the difference, $1400 - 1050 = 350 = Y_1$. The population after 3 weeks of fishing is the initial population number minus the catch, or $1400 - 700 = 700$, which is composed of 350 brook trout and 350 cisco.

Approximate variance for $\hat{X}_1$, using the formula for estimating variance of $\hat{p}_i$ without replacement is given by:

$$\hat{V}(\hat{X}_1) \doteq \left[1400^2(0.50)^2 \left(\frac{1400 - 200}{1400} \right) \frac{(0.75)(0.25)}{199} \right.$$

$$\left. + 700^2(0.75)^2 \left(\frac{700 - 60}{700} \right) \frac{(0.50)(0.50)}{59} \right] \Big/ 0.75 - 0.50$$

$$= 5854.10.$$

Assuming normal theory approximations are appropriate, the 95% confidence interval is:

$$P(973 \leqslant N \leqslant 1127) = 0.95.$$

Correlated population method. Certain species of fish may be more readily estimated by estimating a closely-related population, as for example using samples of eggs to determine population number through fecundity relationships of the population. This method is discussed in detail by Cushing (1957), English (1964) and Saville (1964).

Population number may be estimated using eggs spawned as a correlate by the formula:

$$\hat{N} = \frac{\hat{r}_n \hat{E}}{\hat{e}}$$

where E is the total number of eggs spawned, e is the mean number of eggs per female and

$$r_n = \frac{N_{\female} + N_{\male} + N_I}{N_{\female}}$$

with $N_{\female}$, $N_{\male}$ and N_I corresponding respectively to the number of sexually mature female, sexually mature male and sexually immature fish beyond a given age or size.

Total biomass may be analogously estimated by

$$\hat{p} = \frac{\hat{r}_p \hat{E}}{\hat{k}}$$

with

$$\hat{k} = \frac{e_1 + e_2 + \ldots + e_{N_{\female}}}{w_1 + w_2 + \ldots + w_{N_{\female}}}$$

and

$$\hat{r}_p = \frac{P_{\female} + P_{\male} + P_I}{P_{\female}}$$

and assuming that the average number of eggs per female e is directly proportional to the weight of the female, i.e. $e = kw$.

Three separate sampling problems are involved in obtaining an estimate of either N or P by these means. The r ratios must be obtained either from an experimental fish-catching survey or from sampling of the commercial catch. Some of the many statistical problems that arise in sampling fish populations are mentioned in Chapter 2. The estimate of the total number of eggs spawned involves taking random samples either of known volumes of water for pelagic eggs, or of known areas of bottom for benthic eggs. English (1964) has discussed estimation problems with pelagic eggs, and the discussion of Lambou (1963) is also relevant; Rothschild (1961) studied an instance of stream-spawned benthic eggs; and the problems in estimating fecundity are discussed in Chapter 7.

In carefully designed studies, where sampling variances of each of the parameters r, E and e or k can be estimated, an approximate sampling variance of $\hat{N}$ or $\hat{P}$ can be obtained by the delta method (Seber 1973).* The $\hat{N}$ or $\hat{P}$ will in most cases have no precise connotations since the population will very likely not be closed during the spawning interval; we can expect the estimates to fall somewhere between the maximum and minimum populations during this time interval. Since the population will probably always be open, at least to recruitment and death between spawning periods, it would probably not be worthwhile to seek mortality estimates from estimates of total population made in this manner a year apart, though in conjunction with age-composition data, estimates of the mortality of year-classes may be obtained.

Catch-effort methods

The rationale for catch-effort methods is that for a closed population the catch per unit effort is proportional to the population number present at that time. A series of samples should therefore show a decline in catch per unit effort. The sampling effort may be variable or constant; we will present two methods applicable to most freshwater situations where the assumptions seem reasonable. These methods are the Leslie method (Leslie & Davis 1939) for variable effort and the Moran–Zippin method (Moran 1951; Zippin 1956, 1958) for constant effort. A statistical review of these and other methods for closed and open populations may be found in Seber (1973).

Leslie method. This method assumes the probability of capture is equal for all fish and that this probability of capture is proportional to the effort extended for the sample, i.e. $p_i = q f_i$ where p_i is probability of capture, q is the catchability coefficient and f_i is effort for the ith sample, $i = 1, 2, \ldots, s$. The population number at any time i is equal to the initial population N less

---

*The delta method, also called the propagation-of-error method, is an approximate method of estimating the variance by use of the first few terms of a Taylor series expansion.

what has been taken in the previous $i - 1$ samples. Let

$$K_i = \sum_{j=1}^{i-1} C_j$$

be the accumulated catch up to but not including the ith sample period (C_j is catch for an individual sample), then the expected catch per unit for the ith sample given that K_i have been taken from the population is:

$$E(C_i/f_i \,|\, K_i) = qN - qK_i.$$

This is just a linear regression of catch per unit effort, C_i/f_i, on accumulated catch, K_i. The least-squares analysis provides an estimate of the slope, q, which is the average catchability coefficient over fish and sample periods. The population number N may be estimated as

$$\hat{N} = \bar{K} + \overline{(C/f)}/\hat{q}$$

where $\bar{K}$ and $\overline{(C/f)}$ are average values for K_i and C_i/f_i respectively. The approximate estimated variance of $\hat{N}$ is given by

$$\hat{V}(\hat{N}) = \frac{\hat{\sigma}^2}{\hat{q}^2}\left[\frac{1}{s} + \frac{(\hat{N} - \bar{C})^2}{\Sigma(K_i - \bar{K})^2}\right]$$

with $\hat{\sigma}^2$ representing the residual mean squared error in regression analysis. Procedures for confidence intervals are reviewed by Seber (1973).

Moran-Zippin method. Under assumptions of a closed population, equal probability of capture for each fish in a given sample, and a constant sampling effort such that the probability of capture, p, remains the same for each sample, the estimate of N is taken as

$$\hat{N} = \frac{C}{1 - z^n}$$

where

$$z = 1 - p, \qquad C = \sum_{i=1}^{n} C_i$$

and n is the number of samples. It is first necessary to estimate z, the probability of not being caught and this is done by iterative solution of the equation:

$$\frac{\hat{z}}{1-\hat{z}} - \frac{n\hat{z}^n}{1-\hat{z}^n} = \frac{\sum\limits_{i=1}^{n}(i-1)C_i}{C}.$$

Zippin (1956) provides graphs for estimating $p = 1 - z$. Estimated variances for $\hat{N}$ and $\hat{p}$ are:

$$\hat{V}(\hat{N}) = \frac{\hat{N}(1 - \hat{z}^n)\hat{z}^n}{(1 - \hat{z}^n)^2 - (\hat{p}\hat{z})^2 \hat{z}^{n-1}}$$

and

$$\hat{V}(\hat{p}) = \frac{(\hat{z}\hat{p})^2(1 - \hat{z}^n)}{\hat{N}[\hat{z}(1 - \hat{z}^n)^2 - (n\hat{p})^2 \hat{z}^n]}.$$

The case for $n = 2$ reduces to (Seber & LeCren 1967):

$$\hat{N} = \frac{C_1^2}{C_1 - C_2}$$

$$\hat{p} = 1 - \frac{C_2}{C_1}$$

with estimated variances

$$\hat{V}(\hat{N}) = \frac{C_1^2 C_2^2 (C_1 + C_2)}{(C_1 - C_2)^4}$$

$$\hat{V}(\hat{p}) = \frac{C_2(C_1 + C_2)}{C_1^3}.$$

Direct enumeration
Certain situations, e.g. migratory species passing through a fish ladder, or for a section of stream, may allow the entire number of fish to be counted. Practical aspects of estimating population number under these conditions have been discussed by Rounsefell & Everhart (1953), Lambou & Stern (1958) and Lambou (1963). The statistical treatment of this and other types of direct

counting have been reviewed by Seber (1973). Sampling design and methods for determining variance for a variety of estimators may be found in treatments of sampling theory, e.g. Cochran (1963).

The area or time space occupied by a fish population is divided into A size units with a of these selected at random for counting the contained population. For each of the a units there are thus error-free counts of the number of fish, i.e. $N_1, N_2, \ldots, N_a$ corresponding to subspaces $1, 2, \ldots, a$ respectively. The population number over the entire area or time space is then estimated by

$$\hat{N} = \frac{A}{a} \sum_{i=1}^{a} N_i.$$

The estimated variance of this estimate is given by

$$\hat{V}(\hat{N}) = \frac{A^2 - aA}{a} \left[\frac{a \sum\limits_{i=1}^{a} N_i^2 - \left(\sum\limits_{i=1}^{a} N_i \right)^2}{a(a-1)} \right].$$

This estimate is valid regardless of the dispersion of the population but the ideal partition of the population would be one achieving uniformity in number of fish per unit, resulting in a small value for $\hat{V}(\hat{N}.)$.

Mortality rates

Knowledge of the mortality rates is of prime importance in expressing the dynamics of fish populations. One of the reasons for estimating population number is to determine mortality. It is customary in fish population analysis to assume the following as representing survivorship:

$$N_t = N_0 S^t = N_0 \exp[-(F + M)t]$$

where S is survival rate, F is a coefficient of fishing mortality and M is a coefficient of natural mortality. A general assumption concerning relations between various components of mortality is:

$$\frac{E}{F} = \frac{1 - S}{F + M}$$

where E is called exploitation rate.

A wide variety of methods has been and is still being developed for estimating survival. Many of these methods have been reviewed by Seber (1973) and Ricker (1975). We will consider three general methods appropriate for work with freshwater populations.

Survival rate

The ratio of the number of fish alive at the end of a time period relative to the number of the same group which were alive at the beginning of the time period is defined as survival. This group may be a cohort or a total population; however, it is assumed that the group is closed except for mortality. The estimate of survival is therefore

$$\hat{S} = \frac{N_{i+1}}{N_i}.$$

If the N_i are total counts then N_{i+1} given N_i is binomially distributed thus providing the estimated variance for $\hat{S}$ as:

$$\hat{V}(\hat{S}) = \frac{\hat{S}(1 - \hat{S})}{N_i}.$$

However, in most cases the N_i are estimated resulting in a variance being associated with each estimate. The estimated variance of $\hat{S}$ is then much more complex and has not been dealt with to any great extent in fishery literature. Robson (1971) developed an estimator for the variance of survival from the situation reported below. We consider here the one estimate of survival resulting from using the sequential estimates of population number for the case given in the section Multiple Mark–Recapture with Mortality. In that section two estimators $\hat{N}$ and $\tilde{N}$ were given for the experiment resulting from a capture–mark release programme over some period of time. If the marking occurs as an annual event, survival may be estimated as:

$$\tilde{S}_i = \frac{\tilde{N}_{i+1}}{\hat{N}_i}.$$

We use $\hat{N}$ in the denominator since when in the denominator the random variable part of $\hat{N}$ namely r_i ends up in the numerator. The estimated variance for $\tilde{S}_i$ may now be calculated as:

$$\hat{V}(\tilde{S}_i) = \frac{r_i(r_i - 1)}{m_i(m_i - 1)c_i(c_i - 1)}\left[\hat{V}(\tilde{N}_{i+1}) - \frac{m_i + c_i}{m_i c_i}N_i^2{}_{+1}\right] +$$

$$+ \frac{r_i}{m_i c_i}\left[\frac{1}{m_i c_i} + \frac{(r_i - 1)(r_i - 2)}{(m_i - 1)(m_i - 2)(c_i - 1)(c_i - 2)}\right]\tilde{N}_{i+1}^2.$$

Letting $\hat{\lambda} = \tilde{S}_i^2 / \hat{V}(\tilde{S}_i)$, a 95 % confidence interval estimator of S_i is given by:

$$\frac{2\hat{\lambda}_i \tilde{S}}{\chi^2[0.975(2\hat{\lambda}\,\text{d.f.})]} < S_i < \frac{2\hat{\lambda}\tilde{S}_i}{\chi^2[0.025(2\hat{\lambda}\,\text{d.f.})]}.$$

For $\hat{\lambda}$ large ($\hat{\lambda} > 50$) this becomes essentially the normal approximation.

$$\tilde{S}_i - 1.96\sqrt{[\hat{V}(\tilde{S}_i)]} < S_i < \tilde{S}_i + 1.96\sqrt{[\hat{V}(\tilde{S}_i)]}.$$

Variance estimates for other estimates of the form $N_i^*{}_{+1}/N_i^*$ where N^* is an estimator of survival other than $\tilde{N}$ and $\hat{N}$ have not been developed.

EXAMPLE. Data from the section on estimation of population number with multiple mark–recapture allowing for unknown mortality are used below to show calculation of survival and resulting confidence interval. Survival between the 1971 and 1972 samples may be calculated from the ratio of the two population estimates $\tilde{N}_{72}$ and $\hat{N}_{71}$ as follows

$$\tilde{N}_{72} = \frac{(m_{72} + 1)(c_{72} + 1)}{(r_{72} + 1)} - 1$$

$$= \frac{(100 + 1)(78 + 1)}{(15 + 1)} - 1 = 498$$

with estimated variance

$$\hat{V}(\tilde{N}_{72}) = (498 + 1)(498 + 2) - \frac{(100 + 1)(100 + 2)(78 + 1)(78 + 2)}{(15 + 1)(15 + 2)}$$

$$= 10130.00$$

and

$$\hat{N}_{71} = \frac{m_{71}c_{71}}{r_{71}} = \frac{200 \times 163}{30} = 1087.$$

Therefore survival is estimated as

$$\tilde{S}_{71} = \frac{\tilde{N}_{72}}{\hat{N}_{71}} = \frac{498}{1087} = 0.458.$$

The estimated variance of the estimate is

$$\hat{V}(\tilde{S}_{71}) = \frac{(30)(30-1)}{(200)(200-1)(163)(163-1)}\left[10130\cdot00 - \frac{(200+163)}{(200)(163)}498^2\right]$$

$$+ \frac{30}{(200)(163)}\left[\frac{1}{(200)(163)} + \frac{(30-1)(30-2)}{(200-1)(200-2)(163-1)(163-2)}\right]498^2$$

$$= 0\cdot0061 + 0\cdot0072$$

$$= 0\cdot0133.$$

The 95% confidence interval of S_{71} is found first by determining $\hat{\lambda} = \tilde{S}_{71}/\hat{V}(\tilde{S}_{71}) = 0\cdot458^2/0\cdot0133 = 15\cdot77$ and then, since $\hat{\lambda} < 50$, by the relation

$$P\left(\frac{32 \times 0\cdot458}{49\cdot5} < S_{71} < \frac{32 \times 0\cdot458}{18\cdot3}\right) = 0\cdot95$$

$$P(0\cdot30 < S_{71} < 0\cdot80) = 0\cdot95.$$

Chapman-Robson method

In some situations it may be reasonable to assume that recruitment and survival are relatively constant for a given population resulting in a stationary population at least on an annual basis. Under these assumptions a method for estimating survival which is the minimum variance, unbiased estimate of survival has been developed by Chapman & Robson (1960) and Robson & Chapman (1961). Since many types of sampling gear may be biased, particularly against younger age groups (see Chapter 2), they also provide a test for the model.

This procedure assumes some knowledge of the age structure for the population above some minimum age as determined by sampling gear, and three alternatives are given: (1) all ages in the sample are estimated and represented in the sample, (2) ages are estimated up to some age but not estimable for the remainder although all ages are represented in the sample, and (3) age distribution is truncated at some age greater than the first fully recruited age.

Case 1. For samples in which age can be determined for all fish and for which the age distribution is representative of the entire population, i.e. not truncated with respect to older age classes, survival beyond the first fully recruited age may be estimated by:

$$S = \frac{T}{n + T - 1}$$

with estimated variance

$$\hat{V}(\hat{S}) = \hat{S}\left(\hat{S} - \frac{T-1}{n+T-2}\right)$$

here n is sample size and T is a statistic. T is calculated as the sum of the coded ages times their frequencies when coded age is found by setting the youngest age in the sample to zero, the next age to one and so forth.

A chi-square test of agreement between sample observations and the model may be calculated as follows:

$$\chi^2_{\text{1d.f.}} = \left(\hat{S} - \frac{n - n_0}{n}\right)^2 \Big/ \frac{T(T-1)(n-1)}{n(n+T-1)^2(n+T-2)}.$$

This test is directed towards the youngest age in the sample. Should the chi-square value turn out to be greater than expected, the process may be repeated using the next age group coded to zero.

EXAMPLE. Robson & Chapman (1961) provide an example of this method with data of rock bass taken by trapnet from Cayuga Lake, New York. Age VI+ was the youngest age in the sample and therefore coded to 0. The data set was as follows:

Age	Coded age	Number in catch
VI+	0	$n_0 = 118$
VII+	1	$n_1 = 73$
VIII+	2	$n_2 = 36$
IX+	3	$n_3 = 14$
X+	4	$n_4 = 1$
XI+	5	$n_5 = 1$
	Total sample size,	$n = 243$

The T statistic is calculated as:

$$T = (0 \times 118) + (1 \times 73) + (2 \times 36) + (3 \times 14) + (4 \times 1) + (5 \times 1) = 196$$

The estimate of survival S is:

$$\hat{S} = \frac{T}{n + T - 1} = \frac{196}{243 + 196 - 1} = 0.4475.$$

The estimated variance of this estimate is

$$\hat{V}(\hat{S}) = \hat{S}\left(\hat{S} - \frac{T-1}{n+T-2}\right) = \frac{196}{438}\left(\frac{196}{438} - \frac{195}{437}\right) = 0\cdot000566.$$

An approximate 95% confidence interval for S may be found by taking the estimate plus or minus two standard errors: i.e.

$$\hat{S} \pm 2\sqrt{[\hat{V}(\hat{S})]} = 0\cdot4475 \pm 2 \times 0\cdot0238$$

or

$$0\cdot40 \leqslant S \leqslant 0\cdot50.$$

The agreement of data and model are tested as:

$$\chi_1^2 = \frac{\left(\hat{S} - \dfrac{n - n_0}{n}\right)^2}{\dfrac{T(T-1)(n-1)}{n(n+T-1)^2(n+T-2)}} = \frac{\left(0\cdot4475 - \dfrac{243 - 118}{243}\right)^2}{\dfrac{196 \times 195 \times 242}{243 \times 438^2 \times 437}} = 9\cdot958.$$

Since 9·858 is greater than 3·841, chi-square with one degree of freedom, one would reject the hypothesis that the observed difference is due to sampling error. The next step is therefore to eliminate age VI+ and start with age VII+ as coded age 0 and repeat the entire procedure of estimating survival and testing the model against the new age frequency distribution. In so doing the new $T = 71$, the new $n = 125$ resulting in a new estimate of $S = 0\cdot3641$. Again the test of the model results in a chi-square value of 4·032 which is greater than 3·841. Age VIII+ would then be coded to age zero with T and n now equal to 19 and 52 respectively giving $\hat{S} = 0\cdot2714$. The test this time results in a chi-square of 1·328. We conclude from this that ages VI+ and VII+ were not fully recruited to the sampling gear.

Case 2. Age determination may be accurate or possible for only part, generally the younger ages, of an age frequency distribution in which case the following estimator of Chapman and Robson is appropriate:

$$\hat{S} = \frac{T}{n - m + T}.$$

In this case ageing is possible through coded age k but ages $k+1$ and older are not determined. The T statistic is calculated as:

$$T = (0 \times n_0) + (1 \times n_1) + \ldots + (k \times n_k) + (k + 1)m$$

where m is the sum of the frequencies for all ages $k + 1$ and older. The estimated variance of this estimate is given by:

$$\hat{V}(\hat{S}) = \frac{\hat{S}(1 - \hat{S})^2}{n(1 - \hat{S}^{k+1})}.$$

Tests for the model for this case and the following case have not been developed.

Case 3. The estimate of survival for the case of a truncated sample is no longer explicit but is determined by iteration although Robson & Chapman (1961) provide a table of solutions for various values of S and k. The estimate of survival is taken as the solution of the following equation:

$$\frac{T_k}{n} = \frac{\hat{S}}{1 - \hat{S}} - (k + 1)\frac{\hat{S}^{k+1}}{1 - \hat{S}^{k+1}}$$

where T_k denotes the sum of the coded age times frequency up to and including the last coded age k; ages $k + 1$ and greater are not in the sample. The estimated variance of this estimate is given by:

$$\hat{V}(\hat{S}) = \frac{1}{n} \bigg/ \left[\frac{1}{\hat{S}(1 - \hat{S})^2} - \frac{(k + 1)^2 \hat{S}^{k-1}}{(1 - \hat{S}^{k+1})^2} \right].$$

A tag-recapture model
Estimates of survival and exploitation rates are possible through the use of numbered tags and their subsequent recaptures for situations in which recruitment is not known, and for which age determination is not possible. Models are available for both open and closed populations and are reviewed by Seber (1973) and Ricker (1975). The one presented here, arrived at independently by Seber (1970) and Robson & Youngs (1971), would seem of particular value for freshwater work where advantage may be taken of angler-reported tag recaptures. Considerations for determining sample size and tests of the model are given in Youngs & Robson (1975). This method has also been applied to waterfowl populations (Anderson 1975) and in a more generalized expansion to models appropriate for a variety of assumptions concerning age-dependent survival and exploitation rates (Brownie & Robson 1976).

This method assumes year-specific but age-independent rates of survival and reported exploitation rates. The method is based on the return of tags by anglers assuming that the year of capture is accurately reported by the angler. A sample of fish is tagged with serially numbered tags as an annual event just prior to open season. Angler reported recaptures are accountable to a given tagging year on the basis of the tag number. After k years an array of recapture results as shown below.

Year tagged	Number tagged	Reported as recaptured in year					Total recaptures
		1	2	3	...	k	
1	M_1	R_{11}	R_{12}	R_{13}	...	R_{1k}	R_1
2	M_2		R_{22}	R_{23}	...	R_{2k}	R_2
3	M_3			R_{33}	...	R_{3k}	R_3
.	.				.	.	.
.	.				.	.	.
.	.				.	.	.
k	M_k					R_{kk}	R_k
Total recaptures for a given year		C_1	C_2	C_3		C_k	

A statistic T_i is defined as follows: $T_1 = R_1$, and $T_{i+1} = T_i + R_{i+1} - C_i$ for $i = 1, 2, \ldots k - 1$. The year-dependent estimates of minimum exploitation rate E^* are given by:

$$\hat{E}_i{}^* = \frac{R_i}{M_i} \frac{C_i}{T_i} = r_i \frac{C_i}{T_i}.$$

Survival rate is estimated as:

$$\hat{S}_i = \frac{r_i - E_i{}^*}{r_{i+1}}$$

in which $E_i{}^*$ is a minimum estimate because not all tags will be reported, the estimate of S_i is not influenced by reporting. Estimates of E are possible under some conditions (Youngs 1974).

Approximate variances for $\hat{E}_i{}^*$ and $\hat{S}_i$ respectively are

$$\hat{V}(\hat{E}_i{}^*) = \frac{\hat{E}_i{}^*}{R_i M_i} \left[\hat{E}_i{}^*(M_i - R_i) + \frac{R_i(R_i - \hat{E}_i{}^* M_i)}{T_i} \right]$$

and

$$\hat{V}(\hat{S}_i) = \hat{S}_i{}^2 \left[\frac{M_i - R_i}{M_i R_i} + \frac{M_{i+1} - R_{i+1}}{M_{i+1} R_{i+1}} + \frac{\hat{E}_i{}^* M_i}{T_i(R_i - M_i \hat{E}_i{}^*)} \right].$$

A chi-square contingency test of the model may be applied to recapture data in a series of $k - 2$ tables of the form:

Year tagged	Year of recapture				Total
	2	3	. . .	k	
1	R_{12}	R_{13}	. . .	R_{1k}	$T_2 - R_2$
2	R_{22}	R_{23}	. . .	R_{2k}	R_2
Total	C_2	$R_{23}{}^*$	. . .	$R_{2k}{}^*$	T_2

Year tagged	Year of recapture				Total
	3	4	. . .	k	
1 or 2	$R_{23}{}^*$	$R_{24}{}^*$	. . .	$R_{2k}{}^*$	$T_3 - R_3$
3	R_{33}	R_{34}	. . .	R_{3k}	R_3
Total	C_3	$R_{34}{}^*$	. . .	$R_{3k}{}^*$	T_3

which continue in obvious manner. These individual chi-squares may be added for a combined test with $(k - 1)(k - 2)/2$ degrees of freedom. Grouping of recaptures is done if marginal totals become too small for validity of the chi-square approximation.

EXAMPLE. Data below are for a hypothetical largemouth bass population sampled by trap net just prior to angling season.

Year tagged	Number tagged	Recaptured in year					Total recaptures (R_i)
		1973	1974	1975	1976	1977	
1973	700	193	104	48	10	10	365
1974	800		264	123	26	25	438
1975	1000			379	79	78	536
1976	900				194	190	384
1977	600					255	255
C_i		193	368	550	309	558	

The T_i are calculated as $T_1 = R_1 = 365$, $T_2 = T_1 + R_2 - C_1 = 365 + 438 - 193 = 610$, $T_3 = 610 + 536 - 368 = 778$, $T_4 = 778 + 384 - 550 = 612$, and $T_5 = 612 + 255 - 309 = 558$. As a check $T_k = C_k$, i.e. $558 = 558$ for this example. The estimates of $E_i{}^*$ and S_i are straightforward from the formula, for example,

$$\hat{E}_3{}^* = \frac{C_3}{T_3}\frac{R_3}{M_3} = \frac{550}{778} \times \frac{536}{1000} = 0\cdot3789;$$

$$\hat{S}_3 = \frac{r_3 - E_3{}^*}{r_4} = \frac{\dfrac{536}{1000} - 0\cdot3789}{\dfrac{384}{900}} = 0\cdot3682.$$

The test of the model is critical and is shown below. The first set of data is:

Year tagged	Year of recapture				Total
	1974	1975	1976	1977	
1973	104	48	10	10	172
1974	264	123	26	25	438
Total	368	171	36	35	610
		$\chi_3{}^2 < 1$			
1973 or 1974		171	36	35	242
1975		379	79	78	536
Total		550	115	113	778
			$\chi_2{}^2 < 1$		
1973, 74 or 75			115	113	228
1976			194	190	384
Total			309	303	612
				$\chi_1{}^2 < 1$	

Addition of the individual chi-square statistics provides a combined test of the model; in this case the resulting chi-square, with 6 d.f. is also less than one.

7

Eggs and Early Life History

T B Bagenal and Erich Braum

Introduction

Increasing attention is being given to the numbers of eggs developing in female fish prior to spawning and the survival of early stages after hatching. It has been shown that these early stages contribute a major proportion to the annual production, and a knowledge of the fecundity is necessary to delimit the start of an Allan curve (page 203). Therefore a study which does not include estimates of the population fecundity and larval growth and mortality is likely to miss a significant part of the production. Another goal of these studies is to obtain data relating to population stability and to year-class fluctuations. These fluctuations reach extreme proportions in some species, and may be a major factor determining variations in production from year to year. Mortality is usually very great during the early stages of life, and a small change in the daily or weekly rate of mortality can add up to a severe total effect, so that the year-class is 'weak' or even 'blank'.

Considerable theoretical discussion has taken place on the pattern of changes in survival from eggs to young fish ('recruits'), in relation to population density. *Percentage* survival will generally decrease continuously with increasing population. The *number* surviving will at first increase with increasing population; then it may level off, or there may be some maximum point beyond which the total number surviving decreases with further population increase. If such a decline is rapid enough, it can produce oscillations in abundance of the stock (Ricker 1954). However that may be, for most species there is little quantitative information concerning the factors that cause the death of eggs and young fish. More information is needed on this point, and on how the actual mortality factors may be related to population density. Specifically, direct experimentation is likely to shed light on this question.

This chapter presents methods of measuring fecundity, rearing young fish in the laboratory, and sampling eggs and larvae in nature. With these methods egg-laying fishes can be studied with regard to: (1) number and weight of eggs produced by a population, (2) metabolism of fish larvae, (3) effects of starvation, (4) time of hatching, (5) time of first feeding, (6) size and kinds of food material, (7) rate of growth, (8) movements and abundance of fish larvae in nature, (9) feeding in relation to size and species of plankters, (10) relation of changes in the chemical and physical environment to the size of populations of fish larvae, and many other problems contributory to an understanding of fish populations. Several aspects of young fish biology are considered in the volume edited by Blaxter (1974).

PART I. FECUNDITY

T. B. BAGENAL

The fecundity of fish is defined here as the number of ripening eggs in the female prior to the next spawning period. I have published elsewhere (Bagenal 1978) a review which summarizes much of the background information on aspects of fish fecundity. It is essential that this review should be read with the present chapter which deals with methods only. These fall conveniently into three phases: (1) catching an unbiased sample, (2) estimating the number of eggs, and (3) analysing the results in relation to the other population statistics.

Sampling

The method used for catching the adult fish must be chosen so that as far as possible the catch is a random sample of the population with respect to length, weight and age as well as fecundity. The kinds of gear available are described in Chapter 2, with some account of the peculiarities of each. One obvious source of bias would be to sample with a gill net in which the fatter and more fecund fish of a length or age group would be selected.

Sampling bias may be introduced in many unexpected ways, in addition to what arises from the nature of the gear used. For example, the onset of spawning may be related to fecundity both within an age-group and between different age-groups, so the timing of the sampling may be important. With European plaice the older fish spawn first (Simpson 1959b) while with pike the young spawn earlier than the more fecund old ones (Svärdson 1949).

Once eggs have passed a certain stage in maturity they become translucent and approach the ripe and running condition and their preservation becomes more difficult. With some fish, for example the perch, all the eggs are shed almost simultaneously; among others, eggs may be shed a few at a time, over a long period. The methods to be used in this case are dealt with on page 172.

If possible it is best to obtain all the fish needed for a fecundity study on the same date, since all the specimens are then likely to be near the same stage of development and fecundity can be related to somatic weight and gonad weight. Such relationships cannot be recognized if the species show marked seasonal changes in condition and the samples have been collected over a long period. This point is important.

Estimation of fecundity

Initial observations

Once the fish have been caught, the following data should be kept for each individual separately: the fish's length, body weight, gonad weight, and age as determined from scales, bones or otoliths (see Chapter 5).

Live or dead fish

In some cases fecundity may have to be determined by stripping the eggs from the fish so that the parent is not killed. Pope *et al.* (1961) show that the efficiency of stripping is not constant. Their results indicate that eggs should only be obtained by stripping if it is absolutely necessary and then the limits of the error determined from a few specimens by dissection and counting the eggs retained in the ovary. It is more satisfactory to dissect out the ovary and estimate the number of either fresh or preserved eggs.

Counting fresh or preserved eggs

With valuable fish such as salmon it may only be possible to work with fresh eggs that will later be used for hatching. Pope *et al.* (1961) used a variety of methods in their work on Atlantic salmon. With some of the fish the eggs were stripped from ripe females, fertilized, washed and allowed to harden. They were then estimates by the ratio method described by Burrows (1951). This involves finding the total volume of water displaced by all the eggs and also the number of eggs that displaces a unit volume of water. They also used a hatchery method of counting eggs (Lindroth 1956) in which the eggs are allowed to fall into 100 small holes in a plastic plate. In this case all the eggs are counted and not just a sample.

It may also be practical to estimate the fecundity with fresh eggs by weighing the ovary, counting a known weight of eggs and estimating total fecundity by proportion (Kipling & Frost 1969). Fry (1949), working with lake trout in Canada, used a complicated method based on the total weight of the ovary and the mean diameter of 10 eggs dissected from the ovary. The total number of eggs was estimated from the conversion diagram which gave the number of eggs per gram of ovary plotted against the diameter of the maturing eggs, and which was based on 88 fish from two lakes. However it is more usual and, except with large eggs, more satisfactory to work with preserved eggs. Some workers have weighed the ovary and several sub-samples of eggs fresh, and have then preserved the subsamples for counting later.

Preservation of eggs
Preservatives. Three different methods of preservation have been used:

(a) GILSON'S FLUID. Simpson (1951) modified this fixative and preservative by doubling the amount of acetic acid so that the mixture became:

> 100 ml 60% alcohol
> 880 ml water
> 15 ml 80% nitric acid
> 18 ml glacial acetic acid
> 20 g   mercuric chloride

This modified Gilson's fluid has been used by many investigators and has been found to act satisfactorily with a wide range of species. Not only does the mixture harden the eggs, but it also helps to liberate them and break down the ovarian tissue. It is strongly recommended as the best preservative.

(b) FORMALIN. 4% or 5% formalin has been used by some workers (Scott 1962). However in my experience formalin has not been satisfactory since the whole ovary tends to become fixed in a hard mass and it is difficult to separate the eggs from themselves and from the ovarian tissue. This trouble was apparently encountered by Wagner & Cooper (1963).

(c) BOILING. Some early authors, for example Reibisch (1899) and Mitchell (1913), fixed the ovaries by boiling them in water and then preserved them in formalin. Van Leeuwen (1972) advocates boiling the ovaries and then drying the eggs at 70°C for 48 h.

Details of preservation. If Gilson's fluid is used, as recommended here, the treatment should proceed as follows. The ovaries, after they have been removed from the fish, should be split longitudinally and turned inside out to assist penetration by the preservative. Large ovaries should be cut into separate portions. The ovaries should be preserved in labelled jars, shaken vigorously and left for at least 24 h. Repeated shaking helps separate the eggs from the ovarian tissue and assists the penetration of the preservative. The samples may be left for several months without disadvantage. If the eggs are not sufficiently hard to withstand handling by the time one wishes to count them, I have found that gentle heat in an oven will hasten the process. Simpson (1959a) reports that he has been able to work on ovaries preserved for as short a time as 24 h. Pitt (1964) found that the best results were obtained if the eggs were in the Gilson's fluid for 3 months; after longer periods the outer ovarian wall became soft and could not be peeled away.

Washing. To clean the eggs the Gilson's fluid should be decanted and replaced by water. The periodic vigorous shaking will have liberated most of the eggs but the remainder will have to be removed manually. Wenner & Musick (1974) broke up the egg masses after 3 months in Gilson's fluid with a sonic cleaner. The ovarian tissue free of eggs should be removed. The jar will now contain the free eggs in dilute Gilson's fluid made cloudy with minute fragments of ovarian tissue. By repeated filling with water and decanting the supernatant liquid the eggs will become sufficiently washed. Simpson (1951) originally recommended washing with 70% alcohol to prevent the eggs swelling and bursting, but water may be used providing the eggs have been well preserved and are sufficiently hard. De Silva (1973) washed the eggs through a series of sieves to remove resting oocytes.

Total counts

In some cases all the eggs may be counted, for example with the bullhead (Smyly 1957), small salmonids (McFadden & Cooper 1964) and the spurdog (Holden & Meadows 1964). However, with the more fecund species it is more reliable to count the number of eggs in a series of replicate subsamples. It is easy to make a gross error when counting several thousand eggs, but replicate subsamples of a few hundred should check against each other and yield a more constant and reliable result.

Automatic fish egg counters have been described and used by several workers (Parrish *et al.* 1960; Davies & Paulik 1965; Boyar & Clifford 1967).

These must be thoroughly tested by running with known numbers of eggs. My experience with a similar machine and the eggs of perch has not been very encouraging, due to difficulties with separated egg cases and bits of ovarian tissue.

Subsampling

Regardless of which method of subsampling is used, the final estimate must be based on the mean of replicate subsamples. In nearly all cases it is advisable to reduce the size of the subsamples slightly and increase their number. It is often better to have a larger known error than a supposedly smaller but unknown one. With a number of species I have taken four subsamples and found this satisfactory.

Volumetric subsampling. Volumetric subsampling is usually carried out with wet eggs. Simpson (1951) and Raitt (1968) used a Stempel pipette for subsampling plaice and Norway pout eggs. This pipette was designed for subsampling marine plankton (Hensen 1887; Jenkins 1901) but is expensive and difficult to make. Kändler & Pirwitz (1957) had initially tried using a Stempel pipette; they found that the eggs settled too quickly for a representative subsample to be taken. Bagenal (1957a, and 1966 for other papers) used a cylindrical museum jar half full with 2 litres of the eggs and water. The mixture was stirred so that the eggs were well distributed through the water and then a subsample was taken quickly with small glass or Perspex tube attached to a rod. In the later work the Perspex tube held exactly 5 ml and four aliquot subsamples were taken. It was essential to be certain that the eggs and water were well mixed while the subsample was taken.

Kändler & Pirwitz (1957) poured the cleaned eggs into a tall measuring cylinder in which they soon settled down. The total volume of eggs was noted and then a specific volume, either 0·5, 0·25 or 0·1 ml of eggs was removed and counted. Care had to be taken that eggs did not stratify according to size and sinking rates. Bias from this was overcome by shaking and stirring with only a small quantity of water. With three different species the mean deviation from the average number of eggs in 20 replicates varied from 3·8 % to 4·5 %. Mann (1973) working with roach measured the total volume and five aliquots poured into a measuring cylinder with 0·1-cc gradations.

Pitt (1964) and Winters (1971) used a whirling flask as described in detail by Wiborg (1951) for subsampling plankton. The apparatus was used 2 or

3 times to give 4 or 8 samples which by combining two 1/100 subsamples gave either 1/500 or 1/1000 of the total number of eggs. The fecundity was taken as the mean of the 4 or 8 counts.

Gravimetric subsampling. The eggs must be subsampled gravimetrically, either wet or dry. The advantage of weighing the eggs wet is that after the sub-samples have been weighed and preserved, the rest of the ovary may be disposed of. With large ovaries (e.g. pike) this may be the only practical course. The advantages of the dry method are that the eggs are easier to store and if air dried will be in equilibrium with the ambient humidity. This should give more accurate and consistent results.

WET METHOD. McGregor (1922) carefully weighed the ovaries after removing excess water on filter paper and counted the number of eggs per 10 g, and then calculated the total number. He states that the method is accurate to 1 %. Some allowance should be made for the weight of ovarian tissue if the eggs have not been separated from it. Carscadden & Leggett (1975) estimated the number of eggs gravimetrically in four separate size groups from sieving.

DRY METHOD. This is often wrongly referred to as Simpson's (1951) method (e.g. by Baxter 1959; Bridger 1961) but in his 1951 paper Simpson actually describes the use of a Stempel pipette. He described his dry method only in a multigraphed manuscript (Simpson 1959a). The preserved and washed eggs were poured into a filter paper in a funnel. When the liquid had drained away the paper and eggs were spread on blotting paper to remove excess moisture. After about 20 min the eggs were spread on a filter paper tray made from sheets 30 × 45 cm or 45 × 60 cm, with the edges turned up. They were then left to dry until they could be moved without raising the surface of the paper. They were left to air dry and were moved about with the fingers to prevent clumps forming. Plaice eggs turned from a creamy white to a translucent golden yellow and became very hard. When they were thoroughly dry they were stored in specimen tubes.

The fecundity estimate is obtained by weighing all the eggs and two or more random samples of 200 (Simpson 1959a), 250 (Bridger 1961) or 500 eggs (Baxter 1959) and multiplying by the ratio of total weight/weight of subsample. For this method a balance weighing to 0·1 mg is essential with small eggs. Two precautions should be taken: firstly the subsamples must be from randomly mixed eggs, and the moisture content of the eggs must be in equilibrium with the air of the room where the counting and weighing is being done. Simpson reports that repeated weighings of 2 lots of 200 different eggs gave a mean variation of $\pm 3\%$ of the mean of the estimates.

SUBSAMPLING BY AREA. Hickling (1940) spread the separated eggs in a layer one egg thick in a rectangle. He then counted the eggs on two adjacent sides and the product of the two gave an estimate of the total. This was checked by counting the other two sides. Presumably his estimate was based on the mean of these two estimates. Bridger (1961) has checked this method against Simpson's dry method. He found it very laborious, and with two fish it consistently gave an underestimate. Mitchell (1913) spread the weighed subsample over a grid of centimetre squares and either counted all the eggs or only those lying in some of the squares.

COMPARISON OF METHODS. Most good papers give the extent of the variability in the fecundity estimates, but few workers have made comparisons of different methods. Wolfert (1969) reports that his gravimetric method was less variable than his volumetric one. With the gravimetric estimate the error ranged from $-1\cdot3$ to $2\cdot8\%$, whereas with the volumetric method it ranged from $-15\cdot0$ to $4\cdot7\%$. More comparative work on these lines is needed.

Fecundity of multiple spawners

The methods enumerated in this chapter are suitable for most temperate fish, both marine and freshwater, which have a definite spawning season during which all the ripe eggs are shed at approximately the same time. However some species, for example the bleak (Mackay & Mann 1969), the tench (Moroz 1968), the crucian carp (Astanin & Podgorny 1968) and other cyprinids spawn intermittently throughout the breeding season, and with these different methods may have to be used. Furthermore some tropical fish spawn more or less continuously over a long period.

In temperate species with multiple spawnings, it is found that if the developing eggs in the ovary are measured early enough in the season, the oocytes are of two kinds, and exhibit two modes in their size frequency distribution. The diameter of the eggs may be measured under a microscope with an eyepiece micrometer. For this work the ovaries must be fixed whole, and formalin may be used, and the eggs measured in subsamples cut from them. Care must be taken to ensure that the proportion of large and small eggs, and their absolute sizes are representative of the ovary as a whole. The smaller of the eggs form the recruitment stock and the larger ones are usually white and opaque and are the eggs which will be spawned during the coming season. In some species the total number of eggs to be spawned (apart from those resorbed) can be estimated by counting the larger eggs. These counts must be made early in the season before any eggs become more yolky and turgid and there is a possibility of some having been shed. In other species there may be evidence that there is continuous recruitment from the small eggs, in which case the fecundity will be much more difficult to determine.

If the size distribution of the eggs of repeated spawners is determined later in the season, it may be found that the opaque eggs with yolk show signs of being multi-modal; and later those of the largest mode may become even more yolky and a yellow or golden colour, so the ovaries now contain three types of eggs. This situation suggests that the species spawns more than once during the season, in which case later examination will show that the largest type of egg is missing in some of the fish. By taking regular samples and finding the percentage of females with the largest orange/golden eggs, and of females in which they are missing, it is sometimes possible to find the number of spawning times in the season from the peaks in the fluctuations of these percentages. The number of these peaks should agree with the number of modes in the egg size frequency distribution, and should also agree with the modes in the size distribution of the larvae and very young fish if these can be caught. It may also be possible to estimate the number of females spawning on each occasion. Macer (1974), who worked with the marine horse mackerel, discussed the problems of multiple spawners, particularly how to distinguish between reserve and developing oocytes and how to determine the number of batches shed. His paper, and Mackay & Mann (1969), should be consulted by anyone studying the fecundity of multiple spawners.

In *Pomatoschistus minutus* (Pallas) (Healey 1971) some recruitment eggs separate from the rest and ripen for spawning in the posterior part of the ovary which is at first connected to it by an isthmus, but later breaks away completely. Directly after shedding the first batch of eggs the female begins to develop a second. During the season (from January to June) the separated portion contains more eggs, and this is not explained by being the second or subsequent batch.

The fecundity and spawning frequency of mouth-brooding *Sarotherodon* spp. have been discussed by Fryer (1961), Riedel (1965), Lowe (1965) and Welcomme (1967). The fecundity can be determined in the usual way by estimating the number of ripening eggs in the ovary. Welcomme kept eggs in an artificial mouth and made a table of developmental stages of the eggs and fry (which is dependent on the water temperature). From this and an

Chapter 7

examination of the development of the ovaries of females which were brooding, he obtained some idea of the speed of re-ripening and the frequency of spawning. Fryer (1961) made comparable observations using marked fish.

Welcomme also studied the relation of brood size and fecundity and found that although in general the average fecundity at each length was greater than the brood size, the maximum brood could be greater than the minimum fecundity, so fluctuations in fecundity might under some circumstances affect the number brooded. Fryer concludes that most of the eggs produced can be safely gathered into the mouth.

Statistical analysis

Results of typical fecundity investigations have shown that there is very great variability in the number of eggs in fish of the same length, weight and age. This variability must be taken into account if it is desired to find differences in fecundity between different populations, or to give an estimate of the precision of the fecundity, or to find which parameter to use for prediction in production studies. It is therefore essential that the data should be analysed statistically.

The first step is to plot fecundity against the other variables in separate scatter diagrams. Figure 7.1 shows a typical result of plotting fecundity against fish length. The very great variability will be seen in this figure as the scatter about the line, which in this case is obviously a curve. If the size range of the fish is small it may appear to be a straight line, though in fact being part of a curve of the form:

$$F = ax^b$$

where F = fecundity, x = length, weight or age, a = a constant and b = an exponent. The curve is transformed to a straight line by a logarithmic transformation:

$$\log F = \log a + b \log x$$

b usually is about 3 when fecundity is related to length (i.e. $F \propto L^3$) and may be about 1 when related to weight or age. The analysis should be carried out on the logarithmic values since the linear relationship not only allows standard statistical techniques to be used, but also stabilizes the variance with regard to fish size (Baxter & Hall 1960; Pope *et al.* 1961). Details of the methods of regression analysis and analysis of covariance can be obtained from standard textbooks. Most standard statistical textbooks however do

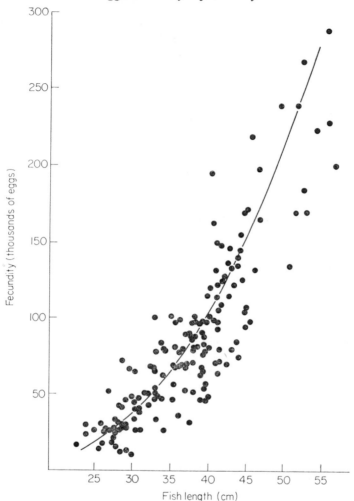

Figure 7.1 Scatter diagram showing a typical relationship between fecundity and fish length.

not deal with logarithmic transformations adequately, and care must be taken in interpreting the results. The antilogarithm of a fecundity estimate derived from the equation on page 174 will always tend to give an under-estimate. Pope *et al.* (1961) and Raitt (1968) apply a correction of:

$$1\cdot15\left(\frac{n-1}{n}\right)s^2$$

where s^2 is the residual variance of the log values. The relations of certain parameters following a logarithmic transformation have been explained by Bagenal (1955). Simpson's (1951) data for plaice provide a good example of the kind of problem that can arise and needs care in interpretation (Bagenal 1957b). The geometric mean fecundity was found to be greater in one year, whereas the arithmetic mean fecundity was greater in the other. The reason for this could be found in the relation between the two means, which may, for normal distributions, be written:

$$\text{G.M.} = \text{A.M.}/(1 + \sigma^2/\text{A.M.}^2)^{\frac{1}{2}}$$

where G.M. and A.M. are the geometric and arithmetic means and σ^2 is the variance. The difference between the ranked orders of the means is due to large differences in the variances of the two sets of data.

Ricker (1973) recommends using a G.M. regression which is a functional regression whose coefficient

$$v = \sqrt{(b_1 . b_2)}$$

where b_1 and b_2 are the standard regression coefficients of X on Y and Y on X. The G.M. regression has not yet been generally accepted by fishery statisticians.

The population fecundity (that is the total number of eggs in all the females in one season) may be obtained from the product of the expected fecundity of an average-sized female and the total number of breeding females. Pitcher & McDonald (1973) pointed out that with the usual logarithmic transformation this will give an underestimate which increases with the regression coefficient and the length range. They give a diagram from which the magnitude of the error may be judged if the regression coefficient and mean length and its variance are known.

Bagenal (1957a, and 1966 for other papers), Baxter & Hall (1960), Hodder (1963), Macer (1974), Pantulu (1963), Pitt (1964), Pope *et al.* (1961), Raitt (1933), Raitt (1968) and Wolfert (1969) among others all give adequate treatments of fecundity analyses. In production studies weight is a basic parameter, so it may be necessary to relate fecundity to this. Some authors have expressed their results as 'relative fecundity', i.e. the number of eggs per unit weight of fish. If the weight includes the gonads this may lead to a spurious correlation, while if the gonad weight is not included difficulties may arise if there are marked changes in condition either as the spawning season approaches, or from year to year, or place to place. I have discussed these difficulties and others in some detail (Bagenal 1978), and my paper should be consulted so that the snags may be recognized and possibly overcome.

The population age structure is also of importance in production studies, and fecundity (F) can sometimes be related to age (t) by the expression:

$$\log F = a + bt$$

but a test for linearity should be made. There is usually an enormous amount of variability within each age group, particularly with short-lived species and those with much size variation within each age group. This variability may make prediction from age difficult. These and other aspects of fecundity and age are discussed by Bagenal (1978).

Fecundity and the environment

It must be realized that any change in the environment may result in significant changes in fecundity and so alter production estimates. An increase in food supply, for example, may not only increase the growth rate and so the gonad weight for a given age, but also the fecundity for a given length may increase (Bagenal 1966; 1969a; Scott 1962) and the amount of fat and yolk in the eggs may also increase. Many examples of these changes are given by Nikolsky (1965, 1969).

Fecundity and egg quality

The eggs of most species vary in size (Bagenal 1971) and chemical composition, and some of these variations will be important from the point of view of fish production. While the extent of these variations has been recorded for many species, its importance in terms of survival of the progeny under natural conditions has been demonstrated adequately less often, and until this has been shown, it is hardly appropriate to talk of egg 'quality'.

A relationship between the fat content of the female parent and the egg size and quantity of the yolk has been shown in a number of species, for example in herring (Anokhina 1963), threespine stickleback (Potapova *et al.* 1968) and roach (Cheprakova & Vasetsky 1962). Vladimirov (1965, 1970) and his colleagues have shown that the fatness of the parents affects the survival of roach, bream and sturgeon in the Lower Dneper. The effect of egg size on larval growth and survival has also been studied by Blaxter & Hempel

G

(1963) in Atlantic herring and Bagenal (1969b) in brown trout. The effect of the age of the parent fish on the progeny has been investigated by several Russian workers whose results are quoted by Nikolsky (1969).

It is not intended in this chapter to consider the chemical methods of fat and other analyses for the determination of egg and parent 'quality', but only to draw attention to the necessity of considering this very important aspect of fish production studies. These methods are discussed on page 236.

PART II. THE EGGS AND LARVAL PHASE

Erich Braum

Introduction

The great natural mortality during the egg and larval phase is a fundamental aspect for the assessment of fish production. Though data about mortality rates in various age groups of freshwater fishes during pre-recruit phases are scarce, the existing information shows clearly that mortality during the first year is highest (Allen 1951; Le Cren 1962; Ricker & Foerster 1948). Thus, it is of greatest interest to obtain more information about survival for short-time intervals during early life. Recently Bannister *et al.* (1974) investigated abundance and mortality of plaice eggs and larvae. In 'normal' years mortality was in excess of 99% and occurred within the first 130 days of life.

Information may be obtained by ecological methods, and sometimes by using complementary rearing experiments that will reveal the incubation time of eggs at different temperatures, the behaviour of larvae, and so on. Techniques developed for sampling eggs or larvae of a particular type must usually be changed to make them applicable to eggs and larvae of another type. The availability of eggs and larvae from rearing experiments is sometimes helpful in working out suitable field methods.

This section therefore seeks to give both techniques for field investigations and some rearing methods for an experimental approach.

Spawning site and egg deposition

One can assume that during the egg stage fishes are more dependent upon their environment than at any other stage of their life cycle. They are threatened by numerous unfavourable changes in biotic or abiotic factors at the spawning site.

Because of the great differences in modes of reproduction among fishes, widely-different methods are needed to obtain data about mortality and survival during early life stages.

Nikolsky (1963a, b) gives a classification of ecological groups of fishes developed by Kryzhanovsky (1949); it is based particularly on the spawning sites, and this is reflected in the names adopted. Lithophils spawn on stony grounds, phytophils among plants, psammophils on sand, pelagophils in the water column and ostracophils in the mantle cavity of molluscs.

Most oviparous freshwater fishes produce eggs of the non-buoyant type. They may be adhesive, like the eggs of pike and most cyprinids, or they may be non-adhesive like many salmonid eggs. A survey of the egg characteristics of different systematic categories is given by Breder & Rosen (1966).

Recently Balon (1975) extended earlier classifications of fish reproduction and established categories suitable to cover the breeding habits of all living species of fish.

Among the ecological features of different spawning sites, the temperature, water flow and oxygen supply are easily measured parameters of fundamental importance for egg development and survival. Technical difficulties may arise in getting water samples for reliable oxygen determinations out of gravel and sediment, or from the mud–water interface, where eggs of some species, e.g. some whitefish, develop. Oxygen content may be extremely low in these two environments and may become a limiting factor for egg development; problems and available methods are discussed by Hayes (1964) and Wickett (1954). In particular, shallow spawning sites in stagnant water have extreme fluctuations of light, temperature, oxygen, etc. Very little is known about the effect of these fluctuations upon egg development.

During the time from fertilization to hatching, eggs require primarily a suitable range of temperatures and a sufficient oxygen supply. Oxygen demand increases continuously during embryogenesis and is influenced by temperature. Both the temperature and the oxygen supply of the environment may accelerate or retard the morphogenetic process of development. Together with the time at which development starts, external factors and egg quality are of importance for the survival prospects of the larvae. Nikolsky (1969) discusses inter-relationships of the various factors concerned with the course of spawning and the survival of eggs and young. Physiological mechanisms controlling the onset of spawning are based on the endocrine system, and in addition are connected with external cycles such as seasonal changes of photoperiod, temperature, etc., to ensure reproduction at a time and place most favourable for development.

Observations on the mating behaviour of commercial freshwater fish such as char, whitefish and burbot were made by Fabricius & Gustafson (1954), Fabricius & Lindroth (1954) and Fabricius (1954), while brown trout and salmon were studied by Jones & Ball (1954). These ethological investigations revealed that spawning is the final act in a chain of events which require a definite sequence of actions as between male and female. It is of some interest that females distribute eggs over a considerable area, and that the spawning period is usually protracted. There are repeated mating acts, with the extrusion of small numbers of eggs each time. Wide distribution of eggs and a protracted spawning period doubtlessly increase the likelihood that some of the eggs will survive unfavourable periods during development.

Many reports exist on the behaviour of fish that guard their eggs, e.g. cichlids. A survey of the biology and behaviour of this important fish group is given by Fryer & Iles (1972).

Egg sampling techniques

Egg sampling techniques are used to determine the total number of eggs laid, and to estimate their survival rate. However many difficulties arise because of the great variability in egg properties and in ecological features of the spawning grounds, so no universal technique exists.

As mentioned above, most eggs laid in freshwater are non-buoyant. Very few fish have truly buoyant eggs, actually lighter than the water in which they are spawned; examples are the snakehead (Channa), whose eggs float at the surface, sometimes guarded by the adults and the sheephead (*Aplodinotus grunniens*) (Davis 1959). There is a larger group of species having semi-buoyant eggs, which are only slightly heavier than water (or than the water-silt suspension in which they frequently occur). In the big rivers of eastern Asia fishes with semi-buoyant eggs are common, for example in the Amur 20 species, or 27 % of the total fauna are of this type (Kryzhanovsky *et al.* 1951). The most important species are the large cyprinids of the Chinese complex—the grass carp, silver carp, bighead and black carp. Semi-buoyant eggs are also characteristic of certain whitefishes and ciscoes, goldeye, burbot, white perch and even maskinonge (Battle & Sprules 1960). Among anadromous species, they occur in the striped bass and the European and American shads (but not the alewife). Depending on whether or not a current is present, such eggs will be found either in a thick suspension near the bottom, or suspended throughout the water column.

(a) **Semi-buoyant eggs.** In sampling eggs that float free in the water column, nearly all the sampling methods of quantitative plankton research can be used. A common method used by marine biologists is a vertical haul with a plankton net from bottom to surface, which gives the number of eggs below a unit area of water surface. The net type about which most experience exists is the Hensen net (Fig. 7.2). Using a net of standard shape and with bolting silk

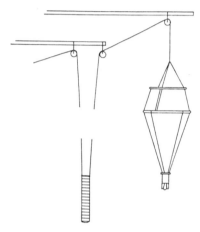

Figure 7.2. Vertical net for quantitative sampling of buoyant eggs as arranged by Buchanan-Wollaston. The counterweight (left) continues to raise the net whether the ship is rising or falling. (Adapted from Graham (1956) and Bückmann (1929).)

of 24 threads per centimetre, the net is hauled vertically at a speed less than 1 m in 3 s, which guarantees the best filtering effect. Figure 7.2 shows an arrangement with a counterweight by Buchanan–Wollaston, which improves the evenness of hauling the net when the ship is rolling (Bückmann 1929; Graham 1956).

Sette & Ahlstrom (1948) inserted a flowmeter in the mouth of the net to measure the column of water filtered, when hauling the net diagonally from a slowly moving ship.

In rivers of moderate to fast current semi-buoyant eggs can be caught in plankton nets suspended from a stake, boat or anchored float. Usually such nets rapidly clog up with debris, so that it is necessary to tend them almost continuously and it is difficult to maintain a constant filtering capacity.

In slow currents, semi-buoyant eggs tend to be commoner near the bottom, so that catches at different depths are required in quantitative sampling. Hass (1968) caught eggs of the twaite shad using a horizontally-arranged plankton net from an anchored boat. Thus he could expose the net at different depths for definite times and, in combination with a current meter, the volume of water filtered was measured (Fig. 7.3).

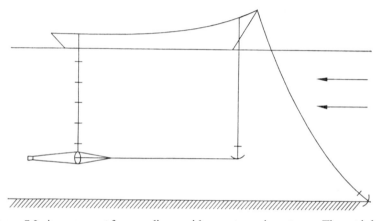

Figure 7.3. Arrangement for sampling semi-buoyant eggs in a stream. The net is kept in position against the current by means of two vertical lines with weights, from Hass (1968).

Another type of quantitative net for sampling eggs close to the bottom is mounted on a sled and hauled by boat (Bückmann 1929). For further sampling techniques used in planktology see Schlieper (1968), Schwoerbel (1966), UNESCO (1968), and the survey of sampling problems of fish eggs and larvae by Nellen & Schnack (1974).

(b) Non-buoyant eggs. Extensive investigations of egg survival have been made in trout and salmon redds by excavation (Hobbs 1937; Allen 1951; Stuart 1953). Newly-constructed redds are characterized by their hummocky appearance and the colour of the turned gravel, so it is possible to count the redds in an area and to estimate the number of eggs laid if the mean number of eggs in a redd is known (Allen 1951; Hobbs 1948). For example, trout eggs in Selwyn River are placed in pockets of 100–2000 eggs each, and 3–4

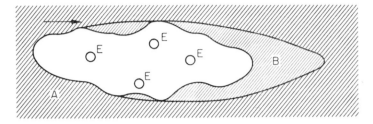

Figure 7.4. Brown trout redd from above, from Hobbs (1948).
A: undisturbed stream bed.
B: disturbed material.
E: egg pockets in the excavated area.

egg pockets were found in most redds (Figs 7.4 and 7.5). Because redds after construction become less recognizable it is advisable to mark them for later excavation. Briggs (1953) marked the redds of cohoes, chinooks and steelheads immediately after spawning by means of numbered stakes painted white. These were driven into the bank above the high-water mark and by measurement with a tape the exact location of each redd could be found. Briggs used the following sampling technique: (1) shovelling across the width of the redd to a depth of about 60 cm; (2) the gravel was carefully turned over, up and down the length of the redd; (3) when eggs or larvae were discovered a net with a solid entrance frame was mounted 1·5 m downstream from the site of excavation to collect them. Material from the redd was thrown up into the current, and the lighter eggs and larvae were carried downstream into the net (Fig. 7.6). Roth & Geiger (1961) fastened an acute-angled metal baffle upstream from the redd which permitted excavation in quiet water.

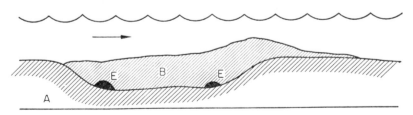

Figure 7.5. A section through a brown trout redd showing the depression in the stream bed, the disturbed material (B) and the egg pockets on the bottom of the redd (E), from Hobbs (1948).

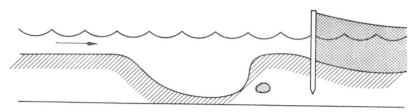

Figure 7.6. Method of sampling eggs and larvae of trout used by Briggs (1953) (explanation in the text).

Centrarchids, some tilapia, etc., construct nests on the surface of the substrate. Eggs can be removed using a pipette, or nests can be counted in a quantitative survey.

Rothschild (1961) developed an interesting technique for sampling non-buoyant adhesive eggs of smelt. 'Sampling units' were exposed at different stations as a spawning substrate. A sampling unit consisted of a glazed black ceramic tile 115 mm square, with two egg-depositional surfaces of heavy black canvas strips 50 mm wide and about 125 mm long. The 50-mm ends of each strip were joined by a rubber band, stapled to each end, which formed a collar-like arrangement that permitted each to be slipped easily on and off the tile. Smelts spawned during the night and sampling units were checked every morning. The eggs on one surface of a unit were enumerated and then the eggs were destroyed or the surface was replaced by a new one. The second surface of each unit remained in its position on the tile, so that eggs accumulated and developed in the natural environment until just before the hatching period. The temporary surfaces gave data on egg production and the permanent surfaces were used to determine egg survival.

Tibbo *et al.* (1963) investigated adhesive eggs of herring using free-diving techniques. The divers measured the size of the whole spawning bed, took quantitative egg samples and gathered many fundamental observations about spawning substrates, and accumulations and density of eggs deposited.

Elster (1933) studied survival of Blaufelchen eggs, which are non-buoyant and non-adhesive. The eggs were laid on lake sediments at depths between 100 and 200 m, and were sampled by dredging.

Examination of eggs

In investigations of production and survival of eggs it is necessary to enumerate the eggs sampled and to distinguish between living and dead ones.

In addition, information about spawning date, prediction of hatching date, damage to the embryos, etc., can be obtained by examining their stage of development.

Living eggs usually are translucent and have a perivitelline space, while dead eggs are white or opaque. Though these properties are more noticeable in unpreserved eggs, in most investigations it is necessary to preserve samples for later examination. Bückmann (1929) recommends a 2% solution of formaldehyde. The low concentration of formalin prevents shrinking, so that measurements of diameter give reliable data for egg identification.

For examination of the embryo in an egg the method of Bau (1922) gives good results. The eggs are put for 3–5 min into a mixture of 3–5 ml glacial acetic said and 100 ml of 0·7% NaCl solution. (The farther the embryos have developed, the less glacial acetic acid is needed.) Shells become transparent, embryos are white and the yolk remains coloured. For preservation, eggs must be transferred to 10% formaldehyde solution containing 2–5% acetic acid or the same percentage of hydrogen peroxide. This is suitable for both old and young stages.

Various forms of slides have been developed for separating non-adhesive eggs from plankton and for examining the eggs under the microscope. Graham's (1956) slide has a glass or Perspex base on to which is cemented a Perspex rectangle divided into strips by rods of drawn glass cemented in position with Perspex cement. The distance between the glass rods should be slightly greater than the diameter of the eggs, so the eggs align themselves and can be examined in sequence.

The surface of non-buoyant eggs may be covered with fine sediment, microorganisms, etc., which make the eggs so opaque that the embryos are not visible. This material can be scraped off with a blunt needle while the egg is held by forceps. Adhesive eggs usually form clumps several layers thick, and must be separated for further examination.

Identification of eggs in samples is relevant if spawning of different species overlap in time and spawning site. For example, in several lakes cyprinid species may spawn more or less simultaneously in the same area, and their eggs are of the non-buoyant type. The main usable features in identification are the diameter of the egg, the structure of its yolk, the presence and distribution of oil droplets, the size of the perivitelline space, and the shape and colour of the living egg.

Pictures and descriptions of freshwater fish eggs are widely scattered in the literature. Kryzhanovsky (1949) gives descriptions and excellent pictures of eggs, larvae and fry in cyprinid, silurid and cobitid fishes (56 species). Some examples of this work are quoted by Nikolsky (1963). Bracken & Kennedy (1967) give keys for identifying Irish freshwater fish eggs and larvae. However, many egg characteristics vary within a species. The extent of these variations depends on environmental conditions such as the food of the parents, or is a result of genetic differences between populations. Egg identification often requires the comparison of the sampled eggs with artificially reared eggs of the population used.

Egg development

Usually sampled eggs are not of the same age, so that they differ in their stage of development. The rate of development is directly related to the temperature and varies considerably between different species. Knowledge of the course of morphogenesis at different temperatures, and of the temperature at the spawning site, makes possible a rough determination of the age of sampled eggs. By knowing the rate of development at the prevailing temperature and the age of the eggs in a given sample it is possible to back-calculate the time of spawning and to predict the time of hatching. The applicability of this method is limited because it requires rather constant temperatures, salinity or oxygen pressure.

Rate of development and its relation to temperature can easily be obtained by fertilizing eggs artificially and rearing them at several constant temperatures.

Fertilization and incubation of eggs

Eggs and milt should be taken from running-ripe fish only (see Table 2.3). Because motility of sperm in water may last less than a minute the 'dry fertilization' or Russian method, introduced by Vrassky, is generally used in artificial fertilization techniques for non-adhesive eggs.

Using gentle pressure along the ovaries towards the genital aperture, the eggs are extruded. The expelled eggs and milt are contained in a receptacle. After careful mixing of eggs and sperm, water is added until the eggs are covered to a depth of 1 or 2 cm, then water and eggs are stirred again for a moment. When the eggs have settled for 10 or 15 min, water is decanted and renewed several times until it becomes clear and the eggs can be transferred into an incubation apparatus.

For adhesive eggs slides of glass or Perspex are a suitable substrate, when only small numbers of eggs are incubated for experimental purposes. The slides can be put on the bottom of a flat container covered with water before the eggs are expelled. Then the eggs and milt are brought into the water as close to the same time as possible and the eggs must be distributed evenly on the slides. Woynarówitch (1961) describes a fertilization method for adhesive carp eggs. The application of NaCl and carbamide $CO(NH_2)_2$ solutions extends the sperm swimming time, eliminates the stickiness of eggs and makes incubation in breeding glasses possible. Prokês (1975) eliminated the stickiness by rinsing the eggs of *Coregonus peled* with slightly acid water (pH 6·2–6·7).

Changes in temperature and mechanical disturbance should be avoided as much as possible during transportation of the fertilized eggs from the field to the laboratory. The principles of incubation methods are simple; any technique which supplies water of suitable temperature and oxygen content will be successful. Two main systems are in use: (1) rearing eggs in glass jars with turbulent water in which the eggs are constantly mixed and (2) rearing eggs on a substratum where water flows over them.

Incubators for non-adhesive eggs such as are used primarily in commercial hatcheries are shown in Fig. 7.7. In a glass of the Weiss-type (left) the water flows into the bottom through a short conical funnel within the narrow neck. A disc mounted on a metal shaft is freely movable and distributes the inflowing water, which flows out over the upper edge of the glass into a channel below (not visible). Kannegieter's glass (middle) consists of two parts, one inside the other. The inner part works in the same manner as the glass on the left, while the outer part is a stand which the water enters through hose pipes The function of the McDonald glass is apparent from Fig. 7.7 (right).

Trout and salmon eggs, which are damaged by movement before eye pigmentation occurs, are placed on sieves, wire screens, etc., preferably in a single layer. Water penetrates from below or flows horizontally along them. Modern trout farms use vertical drip or vertical flow incubation systems where the eggs are in trays of fibreglass or metal like drawers in a dresser. These arrangements save space and water and make inspection easy.

A remarkable method for commercial rearing of pike–perch (*Stizostedion lucioperca*) egg masses has been introduced by Woynarówitch (1955). The eggs are attached by the fish to bundles of roots, etc. These bundles are then removed from the water and hung in a chamber, where they are sprinkled by a water spray. Immediately before hatching the eggs are transferred into

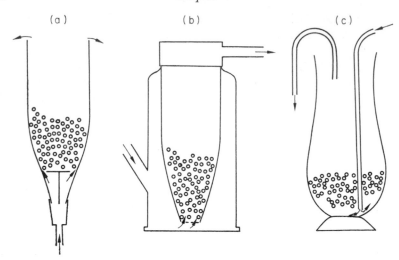

Figure 7.7. Glasses used for incubation of fish eggs: (a) Weiss type; (b) Kannegieter type; (c) McDonald type.

water, where the larvae hatch. The method ensures a good oxygen supply from air which penetrates to the centre of the egg mass.

Incubation experiments at a constant temperature require automatic cooling and heating systems which are available in a laboratory.

The present stage of incubation and rearing techniques of fish species from different parts of the world is compiled in standard books about aquaculture, e.g. Bardach *et al.* (1972), Hickling (1971), Huet (1970), Meske (1973) and Pillay (1973).

Stages of development
From fertilization to hatching, embryogenesis proceeds from a single egg cell to the highly organized larvae. The process occurs within 12 h in *Danio rerio*, while it takes more than 100 days in some salmonids. However the number of stages distinguished during development depends partly on the observer, and on the necessity for reporting small differences. A detailed description and illustration of teleostean fish development is presented by New (1966).

Apstein (1909), who introduced age determination of eggs into fishery research, distinguished 20–30 stages of embryonic development. Some essential stages of development are shown in Fig. 7.8. The initial division produces 2 cells (a), and the 8-cell stage (b) is soon reached by vertical cleavage. Subsequent cleavages increase cell numbers while cell sizes decrease, but at stage (c) the whole blastoderm mass is not yet enlarged. By flattening out over the yolk the blastoderm forms the embryonic disc, which migrates outward over more and more of the yolk. The margin then becomes thickened, forming the germinal ring (d). One portion of the germ ring thickens obviously when gastrulation begins, and the embryonic shield appears. Epiboly continues and the blastopore is reduced to a small opening, while the embryonic shield increases in length and width, and the embryonic axis is formed with optic vesicles (e). During further development the eye lens, optic vesicles, myomeres and brain appear (f, g). The tail grows and lifts off the yolk, eyes become pigmented, and the embryo reaches the hatching stage (h).

Temperature and development

Within certain limits, development from fertilization to hatching is prolonged by low temperatures and accelerated by high temperatures. Moreover incubation temperature determines certain morphological features, the hatching rate, and early behaviour of the larvae when hatched. Temperature seems to be the most important external factor, because it has a direct influence on the timing of ontogenetic events.

The product of time in days needed to reach a certain stage of development and the prevailing temperature in degrees Celsius—called degree-days—was assumed to be constant by Apstein (1909). The theoretical basis of this assumption would be a linear relation between temperature and incubation time. But incubation experiments at several constant temperatures have revealed curvilinearity over the whole range of suitable temperatures. This means that the product of temperature and time is not constant; rather, it decreases with decreasing temperature, and vice versa. Approximate linearity exists only in a narrow temperature range. This reduces the applicability of degree-days, which can give only rather rough information if applied to a wider range of temperature. On the assumption that degree-days obtained by experiment are constant for several small temperature steps, time of incubation can be calculated for the intermediate temperatures with sufficient reliability. The theoretical background of temperature and the rate of development, which follows an exponential function, has been surveyed by Blaxter (1969). The relation between egg development and temperature from

Figure 7.8. Stages of development of fish eggs. For each stage is shown the chorion (outer circle), the perivitelline space, and the embryo on the yolk.
a. 2-cell stage
b. 8-cell stage
c. embryonic disc
d. early gastrula, with embryonic shield formed
e. embryonic shield enlarged, blastopore still open
f. blastopore closed; the embryo half surrounds the yolk; myomeres appear in the middle of the trunk
g. tip of tail free of the yolk sac; eyes well developed; myomeres numerous
h. larva before hatching.

fertilization to hatching is given in Fig. 7.9 for pike, trout and whitefish eggs.

An example of an optimum temperature range is given by Price (1940), who has shown that the lake whitefish has a total incubation range between 0·5°C and 12°C, with an optimum near 0·5°C, where the larvae hatched are most viable. Hokanson & Kleiner (1974) found optimum survival and development rates of embryonic and larval yellow perch with a rising temperature regime.

Age determinations of sampled eggs are reliable only when the temperature of the spawning site is rather constant, and when there are experimental data about egg development at this temperature. Some well-marked developmental stages, such as the appearance of the embryonic shield, size of blastopores, number of myomeres, length of the trunk, pigment performance, etc., should be selected as parameters of development.

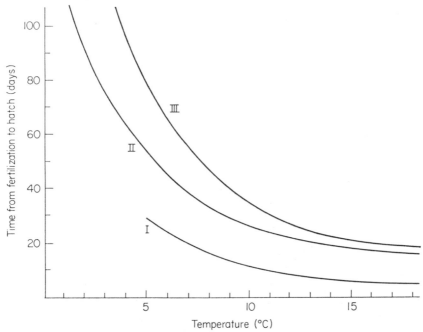

Figure 7.9. Duration of development (D) from fertilization to hatching, at different temperatures (t).

   I. *Esox lucius*, $D = 4 + 1·29^{19-t}$ (Lindroth 1946)
  II. *Coregonus wartmanni*, $D = 15 + 1·26^{20·7-\cdot}$ (Braum 1964)
 III. *Salmo gairdneri*, $D = 15 + 1·26^{23-t}$ (Lindroth 1946)

TABLE 7.1. Duration of egg development from fertilization to hatch in some freshwater fishes

Species	Days	Temp. °C	Author
Goldfish	3·2	25	Battle (1940)*
Lake whitefish	141	0·5	Price (1940)
Lake whitefish	29·6	10·0	Price (1940)
Blaufelchen	100	2·1	Braum (1964)
Carp	10	15·0	Schäperclaus (1961)
Pike	9	12·2	Lillelund (1967)
Pike-perch	11	10·0	Schäperclaus (1961)
Smelt	20	8·5	Lillelund (1961)
Striped bass	2·0	19·5	Bigelow & Schroeder (1953)*
Brown trout	97	4·5	Embody (1934)
Rainbow trout	75	4·5	Embody (1934)
Brook trout (N. America)	90	4·5	Embody (1934)

*Reference from Breder & Rosen (1966).

In shallow water, overflow areas, etc., where many fish have their spawning sites, temperature variations of 10° and more are common, for example, through diurnal fluctuations. Age determination of eggs from such an environment is impossible. Average temperature data cannot be used because an increase of 5°C, for example, accelerates development more than a decrease of 5°C retards it.

The larval stage

The larval phase begins with hatching and is a fundamental stage of early life history. The innate behaviour of newly-hatched larvae differs widely among species. Pike larvae, for example, remain rather inactive during the yolk sac period. They are stuck by the head to plants or other substrate by means of special glands. Trout larvae after hatching show a positive geotaxis and a negative phototaxis. This stimulates them to descend in the gravel, where they are rather inactive, moving only from time to time. At the end of the yolk sac period their reactions are reversed; the larvae ascend and emerge from the gravel (Roth & Geiger 1963). *Coregonus* larvae spend the yolk sac period swimming (Braum 1964).

Morphological characteristics may vary over a certain range at time of hatching, because hatching is not correlated with a definite morphological stage. For example, body length, yolk sac size, and the differentiation of head and trunk are variable features among newly-hatched larvae. However, temperature during incubation influences the larva's morphological stage at hatching. The egg shell ruptures after it is weakened by larval enzymes and the larva's motion inside it. The hatching behaviour of fish larvae was described by Poy (1970).

Sampling larvae*

Surveys of fish larvae and fry in inland waters are needed for assessment of a number of ecological aspects, such as larval survival, stock recruitment, species distribution, food requirements, pollution effects, etc.

Many freshwater fish larvae live in shallow water, among plants as, e.g. young cyprinidae. Larvae and fry of other groups live more in the pelagic region as, e.g. yellow perch and whitefish. Knowledge about the ecological requirements of larvae, their behaviour, orientation and swimming speed gives helpful information for the application of the suitable sampling technique.

Existing data about physiology and behaviour of fish larvae are summarized by Blaxter (1969). Early larvae in many cases can be captured by the same devices as described above for eggs, including sampling of nests or redds, and coarse plankton nets or fixed nets in streams for free-floating types. Faber (1963) used a conical plankton net 1·5 m long and 76 cm in diameter, towed from a boom that projected in front of the boat.

A quantitative push-net system for transect studies of larval fish and macrozooplankton was developed by Miller (1973). Two standard bongo nets are pushed by a catamaran powered by two motors. The sampling device is suitable for surface catches in shallow waters. The samples are easy to remove through the well in the floor (Fig. 7.10). Continuous sampling and its operability by two investigators are principal advantages of the push-net system. Larvae from 2 to 25 mm length were still in good condition at boat speeds of 3 mph, when samples were removed after 3 min.

The efficiency of the Miller high-speed sampler (Miller 1961) which was constructed for catches of marine eggs and larvae (Fig. 7.11) was measured by Noble (1970) in Oneida Lake, NY (Fig. 7.12). He found an avoidance by yellow perch fry (*Perca flavescens*) of 8 mm length and larger, which was in part a response to optical stimulus. The study reveals the need to evaluate the sampling techniques for quantitative studies of pelagic fry and discusses technical improvements. Similar surveys of larval walleyes (*Stizostedion*

*This section is based principally on material supplied by Dr R. G. Werner.

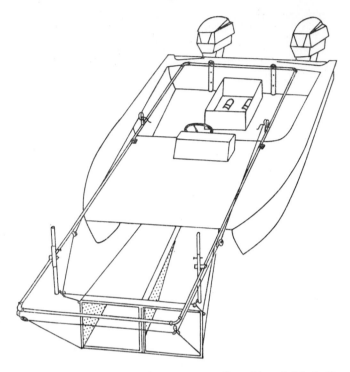

Figure 7.10. The push-net system for transect studies of larval fish (Miller 1973).

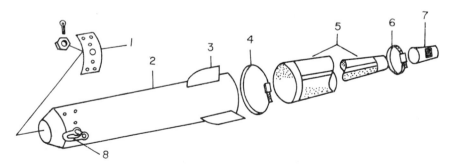

Figure 7.11. Details of the Miller high-speed sampler (Miller 1961).
(1) Reinforcing plate, (2) sampler body, (3) fin, (4) hose clamp, (5) net, (6) hose clamp, (7) collecting bucket, (8) towing shackle.

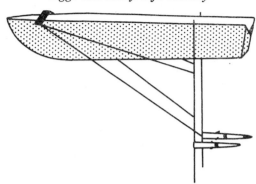

Figure 7.12. The attachment of two Miller high-speed samplers to aluminium pipes as used by Nobel (1970).

vitreum) were carried out by Forney (1975) by means of towed Miller high-speed samplers. No avoidance by larvae of 7–14 mm length was found at towing speeds of 3·6 m/s. Repeated sampling and experiments with introduction of known numbers of larvae revealed the reliability of the sampling technique.

Bagenal (1974) showed that net avoidance by young roach *Rutilus rutilus* (L.) could be reduced with a net which came up from below. He devised a release mechanism which allowed a 1-m buoyant net to ascend some time after he had gone away, and the catch could be retrieved later.

Most tow-net techniques are used for sampling pelagic larvae in large lakes; many of them are not applicable in smaller rivers. Brown & Langford (1975) constructed a tow-net consisting of a metal framework which could be towed below the water surface buoyed by floats as well as over the river bed in shallow water by means of skids underneath the net (Fig. 7.13). The sampling device was used for a survey of coarse fish fry from the 0+ age group. At 4 km/h the net caught fry from 11 to 46 mm in length. It apparently caught the whole size range of the 0+ year-class.

Breder (1960) designed a very effective trap for capturing young fishes. With minor modifications, his trap can be used to sample larvae in the open water of a lake. The trap may be of any size, but the one described below has been found to work well in many inland lakes.

It is constructed from pre-cut pieces of clear plastic (Plexiglass) 6·3 mm thick, joined by either a plastic solvent or Duco cement. The plastic should be cut so that for each trap there are the following pieces:

2 — 305 × 152 mm   2 — 305 × 165 mm
2 — 456 × 152 mm   1 — 152 × 152 mm
2 — isosceles triangles (127 mm base, 127 mm altitude) 1 m
    of 6·3 mm stripping.

These parts are assembled as shown in Fig. 7.14. The wings are removable, being attached to the box by rubber bands that encircle them and hooking on to lugs cemented to the outside of the trap. The trap can be set on the bottom or suspended at any depth from a float. It is raised out of the water with the wings upward so that the catch will not be lost.

The size of fish caught depends to some extent on the width of the entrance aperture. Too wide an aperture invites the attention of larger fish that will eat the fry. When used on the bottom among weeds, the wings can be extended.

For larger larvae and young fry or fingerlings more active measures must usually be used. An otter trawl designed by Barraclough & Johnson (1956) has been used in large freshwater lakes. Numerous sampling systems were developed to investigate the early life history of salmonid fishes. To capture fry as they emerged from their redds, Heard (1964) constructed a rectangular screen box, without top or bottom, long enough to extend above the water-

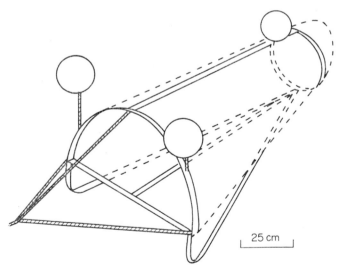

25 cm

Figure 7.13. The tow-net described by Brown & Langford (1975) can be towed below the water surface in deep water buoyed by floats, or in shallow water on skids.

Figure 7.14. Plastic trap for catching larval and fingerling fish. (Courtesy Dr R.G. Werner.)

line and to penetrate a short distance into the stream bed. The wall of the box on the downstream side is tapered and leads to a detachable nylon bag. The same principle has been used on centrachid nests by surrounding them with a cylinder of fine wire gauze. When the fry rise they are dipped out. Johnson (1956) towed a circular net from two boats at dusk to catch young sockeye as they came into the surface waters (see also Chapter 2). Fixed weirs or fences have been used for many years to capture the entire run of downstream-migrating fry and fingerlings (Foerster 1930).

Shetter (1938) constructed a two-way trap with entrances both from upstream and from downstream. Wolf (1951) added a trapping device that operates on the basis of an inclined plane.

Larval development

Two obvious features of newly-hatched fish larvae are the yolk sac, which keeps them independent of an external food source during the first days of life, and a primordial fin fold in the sagittal plane. Duration of the yolk sac period differs widely among species and is related to temperature. Morphological development continues during the yolk sac period and the larva becomes fit to shift from internal to external food sources.

After yolk resorption most authors use the term 'postlarva', while 'larva' is used for the time from hatching to the beginning of first feeding.* Yolk resorption is generally considered to be finished when external feeding starts, though this is not exact because a small yolk reserve is usually still present and there is a short period of mixed feeding. However, the transition to the postlarval phase is often associated with a rather sudden change in behaviour patterns.

Growth during the larval period can be expressed in terms of body length, as wet or dry weight, or in terms of energy. The efficiency of yolk conversion into body tissue is an important factor affecting survival rate. It is related to egg size and temperature throughout the egg and larval stages, and after hatching yolk utilization is influenced additionally by factors that affect larval activity, such as light and temperature.

Most of the existing data, summarized by Blaxter (1969), were obtained by determining the dry weight of yolk and of body tissue from time of

---

*The term alevin is synonymous with larva as defined above. American authors usually use the word fry in the same sense (or extend it somewhat past yolk absorption) and use fingerling for later stages (postlarval and juvenile) up to a year old. In Britain fry usually signifies the postlarval and juvenile stages.

fertilization up to the time of maximum body weight of the postlarva. Efficiency values between 40 and 70% were calculated from measurements made by different methods (dry weight, wet weight, calorific values). Figure 7.15 illustrates the increase of embryonic tissue and the decrease of yolk in Atlantic salmon development at 10°C (Marr 1966). After hatching at 146 days, growth rate increases considerably and the larva reaches maximum weight about 180 days after fertilization. Because more and more energy is required for maintenance, activity, etc., the weight of the whole embryo begins to fall off before all the yolk is resorbed unless external feeding begins.

As mentioned above, the stage of first feeding is marked by considerable change in behaviour. Most fish larvae recognize their first prey visually and they try to engulf it, using darting movements. Feeding behaviour usually appears rather suddenly, as in Blaufelchen and pike larvae for example (Braum 1964). During early feeding only 3% of feeding movements are successful in Blaufelchen, but 30% in pike. Feeding success is influenced by temperature. Copepods were the most important food for Blaufelchen, while *Daphnia* was the essential diet for pike.

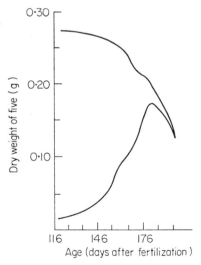

Figure 7.15. The proportion of yolk and embryo in Atlantic salmon larvae, based on the mean weight of 5 specimens taken at 2-day intervals. Hatching was at 146 days after fertilization (adapted from Marr 1966).
Upper curve: weight of embryo with yolk.
Lower curve: weight of embryo without yolk.

Blaxter & Hempel (1963), on the basis of experiments with herring larvae, introduced the concept of the 'point of no return', which is the stage after yolk resorption at which unfed larvae become too weak to start feeding. Their experiments made it possible to predict the time, from fertilization, at which larvae must encounter adequate food in order to have a chance of surviving.

During further development the postlarva changes from the larval to the juvenile form, which is much the same as the adult. The shape of the head and trunk gradually change, fin rays and scales are laid down, and guanin appears in pigmentation. However these changes during metamorphosis are of different degrees of importance among different species.

Examination of larvae

For preservation of larvae, a 4% formaldehyde solution is usually used. Length measurements, stomach investigations, etc., may become difficult after preservation if the larvae are bent. By using a 1% urethane solution before preservation bending can be reduced. A similar concentration of ethyl urethane is a suitable anaesthetic for inspecting living larvae, or for making repeated measurements on the same larva in rearing experiments. For the latter purpose it is essential that the temperature of the anaesthetic solution be the same as that of the water in which larvae have been living. As soon as body movements stop, larvae should be transferred into water with excellent aeration. M.S. 222 Sandoz (tricainmethansulfonate) is also suitable, while 2-phenoxyethanol is said to have a wider range of usable concentrations. Bell (1967) gives a review of the properties of fish anaesthetics.

The relation between behaviour of feeding larvae and the density of suitable food items in nature is an important aspect of survival investigation. Studies of food in the alimentary tract can give information about quality and quantity of foods consumed. Information on food selection can be obtained by comparing the natural food supply with the stomach contents. Food analyses of early postlarval stages are usually easiest by the numerical method (Chapter 9). Generally the food items are readily identifiable and not too numerous. The food canal of many postlarvae is a straight tube which is easy to remove, and items such as plankton organisms often occur in a single row along the tube. Because of the transparency of many postlarvae, food items are sometimes visible through the skin and gut wall, and this makes it easy to distinguish larvae with and without food. Theoretical models and experimental results concerning fish feeding are given by Ivlev (1955, 1961).

Some of the features used in the identification of larvae are the ratio of length to height, shape of the yolk sac, distribution of chromatophores, number of myotomes, etc. Descriptions and illustrations of freshwater fish larvae and young are widely scattered in the literature. Kryzhanovsky (1949) has published a series of illustrations of eggs, larvae and fry of cyprinid, silurid and cobitid fishes. The most reliable method of identification is to rear larvae of the species being studied, and compare reared and wild larvae.

Survival of eggs and larvae

Mortality among deposited eggs differs widely within a spawning area. For example, Rothschild (1961) found a mean relative egg survival of 24 %, yet estimated a total egg mortality during incubation of 99·5 % in smelt eggs under natural conditions. He believed that one reason for large mortality was the high density of the eggs.

For brown trout eggs in New Zealand streams, Allen (1951) pointed out that egg losses in different redds varied between 0 and 82%, but mean loss was only 11 % and in 84 % of the redds examined losses were less than 20 %. Mortality of developing trout eggs is mainly caused by dislodgment by later spawners or by floods. Since trout larvae remain in the gravel after hatching, their mortality is roughly 1 % (Hobbs 1948). In brown trout, mortality of alevins from small eggs is higher than for large eggs (Bagenal 1969). Salmon fry survival has been determined by releasing free-swimming fry and counting the yearling stock they produce. Ricker & Foerster (1948) found the survival rate of hatchery-reared sockeye fry to be between 3·87 and 13·13 % in different years and with different degrees of predation by other fishes.

In rearing experiments there has sometimes been a catastrophic mortality when larvae change to the postlarval stage. The phenomenon is called the 'critical period' for the larvae, and has been associated with a lack of suitable food when external feeding begins. Marr (1956) reviewed studies on pelagic marine fish larvae, but could find little evidence for a period of catastrophic mortality under natural conditions. Instead survival rate is either fairly steady or gradually increases.

Investigating the survival and production of brown trout eggs and larvae, Le Cren (1965) planted trout eggs into screened sections of small streams in England and observed that mortality was highest during the first 3 months after hatching. Because of the trout fry's territorial behaviour, production and mortality rates are density dependent, and above a fairly low rate of stocking, biomass remains constant. Final densities were 7–10 fish per square metre at the end of the summer. The current status of reasearch about mortality and survival of eggs and larvae was reviewed at a symposium edited by Blaxter (1974).

8

Production

D W CHAPMAN

Introduction

Earlier chapters have outlined methods of assessing the seasonal and annual course of fish growth and population size. One of the more important uses of these data is as statistical components of fish production computations.

The general concepts involved in organic metabolism and growth that were recommended for use in the International Biological Programme have been defined in Chapter 1. Here we will be concerned especially with the following:

B_1, B_2 = biomass or biocontent (energy content) at times t_1 and t_2
$\qquad (t_2 - t_1 = \Delta t)$
$\bar{B}$ = mean biomass or biocontent during Δt
P = production during Δt (in terms of mass or energy)
N = number of individuals
$\bar{w}$ = average weight of an individual ($N\bar{w} = B$)
G = instantaneous rate of increase in weight
Z = instantaneous rate of mortality.

Production is defined as the total elaboration of fish tissue during any time interval Δt, including what is formed by individuals that do not survive to the end of Δt (Ivlev 1945, 1966). It may be measured in terms of wet weight, dry weight, nitrogen content or energy content. Of these units, energy is the most flexible, universal and realistic, particularly when the dynamics of an entire ecosystem are under study. On the other hand, nearly all production studies are based on measurements of weight (usually wet weight) in the first instance, and energy contents are computed secondarily if at all. If conversions to energy are to add anything, they must be based on frequent determinations of energy content per unit weight, so that variations due to season (fat content), age, sex, etc., are taken into account. Otherwise nothing is gained.

Components of production that are frequently ignored or overlooked are the sexual products—eggs and sperm—that are discharged from the fish's body. These are discussed separately below.

Ricker (1946) and Allen (1950) formulated production during Δt as:

$$P = G\Delta t\bar{B}. \tag{1}$$

This formula is realistic for any interval Δt during which G is constant. It is based on the exponential model of growth (and of survival if $\bar{B}$ is calculated using exponential rates), but this does not mean growth and mortality must necessarily be exponential functions. In general the exponential rates are good approximations to the real situation over any time interval within which growth and mortality coefficients are small, or vary proportionally.

Production may be estimated either numerically or graphically. Both methods require data on growth and survivorship of fish over the time span of interest.

Graphic method of estimating production

In Allen's graphic method the number of individuals (N) in the population at successive instants of time is plotted against the mean weight ($\bar{w}$) of an individual at the same instants. The rationale of graphic estimation of production is illustrated in Fig. 8.1. The production in a small unit of time (Δt) would be approximately equal to $N_t\Delta\bar{w}$, where $\bar{w}$ is the growth in mean weight of the population in the time interval, i.e. production is the shaded rectangle in Fig. 8.1. If $\Delta\bar{w}$ is made very small, approaching zero, $N_t\Delta\bar{w}$ in the very

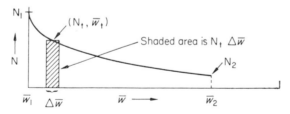

Figure 8.1. Theory of graphical estimation of production (see text).

small unit of time would approach P in that time. Summing $N_t\Delta\bar{w}$ for all increments $\Delta\bar{w}$, which is equivalent to measuring the total area between the curve and the horizontal axis, gives production from t_1 to t_2. A hypothetical example from an experimental pond may help illustrate the use of this curve (Fig. 8.2).

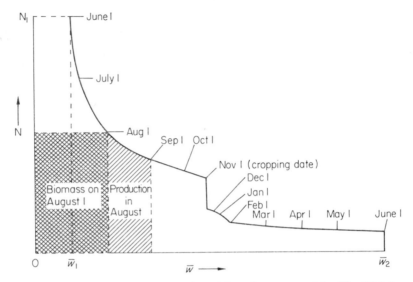

Figure 8.2. Seasonal changes in numbers (N) and average weight ($\bar{w}$) of fish in a pond, illustrating the graphical method of computing production.

Dates on the curve are times when estimates of population numbers and mean size were made. Production in August is equal to the lined area beneath the curve. Biomass on August 1 is also shown on the graph, by cross-hatching. (Note that the abscissal scale must begin at 0 for $N\bar{w}$ to equal biomass, although area determinations of P must begin at $\bar{w}_1$.) Annual production is the entire area beneath the curve from June 1 to June 1 a year later. Areas can be measured on the graph by using a planimeter. If the curve is plotted on graph paper, areas can be measured by counting squares. In the example, 40% of the stock was harvested on November 1.

In using the Allen curve no fixed mathematical model of growth or mortality is required. Data obtained in sampling are plotted to form the curve. However, during the time intervals between estimates of the number and mean size of the fish in the cohort, some decision is necessary as to how to interpolate between the estimates. Where sampling is done sufficiently often, the series of point estimates (and their confidence limits, if available) will give sufficient guidance in placing the curve, as illustrated in Fig. 8.3. This method is more logical than merely connecting the points by straight lines. It may be

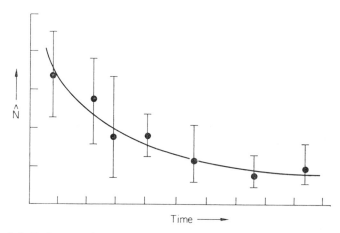

Figure 8.3. Estimates of population (dots), and their confidence limits (vertical lines), with a smoothed curve of change in population size.

most convenient to first prepare separate curves for survivorship and growth, then to take values from each curve at given times for plotting an Allen curve.

When point estimates are separated by long time intervals the possible positions of the curve between them are quite varied. In the example of Fig. 8.4 points A and B are weight-survivorship points on an Allen curve, with no information available between or outside the points. Extreme possible paths for the Allen curve would be:

(i)   APB (no deaths until size $\bar{w}_B$ is reached, so that production is area APDC)

(ii) AQB (all deaths suddenly at size $\bar{w}_A$, in which case production is area QBDC).

Between these extremes there are various alternatives. If we connect A to B by a straight line, production is ARBDC. If we assume decrease in N is exponential but increase in $\bar{w}$ is linear (hence G decreases with time) then production is ASBDC. If both N and $\bar{w}$ are assumed to change exponentially (G and Z constant, or G/Z constant), then production would be ATBDC.

Here we must rely on experience, or on assumed models for survivorship

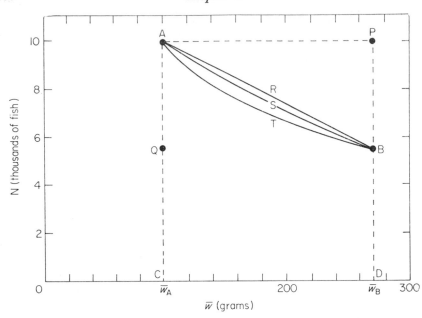

Figure 8.4. Methods of interpolating on an Allen curve (see the text). (In this example the overall instantaneous rate of mortality from A to B is $Z = 0.6$, and the overall rate of growth is $G = 1.0$.)

and growth, or else make a more or less arbitrary choice. There is some information suggesting that exponential decrease in N is realistic as long as there are no sudden spurts of emigration, immigration or fishing activity. For very young fish in the first year of life, exponential increase in $\bar{w}$ can be close to the truth (G constant). Among older fish G decreases with time; in fact increase in weight is often approximately linear from year to year. In the example of Fig. 8.4, using the foregoing assumptions, ASB on the Allen curve might be typical for older fish, while ATB would apply to young fish. APB would characterize experimental stocks where mortality is non-existent during the period of interest (and cropping occurs at the end).

Numerical estimation of production

Numerical estimates of production are made by computation between the times at which estimates of population abundance and average fish size are available (these latter estimates may first be smoothed, if necessary, as indicated in Fig. 8.3). The exact form of the computation depends on what models are used for decrease in numbers and increase in weight. All such models are approximations to the true state of affairs. They should be chosen with an eye to both verisimilitude and convenience.

Exponential models of growth and mortality
When growth is considered to be exponential, its instantaneous coefficient G is estimated by:

$$G = \frac{\log_e \bar{w}_2 - \log_e \bar{w}_1}{\Delta t}. \tag{2}$$

where $\bar{w}_1, \bar{w}_2$ = mean weights of the fish at times t_1 and t_2 respectively. Similarly, if population decrease is exponential, the instantaneous coefficient of mortality Z is:

$$Z = \frac{-(\log_e N_2 - \log_e N_1)}{\Delta t}. \tag{3}$$

where N_1, N_2 = numbers of fish present at times t_1 and t_2.
The difference $G - Z$ is the net rate of increase in biomass during Δt, from B_1 to B_2 (negative values indicate a decrease). Assuming that the stock is increasing or decreasing exponentially, its average biomass $\bar{B}$ is:

$$\bar{B} = \frac{B_1[\exp(G - Z)\Delta t - 1]}{(G - Z)\Delta t} \qquad (G > Z) \tag{4}$$

$$\bar{B} = \frac{B_1\{1 - \exp[-(Z - G)\Delta t]\}}{(Z - G)\Delta t} \qquad (G < Z). \tag{5}$$

Values of these expressions are tabulated by Ricker (1958, Appendix II). Production is of course computed from (1) as $P = G\bar{B}$.

Generally speaking, neither growth nor mortality is likely to be exponential for any long period of time, but these expressions can be used as approximations, being the better, the shorter the interval Δt. However, growth during the first year of a fish's life, or at least the earlier part of it, tends to be exponential.

Exponential model of growth; linear change in biomass

The exponential curves are concave upwards, whether $G - Z$ is positive or negative. For short time intervals between B_1 and B_2 they are not greatly different from a straight line, so the latter can be used as an approximation. In any event the true shape of a graph of the biomass of a year-class plotted against time is likely to be convex rather than concave during the period of increasing biomass; hence a straight line may be at least as generally useful a representation of increase or decrease in biomass as is the exponential curve. When change in biomass is linear, mean biomass is given by:

$$\bar{B} = \frac{B_1 + B_2}{2}. \qquad (6)$$

This $\bar{B}$ can be multiplied by the G from (2) to get an estimate of production. (This implies of course that change in N cannot be exactly exponential.)

The arithmetic mean from (6) is used in the estimates of confidence limits given in a later section.

Exponential model of mortality; von Bertalanffy model of growth

For older year-classes the exponential model of *mortality* is frequently appropriate, or at any rate is used in the absence of exact information; often a constant value of Z is assumed over a whole year or even several years. The *growth* of older year-classes, however, cannot be realistically described as exponential with constant G over long periods, but frequently the von Bertalanffy growth model will be applicable over a period of years (Chapter 5). For the combination of exponential mortality and von Bertalanffy growth, Allen (1971) shows:

$$P = 3KN_0W_\infty\left(\frac{1}{Z + K} - \frac{2}{Z + 2K} + \frac{1}{Z + 3K}\right). \qquad (7)$$

The symbols used above are defined in Appendix I. Notice that this expression presupposes that growth of the fish is isometric (Chapter 5) or close enough to it to be a useful approximation.

Other models

Allen (1971) explored consequences of using different models for production components. The models described above will suffice for most studies of fish production. Where other models appear necessary, Allen's paper indicates ramifications.

Computational procedures

Table 8.1 contains hypothetical data for a single age group over 12 months. We can compute production or estimate it graphically with these data. In the table $\bar{B}$ is computed by averaging adjacent monthly biomass estimates arithmetically.

TABLE 8.1. Computation of production

Species Date	Mean weight $\bar{w}$	Days Inst. growth G	Temp. °C Stock numbers N	Stock biomass B	Author Mean biomass $\bar{B}$	Production P
	g			kg	kg	kg
May 1	1·5		8000	12		
		0·29			10·5	3·0
June 1	2·0		4500	9		
		0·22			8·8	1·9
July 1	2·5		3500	8·7		
		0·34			9·6	3·3
Aug 1	3·5		3000	10·5		
		0·26			10·8	2·8
Sept 1	4·5		2500	11·2		
		0·37			11·6	4·3
Oct 1	6·5		2000	13·0		
		0·06			13·0	0·7
Nov 1	6·9		1900	13·1		
		0			12·4	0
Dec 1	6·9		1700	11·7		
		—0·01			10·9	—0·1
Jan 1	6·8		1500	10·2		
		—0·03			9·7	—0·3
Feb 1	6·6		1400	9·2		
		0			8·9	0
Mar 1	6·6		1300	8·6		
		0·04			8·0	0·3
Apr 1	6·9		1100	7·5		
		0·07			7·2	0·5
May 1	7·4		1000	7·0		

Annual production = ΣP = 16·4 kg

H

Using Allen's graphic method of estimating production, we can use $\bar{w}$ and
N for plotting the weight–survivorship curve (Fig. 8.5). Using a planimeter, or

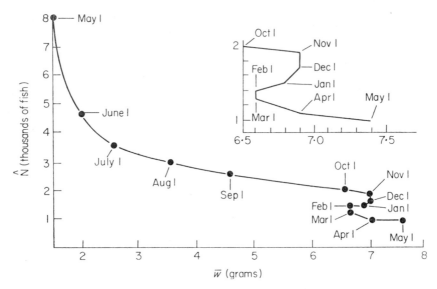

Figure 8.5. Graphical estimation of production for the population of Table 8.1.

by counting squares on graph paper, we can measure the area beneath the
curve and arrive at virtually the same estimate of P as obtained in Table 8.1.
The enlarged segment of the Allen curve includes a period of negative production. Production in October is the area between the curve and weight
axis, or about 0·8 kg. Because no growth occurred in November, there is no
area to add for production in the month. In December and January, weight
loss occurred, and the area (production) beneath the curve in these months
should be subtracted. No production took place in February. Subsequently
tissue was elaborated by the population and the area beneath the curve for
March and April should be added.

Negative production (weight loss by population members) in December
and January and the new production of tissue that replaces lost weight are
summed together in Table 8.1. This situation is discussed by Chapman (1967)
from the separate viewpoints of population ecology and of community
ecology. In the calculations above the population viewpoint is assumed. If

we were interested in community metabolism we should omit negative production from P since we probably would want to compute assimilation and production efficiencies for adjacent trophic groups. In this case total annual production would be 16·8 kg.

The tabular method of computation shown in the hypothetical example of Table 8.1 was used partly to illustrate the handling of negative production. Ricker & Foerster (1948) show actual data for young sockeye in Cultus Lake.

Where immigration or emigration affect N, there is no need to correct production data for the income or outgo, provided population size and growth (by age-group or size-class) are estimated frequently enough to assess accurately the abundance and growth of the animals actually in the area of interest during each time period of interest.

In some instances it may be impossible to obtain direct estimates of N and G for newly-recruited fish. Gerking (1962) had this difficulty in his study of a bluegill stock. He obtained an estimate of the production of very young fish by assuming that if a fishable stock is in a steady state recruitment must replace deaths from natural and fishing mortality. Biomass of the fish newly recruited during a year must in that case be equal to the total biomass of annual mortality of the recruited stock.

Because small fish are usually in the fastest-growing period of their lives (Gerking 1962; Allen 1951; Hunt 1966) the production of the youngest age-group may sometimes be greater than that of all other age-groups combined. Gerking (1962) estimated (by assessing biomass of mortality) that for a blue-gill stock in a steady state the production of the youngest age-groups (0 and 1) was 58% of the total production of all age-groups. Mathews (1971) reported that 0+ age fish made up most of the fish production in an environment in the River Thames. Allen (1951) estimated that 95% of brown trout production by a year-class in Horokiwi Stream was contributed in the first two years of life. Hunt (1966) showed that 80–95% of brook trout production by a year-class was made up by production of fish in the first two years of life.

It may be desirable to use a computer for the routine calculations of production once the component statistics are obtained. Hunt (1966) used a Fortran program in which input statistics are the numbers of fish of each age present and their mean individual weights at the beginning of each month. Output sheets contain monthly tabulations of G, P, $\bar{B}$, B at the start of the month, and the instantaneous rate of biomass increase or decrease. The program can be obtained by writing Mr Robert L. Hunt, Lawrence Creek Research Station, Route 2, Lawrence Creek, Wisconsin, USA.

Estimates of error
Where it is feasible, one should estimate confidence limits for production estimates. Chapman (1967) outlines a method of estimating approximate variance of P. It is necessary to obtain estimates of variance of G and $\bar{B}$, the component statistics used to estimate P.

Assuming samples of population size and growth have been obtained at fairly short intervals, and that:

$$\bar{B} = \frac{B_1 + B_2}{2}$$

we must first estimate variance of B_1 and B_2:

$$\hat{V}(\hat{B}) = \hat{V}(\hat{\omega}\hat{N}) = \hat{\omega}^2\hat{V}(\hat{N}) + \hat{N}^2\hat{V}(\hat{\omega}) + 2\hat{\omega}\hat{N}\operatorname{cov}(\hat{\omega},\hat{N}). \qquad (8)$$

The covariance term can be omitted, so that:

$$\hat{V}(\hat{B}) = \hat{\omega}^2\hat{V}(\hat{N}) + \hat{N}^2\hat{V}(\hat{\omega}). \qquad (9)$$

Variance of $\bar{w}$ is estimated (Cochran 1963) by:

$$\hat{V}(\bar{w}) = \frac{\Sigma w^2 - \dfrac{(\Sigma w)^2}{n}}{n(n-1)} \qquad (10)$$

and $\hat{V}(\hat{N})$ is calculated by the formula appropriate (see Chapter 6). The variance of $\bar{B}$ is estimated by:

$$\hat{V}(\hat{B}) = \tfrac{1}{4}[\hat{V}(\hat{B}_1) + \hat{V}(\hat{B}_2) + 2\operatorname{cov}(\hat{B}_1\hat{B}_2)] \qquad (11)$$

and the covariance term is zero since the samples used to estimate B_1 and B_2 are independent.

The variance of G could be estimated from several, say k, subsamples:

$$\hat{V}(\hat{G}) = \frac{\Sigma G_i^2 - \dfrac{(\Sigma G_i)^2}{k}}{k(k-1)}. \qquad (12)$$

The estimated variance of P is:

$$\hat{V}(\hat{P}) = \hat{V}(\hat{G}\hat{B}) = \hat{G}^2\hat{V}(\hat{B}) + \hat{B}^2\hat{V}(\hat{G}) + 2\hat{G}(\hat{B})\operatorname{cov}(\hat{G},\hat{B}) \qquad (13)$$

where:

$$\text{cov}(\hat{G}, \hat{\bar{B}}) = r\sqrt{[\hat{V}(\hat{G})\hat{V}(\hat{\bar{B}})]} \tag{14}$$

where r = coefficient of correlation between G and $\bar{B}$.

If, as one would expect, G and $\bar{B}$ are negatively correlated, $V(P)$ will be overestimated by setting $r = 0$.

The foregoing process assumes:

(1) The assumptions appropriate for sampling random variables (G and $\bar{w}$) and for estimating N are all satisfied.

(2) Data for estimating $\bar{w}$, G, and B are obtained at the same time. Sizes of fish are usually obtained when fish are marked for release into the cohort, so that this assumption may not be restrictive.

(3) Estimates of $\bar{w}$ are based on actual sampled weights rather than conversions from length to weight. Such conversions would add error to the variance of G that would have to be taken into account in $\hat{V}(P)$.

Approximate 95% confidence limits for P may be estimated from:

$$2\sqrt{[\hat{V}(P)]} \tag{15}$$

The above provides a means of estimating the variance of a single estimate of P. Detailed and careful planning and execution of a study are necessary to provide such an estimate. For other models, e.g. von Bertalanffy, expressions for variance of production are not available.

There is considerable practical interest in estimating production in those waters of a region that are fairly similar. If production is estimated within a randomly selected number of such waters in a region in a series of years, then variances between waters and between years may be estimated directly and compared by analysis of variance methods, and inferences drawn concerning the mean regional and annual production. Some transformations of data will likely be necessary depending on how the variances of individual population estimates (estimated as outlined above) are distributed. Thus even in regional replicated studies it is worthwhile to attempt to estimate separately the variance of each estimate. Estimates of error obtained through replication are usually to be preferred over error estimates that depend upon properties of models.

Frequency of sampling

Production has sometimes been calculated on the basis of estimates made at the start and end of periods up to several months or even a year in length.

If G and Z vary in parallel fashion an interval of this length between estimates is quite satisfactory. But such a circumstance cannot be assumed and is probably rare.

The objectives of the investigator and field circumstances will partly govern the frequency of samples. Where G and Z do not vary sharply in different fashions, observations made monthly or every second month may be satisfactory. In many instances fortnightly production estimates during periods of rapid growth or mortality would be better, preferably with 'paired' data being obtained for fish size and population numbers. Paired observations on numbers and growth are necessary if confidence limits are to be estimated for P. Of course, if fin mutilations are used for marking fish, the possible combinations of fins to be removed are limited, and it may be necessary to settle for monthly paired estimates. When small habitats are being studied, too frequent disturbance may be undesirable.

However, it should be stressed that estimation of production over intervals as great as one year or more, with no intervening samples to estimate growth rate or population size, may yield only a gross approximation to the true value. Further, regardless of the method of calculating production, it is poor practice to subdivide the estimate of production into increments shorter than the periods between population estimates. Models of survivorship or growth are only as good as the empirical data to which they are fitted.

Special situations

Production of heavily exploited stocks when catch statistics are available

For both the graphic and the computational methods, simultaneous estimates of both population numbers and mean weight of the individual fish are required as frequently as possible. However, direct estimation of numbers is usually more difficult and time consuming than estimation of mean weight. In heavily-exploited populations for which the time of occurrence of many of the deaths (often the majority) is known from catch records, quite accurate interpolations may be made of population numbers from estimates made at comparatively long intervals (Regier 1962). That is, the fish taken by angling or netting are subtracted from the population as they are removed, and only natural mortality need be interpolated by means of one of the models discussed above. The trend in stock abundance obtained in this way can be combined with frequent direct estimates of mean weight, which are often fairly easy to obtain.

Production of controlled
experimental populations

In small experimental environments repeated weighing of test animals can be used to measure production. The weight increments of individual fish, summed for all population members during short time intervals, is the production during those periods. Care is necessary, in choosing the intervals between weighings, to avoid omitting periods when weight may change rapidly either positively or negatively. When individual fish die during the time periods of interest, growth of the animals between their last weighing and time of death should be included in the production estimate.

In certain fish-cultural situations where mortality is negligible and growth is always positive, the difference between the initial and final biomass of a stock will approximate its production. Where negative growth can occur, and the context of the production study is trophic efficiency, frequent growth measurements will be necessary.

Production of the youngest age-groups

In the case of newly-hatched or newly-emerged broods, the point of beginning populations size may sometimes be estimated from fecundity and embryonic survival data (Chapter 7). Existing studies of very young fish indicate that their growth in weight and their survivorship may both conform well to exponential models. Hence, having estimated fish size and abundance at the start and the end of the first year of life, we can estimate G and Z for the year, and from them compute a rough estimate of P, using expressions (4) and (1); expression (6) will not be useful because Z is large and numbers are changing rapidly. In addition, maximum and minimum estimates for P can be made by using whatever extreme forms the survival curve might conceivably take (Le Cren 1962); the Allen curve is useful in this operation.

Production of sexual products

Generally speaking, production of eggs and sperm must be estimated separately from that of somatic tissue (Mann 1965; Backiel 1971). This is done by making special determinations of the weight of the products released. Caloric content should preferably also be determined, because eggs and sperm frequently differ from somatic tissues in this respect. Production of sexual products is then added to production of somatic tissue for the year, if an estimate of total production is required.

In temperate regions sexual products are typically released once a year.

For any interval Δt shorter than a year, if Δt includes a discharge of sexual products this fact can distort or complicate the estimate of production. It makes the final average weight $\bar{w}_2$ of the fish less than it would otherwise be; in fact $\bar{w}_2$ can even become less than the initial weight $\bar{w}_1$. If Δt is of the order of only a month or so, a good approximation to the production *of somatic tissue* during that time is obtained, from $P = G\bar{B}$, by first subtracting the average weight of sexual products discharged during Δt from $\bar{w}_1$. This will reduce the estimate of B_1 and hence also $\bar{B}$, while it will increase the estimate of G obtained from expression (2). However, the product $G\bar{B}$ will in general be larger than if the actual $\bar{w}_1$ is used. Backiel (1971) reported that shed gonadal products amounted to 10% of annual production for predatory fish in the Vistula River.

Production and standing crop

Estimating production, by whatever method, requires considerable expenditure of time, so that there are situations where the only clue to production may be the size of the standing crop. For invertebrates the concept of 'rate of turnover' has been employed, by Juday (1940) for example, but what exactly was meant by it has usually been rather vague. Waters (1969) defined the *turnover ratio* (T) as the ratio of production to mean standing crop over a time interval (Δt) that preferably should be equal to the life-cycle of the species concerned (or some multiple of it):

$$T = \frac{P}{\bar{B}}. \tag{16}$$

Waters found that for a series of freshwater invertebrates the value of T for a single life-cycle varied only between 2·5 and 5, with a mean at 3·5.

The same principle can be applied to fish populations. The computations should preferably be made by following one or more year-classes from hatching to final disappearance. However if there are no major variations in year-class strength, a reasonably good answer can be obtained by considering all the fish present in a population over a year's time. For example, if $T = P/\bar{B}$ has been estimated for species X, but only $\bar{B}$ is known for a species Y which has generally similar growth and mortality rates, then the T value for X can be multiplied by the $\bar{B}$ for Y to obtain a rough estimate of the production of the latter. A systematic compilation of values of T from published sources would be useful for this purpose. Chapman (1978) prepared such a listing, finding, for example, that $P = 2\bar{B}$ for most stream-dwelling salmonids where the salmonid component dominates the ichthyofauna. This multiplier (2) can be considered as a secondary productivity function of use in estimating P; perhaps 1·5 would be more appropriate in cold environments, 1·7–2·0 in warmer streams. This does not, of course, obviate necessity to obtain an accurate estimate of mean biomass. Also one should note that $P:\bar{B}$ need not equal G if unusual model combinations are employed (Allen 1971).

In general, $T < 2·5$ for fish populations, considerably less than for the freshwater invertebrates listed by Waters (1969).

Mathews (1970) demonstrated that $P:\bar{B}$ and G, independently determined, were comparable for several lowland cyprinid fish populations in England. The ratio $P:\bar{B}$ ranged from 0·60 to 1·11. These data, and those listed in Chapman (1977) suggest that $P:\bar{B}$ ratios should be useful in ecologically similar waters for estimating production. Backiel (1971) reported $P:\bar{B}$ ratios of 0·30 to 0·70 (mean = 0·40) for predatory fish in the Vistula River, and noted the similarity to Mathews' (1970) results, suggesting that a species with 7 or more age groups may commonly have $P:\bar{B} < 1·0$.

Production in relation to community dynamics

In unexploited populations or in populations subjected to fishing at a steady rate over a considerable period, production may remain fairly stable from year to year. However, the initiation of cropping, or any major change in its intensity, can alter production levels. For example, reduction in biomass may bring about a compensating increase in the instantaneous growth coefficient. Production should be considered as a dynamic parameter, one that is influenced by changes in biomass or growth rate caused by cropping or by natural environmental variables.

Partly for this reason, production is not a satisfactory measure of the importance of fish as a trophic group in the aquatic community. Energy consumption by fish is a far more useful statistic in studies of total energy turnover. Davis & Warren (1965) have shown that during a year or period of years when biomass is (temporarily) unusually high, the production may be nil, yet the population is consuming and metabolizing important quantities of food (energy).

Methods for Study of Fish Diets
Based on Analysis of Stomach Contents

JOHN T WINDELL and STEPHEN H BOWEN

Introduction

Much of our current understanding of the autecology, production and ecological role of fish populations is derived from studies of the diet based on analysis of stomach contents. In this chapter, methods used in such studies are described and their relative advantages and limitations for different types of investigations are discussed. Many recent studies of the diet have proceeded to a point at which chemical analysis of the diet is required and thus a section on chemical methods is included.

It is appropriate to begin with a word of caution. For some time, fisheries biologists have appreciated that stomach contents, *per se*, may not accurately reflect the consumer's diet (Lagler 1956). Some important components of the diet may be processed so rapidly that they leave little or no recognizable remains. Tubificids ingested by roach are largely destroyed through mastication and only the minute chaetae remain in the stomach. As a result, the importance of tubificids as a food for roach went unrecognized for more than two decades until heavy infestations of an intestinal parasite that requires a tubificid vector were noticed (Kennedy 1969). A second problem arises in that different rates of food progression for various items may lead to selective accumulation of those food items or parts which are digested more slowly. Thus relative abundances of food items in the stomach may not reflect the proportions in which they were ingested (Mann & Orr 1969). Although workers have been aware of this potential problem for some time, its real significance is yet to be established and the critical worker must keep it in mind.

Collection and preservation

In addition to those considerations routinely required to obtain a representative sample of a fish population, three special considerations are required in

Chapter 9

collection of specimens for analysis of stomach contents. Collection methods should be chosen which minimize (1) regurgitation of food, (2) feeding under abnormal conditions, and (3) digestion after capture. Struggling fish in gill nets may regurgitate their food. Fish caught in traps may feed atypically from substrates in contact with the trap or on other organisms in the trap. Any method of collection that holds the fish for more than a few minutes after capture will allow digestion to continue and result in a loss of information. Preferred methods minimize the time interval from collection to preservation. Seines, trawls, cast nets, electrofishing apparatus and hook and line have all been used with satisfactory results.

Several workers, including Keast & Welsh (1968) and Elliott (1970) have found that diet and feeding intensity can vary during the diurnal cycle. Thus, it is best to begin a study of the food and feeding of a fish population with a series of collections made at regular intervals over one or more 24-h periods. This would be expected to reveal the hour of day when specimens would be most likely to contain food in their stomachs, and would determine whether or not specimens collected throughout the day could be treated as samples from the same feeding population with respect to composition of the diet.

As soon as possible after capture specimens should be fixed in an aqueous solution of formaldehyde. Four percent is the concentration most commonly used. Fixation is allowed to continue until all tissues are rigid. The specimen is then transferred to alcohol for storage. Seventy percent solutions of methanol, ethanol and isopropanol are all satisfactory preservatives and are considerably less noxious than formaldehyde, to which many workers develop heightened sensitivity after repeated exposure.

If the whole fish is to be fixed, the coelom should be opened to admit the formaldehyde that will minimize post mortem digestion. In many cases it is convenient to fix and preserve only the stomach or stomach contents after the relevant data have been collected from the rest of the specimen. The stomach or stomach contents of each specimen should be stored separately pending examination. Pooled stomach samples can be recommended only for those rare studies in which within sample variation has been established under a wide variety of circumstances.

Analysis of stomach contents

The three methods of analysis commonly used are described separately and then discussed together.

Numerical analysis

The stomach sample is examined at several levels of magnification and food items present are identified and counted. Identification is usually to species where practical, but in some cases the goals of the study are adequately served by less precise identification. Data from enumeration of food items are commonly treated in two ways. Firstly, the number of stomach samples in which one or more of a given food item is found is expressed as a percentage of all non-empty stomachs examined. This figure estimates the proportion of the population that feeds on that particular food item and is referred to as the *frequency of occurrence*. Secondly, the number of food items of a given type that were found in all specimens examined is expressed as a percentage of all food items to estimate the relative abundance of that food item in the diet. This figure is often called the *percentage composition by number*.

Volumetric analysis

For direct volumetric analysis, food items are sorted into taxonomic categories and the displacement of the group of items in each category is measured in a partially filled graduated cylinder. Since a wide range in the volume of different categories is usually found, it is often necessary to use a series of different sized graduated cylinders to achieve reasonable accuracy. To obtain meaningful results, superficial water attached to food items must be removed before displacement is measured. Blotting food items between paper towels and low speed centrifugation in specially constructed baskets have both proved satisfactory.

If it is not possible to measure the volume of food items directly, their volume may be estimated as the volume of one or more geometric solids that together approximate the shape and dimensions of the food item. This approach is particularly useful for estimation of the volume of micro-organisms. Errors in estimation of volume are usually trivial when compared to errors in enumeration.

Volumetric data are usually presented for each category as its percentage of the total volume of all stomach contents examined.

Gravimetric analysis

Food items in a sample are divided into taxonomic categories and the group of specimens in each category is weighed. Both wet and dry weights have been used. If wet weights are used, superficial water must be removed as discussed above. When dry weights are used, food items should be dried to constant weight and cooled in a desiccator prior to weighing. Consensus is lacking as to the temperature at which samples should be dried. Some workers believe that volatile lipids may be lost at temperatures above 80 °C and suggest that lower temperatures should be used. Other workers routinely dry samples at 105 °C. A quick check performed by heating samples previously dried at a temperature below 80 °C at 105 °C will help determine if sufficient weight is lost at 105 °C to justify the additional expenditure of time required to dry samples at lower temperatures.

If it is not feasible to sort or weigh food items, their weight may be estimated. First the volume of the food items is estimated as described above, and then the volume is multiplied by the item's specific gravity. If the specific gravity cannot be determined directly and a value is not available in the literature, an estimate of S.G. = 1 may be acceptable. As with the volumetric method, indirect estimation is most frequently applied to microorganisms.

The measured weight of food in the stomach is equal to the weight of food ingested minus the weight that has been digested and passed to the intestine. The extent to which food is digested in the stomach varies greatly with the species and its diet. Gastric digestion is most extensive in fish that feed on large prey, especially those that feed on other fish. Because such predators usually contain fewer food items, variation in the degree of gastric digestion can result in considerable variation in gravimetric (also volumetric description of the diet. The method of *reconstructed weights* has been developed to obviate this difficulty. The original weight of a partially-digested food item is reconstructed from the dimensions of some indigestible hard part of the item such as an otolith, vertebrae or other bone, carapace, or some easily distinguished element of a compound appendage (Popova 1967). The relationship between the weight of the prey and the dimensions of the indigestible part is established for an appropriate range of prey sizes using specimens collected from the feeding habitat.

Data from gravimetric analysis are usually expressed for each food category as its percentage of the total weight of stomach contents analysed.

Selection of a method

For a given study, one method will be better than the others depending on the goals of the study and the nature of the food to be analysed. The uniqueness of each situation studied prohibits hard and fast rules for selection of a method, but some rough guidelines may be drawn from the relative advantages and limitations of the three basic methods.

Apart from simple descriptions of the diet, studies based on analysis of stomach contents can be divided into two classes with regard to their goals. Studies in the first class attempt to compare diets of different groups of fish, or the diet of one group with the available food. Studies in the second class attempt to assess the energetic and/or nutritional significance of the diet or its components.

In the first class of studies, comparisons are made on the basis of relative abundances of different food items. Numerical analysis is usually the best way to establish relative abundances because it requires the least time and apparatus. It is inadequate only when a significant component of the diet does not occur in discrete units of uniform size. Examples of such problem food items are macrophytes, detritus and filamentous algae. Either volumetric or gravimetric analysis is required to quantify these food items.

Data from numerical analysis provides little information on the food value of different items in the diet, so either volumetric or gravimetric analysis must be used for studies in the second class. Although volumetric analysis requires the least time and apparatus it is necessary to use several assumptions or approximations to draw conclusions about energetic or nutritional features of the diet from volumetric data. Gravimetric analysis by wet weight is subject to similar limitations. Gravimetric analysis by dry weight is the best approach since it quantifies only the dry biomass that has potential food value and results in a dried sample that is available for chemical analysis.

Before leaving this section, some mention should be made of the 'points' method of analysis used by a few workers (Hynes 1950). Food items are sorted into categories, usually species, and each category is assigned a number of points depending on: (1) the number of items present and (2) the size of items in the category. The 'points' method can be described as a sort of numerical-volumetric hybrid applied subjectively. Several workers have chosen this approach because they believed it represented a compromise between the conceptual inadequacies of the numerical and gravimetric methods. They reasoned that the numerical method was not entirely satisfactory for analysis of the diet since small organisms in the diet have the same impact on the analysis as larger organisms, but are clearly of less nutritional value. They considered volumetric analysis to be of limited value because it overemphasizes the importance of predation by fish on the larger food organisms in the community when a great many small organisms are also eaten. Such reasoning reflects a failure to clarify and define the goals of the study before a method of analysis is chosen. As discussed above, numerical and volumetric methods are appropriate to different types of studies, but the 'points' method results in data that is of doubtful value for the solution of any clearly defined question. Workers who have used the points method in conjunction with the numerical and volumetric methods (Fagade 1971; Munro 1967) have generally drawn their conclusions from the latter and found points to be of little use. Another disadvantage of the points method is that its subjective basis makes it impossible to use statistical analysis of the data or to compare points data from two different workers. In summary, we must conclude that the points method does not meet the modern requirements for a method used in critical scientific investigation.

Data analysis

Biologists engaged in analysis of stomach content data have spawned a variety of indices intended to illuminate one aspect or another of the data and to facilitate comparisons of samples. Although most indices have been used only once or twice, a few, for example Ivlev's electivity index, have come into general usage. It is possible to replace each of these indices with a standard statistical method. Consider Ivlev's index as an example. The purpose of Ivlev's index is to compare the relative abundance of a food item in fish stomach samples with the relative abundance in the feeding environment. The greater the difference between relative abundances in stomach contents and the environment, the greater the calculated value of the index. Essentially the same analysis can be made using the χ^2 or G test (Sokal & Rholf 1967). Relative abundance in the environment may be taken as the expected frequency and relative abundance in stomach samples as the observed frequency to test the null hypothesis that the two are equal. The greater the difference between the two, the greater the χ^2 or G value calculated. To compare the degree of selection in different samples or for different food items, the calculated χ^2 or G may be divided by its critical value to obviate the effects of different degrees of freedom.

Standard statistical methods have three advantages over fisheries indices. Firstly, the average scientific reader is unlikely to be acquainted with most fisheries indices but should be familiar with basic statistics. The use of a standard statistical procedure will therefore more readily communicate the purpose and design of the analysis presented. Secondly, while indices may emphasize trends in the data, only standard statistics can reveal the significance of the observed trends. Thirdly, statistical techniques have considerably more analytical power than simple indices. Various components of the data can be isolated and analysed separately, and interaction between components of the diet can be studied. To make analysis of stomach content data more readable, conceptually clear, and to have confidence in the results, fisheries indices that have been used in the past should be replaced by the statistical techniques that are now a basic component of a biologist's working knowledge. Present trends are clearly in this direction.

Chemical analysis

Every consumer population is confronted with the basic problem of selecting a diet which supplies it with adequate dietary energy and protein to support maintenance, reproduction and growth. The role of dietary energy is now generally appreciated. The significance of dietary protein, or more specifically the digestible protein–digestible energy ration, is discussed by many authors, including Harper (1967) and Russell-Hunter (1970). To answer basic questions about the nutritional significance of different diets or dietary components, it is often necessary to complement use of the essentially taxonomic analyses discussed above with chemical analysis.

Chemical analysis for nutritional considerations necessarily involves two steps. First, the concentration of the chemical characteristic in the diet is determined, and then the extent to which that characteristic is assimilated from the diet is determined. From this data it is possible to calculate the yield from the diet to the consumer in such units as Joules or milligrammes of protein per gramme of food ingested.

To determine the concentration of a chemical characteristic in the diet, either stomach samples or samples of the food taken from the environment may be analysed. The samples should be dried immediately after collection and stored in a desiccator pending analysis. Methods for determination of energy in organic materials are described by Phillipson (1970) and Cummins & Wuycheck (1971). Protein in animal tissues may be estimated as total N times 6·25, but this estimate is not applicable to plant materials or detritus which frequently contain large amounts of non-protein nitrogen (Riley 1970; Harrison & Mann 1975). Techniques for estimation of plant proteins are described by Pirie (1955), Price (1965) and Kaushik & Hynes (1968). The technique of the latter authors has been used successfully in analysis of samples that contained large amounts of amorphous detritus (Bowen 1976).

Assimilation efficiency is the difference between the amount of a substance ingested and the amount defecated expressed as a percentage of the amount ingested. It is measured under laboratory conditions chosen to approximate conditions in the environment and details are reviewed in the following chapter.

Experiments for determination of assimilation efficiency should be conducted in a way that minimizes disturbance of the fish. In some species, gastric digestion comes to an abrupt halt when the fish are disturbed (Moriarty 1973; Bowen 1976). Faeces should be collected almost immediately after they are released. After one hour, considerable organic matter can be leached from faeces (Windell, in press), and after 6 h the chemical composition may be drastically altered by microbial activity (Newell 1965).

The methods described above are the basic tools available for the study of the diet of a fish population. They possess considerable untapped analytical power, and it is likely that they will continue to be used without substantial alteration for some time.

10

Estimating Food Consumption Rates of Fish Populations

JOHN T WINDELL

Introduction

This chapter presents five general methods that have been used to estimate the magnitude of food consumption of fish populations in natural, laboratory and hatchery situations. These are the (1) bioenergetic balanced equation, (2) Winberg balanced equation, (3) nitrogen balanced equation, (4) radio-isotope and (5) food progression method. Each of these methods have possible applications, but also their own inherent peculiarities, weaknesses and assumptions. Careful consideration should be given before selection of any one of the methods because none are yet perfected and may require substantial modification, refinement and imagination for different types of fish populations, ecosystems and trophic levels. For accurate estimates of food consumption many different types of data are required from several different experiments. Population density, age structure, growth rates, metabolic expenditures, egestion rates, excretory rates, and food consumption rates on a daily, seasonal, and yearly basis are essential pieces of information when one strives for an ideal study. Unfortunately the ideal has not been reached in spite of the need to be able to predict yield and production of fish populations. No attempt has been made in what follows to review the mass of published findings and contrasting views of the cited and uncited works. Emphasis has been placed on the essential outlines of methodology and studies cited to permit easy and quick access to more detailed published descriptions.

Bioenergetic balanced equation

The bioenergetic method has been tested by Mann (1964, 1965). The literature to 1966 has been summarized in the contributions of Warren & Davis, Mann, Beamish & Dickie to the symposium volume edited by Gerking (1967). More recent reviews include that of Mann (1969), Davis & Warren (1971) and Weatherly (1972). Solomon & Brafield (1972) were the first to measure all parameters, continuously record oxygen consumption and compute metabolic rate while fish were growing. From their data it was concluded that the majority of the assumptions often made in energetic studies are valid. In contrast, Healey (1972) following a study on the bioenergetics of sand gobies (*Pomato-schistus minutus*) where consumption and growth were measured in a natural population, resting metabolism measured by respirometry and egestion estimated from published data concluded that until contradictions are solved, energy budgets of natural populations of fishes must remain at best crude approximations. These contrasting views and others emphasize the need for careful planning prior to initiating these types of investigations.

Warren & Davis (1967) presented a modified equation proposed by Ivlev (1939a, b, 1945, 1966) for the quantitative measurement of food consumption by fish populations. The terms of the equation are defined so as to be independent and measurable. In the terminology of Ricker, page 3, Chapter 1, the energy budget of an animal or of a population may be written as:

$$C = F + U + \Delta B + R$$

where:

C = *Consumption*—total intake of food by an individual or population during a specified time interval.

F = *Faeces* (*Egesta*)—that part of the total food intake which is not digested or absorbed and leaves the alimentary canal.

U = *Excreta* (*Urine*)—that part of the food intake which is absorbed and passed from the body either in the urine or through the gills or skin.

ΔB = *Growth*—for an individual fish or increase in biomass or biocontent of an individual or population.

R = *Respiration*—that part of assimilation which is converted to heat or mechanical energy and is used up in life processes. Usually measured by oxygen consumption.

The basic assumption is that the amount of food intake expressed in material units such as living or wet weight, dry weight, ash-free weight, nitrogen content, calories, etc., equals the sum of the amounts lost in (1) egestion, (2) excretion, (3) metabolism, and (4) the amount retained in growth. Experiments are usually designed to measure growth, maintenance and efficiency under specified laboratory, simulated field and field conditions for a sufficient time period, i.e. long enough to record significant growth and short enough to permit additional experiments at a range of temperatures, fish sizes, and food types. Egestion, excretion and growth may be measured directly and the metabolic rate determined indirectly by respirometry in a separate experiment. The terms of this equation are most conveniently expressed in calories per fish over an interval of time long enough that changes in weight or total caloric content of the fish body are sufficiently large to be reliably determined.

Because metabolism is considered to consist of several distinct components with values which depend upon rates of growth (ΔB) and food consumption (C) the respiratory (R) category can be further partitioned as:

$$R = R_s + R_d + R_a$$

where:

$R_s = $ *Standard Metabolism* (S_{met})—that energy equivalent to that released in the course of metabolism of unfed and resting fish.

$R_d = $ *Specific Dynamic Action* (SDA)—additional energy released in the course of digestion, assimilation, storage of materials consumed and deamination of amino acids.

$R_a = $ *Active Metabolism* (A_{met})—additional energy released in the course of swimming and other activity.

Warren & Davis (1967) have discussed the categories of uses and losses of the energy of consumed food materials by fish as shown in equations and a model (Fig. 10.1) similar to that of Needham (1964), Kleiber (1961) and Davies (1964).

Consumption measurements (C)

The daily food consumption (C) of wild fish is affected by a large number of factors which include size of the fish, amount of food eaten in a meal, number of meals in a day, rate of gastric clearing, water temperature, activity of the fish, type of food eaten, availability of food organisms and prior feeding history (Elliott 1975a, b, c). Measurement of food consumption is further complicated because of interaction between some of these factors. Many studies have simultaneously measured consumption and growth under laboratory conditions by feeding known amounts of food over varying periods of time (Brett *et al.* 1969; Brett 1971b, c; Elliott 1975a, b). Some workers have based estimates of consumption upon gastric clearing rate in relation to temperature and quantified gut contents from field observations of daily and seasonal feeding activity for different size groups (Healy 1972;

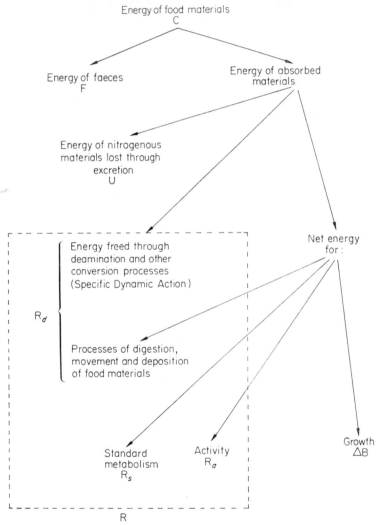

Figure 10.1. Model of categories of losses and uses of the energy of consumed **food** materials.

Cameron *et al.* 1973). Models have been developed from which consumption could be predicted from field measurements of gut contents at different water temperatures (Healy 1972), or metabolism and food requirements computed from growth data with a metabolic submodel (McKinnon 1973). In an attempt to evaluate the assumption that fish in the laboratory have the same energy requirements and growth efficiency as fish in nature, Carline & Hall (1973) estimated food consumption rates and growth for coho salmon (*Oncorhynchus kisutch*) by feeding known amounts of food to fish held in a simulated stream environment and in adjoining aquaria. All groups had similar growth efficiencies over a wide range of rations and it was concluded that laboratory derived food and growth data may provide reasonably accurate estimates of food consumption in nature.

Analysis of hunger and appetite. Most fishes feed at a high rate until their stomachs are full or nearly full. Rate of eating remains at a low level as long as the stomach is full and hunger is presumed to be zero. Volume of stomach contents is directly related to ingestion, digestion and food progression which is strongly influenced by water temperature. When stomach fullness decreases, hunger increases and the probability of eating rises. High levels of hunger tend to occur with a more or less empty stomach. Fortmann *et al.* (1961) reported that starved trout were caught by anglers in much higher proportion relative to their abundance than previously fed trout. Prolonged periods of food deprivation result in a lowered metabolic level and anatomical changes in the alimentary canal and especially the pyloric cecae which result in a slower rate of food progression (Windell 1967).

The approach to the investigation of hunger and appetite is largely one of the ethologist and comparative psychologist or physiologist. Little agreement exists on what hunger and appetite are and how they should be measured. However, the most accepted view is that hunger is only relevant as far as it finds expression in behaviour (Beukema 1968).

Workers have found it almost impossible to measure hunger in fishes in a direct way under completely natural circumstances. Little or no explanation exists for numerous reported observations of fish within the same population that have empty stomachs in the presence of food abundance. Therefore indirect approaches have been used to determine degree of hunger by utilizing *ad libitum* feeding and varying periods of food deprivation.

Beukema (1968) working with the stickleback, *Gasterosteus aculeatus* L., provided an excess of living tubifex worms on the bottom of aquaria for an

8-h period on observation days. On other days no food was present (deprivation). The number of prey was determined every hour by counting the number left on the bottom. Individual food intake showed some day-to-day fluctuation, but no significant trend was present for well-acclimated fish.

The length of food deprivation may be expected to exert an important influence on hunger for subsequent food intake. Rozin & Mayer (1964) found in goldfish, *Carassius auratus* (L.), an increase in the 1-h food intake with increasing length of deprivation time up to 4 h. However, the mouthbrooder, *Sarotherodon melanotheron*, showed an increase in the quantity of food required to reach a level of satiation up to 4 days of deprivation. Beukema (1968) found that food deprivation of 16–88 h did not alter the quantity of food consumed over an 8-h period but produced a substantial influence (doubling) on the rate of eating in the first hour. By varying the length of the deprivation time under specified conditions of temperature, time of day, feeding–deprivation schedule, and kind of food eaten before the sticklebacks were brought into well-defined hunger states. A number of elements in feeding behaviour were found to increase and decrease with time of deprivation and feeding, respectively (Beukema 1968; Chiszar & Windell 1973).

Behavioural elements such as rates, intensities and durations of feeding appear to fluctuate in parallel and provide evidence for a common causative internal mechanism called a feeding or hunger mechanism (Miller 1959; De Ruiter 1963; Beukema 1968). Beukema (1968) defined hunger for the stickleback as the activity state of the internal mechanism controlling feeding behaviour. Feeding behaviours such as encounter, neglect, fixating, grasping, rejection and eating were measured as complete or incomplete responses. The predatory sequence is dependent upon prey properties such as recognition of palatable food, buoyancy, susceptibility to capture, appropriate size, taste, concentration, and conspicuousness (Chiszar & Windell 1973).

Analysis of satiation. Maximum food intake (satiation) in the laboratory has been studied using several variations of a similar experimental design (Ishiwata 1968a, b, c, d, e, f; Brett 1971a; Elliott 1975a, b). After appropriate acclimation fish are individually compartmentalized and conditioned to feed on the chosen food type. Following a previously determined food deprivation period of 2 or 3 days a feeding bout is conducted whereby natural or commercially prepared food items are offered at timed intervals until the fish refuse to feed. The experimental apparatus is constructed with a false bottom so that uneaten food items become unavailable and easy to remove without disturbance to the fish. The difference between the number of food items offered and the number removed is the total number consumed. This number is usually converted to dry weight by using mean dry weights derived from a separate analysis.

The 'satiation time' is recorded to the nearest minute for each meal and defined as the time from the start of feeding to voluntary cessation. Therefore, when fish no longer accept food in the presence of excess, after a period of feeding, they are considered satiated. Satiation time (with 95% confidence limits) was estimated from multiple regression equations for brown trout fed *Gammarus* at 15 temperatures (Elliott 1975a). Estimates from the regressions were applicable to a wide range of organisms and appetite varied with temperature. Size of individual particles have some effect on the point at which stomach wall distension prevents further consumption.

Satiation times for sockeye salmon, *Oncorhynchus nerka* (Brett 1971a), jack mackerel, *Trachurus japonicus*, rainbow trout, *Salmo gairdneri* (Ishiwata 1968a) the puffer, *Fugi vermicularis* and the file fish, *Stephanolepis cirrhifer* indicate marked species differences. In skipjack tuna, *Katsuwonus pelanis* the proportions of prey items attended to and attacked decreased as satiation progressed (Magnuson 1969). Data on deprivation suggest that initial feeding rate and amount eaten in relatively short bouts reflect deprivation but, paradoxically, that if food is available for long periods fish eat amounts independent of deprivation.

Faeces and urine measurements $(F + U)$

There is little accurate information on the energy losses in the excretory products of fish save one recent notable exception (Elliott 1976). In practice it often is impossible to separately measure F (egesta or faeces) and U (excretion or urine) and many workers have measured C, ΔB, R, and effectively balanced the equation by assuming that $C - (\Delta B + R)$ represents the unassimilated portion of the food. This is not quite correct because urine and other excretions are derived from food which has been first assimilated (Mann 1969).

Winberg (1956) suggested that under natural conditions natural foods are about 85% digestible and assimilatable. The remaining 15% becomes F (faeces-egesta) moving on through the fish. He also proposed that 3–5% of the energy intake was lost as U (excretory products) and erroneously assumed that the energy value of ammonia was negligible. Therefore it was proposed that the average amount of energy available for growth and metabolism is 80 % of the daily energy consumption (C) and that the remaining 20 % is lost as waste products $(F + U)$. Since that time workers have calculated energy budgets from the relation $0.8C = R + \Delta B$. Recent reports indicate that these assumptions do not apply to all species and that greater care should be given to actual measurements (Ricker 1973; Elliott 1976).

Estimation of the values for U have included holding fish in the smallest amount of water possible in order to assess accurately the concentration of ammonia-nitrogen and urea-nitrogen. Details of acceptable methods can be found in Elliott (1976). Solid faecal matter (F) has been collected by a variety of techniques including siphoning, filtration, centrifugation, or use of a faecal trap (Solomon & Brafield 1972). Dried samples have been analysed by oxygen bomb calorimetry or wet combustion methods (Maciolek 1962). Some workers have determined the proximate amounts of protein nitrogen by the Kjeldahl method, amount of fat by ether extraction and used appropriate calorific conversion factors (see page 236).

Growth measurements (ΔB)

Methods for obtaining data on growth have been extremely variable. Most workers have been conscientious of the extreme sensitivity of fish to handling and conducted their experiments accordingly. Collection and transportation of the animals to the laboratory takes a variety of forms and depends mainly on local available equipment and facilities. Periods of acclimation have not always been reported but should be substantial before beginning an experiment. Most experiments utilize replicate groups or individuals and begin with narcotization, measurement to the nearest millimetre and weighing (see below) to the nearest practical measurement. Often fish are starved prior to weighing for a period suitable (but no longer) for the alimentary canal to be emptied. Weight (and length) measurements may or may not be taken at weekly or biweekly intervals.

In many growth experiments each fish group is weighed according to the following procedure. Fish are netted in a deep-bodied net, lifted from the water, allowed to drain for a full 30-s interval and poured into a pre-tared container containing sufficient water to eliminate stress. Total weight to the nearest gramme is determined on a suitable (solution) balance and the fish immediately returned to their water environment. In routine operations the elapsed time from removal to return to water is approximately 2 min or less.

When weighed at biweekly intervals it is often desirable to predict growth for each period and increase the ration daily. At the end of the experiment the fish are again fasted, weighed and measured. Most workers randomly select subgroups of fish for chemical analysis at the beginning and end of each growth experiment. Wet weights are taken followed by drying at 60–80 °C until a constant dry weight is achieved. Samples are ground with a Wiley mill or mortar and pestle and frozen or stored in a desiccator until further analysis.

Growth (ΔB) is usually expressed as a change in weight over a given period of time. However the body composition of fish may vary considerably and for most purposes growth is better expressed in terms of the body energy content or a summation of the component mineral, protein, fat and carbohydrate fractions.

Metabolism measurements (R)

Recognizing that routine energy expenditures are difficult to estimate for wild fish populations, Winberg (1956) recommended as an approximation that A_{met} was roughly twice the S_{met} level measured under appropriate experimental conditions. Although this assumption has been indirectly supported (Mann 1967) current evidence is circumstantial. The assumption has been criticized by Warren & Davis (1967), who present cogent arguments suggesting why fish metabolism subject to different nutritional levels and diets is unlikely to be a constant multiple of S_{met}. Ware (1975a) made new calculations based on Ivlev's (1960) work which indicated that field metabolism of young, actively growing fish may be closer to 3 times the S_{met} rate, rather than the factor of 2 suggested by Winberg (1956). After all considerations it appears fact that many of the conclusions drawn from bioenergetic studies of natural populations rest upon a foundation of questionable assumptions (Ware 1975a).

Following food consumption the metabolic rate of a fish measured by oxygen consumption increases abruptly to a maximum and thereafter decreases gradually or in some cases irregularly to pre-feeding levels. This increase is attributed to what is known as specific dynamic action (SDA) of the food. The most thorough investigation of apparent SDA is that by Averett (1969) on the effects of ration size, season and temperature on coho salmon, *Oncorhynchus kisutch*. Similar studies have been reported by Muir & Niimi (1972) on aholehole, *Kuhlia scandvicensis* and Beamish (1974) on largemouth bass, *Micropterus salmoides*. Although the biochemistry of SDA effect is not well understood the energy expenditure is generally assumed to be largely the result of the deamination of amino acids. Beamish (1974) recommends that the term apparent SDA or heat increment be used to distinguish between the energy required for deamination and that for absorption, digestion, transportation and deposition of food materials. These latter processes are difficult to separate experimentally and are presumed to require minimal energy.

Apparent SDA has been determined by forced swimming at a fixed speed in a respirometer prior to and following consumption of different meal sizes and fish size (Beamish 1974), season and temperature (Averett 1969). Elevated oxygen consumption over time following ingestion is summed, expressed as milligrams of oxygen consumed and equated to apparent SDA.

Rough estimates of SDA have been derived indirectly by measuring the amount of energy lost by a separate group of fish starved for the duration of an experiment (Warren & Davis 1967; Kionka 1972; Sarokon 1975). It is assumed that amount of energy lost is equivalent to the energy required for standard metabolism and activity. This value plus the energy of growth is subtracted from the amount of energy absorbed to provide the SDA estimate.

Proximate analysis of samples

Usually random subsamples of fish are removed from each experimental group at the onset and at the end of each experimental period, and weighed. These samples of food, fish and faeces are dried to a constant weight at 60–80 °C, homogenized and stored for analysis. Dry weight measurements without caloric information on the materials involved are not satisfactory for bioenergetic studies. Calorific values are determined by oxygen bomb calorimetry (Phillipson 1964), or by the wet oxidation method with dichromate/acid mixture (Maciolek 1962).

In the absence of a bomb calorimeter the energy values may be estimated if the protein and fat composition is known for the material after it has been dried at 80 °C and homogenized.

Protein nitrogen can be estimated as 6·25 times the total N, which may be determined by the Kjeldahl technique as outlined by the Association of Official Analytical Chemists (1960) and Allen *et al.* (1974). It may also be necessary to allow for non-protein nitrogen (Niimi 1972; Craig 1977), for which Gerking (1955) describes a determination method. The calorific value for protein is obtained by the conversion factor of 5·65 kcal/g.

For fats the conversion factor is usually taken as 9·45 kcal/g after the lipids have been determined by Soxhlet or other method of reflux distillation, with petroleum ether or chloroform. Alternatively the analysis may be based on the Bligh and Dyer method (Hanson & Olley 1963). The conversion factor of 9·45 has proved to be too high in some cases (Beamish, Niimi & Lett 1975; Craig 1977), probably owing to the form of the fatty acid chains and impurities carried over in the fat (Ackman *et al.* 1967; Hanahan 1960).

Carbohydrates are usually present in fish material in negligible quantities and can be ignored, but should they have to be considered, the method of Mendel, Kemp & Myers (1954), as described by Winberg (1971), may be used. However, care must be taken since carbohydrates may be lost by drying, even at 80 °C. The energy value is obtained from the conversion factor of 4·1 kcal/g.

It is advisable to analyse some samples by more than one method and also to complete and check the analysis to 100 % of the dried tissue by estimating the ash content by heating some of the material in a muffle furnace at 600 °C. If possible chemical analyses should be checked by bomb calorimetry and vice versa.

In all cases the analyses and bomb calorimetry should be replicated sufficiently to calculate the 95 % confidence limits. Finally the total energy values in calories may be converted to joules by 1 cal = 4·184 J. In so far as possible the conventional terminology should be followed as recommended and described by the American National Research Council (NRC) (Crampton & Harris 1969).

Food conversion efficiency measurement

Daily, monthly and seasonal food consumption by fish populations ultimately leads to a consideration of the efficiency with which food is utilized for growth, maintenance, and reproduction. The two most often reported efficiencies are total or gross efficiency and partial or net efficiency (Kleiber 1961). These correspond to the 'coefficient of the first order or K_1' and 'coefficient of the second order or K_2' of Ivlev (1945) and Ricker (1946). However these latter terms are objected to because K_1 and K_2 are expressed in percent and are not coefficients (Pandian 1967).

Total or gross efficiency. Total or gross efficiency is derived by initially weighing replicate groups of fish, feeding them measured amounts of food over a time period and reweighing them at the end of the time period. Total growth efficiency, E_t, of the food is computed according to the following:

$$E_t = \frac{\Delta B}{C}$$

where

$\Delta B =$ growth, i.e. energy of the animal product, and
$C \ \ =$ intake, i.e. energy in food during the period at which the product is
       formed.

Total efficiency is zero at the maintenance ration and asymptotically approaches a maximum at the maximum ration if net efficiency is constant. If net efficiency declines with increasing rations, gross efficiency will increase to a maximum as rations increase up to some intermediate level, and then decline with further increase.

Maintenance ration and measurement. The maintenance ration is that amount of food intake measured as dry weight or in energy equivalents that results in no net gain or loss in the body tissue measured as wet weight. Little or no attention has been given to whether the fish have been in a producing (i.e. reproductive) or non-producing condition. However, each species biology, previous feeding history and temperature acclimation should be acknowledged. Body maintenance includes energetic expenditures for swimming, standard metabolism, processes of digestion, assimilation and storage of food materials.

Maintenance ration values have been derived by several variations of the same general method. Replicate subgroups of fish, after appropriate acclimation to temperature and feeding are initially fasted for a sufficient time to ensure that the stomachs are empty (but no longer). They are then anaesthetized, and weighed. After recovering from this procedure the fish are fed according to schedule for a period of weeks being weighed at weekly or biweekly intervals. Changes in weight after each week are used to recalculate the feeding levels for the next week. An alternative procedure utilizes several subgroups which are fed predetermined amounts of food which may range from maximum consumption to maintenance and starvation.

Partial or net efficiency measurement. Partial or net efficiency, E_{pg}, values are derived in experiments similar to that for determination of total or gross efficiency but requires a value for the maintenance ration. The formula for computing partial growth efficiency is:

$$E_{pg} = \frac{\Delta B}{C - M}$$

where M = maintenance ration.

Partial growth efficiency is the efficiency with which a fish species utilizes for growth that part of its ration in excess of the maintenance requirement. Net efficiencies tend to decline with increasing ration size because of increased energy costs and declining absorption efficiency. However under some conditions partial growth efficiency can be remarkably constant over a wide range of ration sizes.

Partial maintenance efficiency. Partial maintenance efficiency, E_{pm}, expresses the efficiency with which an animal utilizes rations at or below the maintenance rations to maintain its tissues or to prevent them from being catabolized (Kleiber 1961). This efficiency can be determined only when data on weight change corresponding to two different rations at or below the maintenance ration is established. It is the ratio of the difference between tissue lost at the two rations to the corresponding difference between the two rations, calculated as follows:

$$E_{pm} = \frac{L_p}{I_p}$$

where L_p = tissue loss prevented, and
I_p = part of ration preventing loss.

Although not studied by fishery scientists partial maintenance efficiencies are of theoretical and practical interest. Considerable knowledge is available to indicate that temperate zone freshwater fish grow only during part of each year. However, the efficiency with which populations maintain themselves under stressful environmental conditions and during periods of starvation or at low food availability would be instructive (Davis & Warren 1971).

Absorption efficiency measurement (digestibility)
Anatomical and physiological differences in the digestive tracts of fishes are responsible for large variations in the ability to utilize different types of foods. The nutritional usefulness of food for fish populations depends in part on the extent to which it is digested. As a general measure of nutritive

value of food, coefficients of digestibility are used to compute its content of total digestible nutrients (TDN). Early studies related the total quantity of food consumed over the experimental feeding period to the total amount of faecal matter produced in terms of the nutrients, such as protein, fat, carbohydrate and their calorific values. Although data for 'digestible ash' have been frequently reported they are of no real significance (Maynard & Loosli 1969).

Methods for the determination of digestibility coefficients have typically involved either a direct or an indirect quantitative measurement of the amount of nutrient ingested and subsequently egested. A digestibility trial involves prior measurement of samples for nutrients in the food type fed and later measurement of the amount voided in the faeces. A trial must involve several animals and the results averaged to minimize the factor of individual variability. Nose (1967) emphasized the importance of negative bias resulting from the presence of abraded intestinal epithelial cells, and residues of digestive juices which contribute to the nitrogen content of the faeces. Therefore the term 'coefficient of apparent digestibility' has been coined since the digested portion is not determined directly in the case of any of the nutrients. When a correction factor is applied the 'true digestibility' can be estimated. However, the only published correction factors are based on the work of Nose (1967) whereby protein faecal content was measured from a diet containing no protein.

Direct method. The direct method involves collection and measurement of total quantities of faeces excreted by fish in the aquatic environment (Tunnison *et al.* 1942). Most workers have quantitatively collected faeces from one to several times daily or at several-day intervals following feeding of a known quantity of food. Collection methods have included total removal of faeces from aquaria, troughs or tanks by water filtration, fine mesh dip nets or siphoning and filtration. Faeces have been concentrated by centrifugation, dried in an oven at 60–105 °C and stored in a desiccator prior to chemical analysis. Nutrient and crude fibre analysis is usually according to the prescribed methods of the Association of Official Analytical Chemists (1965). Coefficients of digestibility are expressed as percentages and computed as follows:

$$\text{Digestibility coefficient } \% = \left(1 - \frac{\text{Egested material}}{\text{Ingested material}} \right) \times 100$$

Indirect method. An indirect method of comparatively recent development involves use of an inert reference substance as an indicator. Chromic oxide (Cr_2O_3) or chrome green is the index substance of choice. Calculation of digestibility coefficients by this method is based on the assumption that the amount of chromic oxide in the feed (1 % or less mixture) and the amount voided in the faeces is the same over equal periods of time. Therefore digestion coefficients can be calculated for crude protein, ether extract, nitrogen-free extract (NFE) and the total digestible nutrients (TDN) following appropriate chemical analyses for the nutrients and chromic oxide in the consumed food and the faeces. This method eliminates the necessity of a quantitative collection of all faeces required by direct methods. The calculation is as follows:

$$\text{Digestibility} = 100 - \left(\frac{\% \ Cr_2O_3 \text{ in food}}{\% \ Cr_2O_3 \text{ in faeces}} \times \frac{\% \text{ Nutrient in faeces}}{\% \text{ Nutrient in food}} \times 100 \right)$$

Faecal collection methods. Although the chromic oxide method eliminates the need for total collection of faeces, satisfactory faecal sampling is essential to ensure accurate measurement of the ratio of undigested nutrient to indicator in the faeces. Most workers have ignored the fact that faecal exposure to water for varying lengths of time results in leaching of nutrients into the water. Windell *et al.* (unpublished) have shown that trough collection of faeces is subject to an experimental leaching error of 5–40%. Most nutrient leaching occurs during the first hour after defaecation.

Collection of insoluble excreta from the water by fine nets, filtration or other means is to be avoided. A stripping, milking or squeezing technique utilized by Singh & Nose (1967) likewise is subject to unacceptable experimental error resulting from the addition of milt, ova, blood and body slime. Collection of faeces by dissection from the lower one inch or less of intestine destroys many fish and may be subject to error because of lower intestinal nutrient absorption prior to defecation (Smith & Lovell 1971, 1973). A vacuum suction technique of the lowermost intestinal faecal pellet may be the method of choice (Windell, unpublished).

Chromic oxide analysis by wet acid digestion. Chromic oxide is determined according to the procedure described by Furukawa & Tusukahara (1966).

I

Replicate or triplicate 50–100 mg samples of dried food or faeces containing 1–3 mg Cr_2O_3 are wrapped in a small piece of filter paper and transferred to a digestion flask (microKjeldahl). Following the addition of 5 ml of concentrated nitric acid, and a 5-min waiting period, the sample is heated for 20 min or until a white precipitate forms. After cooling, 3 ml of perchloric acid is added and the green-coloured mixture reheated for 10 additional minutes after changing colour to yellow, orange or red. Slight cooling, addition of 50 ml of distilled water, further cooling to room temperature, is followed by transfer to and filling of a 100 ml volumetric flask. The yellow solution is mixed well, allowed to stand for 5 min, subsamples transferred to colorimetric tubes, and read at 350 mμ in a spectrophotometer. Percent chromic oxide is calculated from a prepared standard curve where $Y =$ the optical density at 350 mμ and $X =$ the Cr_2O_3 content of the sample (mg/100 ml).

Winberg's balanced equation

Winberg (1956) in the process of reviewing the published data on respiration, egestion and excretion in freshwater fish proposed a balanced energy equation that could be applied to whole fish populations. Mann (1964, 1965) utilized the method to estimate the total energy requirements of populations of several species of fish in the River Thames. Since this early work portions of the method have been reviewed by Warren & Davis, Beamish & Dickie, and Mann in the symposium volume edited by Gerking (1967). More recent reviews include that of Mann (1969), Davis & Warren (1971) and Weatherly (1972, 1976).

Winberg's equation attempts to relate metabolic rate, growth rate and food consumption rate for a unit time interval such as 24 h; each in itself difficult to measure in nature. It was proposed that given reliable values for any two of the three parameters the third can be calculated. The basic equation is simplified to read:

Energy of growth (ΔB) + energy of
metabolism (R) = physiologically useful energy

Accepting one of the basic assumptions that under natural conditions 80% of the consumed food (C) is utilized (i.e. 15% becomes faeces and 3–5% becomes excretory waste products $[F + U]$ then:

$$\Delta B + R = 0.80C$$

The equation was developed further to read:

$$C = 0.80(R + \Delta B)$$

or

$$C = 1.25(R + \Delta B).$$

Application of this method requires making a large number of simplifying assumptions that are detailed in the cited literature. Ideally each one should be verified for each species in each situation (Mann 1969). They are:

1 Under natural conditions freshwater fish assimilate 85 % of their consumed food and egest 15 %. It is now known that this is not a constant for all species (Elliott 1976).

2 Excretory products amount to 3–5 % of the unassimulated food energy. As above, this is likewise not a constant for all species (Elliott 1976).

3 The active metabolic rate in nature is two times the value obtained in the laboratory at minimal activity. There appears to be no justification that A_{met} approximates twice S_{met}. It may be much smaller or much larger (close to three times) depending on species and environment (Ware 1975a).

4 Metabolic rate varies with temperature according to the empirical curve of Krogh (1916).

5 Metabolic rate can be determined by measuring oxygen consumption and applying a calorific equivalent of 1 ml O_2 = 4.8 calories.

6 Metabolic rate is not influenced by level of feeding or type of food. This statement is not true inasmuch as the magnitude of SDA depends on quality and quantity of food (Warren & Davis 1967; Kerr 1971a; Beamish 1974; Muir & Nimii 1972; Morgan 1974).

7 Growth energy approximates to 1 kcal for every 1 g of live weight increase.

In theory the equations have generated considerable discussion, speculation and research whereas in practice there has been great difficulty in gathering and reporting acceptable data and eliminating the many assumptions. The equations have led to the publication of notable papers related to analysis of fish metabolism and growth processes (Palaheimo & Dickie 1965, 1966a, b; Kerr 1971a, b, c; Ware 1975a). Ware (1975a) developed a particularly useful approach which converts the basic energy equation into a comprehensive growth equation that considers the relation between feeding rate, food concentration in the environment, cost of locomotion involved in food search and SDA.

Nitrogen balance method

The nitrogen balance method for fish was first described by Meien *et al.* (1937) and utilized by Ivlev (1939a). A detailed description of methods has been published by Karzinkin & Krivobok (1962, 1964). No thorough review of nitrogen balance exists for fish but a number of workers have made significant contributions relating protein metabolism to aspects of growth and production (Gerking 1952, 1955, 1962, 1971; Menzel 1959, 1960; Pandian 1967a, b; Fromm & Gillette 1968; Birket 1969; Savitz 1969, 1971a, b; Iwata 1970).

Nitrogen balance (*NB*) is summarized by the following equation:

$$NB = I - F = A = R + E$$

where: I = nitrogen intake
F = faecal nitrogen
A = absorbed nitrogen
R = retained nitrogen
E = excreted nitrogen.

When the total daily nitrogen intake is less than the total outgo a fish or population is in *negative nitrogen balance*. When nitrogen intake equals outgo the animals are in *nitrogen equilibrium*, and when there is an excess of intake over outgo there exists a *positive nitrogen balance*. Growth in the form of an increase in protein occurs during a positive nitrogen balance condition.

The essentials of the nitrogen balance method involve feeding and growth experiments similar to that discussed in the preceding sections except that food, growth, egestion and excretion are considered in terms of their nitrogen content. Comparisons are made between a 'sample group' of fish and an 'experimental group' collected from nature at the same time. As soon as all fish are feeding well in captivity the sample group is killed and analysed for nitrogen content by the Kjeldahl or other standard methods. These results represent the experimental group at the beginning of the feeding and growth period. The experimental groups are fed on rations of known weight and chemical composition for a period sufficiently long to accurately measure growth. Birkett (1969) utilized a 6-week growth period but found 10–20 days sufficiently long for measurable growth to occur. They are then killed and analysed by the same techniques employed for the sample group. A greater emphasis is placed on changes in nitrogen content than on other body or food constituents. The ideal is to work with sufficient numbers of fish over the entire range of body size and water temperatures encountered in nature.

The ratio of nitrogen content to food item weight is used to compute the daily food consumption rate from the rate of nitrogen intake. Calculation is summarized by the following formula (Karzinkin & Krivobok 1964):

$$C = \frac{NI \times 100}{NC}$$

where: C = consumption as the daily ration
NI = daily intake of nitrogen in mg
NC = nitrogen content in food as percent wet weight of food.

The daily ration and nitrogen intake ration can be expressed in percent of the average fish body weight or regressed against body weight if they are not proportional. When fish consume a mixed diet the variation in the percent nitrogen of the different food organisms must be determined and the estimate of total food consumed based on the nitrogen contents of the various food organisms and their relative contributions to the diets.

Radioisotope method

Kevern (1966) measured the mean annual feeding rate but not the seasonal daily feeding rates for carp (*Cyprinus carpio*) in a natural aquatic environment to test the practicality of the radioisotopic method. Food consumption was based upon calculation of the average amount of radioisotope in the daily ingested food. Calculation depends on measurements of the equilibrium body burden, i.e. the quantity of radioisotope contained in the fish and the rates of assimilation and elimination of the isotope by the fish. Kolehmainen (1974) refined Kevern's method in order to measure the daily feeding rates of bluegill sunfish (*Lepomis macrochirus*). A small impoundment receiving low-level radioactive wastes at a nearly constant rate provided an experimental laboratory where consideration was given to the concentration of radioisotope in the fish; growth of the fish; relationship between temperature and the elimination rates of the radioisotope; concentration of the radioisotope in the food items of the fish, absorption of the radioisotope from different food items, and the proportion of different food items in the diet of the fish. The uptake values of ^{137}Cs from season to season were used to calculate the daily feeding rates for different times of the year.

Feeding rates were obtained by dividing the daily intake of ^{137}Cs by the concentration of ^{137}Cs in the diet. The formula for the daily food intake, r', was (Kevern 1966):

$$r' = \frac{I}{b_i \cdot d_i \cdot f_i}$$

where I was the daily intake of ^{137}Cs, b_i the absorption percentage of ^{137}Cs for the ith food item, d_i the concentration of ^{137}Cs in the ith food item, and f_i the proportion of the ith food item in the diet. Composition of the diet during a year was determined on the basis of stomach samples collected monthly.

It is not necessary to have radioisotopes in the water body in order to use this technique for food consumption studies. Stable elements such as K, Rb, Cs, and many others can be used. The body burden of the element is determined in the fish and the concentration of the element in the diet. Absorption of the element from the food items and elimination rates of the element from the fish can be studied in laboratory experiments. However, the percentage of the element taken up directly from the water must be determined before this technique can be used. In the case of caesium the uptake from freshwater fish is less than 1 % (Kolehmainen *et al.* 1967).

Food progression method

Methods of estimating food consumption rates of fish populations on the basis of digestion rate have not been extensively employed. However it has been assumed that the average rate at which fish in nature consume, digest and pass food through their stomachs must be equal to their average rate of consumption. Therefore it has been proposed that information on food passage rates may provide useful estimates of quantitative food consumption rates in nature. Implicit in this assumption is that estimates will be based upon comprehensive examination of food consumption under natural conditions, during all seasons of the year, at all water temperatures with consideration of diel and/or diurnal variations in feeding behaviour and seasonal food availability.

Prerequisite to calculation of the daily meal and daily ration by the food progression method is quantitative data on the rate at which food passes through the stomach. Digestion rates (gastric evacuation rate) have been reported for a number of species at one or over a narrow range of temperature

(Magnuson 1969) or over a broad range of temperature (Windell, in press) Before discussing how food consumption rates are quantitatively estimated the laboratory methods for gathering food progression data are briefly discussed. Specific details can be found in the cited literature.

Laboratory methods for measuring food progression

X-ray method. Molnár & Tölg (1960, 1962a, b) designed and utilized an ingenious X-ray method for determining gastric digestion in several piscivorous species. The fish remain alive and can be used repeatedly. The skeleton, swimbladder and otoliths of the prey fish in the stomach produce X-ray images that are easy to observe on film. A similar X-ray method was used by Edwards (1971). Mean times for test meals to reach the rectum were obtained when pieces of food were injected with barium sulphate paste, force-fed to fish and later exposed to X-ray film. However, viewing the X-ray image on a fluorescent screen and noting the position of the food mass proved to be more rapid and just as accurate.

Radioisotopic method. Peters & Hoss (1974) tagged small fish and shrimp either individually by injecting 25 uCi ^{144}CeCl$_3$ dissolved in HCl or as a group by holding the organisms for 12 h in sea water containing radioactive cerium (200 uCi ^{144}Ce/litre). Fish were fed to satiation after starvation. The gut of live fish placed in glass jars could be repeatedly measured for radioactivity in a whole-animal scintillation counter. Comparison of this method with the dried digestible organic weight technique (described later) gave similar estimates of the time to reach 99 % gastric evacuation.

Radioactive cesium has been used as a tracer (Kevern 1966) but since it is readily assimilated it is undesirable for evacuation studies. Pappas *et al.* (1973) used chromium oxide (Cr_2O_3) in estimating digestion and absorption of protein, fat, and carbohydrate by neutron activation analysis unavailable to most workers. Radioactive cerium (^{144}Ce) has been suggested as a substitute for digestion and digestibility studies because it is easily analysed in samples, very poorly assimilated by fish, permits determinations on the same fish and requires less effort (Cowey & Sargent 1972; Peters & Hoss 1974).

Water displacement method. Hunt (1960) reported rates of digestion by measuring meals and the partly-digested food recovered from the stomachs upon autopsy as volume by water displacement. The relationship between volume and weight was established by comparing these two measurements of the prey fish, *Gambusia affinis*. Volume was considered to be the equivalent of weight.

Dried digestible organic weight method. A dried digestible organic weight method was described and utilized in several laboratory experiments by Windell (1966). Each food type was analysed for its percentage of organic matter and chitin. Digestible organic matter was defined as dry weight minus ash weight and chitin weight. Rate of digestion was measured as the difference between the weight of food intake and the stomach remains at timed intervals in terms of dried digestible organic matter.

Dry weight method. Windell *et al.* (1969) reported rates of gastric evacuation measured by utilizing a dry weight method. All computations were based on percentage dry weight of the food. Subtraction of dry matter remaining in the stomach at autopsy from dry matter consumed yielded the amount of food evacuated from the stomach per unit time. It is assumed that indigestible materials such as ash, fibre, chitin and debris pose no problem with reference to gastric emptying. Comparison of this method with the dried digestible organic weight method gave equivalent results.

Laboratory feeding techniques for measuring food progression
Individual method. Difficulty in getting groups of wild fish held in individual tanks or trough compartments to simultaneously consume a measured meal requires special handling techniques (Windell 1966, 1968, 1971). A dominant and subordinate behaviour has been reported for bluegill sunfish (Gerking 1955) and many other species (Jenkins 1969). When held in groups the more dominant, aggressive fish when fasted for a short period will feed readily when food is offered. Subordinate fish observe the feeding dominants and feed after some time has elapsed. However, when individually placed in separate aquaria or trough compartments, dominant and subordinate fish often require a substantial conditioning period before feeding regularly. A 'teasing' technique developed by Windell (1966) requires that considerable caution be taken to prevent startling the fish during the feeding period. Individually-housed fish are offered food 3 or 4 times per day. If not consumed in a short period of time the food items are gently removed in 10–15 min. Consequently, most of the subordinate fish are teased into feeding on the desired food item for each experiment.

Group method. Some investigators have preferred to feed groups of fish to satiation over a period of 15 min, perform serial slaughter at intervals, freeze until time of dissection, remove stomach contents and apply the digestible organic weight method (Brett & Higgs 1970; Elliott 1972; Peters & Hoss 1974). Subsample fish groups are sacrificed initially (time 0) and at pre-determined time intervals. Data are compiled as the percentage of organic matter in the fish's stomach as milligrams organic content/100 mg dry body weight. The geometric means of these percentages is determined for each time interval and regressed as the logarithm of the percent of stomach contents against time. Because of variation in the amount of food consumed by individual fish individual measurements are deleted from subsamples on the following basis: (1) no fresh food present in the very early stages of digestion; (2) notable premature empty stomach; (3) highly-divergent contents at intermediate stages of digestion; and (4) when chronic poor or non-feeders are present.

Estimation of food consumption with food progression data
Daily feeding pattern and the modified Bajkov method. In general terms, the rate of food consumption, C, is calculated from a known rate of gut (stomach) clearance or turnover coefficient, K, determined *in situ* or from laboratory studies; and a measurement of average stomach content, $\bar{A}$, in nature. Simply stated:

$$C = K\bar{A}. \tag{1}$$

Values for K have been variously determined as previously discussed. The Bajkov (1935) method reviewed by Windell (1967) states that $K = 24/n$. where $n =$ the number of hours for complete gastric evacuation. Examples of recent applications are those by Biro (1969) and Backiel (1971). Kitchell (1970) modified the Bajkov formula to account for more rapid gastric evacuation rates in more or less continuously feeding fish so that $K = 24/2n_{50}$, where $n_{50} =$ the hours for 50% depletion. Seaburg & Moyle (1964) and Keast & Welsh (1968) performed similar modifications based on estimates of food passage rates *in situ*. The former was based on evacuation rates determined from subsamples of fishes held in food-free cages. The latter was determined by assuming that no food was consumed during a specific short period of the diel cycle and the resulting change in average stomach content represented the evacuation rate. Digestion rate was similarly employed by Fortunatova (Popova 1967) and Darnell & Meierotto (1962) in reconstructing food items for daily ration determinations. More sophisticated analyses of gastric digestion data are reported by Brett & Higgs (1970) and Elliott (1972, 1975b). Tyler (1970) also developed an exponential model of the gastric evacuation process and demonstrated that these kinds of data could be employed in predicting stomach content after sequential meals. Thorpe (MS) effectively coupled the exponential model with *in situ* experiments to determine daily rations.

Fundamental to the application of laboratory information on evacuation rates is the assumption that K varies independently of $\bar{A}$. Studies by Windell (1967), Kitchell & Windell (1968) and Tyler (1970) confirmed the assumption and a more recent report by Norris *et al.* (1973) indicated some features of the homeostatic mechanism.

Thus, temperature becomes the variable of almost singular importance in determining K values. Small fish generally consume proportionately more food per unit weight and an effect has been associated with body size (Shirahata 1966; Kitchell 1970; Magnuson 1969). The latter is quantitatively subtle relative to the thermal effect but becomes important if attempts are made to extrapolate to the total fish population or if mean size differs substantially between laboratory and field applications.

Based on laboratory experiments to determine n_{50} values at 5, 10, 15, 20 and 25 °C (Kitchell 1970), Kitchell *et al.* (1972) reported that K values for 18–32 g bluegill sunfish, *Lepomis macrochirus* were related to temperature, T, by the equation:

$$K = 0 \cdot 067(T)^{1 \cdot 22}. \tag{2}$$

No size effect was perceived; however, the evacuation rates at any temperature were generally more rapid than those reported from comparable experiments with much larger bluegill (Windell 1967). Kitchell *et al.* (1972) reasoned that the relation between K and body size could be determined by setting equation (1) to its upper limit; i.e.

$$K = \frac{A_{max}}{C_{max}}. \tag{3}$$

Maximum stomach content, A_{max}, was derived by feeding 0·5–55 g fish to satiation. The relation between wet body weight, W, of fish and A_{max} in dry weight units was determined as:

$$A_{max} = 0 \cdot 007(W)^{0 \cdot 85}. \tag{4}$$

Values for C_{max} were determined from *ad libitum* feeding experiments at constant 22 °C and 12L:12D photoperiod reported for 2–90 g bluegill by McComish (1970). Substituting into equation (3) gave the resultant relation between K and fish weight as:

$$K = 5\cdot58(W)^{-0.23}. \tag{5}$$

Combining the results of equations (2) and (5) for fish weighing 5–45 g at temperatures of 5–25 °C gave the multiple regression for K values for the bluegill as:

$$\ln K = 1\cdot9602 + 1\cdot2092(\ln T) - 0\cdot2329(\ln W) \tag{6}$$

To evaluate the adequacy of equation (6) it was employed with equation (4) to predict maximum daily rations for comparison with those determined from *ad libitum* feeding experiments under seasonal photo-thermal regimes (McComish 1970). The results are summarized in Table 10.1.

TABLE 10.1 Comparison of calculated and observed maximum daily rations for the bluegill sunfish (*Lepomis macrochirus*). Observed data for fish weight, temperature and maximum rations are from selected monthly periods of *ad libitum* feeding experiments reported by McComish (1970). Calculated values for A_{max} are from equation (4), converted to wet weights as a percent of fish weight, and from equation (6) for values of K. (From Kitchell *et al.* 1972)

| | | | | Maximum daily ration (%) | | |
| | | | | | Observed | |
$\bar{X}$ fish wet weight (g)	$\bar{X}$ temp. (°C)	A_{max} (%)	K	Calculated	$\bar{X}$	Range
6·2	23·1	3·08	4·10	12·4	12·8	11·3–14·3
14·7	26·8	2·71	4·01	10·9	11·5	7·0–13·6
51·4	5·7	2·24	0·46	1·0	0·6	0·5– 0·7
208·0	21·6	1·82	1·67	3·0	3·6	2·4– 5·2
223·0	15·7	1·80	1·11	1·9	1·8	1·2– 2·7

Calculated and observed values generally correspond for the range of temperature and fish sizes considered. However, it appears that K values from equation (6) may slightly overestimate maximum rations at low temperatures. A second overestimate may be introduced with the assumption that A_{max} values are constant for a 24-h period.

As previously stated, recent studies generally confirm the assumption that K and A vary independently; i.e. that a variety of food items common to the bluegill diet are digested at much the same rate (Windell 1967). Although differential rates of evacuation of digestible and indigestible fractions (e.g. chitin) have been documented (Kionka & Windell 1972) the total effect on estimates of food turnover is minimized over extended sampling intervals and/or if the units employed to estimate evacuation rates are wet or dry weight measures of the total stomach content.

Given the above and accepting the application in Table 10.1 as confirmation of predictability, it is concluded that a formulation like that in equation (6) can be applied directly to nature when combined with adequate sampling to determine the temporal variation in A values (Kitchell *et al.* 1972).

Daily feeding pattern and food progression method. A method for a nearly direct estimation of daily food consumption by the herbivorous cichlid fishes *Sarotherodon niloticus* (L.) and *Haplochromis nigripinnus* Regan was developed on the basis of cyclic feed patterns (Moriarty & Moriarty 1973). Fish are caught by trawling for a period of up to 15 min at 2-h intervals daily and seasonally. Collected fish are immediately processed by weighing, measuring, separation into size groups, followed by dissection and removal of stomach and intestinal contents into individual containers. All samples are dried to a constant weight and cooled in a desiccator before weighing. Dry weights of stomach and intestine contents are averaged for each 2-h sample of fish from each size group. Dry weight values are plotted against time of day (hours) using a different plot for each size group of fish. Because the number of fish in each sample are often different, weighted regressions and variance are calculated in order to obtain lines of best fit. This procedure provides not only an estimate for the average quantity consumed per day by individual fish but reliable information on daily feeding patterns.

Accuracy of the food consumption estimates may be influenced by a number of variables. These include variation in the time at which individual fish begin and stop feeding, rate at which they feed, the maximum amount accumulated in the stomach, rate at which food moves from the stomach to the intestine while the fish are feeding and the assumption that food availability is equally accessible to all members of each group. Herbivorous species which feed continuously on a diurnal basis ingest and accumulate material in their stomach at an essentially constant rate. Therefore the rate of passage of algae from the stomach to the intestine during the feeding should also be a constant (Moriarty & Moriarty 1973).

A field-laboratory method of applying digestion data was developed which provides estimates of daily consumption rate for an average individual from a field population (Swenson & Smith 1973). The technique appears suitable for general use and can describe daily consumption for a given day, of individual prey species and feeding chronology within a given day. When used in conjunction with information on food availability, the method permits assessment of influences of food consumption and time of feeding. Estimates of consumption rate combined with information on growth rate allow estimates of conversion efficiency. Evaluation of effects of predation on prey species is also possible.

All sizes of fish and sizes of meals encountered in the field are included in the laboratory work. The method used to estimate food consumption is summarized in the equation:

$$C = \Sigma t \, \Sigma s \frac{(\Sigma f \, SC)}{F}$$

where C = daily food consumption in grammes for the average fish; SC = undigested weight of stomach contents for foods of a given size, not more than 90% digested, consumed during a time period; f = summation corrected weight of stomach content for all fish in the sample, having consumed food of a size, during a time period; F = number of fish in the sample which could have contained food of a size, in a state of digestion not exceeding 90%, during a time period; s = summation of food sizes; t = summation of time. This method is another approach which allows description of consumption for a given day. By making estimates of consumption for all periods of a day a means is provided of estimating possible bias associated with periodic feeding.

Daily feeding pattern and defaecation method. The feeding of the cichlid fish *Sarotherodon mossambicus* in Lake Sibaya, KwaZulu, South Africa, provides a model for estimation of food consumption by means of a defaecation method (Bowen 1976). This method is based upon the assumption that consumption (C) during a given time period is related to the change in the amount of gut content during that time (ΔA) plus the amount of material defaecated (D) during that time. It is assumed that if the amount of food in the gut increases ($\Delta \bar{A} > 0$), consumption will have been equal to that increase plus any material defaecated. If the amount of food in the gut decreases ($\Delta \bar{A} < 0$) consumption will have been equal to any amount by which the amount of material defaecated exceeded that decrease. Consumption is zero when the amount of material defaecated is equal to a negative change in amount of gut content.

Diel seine collections are made at 2-h intervals. Half of each catch of 30 is fixed immediately in formalin and half placed in cages supported by 0·3 m long legs. This holds the fish under wave, light and temperature conditions comparable to conditions in the area where they were collected and allows defaecation, but prevents feeding from the lake substrate. Exactly 3 h after capture, these fish are fixed in formalin. In the laboratory, the gut content is carefully removed, dried to constant weight, cooled in a desiccator and weighed. The fish, including intestinal tract, is dried and weighed in a similar way.

Defaecation rate (D_t), defined as mg of gut content defaecated per hour, is calculated for each 2-h interval starting at time t as:

$$D_t = \frac{\bar{A}_t - \bar{A}H_t}{3}$$

where: $\bar{A}_t$ = mean weight of gut content at time t and fixed immediately, and
$\bar{A}H_t$ = mean weight of gut contant at time t and held for 3 h.

Rate of change in weight of gut content ($\Delta\bar{A}_t$) over the 2-h interval starting time t, expressed in mg per h, is calculated as:

$$\Delta\bar{A}_t = \frac{\bar{A}_{t+2} - \bar{A}_t}{2}$$

where: $\bar{A}_{t+2}$ = mean weight of gut content at time $t + 2$ h and fixed immediately.

Consumption rate for the 2-h interval starting time t (C_t), in mg per h, is calculated as:

$$C_t = \Delta A_t + D_t.$$

Estimated consumption rates are used to calculate the daily meal as mean hourly consumption rate by multiplying by 24 h.

Defaecation rate is used to calculate consumption by assuming that consumption is equal to any positive change in gut content for time periods when defaecation cannot be estimated.

The major objection to the method is that handling effects may significantly affect the rate of defaecation of held specimens and result in over estimation of defaecation.

11

Investigation of Mortalities in the Wild

GORDON R BELL

Introduction

It is the purpose of this chapter to discuss methods and techniques for the systematic investigation of unusual levels of mortality in wild fish populations, a subject previously dealt with from another viewpoint by Paling (1968). Whether or not a level is 'unusual' or alarming will have to remain a subjective decision. Most of the discussion will deal with mortalities that occur over a few hours or a few days; severe rather than chronic losses. In other words, situations where there is likely to be a single cause or single group of causes of the mortalities. Slowly occurring losses are more likely to have a variety of causes each requiring special investigation, and it is not possible to discuss each particular investigative procedure. The general, practical approaches to investigating the causes of fish mortalities will be dealt with to the point where specialized procedures and techniques such as chemical analyses are required. At this point key references, mostly in English, will be given so that the non-specialist reader can seek more detailed information. In the space allotted to this chapter little more than general guidance can be given. Emphasis will be placed on the widespread and valuable trout and salmon species but the principles and procedures should have wide applicability.

Broadly speaking the three most common causes of mortalities are non-infectious ('organic', abiotic) disease, infectious disease and predation. (Disease is defined as an interruption, cessation or disorder of body functions, systems or organs.) More specific causes of mortalities are listed for convenience of discussion under these three categories in Table 11.1 and show the great variety of agents and conditions that may be involved. Non-infectious disease may be caused by natural or man-made conditions, and the naturally-caused disease may arise from physiological changes associated with the life cycle of the fish, or from alteration of the environment. Either of these natural causes can result in the rapid death of many fish but physiological changes will usually only affect one species. Multispecies kills, especially if the species are very different, are most likely to be environmentally caused, but environmental degradation whether natural or man-made can also be selective for species, sex or age. The victim fish may be selected because of their distribution relative to gradients of pollution, their feeding habits, and susceptibility to certain poisons or general environmental degradation. Jones

TABLE 11.1. Some direct and indirect causes of fish mortality. (With selected references)

Non-infectious disease ('organic' or abiotic disease)	Infectious disease* (from indigenous or alien organisms)	Predation
The fish:	Bacteria	Cannibalism
Physiological and metabolic changes, e.g. pre- and post-spawning alterations, overwintering starvation; malnutrition (Ashley 1972; Snieszko 1972)	Algae (Hoffman *et al.* 1965)	Other species of fish
	Fungi	Birds
The environment:	Viruses	Mammals,
(a) Natural causes, e.g. decaying organic matter such as spawned-out fish, phyto- and zooplankton, leaves; turnover of water bodies (producing anaerobiosis, ammonia, H_2S, acids) (Bell & Hoskins 1971); abnormal thermal conditions (Ash *et al.* 1974); Fryer *et al.* 1976); toxic algae (Matida *et al.* 1967);	Protozoan parasites Metazoan parasites Insect infestations (more rarely)	including man Reptiles Invertebrates
(b) Man-made causes (pollution†), e.g. organic and inorganic poisons and/or their effects on food supply; high BOD wastes; supersaturation (Ebel 1969); thermal pollution (Jones 1964; Fryer *et al.* 1976); transfaunation (Hoffman 1970), and transfloration leading to destructive habitat competition. Introduction of disease agents or predators may also be regarded as 'pollution'.		

*Throughout the text infectious diseases will refer to all those caused by living agents, including metazoan parasites.

†There is no universally accepted definition of pollution, nor is there likely to be, but one of the best was given in *GESAMP* (in press) and it is presented here in slightly modified form (proposed amendments to the original definition are included): Pollution means the introduction by man, directly or indirectly, of substances or energy into the environment which results or is likely to result in such deleterious effects as harm to living or non-living resources, hazards to human health, hindrance to man's activities, impairment of quality for use of air, land or water, and reduction of amenities.

(1964) and Tarzwell (1965) dealt with many other biological problems associated with water pollution.

It is naive to expect that biologically caused fish mortalities, especially in the wild, will likely have a single cause but it is reasonable to expect that a major or principal cause can be determined. Infectious diseases of fishes are usually caused by organisms that are a constant component of the host's environment. Snieszko (1974) and Wedemeyer *et al.* (1976) have ably explained the interrelationships among host, pathogen, and environment that can lead to outbreaks of disease. Epizootics can also be caused by exposure of the host to alien organisms such as *Myxosoma cerebralis* (cause of whirling disease) in Michigan and IPN virus in Britain, but thanks in part to present and proposed national and international disease control measures outbreaks of exotic diseases should become relatively less common. Frequently, then, the investigator must deal with an ecological problem in which the ultimate cause of death, say from *Aeromonas liquefaciens* bacteremia, may not be the primary cause (Haley *et al.* 1967). Indeed, one's final assessment of the problem often appears frustratingly, and to some, suspiciously, vague and discursive because of the many interacting factors involved.

Even contemporary literature on the effects of pollution on freshwater fish is so immense that it can best be dealt with here by referring the reader to the relevant section in the annual *Literature Review Issue* of the *Journal of the Water Pollution Control Federation*. (For example, Effects of pollution on freshwater fish, *J. Water Poll. Control Fed.*, **48**(6), 1545 (1976).) The book by Jones (1964) provides useful basic information and concepts on the effects of pollution on freshwater fishes.

In contrast to losses due to severe outbreaks of disease when carcasses and moribund fish (other than larval forms or fry) may be evident, predated fish simply disappear unnoticed except in closely watched populations. (The absence of dead or dying fish in an affected population does not necessarily indicate predation.) Stocks of fish in the wild are continually subjected to predation of fluctuating intensity by some or all of the agents listed under 'Predation' in Table 11.1 and the surplus prey becomes the established population: predator and prey populations are usually in dynamic equilibrium. (The theory and dynamics of predator–prey relationships (including cannibalism) have been discussed by Ricker (1954) and Weatherley (1972).) However, 'when a newly introduced predator population starts to consume a prey population that has been in equilibrium with its competitors and other predators, the first consequence is an increase in the mortality rate of the prey population' (Royce 1972). Predation could also be increased by an increase in the number of sick fish, perhaps a useful mechanism in controlling the spread of fish diseases provided the predator does not act as a disease vector (Eskildsen & Jörgensen 1973) or intermediate host for parasites. This is an instance in which disease could account indirectly for the mysterious disappearance of appreciable numbers of fish. Although we are dealing with fish rather than egg mortalities, it is interesting to note that insects might cause significant losses in stock by preying upon the incubating eggs (Astafyeva 1964; Claire & Phillips 1968). If stocks are declining and fish are unaccountably disappearing, then one might look for new predators or for some disturbing factor that has favoured resident predators. Fishing is a special instance of predation, and if it had been conducted without the knowledge of the investigator, could lead to a frustrating investigation. Sometimes the sudden appearance of numbers of dead scrap fish and/or juvenile food fishes has a simple answer—legal or illegal netting in the area!

Contingency plans for investigating fish mortalities: a 'fish kill team'

Alarming mortalities of fish in the wild are quite common throughout the world, indeed in industrialized countries such as the USA deaths of millions of fish are compiled each year from a multitude of incidents. (The Environmental Protection Agency reported 37·8 million fish killed by pollution in 1973 and a total of 336·5 million reported killed since 1960. Detailed analysis of the reports given are instructive.) Such incidents often reported as 'die-offs' (implying natural causes) and 'kills' (implying pollution) usually require prompt, organized and multidisciplined response for their successful investigation. It would be wise, therefore, if area managers of fisheries resources prepared contingency plans for the investigation of these incidents, and a so-called fish kill team appears to be essential to any plan. The purpose of the team would be to discover the cause(s) of the incident and take or suggest appropriate and feasible corrective action, or to document the case for legal action or for further study.

Also, in anticipation of investigation of fish mortalities, there should be basic information available on normal features of important species of fish—features included in the disciplines of anatomy, histology, haematology and behaviour. In this regard the following selected references are particularly useful (most apply to the widely distributed and valuable salmonids): Hawkins & Mawdesley-Thomas (1972), Blaxhall & Daisley (1973), McCarthy *et al.* (1973, 1975), Anderson & Mitchum (1974), Ezzat *et al.* (1974), Lehmann & Stürenberg (1974, 1975), Meyer (1975), Smith & Bell (1975) and Grizzle & Rodgers (1976). In addition, Yasutake & Wales are preparing a manuscript on the histology of Pacific salmon species (W. Yasutake, personal communication).

Organization

A leader and several deputy leaders should be appointed and the existence and responsibilities of the team should be well publicized. An emergency telephone number should be listed and the team should have priority in calling for assistance and equipment. The leader should be a person able to assess the type of expertise needed, at least for the preliminary investigation, and to co-ordinate the work and findings of specialists. Aside from the leader, the composition of the team may be changed according to the nature of the incident and the availability of appropriate specialists. It is also often advisable to appoint one person to give information to the press concerning findings and progress of the investigation. In some situations the investigator may form a team of one unbelievably versatile and omnipresent person!

Operation

Although the approach to each incident may differ in detail the leader should take the following steps:

(a) Conduct a personal reconnaissance of the affected area and if possible the entire water body, or discuss the situation with someone on site, preferably a biologist who knows the locality and its aquatic life. Many 'panic' situations are over-rated or misunderstood (e.g. crustacean molts, post-spawning deaths of kokanee [*Oncorhynchus nerka*]) and the 'tragedy' is found to be a normal part of the life cycle. In large bodies of water aerial reconnaissance may be advisable and radio contact with and among a ground party may be expeditious.

(b) Consult chosen specialists—using maps and charts of the area—regarding strategy and tactics of the investigation.

(c) Assemble supplies and equipment (see Table 11.2) and proceed to the site.

(d) Collect and preserve representative samples, gather information, make careful observations and/or set up a base of operation in consultation with a person who has useful local knowledge, then proceed with the investigation.

However this is done, speed and care in sampling and preservation of the samples are often critical because conditions can change rapidly and opportunities are lost. Photographs of the incident, or typical features of it, may prove valuable later on.

Further discussion and other approaches have been given by Mackenthun (1969) in his Chapter 4 and by Tracy & Bernhardt (1973).

The investigation will proceed with increasing detail and specialization until the cause is discovered. A guide to the process of discovery is given in the text below.

TABLE 11.2. Suggested basic field kit

Instruments	Nets and containers	Miscellaneous
Dissolved oxygen probe	Long-handled dip nets	Stains (Gram and methylene blue)
pH meter	Gill nets	Formalin or paraformaldehyde
Conductivity meter	Seine nets	Concentrated HNO_3
Water chemistry kit*	Plastic bags, sterile and	Ethanol
Microscopes: Bright field	non-sterile	Sterile swabs and transport me-
and phase contrast (low	Buckets	dium
power, high dry and oil	Bottles, glass and plastic	Heparinized capillary tubes (for
immersion objectives);	Plastic graduated cylin-	preparing blood smears)
slides, coverslips and	cylinders	Propane torch
lenspaper. Stereoscopic,	Hypodermic syringes and	Thermometer
or 3× and 6× hand	needles or 'Vacutainers'	Cloth and/or paper towels
lens	(see footnote, p. 263)	Tape measure
Camera with film and	Ice chest and ice	Scale card
flash; close-up lens		Digital counter
Binoculars		Chest waders
Dissecting instruments		Life jacket
		First-aid kit
		Writing equipment
		Labels
		Standard Methods (Anon. 1976, or later edition)

Preliminary, systematic on-site examination and sampling

If no cause is immediately obvious, the team must begin systematically sampling and gathering information on:

*For example, the Hach Chemical Co., Box 907, Ames, Iowa 50010, USA, produces useful field kits. (Mention of a product is for information only and does not imply endorsement by the Fisheries and Marine Service.)

The aquatic environment

Representative samples of several litres of water should be taken immediately in one or more clean, sample-rinsed ($3 \times$) glass (with Teflon-lined cap) and plastic (hard polyethylene, or polycarbonate) vessels, sealed securely, protected from heat and sunlight and labelled with the date, time, location, depth and any other relevant information. Both types of containers are recommended unless one knows what analyses will be conducted because, for example, polyethylene is better for mercury-containing samples (Traversy 1971) and for fluoride but plastic is generally less desirable because it may leach or absorb organic chemicals. All sampling equipment should be scrupulously clean so that it will not be a source of contamination. Glass bottles for inorganic analysis samples should be rinsed with conc. HNO_3 and then with glass-distilled water. Necessary cleaning methods and the appropriate composition of the collecting vessel are indicated in Anon. (1976). Samples should be identified and safeguarded so as to preserve the continuity of legal evidence needed in possible litigation. In this regard the investigator would do well to read Sullivan & Roberts (1975). It is imperative, particularly in well flushed areas, to obtain a water sample as soon as possible after the incident, so a person on scene should be instructed to do so pending the arrival of the team. Samples should be obtained from the active problem area, and for comparison, from above and below the affected area in a stream, or outside the mortality area in a lake. Note any unusual colour, odour, and if the water is turbid, take and preserve a sample for the microscopic examination of particulate matter, including plankton, using methods given in *Standard Methods* (Anon. 1976).

The method of preservation of the sample depends upon the nature of subsequent tests, no single method being uniformly applicable, but since the tests to be conducted are often not immediately known because such decisions are based on the results of field observations, the best approach is to refrigerate (ca. 4 °C) and/or deep freeze (ca. -20 °C). But samples for inorganic analysis should not be frozen. To be really safe samples should be divided and preserved by a variety of preservation methods, including $\leq 1 \%$ (final conc.) formalin for biological investigations. In any case, samples should be tested and analysed as soon as possible because the composition of the sample may change critically. 'In general, it can be stated that temperature, pH, specific conductance and dissolved gas determinations should be carried out in the field. Samples for metal analysis can be preserved by the addition of nitric acid [to $\geq$ pH 2], and samples for the determinations of such biodegradable substances as nitrates, phosphates, and surfactants can be preserved by the addition of mercuric chloride.* It is advisable, however, to select the method of analysis and determine what preservative is recommended for that particular determination before adding preservative to any sample, as preservatives may interfere with some determinations' (Anon. 1972a, p. V-11). Appropriate preservatives and methods for a variety of determinations are listed in Anon. (1976) along with minimum volumes needed for various tests.

When sample collecting has been completed, note or investigate prevailing currents because carcasses or moribund fish might have drifted away from the affected area.

In submitting samples to a laboratory be sure to state whom the analyst should contact, the degree of urgency, what you want analysed, and include a summary of field observations and any other background information.

For water quality criteria see McKee & Wolf (1963), EIFAC (1973a); for toxicity of power plant chemicals, Becker & Thatcher (1973); for fish toxicity testing, EIFAC (1975).

The terrestrial environment

The investigator should find out the location, nature and discharge areas of nearby industries, including sewage treatment plants. Tactful questioning of managers may reveal some qualitatively or quantitatively unusual operational procedure that might explain the incident. It is often wise also to conduct independent investigations, particularly if one has suspicions. Local residents should be questioned about weather conditions, any unusual activities of man such as insecticide spraying and other agricultural activities. If local weather observations are recorded, these should be examined for unusual patterns that might have affected the body of water (Bell & Hoskins 1971).

Although she discusses marine conditions, Brongersma-Sanders (1957) presents some very instructive case histories of mass mortalities related to climatic conditions.

The fish

Selection of samples and methods of preservation. If the number of moribund specimens is limited, one should immediately take, aseptically if possible, a

---

*Refrigeration is preferred.

blood sample in a vessel ('Vacutainers'* for example) containing an anti-coagulant such as ethylenediamine tetra-acetate (preferred) or heparin (Blaxhall & Daisley 1973; Lehmann & Stürenberg 1974), and also prepare several blood smears according to the method of Amlacher (1970). Cardiac puncture is usually most convenient (Lehmann & Stürenberg 1974) but other sites might be used (Smith & Bell 1975). Blood samples should be refrigerated for chemical determinations, including routine haematology, and smears should be labelled and stored in a slide box for later examination, along with gill and skin mucus smears made at this time (see p. 268). It might also be useful to collect scales and/or otoliths for ageing and history of the fish. Typical victims, along with an identifying label and size scale (Professional Tape Co. Inc., Riverside, Ill. 60546, USA, markets a combined label and scale), should be photographed, preferably in colour. An assessment of the numbers, sizes and species of fish affected should be made, especially if there is a possibility of compensation.

Moribund fish are ideal samples because they are suitable for all types of examination but fish that have been dead for several hours at temperatures of ca. 15 °C or more are poor specimens for histopathology and microbiology because of tissue decomposition and secondary invasions. If there is little or no choice, decomposing specimens might fruitfully be examined for parasite infections and/or chemical contamination. However, at least with salmonids, one can obtain pure cultures of bacteria from the kidney of putrefying fish provided the kidney membrane is intact. As with chemical determinations of the water, diagnostic tests can only be as 'good' (i.e. accurate) as the sample, and choice of the method of preservation depends upon the tests to be conducted. Since these tests are often not decided upon at the time of collection, the safest course is to use several methods: any that permit culturing of disease agents and any that permit histopathology and identification of parasites. If it is possible in the field to deduce at least the general cause of the incident using the rationale outlined below, appropriate methods of preservation can be decided upon. Suggested methods, A to D, are given in the subsequent section and are listed in order of decreasing preference for each deduced cause.

1   Environmental stress or poisoning—synchronous morbidity, often multi-species. (Method A, B, C.)

2   Microbial infections (viruses, bacteria, protozoa and fungi [molds])—

*An evacuated tube and a syringe system marketed by Becton, Dickinson Co., Rutherford, New Jersey.

specimens have grossly visible external and/or internal lesions, haemorrhagic areas, swellings, suppurations, ulcers or discoloured areas. Gills of moribund specimens may be pale, clubbed, and fish covered with heavy slime. Death or debilitation usually occurs over several days or weeks; usually one species affected. (Method A, C, D.)

3   Metazoan infections or 'infestations' (crustaceans, leeches, helminths)—parasites often visible to the naked eye or with a hand lens, but some may not be easily recognizable. Buccal cavity may be invaded and the operculum distended by a mass of organisms. Small gill monogeneans, *Diplostomulum* in the eye (causing cataracts and blindness), and metacercariae such as of *Tetracotyle* around the heart require examination of dissected organs under a stereoscopic microscope. Death and debilitation slow, and host range usually narrow. (Method A, B, C, D.)

Methods of preservation and fixation. The objective of the various methods of preservation and fixation is to retard or halt the degenerative processes in the tissues but in such a way that the cause(s) of the event can be discovered. Fixatives should preserve tissues in as lifelike a way as possible, i.e. without causing artefacts that might mask critical features, or be misleading (Bucke 1972).

Freshly dead, iced fish are almost as useful as moribund specimens but frozen specimens are nearly useless for histopathology because the tissue structure is destroyed. On the other hand, formalin and other fixatives cannot be used, if diagnosis involves the culturing of live microorganisms, because they usually sterilize the specimen. Fixed tissue can, however, be useful if the invading microorganism has a characteristic morphology. Metazoa and many protozoa are identified by microscopic features but bacteria cannot be identified by morphology alone. Helminths and some metazoans are distorted and may be extremely difficult, perhaps impossible, to identify if they are fixed in formalin. They should be killed quickly in 70–80 °C water and then placed in fixative, or killed directly in a hot fixative.

If possible, include several apparently healthy specimens of the same species, sex and size for comparison.

Preservation of live fish
Method A: Shipment in water. Live fry or fingerlings can be transported or shipped over many hours in a polyethylene bag (minimum of 0·1 mm thick-

ness) partly filled with ice-cold water. As a rough rule of thumb, put 10–12 fry and 4–6 fingerlings per half gallon of water. Flush the water with pure oxygen (preferably) or air, and seal the bag (several knots in the plastic will do) leaving 3–5 times as much gas volume as water. Seal this bag inside another and place the double bag in an insulated container, such as a styrofoam ice chest, packed with pieces of ice. Seal and ship.

If the fish are to be retained for observation upon receipt at the laboratory, follow the guidelines given in Anon. (1974a).

Preservation of dead fish, tissues or parasites
Method B: Iced specimens. Moribund fish or ones that have been dead for 1 or 2 h can be effectively shipped on ice in insulated containers (e.g. styrofoam coolers) if they are received within 24 h at the laboratory. Fish that have been dead for several hours at 15 °C or greater are usually poor specimens because of tissue decomposition and secondary invasions. Ice in individual, closed polyethylene bags (domestic thickness would do), or at least separate the healthy from diseased specimens.

Method C: Frozen specimens. Frozen specimens shipped in well-insulated containers (e.g. styrofoam coolers), especially those packed with dry ice (solid carbon dioxide) rather than 'wet' ice, can travel satisfactorily for 1–2 days. Ice in individual, closed polyethylene bags (domestic thickness would do), or at least separate the healthy from diseased specimens.

If dry ice is used, provide adequate venting so that gas pressure does not build up in the shipping container. (Consult shipping regulations about requirements for special labelling of the package (Wolf 1970).) Freeze the specimens and seal, individually if possible, in gas-tight glass or metal containers to prevent the high concentrations of acid-generating carbon dioxide from killing microorganisms which might be cultured for diagnosis. Most fish viruses survive for short periods at least in tissues held at −20 °C or lower (Wolf 1970).

For organic chemical analysis especially, moribund or recently dead specimens should be individually wrapped in acetone-washed aluminum foil and placed in individual polyethylene bags for freezing. As a practical compromise other forms of clean wrapping should suffice.

Method D: Fixation in formalin. Place the moribund or just dead specimens in a glass or plastic container (metal containers often rust undesirably) and add 10–20 times the volume of 10% formalin to the volume of specimen. Most of the musculature can be filleted if it is necessary to reduce the volume of specimen. Fixation is improved if the final solution contains 0·9–1·0% sodium chloride, i.e. 0·9–1·0 g/100 cc of 10% formalin. Further improvement may be obtained by adding an excess of calcium carbonate (chalk or marble chips) to the fixative, or by diluting the concentrated formalin with 0·1 M phosphate buffer, pH 7·2. However, neither of these additions is essential.

To reduce the bulk of the field kit Lowe–McConnell (Chapter 3, p. 54) suggests the substitution of formalin by powdered paraformaldehyde (trioxymethylene).

Fry can be preserved intact but larger fish should be carefully slit along at least two-thirds the length of the abdomen, and through the brain case to facilitate the penetration of fixative. Also slit tissues or tumours that are more than 1 cm thick.

It is unnecessary to submit the whole fish if, for example, a large fish has strictly localized abnormalities. A neoplasm or other affected area can be excised and fixed but identify the locations of the excised specimen, photographically if possible.

The fixed specimen can be shipped immediately, as it is (but only in the full volume of formalin), or after at least 4 days in fixative it may be removed and wrapped in fixative-soaked material. The wrapped specimen can then be shipped in sealed plastic bags suitably protected.

There are many other fixatives and special techniques designed for particular uses (see Bucke 1972) but formalin is probably the best general fixative. Its main disadvantage is that it penetrates slowly. For rapid fixation and good cytological detail Bouin's solution is recommended for fish tissue (J. Bagshaw, personal communication) but it should be replaced in the sample with 70% ethanol after a week or so of fixation, a possible disadvantage in the field. Ethyl, methyl or propyl alcohol should only be used directly as a last resort in preserving fish tissue.

Systematic examination of specimen (gross pathology)

Amlacher (1970), Reichenbach-Klinke (1973) and Klontz (1973) have described procedures for the systematic gross examination of specimens, and the first two authors gave a list of possible causes of disease, mostly infectious, based on clinical signs. (A hand lens or stereomicroscope could be beneficial.) Further information on disease may also be found in the classic texts of Davis (1953) and Schäperclaus (1954), and in the practical treatise of Wood (1974). Healthy or at least asymptomatic fish should be examined first grossly and microscopically unless the investigator is familiar with the species. Particular attention should be paid to the gills of victim fish as a vulnerable and sensitive target organ. If the stomach is full of fresh feed, this suggests that the affected fish was not likely to have been suffering from an infectious disease, which usually debilitates the host over days or weeks, but from a relatively abrupt change in the environment leading to non-infectious disease. On the other hand, an empty stomach could suggest either infectious disease or slowly deteriorating environmental conditions.

Detailed information (suitable also for use in the next section) on parasitic algae, fungi, protozoa and certain metazoa has been given by Bykhovskaya-Pavlovskaya (1962, 1964), Hoffman (1967) and Dogiel *et al.* (1970); on crustaceans by Kabata (1970), and on fungi (molds) by Scott (1964) and Wolke (1975). For more precise taxonomy of the saprolegniales and the genus *Dermocystidium* than given in the papers on fungal infections, consult Dick (1973) and Perkins (1974) respectively. For aspects of fungal pathology see Wilson (1976). Common bacterial diseases, mostly those affecting salmonids, were discussed by Bullock *et al.* (1971), and virus diseases by Wolf (1972) but it is unlikely that one could make other than a tentative diagnosis of disease caused by these agents, malnourishment or poisons, on the basis of gross clinical signs alone. The necessary microscopic and culture techniques will be discussed next.

Microscopic examination, culturing and chemical analysis

If the cause of the incident is still not apparent, it may be necessary to examine samples in much greater detail, and the numerous specialized diagnostic and identification procedures can be time consuming. But the investigator would probably have some suspicions to suggest the course of further work and avoid 'blind' testing. Many fish diseases, especially microbial, nutritional or environmental ones, cannot be diagnosed without the aid of culturing techniques, histopathology or chemical analysis. Ultimately, diagnosis may only be made on the sum of evidence, not on the basis of one test.

Klontz (1973) presented a detailed procedure including photographs, for the systematic post-mortem examination of trout that can apply to many species of fish. Meyer (1972) gave briefer but very useful procedures for presumptively identifying the causative agent of an epizootic and discussed noteworthy instances.

Microscopic examination

Fish. In the absence of any detected abnormalities examination of the fish should proceed systematically from the exterior to the interior (do not incise the intestine accidentally and release massive contamination) as for gross pathology, but if there are only a few intact, fresh specimens suitable for bacterial culturing, then the procedure for culturing (p. 270) should be carried out first lest tissues become contaminated. Otherwise, fresh wet mounts of gill filaments, skin scrapings, peritoneal fluids and expressed faeces should be examined microscopically first because the more involved culturing procedures may be obviated. For example, one might readily detect such ectoparasites as *Costia, Trichodina* or *Gyrodactylus* in skin scrapings. Phase contrast microscopy can be invaluable in detecting and identifying many parasites.

Gill lamellae should be examined under objectives from 10 to 100× for lesions, cysts, swellings, clubbing, excess mucus, protozoa, monogenea and other organisms. Heavy infections of *Flexibacter* spp. and other bacteria can be seen under bright field or phase contrast microscopy but a Gram stain (see any text on bacteriology for this basic procedure) of gill smears is often a more sensitive means of detection. Faeces diluted with physiological saline should be examined for protozoa such as *Hexamita*. The culprit should in all instances show itself in considerable numbers. A few bacteria are normal on the skin, the faeces contain millions per gramme, and the peritoneal fluid should be sterile or nearly so (Bullock & Snieszko 1969).

The brain and the cartilage of the brain case should be examined for parasites, especially *Myxosoma cerebralis* (Anon. 1975b) in the latter. *Myxobolus* spp. that the untrained eye might confuse with *M. cerebralis* can occur in the brain of apparently healthy salmonids (Bell & Margolis 1976). Metacercariae of *Diplostomulum* spp. may also be found in the brain and eyes. Internal organs should be examined for helminths.

Migrating stages of histozoic helminths can cause or lead to mortalities of fishes (Hoffman 1975) and some of these agents can be recognized in fresh mounts. But histological examination discussed below may be necessary for diagnosis in many cases.

Blood films prepared and stained essentially as in mammalian haematology should be examined for the presence of abnormal blood cells (for cell types of many species see Hawkins & Mawdesley-Thomas 1972; some salmonids, Watson *et al.* 1956, Conroy 1972, Klontz 1972, Lehmann & Stürenberg 1975) but more usefully for the presence of foreign organisms, especially protozoans (Becker 1970) and bacteria. (Quantitative and qualitative changes in the blood cells are at present of little specific diagnostic value.) Versions of Romanowsky-Giemsa stains can be used, but to show effectively both blood cells and bacteria special stains such as Giemsa (Fisher Sci. Co., USA, Catalogue 74540) for bacteria and 'Diff-Quik'* are helpful. The Gram stain can also be used on blood films.

Tissue imprints stained as for blood smears can be very useful for detecting foreign cells *in situ* (Ashley & Smith 1963). These imprints are made by gently pressing the freshly cut, blotted surface of an organ or tissue on a microscope slide, and then treating it as a blood film. If no organism can be detected in a necrotic area following staining, then a Ziehl–Neelsen stain may reveal the presence of acid-fast bacteria.

Bucke (1972) gave a detailed description of useful histological techniques, and Hinton *et al.* (1973) have discussed the application of histopathology (including histochemistry) to the detection of certain water pollutants. Interpretation of the results often calls for specialized knowledge and training, or for searching hopefully through myriads of publications on individual pathogens or chemicals but fortunately Ribelin & Migaki (1975) have edited a comprehensive text on fish pathology. The text deals with many basic aspects of the pathology of infectious and non-infectious disease essential to the effective investigation of fish mortalities. Ashley (1972) emphasized the histological aspects of nutritional pathology, including the cytopathology associated with the uptake of organic and inorganic toxicants. Many useful photomicrographs were presented.

Water. 'Water quality affects the abundance, species composition and diversity, stability, productivity, and physiological condition of indigenous populations of aquatic organisms. Therefore, an expression of the nature and health of the aquatic communities is an expression of the quality of the water' (Anon. 1976, p. 1007). Such an expression calls for considerable specialized training and experience, and would involve a great deal of work examining all communities. However, an examination of plankton communities alone would probably be the most fruitful in explaining unusual colours,

*Harleco, Gibbstown, NJ 08027, USA. A 15-s method giving results like Wright-Giemsa.

odours, turbidities, pH reactions and gaseous conditions that could not be directly related to pollution. Methods of sampling, preparation and examination of water samples, and keys for the identification of important species are given in Part 1000 of Anon. (1976) and Edmonson (1959).

Culturing

Bacteria. If there are no obvious areas of infection from which to culture, the kidney is the tissue of choice. The kidney in most species can be sampled via the body cavity if care is taken not to incise the intestine and if there is no peritonitis. (It may be more convenient to reach the kidney through an aseptic incision made in the flank just ventral to the lateral line of a surface-disinfected fish.) The swim-bladder membrane is set aside and the exposed surface of the kidney is seared using a heated metal object. The inoculum for culture plates is obtained by plunging a flamed bacteriological loop or a sterile swab through the sterilized surface. The sample is then streaked directly onto bacteriological culture media, incubated and the growth examined (Bullock *et al.* 1971; Anon. 1975b). If it is impractical to streak immediately in the field, one can preserve and carry the sample to the laboratory using a combination swab and sterile disposable plastic holder containing 'transport' medium. The cooled samples should be plated within 24 h. Several useful versions of this culture system are on the market, one of which is the 'Securline' (Precision Dynamics Corp., Burbank, Calif. 91504).

It is desirable to fulfil Koch's postulates (see any text on bacteriology for an explanation of this concept) before implicating an organism as the cause of an epizootic but unfortunately the experimentally-infected fish are often atypically symptomatic. The problem can be further complicated by the fact that many organisms not usually pathogenic can appear so under the experimental procedures. Dubos (1955) presented a valuable perspective on the aetiology of infectious disease.

Viruses. Wolf (1970) should be consulted for general guidance on the virological examination of fishes, and Anon. (1975b) and Yasutake (1975) for more specific details on techniques and diagnosis. Tissues need not be handled aseptically but they should not be contaminated by other, possibly virus-infected fish. Samples can be pooled, usually in 5-fish lots, in clean, sealed containers and stored for a few days at ca. 4 °C or for longer periods at −20 °C or lower.

If tissue cultures are not available, suspected viral aetiology may be tested *in vivo* using experimental fish held and treated according to Wolf (1970) and in Anon. (1974a). Filtrates (0·45 μm) obtained from moribund specimens must be passed, with effect, serially through at least three or four fish to rule out chemical toxicity.

Chemical analysis

Selection of the analytical procedure(s) depends among other things upon the weight or certainty of implicating evidence gathered and the degree of detail required. For example, analysis for a specific compound would be unwarranted if one had only a general hypothesis regarding the cause of the incident, or if detection of a class of compounds were adequate to conclude the investigation.

Water sample. Publications on specific chemical determinations are legion but there are some basic texts such as Golterman (1971), Sunshine (1969), that of the US Federal Interagency Work Group (Anon. 1972a), Stainton *et al.* (1977), and the classic *Standard Methods* (Anon. 1976). An FAO (Anon. 1975a) publication is also very useful even though it deals almost exclusively with sea water. Publications such as the *Bull. Environ. Contam. and Toxicol., J. Assoc. Off. Agric. Chem., J. Assoc. Off. Anal. Chem., Water Poll. Res.* and *Water Res.* to mention but a few, often contain relevant papers. But for the latest methods on analysis of pollutants in water or fish one should consult the annual *Literature Review Issue* of the *Journal of the Water Pollution Control Federation*, particularly, for example, the section dealing with the 'Nature and analysis of chemical species' (Vol. 48(6), 998–1086). Useful information on quality control in water analysis laboratories may be found in Anon. (1972c).

McKee & Wolf (1963) wrote a still valuable basic text on water quality criteria (including criteria for the propagation of fish) but as its successor the US Environmental Protection Agency has begun publishing a series of volumes such as *Water Quality Criteria,* 1972 (Anon. 1972b) that contains a section on 'Freshwater aquatic life and wildlife'. Criteria for solids, pH, temperature, ammonia, monohydric phenols, zinc and copper for European freshwater fish are given or discussed in EIFAC (1964, 1968a, 1968b, 1969 (the last two on temperature), 1970, 1972a, 1973b and 1976) respectively. Dissolved oxygen requirements of freshwater fish have been discussed by Doudoroff & Shumway (1970), and Davis (1975) gave a fundamental review of the subject.

For the analysis of pesticides one should consult McMahon *et al.* (1975), Biros *et al.* (1970), Biros (1970), and Anon. (1976); for their metabolic products, Menzie (1966). Zitko & Choi (1971) provided helpful information on the occurrence and analysis of halogenated hydrocarbons, including polychlorinated biphenyls (PCB's), in the environment. The governments of many countries require the registration of pesticides and herbicides, and lists of these along with useful information on their formulations, properties and tolerances are published at intervals (Anon. 1968). Spencer (1973) also provides relevant information particularly on methods of analysis of certain agricultural chemicals.

Information on the toxicity of detergents to fish and on their estimation in water may be found in Prat & Giraud (1964).

Fish tissue. Whole fish may be analysed, or tissues, organs or extracts where the suspected toxicant(s) is known to accumulate may be more effectively utilized, e.g. the gill for Cd, Pb, Zn. For specific methods one can refer to many of the same sources mentioned under water analysis. Over the years Kariya and colleagues have published in the *Bulletin of the Japanese Society for Scientific Fisheries* many relevant methods for the analysis of carcasses for organic and inorganic pollutants using critical tissue assays but unfortunately they are mostly in Japanese. The critical tissue concept has been described by Matthews (1972).

McLeod & Ritcey (1973) have compiled and edited analytical methods for pesticides, including certain herbicides, suitable for fish. Some useful methods are also given in Anon. (1974b).

Concluding remarks

Investigation of the cause of an epizootic in nature is essentially an ecological problem with all the complexities that this implies. Deducing cause and effect relationships can be hazardous because indirect (e.g. release of heavy metals by acids), additive, synergistic and/or antagonistic factors can be involved. Interpretation of analytical data can also be difficult because information on the toxicity of many substances is limited, conflicting, or non-existent. If the incident requires it, the investigator may be forced to conduct multifactorial bioassays. The amount and precision of evidence necessary to conclude an investigation will largely depend upon its purpose. Whether, for example, it is only to assure the public that the cause is 'natural', for scientific documentation, or for the ultimate challenge, legal prosecution.

The successful outcome of the investigation will depend heavily upon the wisdom and judgment that the co-ordinator has gained from a vigorous blend of academic and practical experience.

Acknowledgments

I am particularly grateful to Dr L. Margolis for his critical review of the manuscript and for many useful suggestions. My thanks are due to Dr G. Neish for his guidance in selecting valuable references on mycotic diseases and to Miss Pat Cowie for efficiently transforming my script.

Drs M. Waldichuk and R.B. Swingle were kind enough to give their help on some aspects of pollution.

K

12

Assessment of a Fishery

J A GULLAND

Introduction

The production from fresh waters is apparent as the catches of either commercial or sports fishing. Not all the fish population, i.e. the gross increase in biomass through growth of the individual fish, can be caught if the stock of fish is to be maintained. A major theme in the study of fish production is therefore the assessment of the relation of the present catches to the part of the total gross production that could be taken year after year. It has the direct practical aim of identifying where catches can be expanded by intensification of fishing, and where the stocks are already heavily fished, so that increases can only come from the introduction of appropriate management measures. While this is obviously useful in the waters of Europe and North America which are heavily fished (at least for the favoured species), it can be vital in many of the poorest countries of the world. For a large proportion of these, e.g. Bangladesh and other parts of monsoon Asia, and Chad, Mali, Uganda and other land-locked states of Africa, freshwater fish provide a major source of protein. Despite the simple methods used, many stocks of fish in these countries are heavily exploited, or even depleted. It is as equally important to avoid wasting scarce financial and other resources in increasing fishery pressure on these stocks (whether by increasing the number of fishermen, or introducing new technology) as it is to increase the food supply where the stocks allow greater catches.

In qualitative terms the first stage of appraisal is to place the fish stock* of concern in one of three categories:

1 Unfished or lightly fished. Very small catches, with no detectable effect on the stock.

2 Moderately fished. Significant catches, and a detectable effect on the

---

*A stock in this context is usually considered as being a self-contained population of a single species of fish, but particularly in tropical areas could be a group of species.

stock, but appreciable increases in catch could be obtained by increased fishing.

3 Heavily fished. Large catches (at least in the past). The abundance of the stock has been greatly reduced by fishing. Catches can be increased only by suitable controls of fishing.

The next stage is to put these appraisals into quantitative terms, especially in the two latter categories. For moderately or lightly-fished stocks estimates are needed of by how much the catch can be increased, and with what increase in fishing effort. For heavily-fished stocks, where management measures are needed, predictions of the effects of specific regulations, e.g. that increasing the minimum size limit by 2 cm will increase the weight caught by 10 %, are required.

Traditionally appraisals have been carried out for each stock directly and independently. This may be the only way of proceeding in the sea where each body of water is large, the number of stocks is small, and each has very different characteristics from others, and the results of studying the cod stocks of the North Sea can be transferred only in very general terms to the study of halibut in the north-east Pacific, or even to the cod at Newfoundland. Freshwater bodies, and the stocks in them, are smaller, more numerous and there is clearly considerable similarity between stocks in similar water bodies—lakes, ponds, rivers, etc. Comparative studies between stocks can therefore be of considerable help in assessing these stocks, and can be much quicker and cheaper than attempting to assess each stock individually.

Data requirements

Stock assessment consists essentially of the analysis of a small set of basic data—the catch, the effort involved in taking that catch, an index (in absolute or relative terms) of the abundance of the fish stock, and where possible some information on the population parameters of growth, reproduction and, particularly, mortality. At times some or all of these data have to be collected directly on the spot by the scientist concerned, but frequently some can be obtained from other sources. Thus where a commercial fishery exists, statistics of the catch are usually available, as also may be information on the fishing effort, e.g. number of licensed fishermen, or the number of nets used. In many freshwater situations the main part of the catches are taken by sport or subsistence fishermen, neither of whom are likely to provide comprehensive statistics. For these fisheries some type of sampling survey or creel census is necessary to estimate the catch. The statistical procedures are well established (e.g. Bazigos 1974), being fairly direct applications of standard sampling methods used in agricultural or social surveys, e.g. Cochrane (1963).

Effort and catch per unit effort

The other two basic parameters—effort and abundance index—are not independent, and once one, and the total catch, is known, the other can be immediately derived from the relation:

$$C = F\bar{B} = qf\bar{B} \tag{1}$$

where C = catch
F = fishing mortality coefficient
$\bar{B}$ = mean biomass of the fishable part of the stock during the period considered
f = fishing effort
q = constant.

From equation (1) we have:

$$\bar{B} = q \cdot \frac{C}{f}, \tag{2}$$

i.e. biomass is proportional to the catch per unit effort, and

$$f = \frac{1}{q} \cdot \frac{C}{\bar{B}}, \tag{3}$$

i.e. effort is proportional to the catch divided by the abundance.

Traditionally, in fisheries for which good series of catch and effort statistics are available, the most used expression is equation (2), the abundance being estimated from the catch per unit effort. This is acceptable provided there are no changes in the effectiveness of a unit of effort, i.e. changes in the value of q in the relation $F = qf$. Care needs to be taken to choose an effort unit that is least susceptible to such changes, or that takes them into account. For example, in a gill-net fishery a suitable unit might be the number of net-nights, where one net-night is the operation of a gill-net of standard size and mesh for one night. This would be better than the number of nets used if there were any change in the frequency of use. Another change might be the introduction of monofilament nets, which may catch more than traditional nets. In this case, the difference could be measured by direct experiment, showing perhaps that the difference is 2:1. Then the effort data after the change can be expressed in the old standard net-night, by counting each night's operation with a monofilament net as two standard net-nights.

Efficiency can also improve more gradually and continuously, e.g. by the introduction of bigger boats with more powerful engines, by a succession of minor technical improvements in the gear, or by better training or experience of the fishermen. These can be difficult to detect, let alone to measure. Quantitative corrections may not then be possible, but in all cases the historical series of effort and catch per unit effort needs to be looked at with caution, taking account of the changes that could have occurred.

Where several gears are used to harvest the same stock, one gear can be used as standard, and the total effort calculated as:

$$\text{Total effort} = \text{Total catch} \times \frac{\text{Effort by standard gear}}{\text{Catch by standard gear}}.$$

The gear selected should be one where the catch per unit effort is believed to give a consistent measure of the stock abundance; if more than one gear satisfies this, then the two sets of estimates of catch per unit effort and total effort should be calculated. Though the two sets of estimate will differ in absolute value, the year-to-year trends should be the same, and any difference provides evidence on the changes in the efficiency of one or other gear.

In obtaining these basic catch and effort statistics, and in choosing what series to use, the main uses to which they will be put must be remembered. The catch data provides an absolute measure of what is removed from the stock by man. Avoidance of bias is therefore important, but taking account of the usual variability of the natural system and the uncertainties in other estimates concerning the fish stock, a high precision is seldom needed. The main attention, given a set of catch statistics, should be given to ensuring that they are not biased, e.g. through under-reporting, or that part of the catch (e.g. by subsistence fishermen) is not omitted. The specific figures of effort and catch per unit effort (c.p.u.e.) in any particular year are not in themselves of particular significance, being on no absolute scale, and it is the trends in these figures from year to year that are important. Thus the question of bias does not really arise, and the real question is whether or not the relation between abundance and c.p.u.e. (or fishing mortality and fishing effort), i.e. value of the coefficient q, changes from year to year. The main concern is therefore to detect changes, particularly in the type of gear, or the way it is operated, that could cause such changes (see Gulland 1964b; FAO 1976).

Surveys

Where no available series of catch and effort statistics are satisfactory, the abundance of the population may be estimated (in relative or absolute terms) by some type of survey. The effort can then be derived from the total catch. Most surveys will be conducted with some standard type of fishing gear. The general procedures have been described by Lagler (Chapter 2). The choice of gear (or gears) and survey patterns will be determined by the species (and sizes of fish within a species) of major interest, convenience in carrying out the survey, and repeating it from year to year, and the precision aimed at. Of these, ensuring that the surveys will be repeated in comparable, if not identical, form from year to year, is the most important in the present context of providing a continuing monitoring of the stock abundance. It is relatively easy to arrange for a single survey, even if it is quite complex and extensive. It is another matter to ensure that it is repeated year after year, but without repetition the information provided on *changes* in abundance is slight.

A number of other less direct techniques of surveying can also be used. If the stock migrates past some fixed points, e.g. salmon going upstream to spawn, the total number can sometimes be counted, visually or by automatic techniques, or at least relative numbers can usually be estimated. In open water acoustic methods can be used. The number and strength of echos will provide an index of population abundance, and under favourable conditions (e.g. when only one species occurs with the individuals well dispersed, and not too close to the bottom or surface—a condition which is sometimes satisfied by juvenile salmon) the absolute numbers can be estimated. The whole problem of monitoring abundance has been recently reviewed by a Symposium of the European Inland Fisheries Advisory Commission (EIFAC) (Welcomme 1975).

Stock assessment

The actual assessment or evaluation of the state of the stocks depends on relating, in a quantitative manner, changes in the abundance or composition of the stock to the changes in the amount of fishing. Two general approaches have been used—the production model, typified by the works of Schaefer (1954, 1957) in which the stock is treated as a single entity, subject to simple laws of population growth, and the analytic approach, typically of Ricker (1958, 1975) and Beverton & Holt (1957) which considers the abundance of the population as determined by the net effect of the growth, reproduction and mortality of the individual members of the stock.

Production models

The general approach of this type of model is that if the population at any time is less than the carrying capacity of its environment, it will tend to increase, and that the rate of increase will be some function of the population size, i.e.

$$\frac{dB}{dt} = f(B) \tag{4}$$

where $f(B) = 0$ when $B = 0$ or $B = B_{max}$, the maximum population, and $f(B) > 0, \quad 0 < B < B_{max}$.

Clearly, if the rate of catch is kept equal to this natural rate of increase, the population will be maintained at the same size, so that in a steady state

$$C = f(B) \tag{5}$$

or, if the population is changing during the year, the change during the year will be given by:

$$B_1 - B_0 = f(\bar{B}) - C. \tag{6}$$

(This formula is only approximate, because the average rate of increase is not exactly equal to the rate of increase corresponding to the average population $\bar{B}$.)

If some form for $f(B)$ is assumed, then equations (5) or (6) can be fitted to observations of catch, population size and change in population to give assessments of the stocks. The simplest, and best known, form for $f(B)$ is the logistic, as used by Schaefer (1954, 1957) and others:

$$\frac{dB}{dt} = f(B) = aB(B_{max} - B). \tag{7}$$

A more general form has been proposed by Pella & Tomlinson (1969) as

$$f(B) = aB - bB^m \tag{8}$$

where m is any constant. This reduces to the logistic if $m = 2$.

Another way of looking at the same situation is to note that under equilibrium conditions, the abundance will be some (decreasing) function of the fishing effort, i.e.

$$B = g(f)$$

or, in terms of catch per unit effort,

$$\frac{C}{f} = qB = q \cdot g(f)$$

the simplest form for this is a linear decrease of c.p.u.e. with increasing effort, i.e.

$$\frac{C}{f} = a - bf. \tag{9}$$

This is identical (except for constants) to the logistic equation (4) since the latter can be written:

$$C = a\left(\frac{1}{q} \cdot \frac{C}{f}\right)\left(B_{\max} - \frac{1}{q} \cdot \frac{C}{f}\right)$$

which, rearranging, becomes:

$$\frac{C}{f} = q \cdot B_{\max} - aq^2 \cdot f.$$

Usually the decrease of c.p.u.e. with effort is not linear, and a better fit is given by a linear decrease of the logarithm of c.p.u.e. (Fox 1970), i.e.

$$\log\left(\frac{C}{f}\right) = m - nf$$

or

$$\frac{C}{f} = k\,e^{-nf} \tag{10}$$

where m, n, k are constants.

Basically there is little or no difference between these two ways of taking a simplified view of a complex biological situation, but there are differences in the ways in which the relevant equations (7) and (8), or (9) and (10) can be fitted to actual observations, and in the degree to which the fits obtained are vulnerable to departures from the basic assumptions. Both forms, as written here, assumed that the population is in a steady state, and therefore need strictly to be applied to a set of observations, each concerning a period during which the fishing effort and other factors were constant. This condition is unlikely to be met. The failure to meet it can be tackled in different ways. Equation (6) can be used if estimates of the abundance at particular instants in time can be obtained. Alternatively, it may be noted that the determinant of the catch per unit effort at any moment is not merely the effort at that moment, or during the particular year, but the effort also in previous periods. Equations (9) or (10) can therefore be applied, but relating the catch per unit effort in a given year, to the average effort in some period up to and including the current year. A convenient length of period is that equal to the average life-span of an individual fish in the fishery (Gulland 1961).

Analytic models

These models consider the detailed characteristics of the population, especially the growth, reproduction and mortality rates of the individual fish. Of these only the mortality rate is directly affected by fishing so that the best measure of the effect of fishing is obtained directly from changes in the total mortality coefficient. Mathematically, if Z is the total mortality coefficient, this is given by:

$$Z = M + F = M + qf \qquad (11)$$

where M and $F =$ natural and fishing coefficient respectively.

Thus, if a series of pairs of values of f and Z are plotted (and if q and M are constant) there should be a linear regression of Z on f, with slope q, and intercept on the Y-axis equal to M.

In its simplest form this method depends on knowing the fishing effort during some period, e.g. a year, and also the total mortality during that year. The latter strictly requires estimates of the abundance at the beginning and end of the year. Such point estimates are not as easy to obtain as estimates of the average abundance over certain periods (e.g. from the average catch per unit effort during a year). A mortality estimate can for example be obtained from the rates of the abundance of a particular year-class in say 1975 and 1976, and this mortality coefficient can then be related to the average fishing effort in 1975 and 1976.

Other characteristics of the composition of the stock, e.g. the average age, length, or weight of the individual fish, the proportions of different sizes or market categories in the catches, etc., can provide less quantitative measures of change in total mortality, and hence when related to changes in the total fishing effort, can provide estimates of the fishing mortality.

The fishing mortality can also be estimated in other ways. In principle marking and tagging (see Chapter 4 in respect of practical techniques, and Chapter 6 for methods of analysis) provide direct estimates, from the percentage of tagged fish that are returned, of the rate of fishing. However, the catching and tagging process may kill the fish, tags may drop off, or not be detected and returned, and—a critical factor in any body of water larger than a pond or small lake—tagged fish may not be randomly mixed with the whole population. In practice therefore estimates of fishing mortality obtained from tagging must be treated with caution, and it can in general be expected that, except where tagged fish are released near a concentration of fishermen, the estimates will tend to be too low. Estimates of F can also be obtained from equation (1) when independent figures of abundance are available, e.g. from quantitative acoustic or other surveys when these can be used.

Yield curves. Given the estimates of fishing mortality, and of natural mortality and growth rate, it is a straightforward arithmetical task to calculate the yield in weight and numbers to be expected from a given brood of fish reaching a catchable size. In its most general form the expression for yield in weight is the sum, over all time intervals, of the product of the fishing mortality, the number of fish present, their mean weight, and the duration of the interval, i.e. is given by:

$$Y = \int_{c}^{\infty} F_t N_t w_t \, dt \qquad (12)$$

where c = age at which fish reach a fishable size

N_t = numbers alive at age t, which will be determined by the mortality rates, i.e.

$$N_t = R \exp - \left[\int_{c}^{t} (F_t + M_t) dt \right]$$

w_t = mean weight of a fish age t

R = number of recruits, i.e. number of fish alive at time $t = c$.

Similar equations can be devised for catch in numbers, and for characteristics of the population (biomass, numbers present, etc.) (Strictly these will apply to the values occurring under a steady state of constant recruitment, mortality, etc.).

To use equation (12), functions have to be substituted values for the various parameters. For example, following Beverton & Holt (1957), we can use the von Bertalanffy growth curve:

$$W_t = W_\infty \{1 - [\exp(1/K(t - t_0)]^3\}$$

and put $F_t = 0$ up to some age at first capture, r, determined by the selectivity of the gear being used, and $F_t = F = $ constant for $t > r$. Then the yield will be given by:

$$Y = FRW_\infty \exp[-M(c - r)] \left[\frac{1}{F + M} - \frac{3 \exp[-K(c - t_0)]}{F + M + K} + \right.$$
$$\left. + \frac{3 \exp[-2K(c - t_0)]}{F + M + 2K} - \frac{\exp[-3K(c - t_0)]}{F + M + 3K} \right] \tag{13}$$

Equation (13) can be used to study how the yield from a given year-class of fish can be altered by changes in the amount of fishing (i.e. the value of F), and its selectivity (i.e. the value of c). These can be particularly easily studied by using the tables of Beverton & Holt (1964), which gives the yield as a function of (F/M') (M/K') and c.

Stock and recruitment. Equations (12) and (13) are not complete descriptions of the yield to be expected from a given fishing pattern over a long period, because the strengths of the year-classes constituting the future yield can be expected to vary. To the extent that these variations are due to environmental factors (e.g. temperature, food supply of the very young fish), and are independent of the abundance of the parent stock, they are likely to be of relatively minor importance for the present purpose. The actual value of the yield in some future year will depend on, say, the temperature in the preceding spawning periods, but the advantages and disadvantages of different fishing strategies will be unaltered.

The possible effects on recruitment of changes in the parent stock (which will be the way in which fishing might affect recruitment) is much more critical. If, over the range likely to be observed in practice, smaller stocks will, on the average, produce considerably smaller recruitment, heavy fishing can cause disaster—reduced spawning stock resulting in low recruitment, a still smaller spawning, and so on. Fortunately, this is not a typical feature of fisheries. The high fecundity of most fish must mean that, on the average, mortality between egg production and spawning must be correspondingly high. If the adult stock falls, quite a small reduction in this mortality through some density-dependent factor can result in about the same number of recruits. In fact it seems that competition between young fish, or cannibalism or other interference from adults can result in a lower recruitment from very large stocks. This seems to be the case for Pacific salmon (the group of species for which the stock–recruit relation is best known), where damage to the previous spawning by later spawners seems to be an important factor in causing the greatest recruitment to occur at less than the maximum adult stock size. Salmon also provide the clearest decreases in recruitment at low adult densities, probably in part because their fecundity is less than most other fish species. In general the stock–recruit relation is not well known for most stocks, and although it can often be a reasonable assumption that moderate changes in spawning stock caused by changes in fishing practice will not cause significant changes in recruitment, the appraisal of any fishery should include some consideration of whether recruitment is likely to be affected. The problem has been discussed in more detail by Ricker (1954) and Parrish (1973).

Consideration of stock and recruitment in fresh waters should also take account of some of the more drastic effects man can have through changes in the spawning sites (e.g. by drainage, logging, etc.), blockage of the migration routes to the spawning grounds by dams, as well as the direct effects of fishing, especially on fish concentrated on spawning grounds, or on the passage to them.

Comparative studies

Freshwater fish stocks usually consist of a large number of independent stocks, e.g. in different small lakes, with characteristics that are often very similar. These similarities can be used to simplify what would otherwise be the impracticably lengthy work of carrying out assessments of each of these stocks independently. These comparisons can be used in the methods outlined in the previous sections, e.g. the natural mortality of a given species may be reasonably constant over much of its range, or be closely correlated with the (more easily measured) Bertalanffy growth parameter K, so that M/K is constant (Beverton & Holt 1959). More generally, similarities in more basic patterns can be used to advantage. Cushing (1971) has, for example, suggested that all stock–recruit curves belong to a single family, the shape of the curve for any particular stock depending mainly on the fecundity of the species concerned.

The most valuable generalization is that which fits the total potential fish production of bodies of water into a single pattern. A pattern for temperate North American lakes, relating fish yield to a simple morpho-edaphic index, derived from the mean depth of the lake, and the quantity of derived solids has been determined by Ryder (1965). These have been expanded to other regions (Jenkins 1967; Regier *et al.*, 1971), and Henderson *et al.* (1973) show that lakes in different climatic regions fit into a natural progression, the annual yield from a lake of given characteristics decreasing from the tropics to the polar regions. Henderson & Welcomme (1974) have combined these biological characteristics with the estimate of number of fishermen per unit area of lake, to show that the latter can provide, under the relatively similar conditions of African lakes, a reasonable measure of the intensity of fishing. While lakes have been the main objects of this type of study, the principles obviously apply to other classes of water-bodies, e.g. African rivers (Welcomme 1976).

Using this approach the appraisal of a fishery in any given body of water can consist of first determining the general pattern of production for the class of water-body concerned (for an increasing number of classes this can be done by reference to published works, such as those mentioned above); second, making the relatively simple observation (e.g. of mean depth) needed to estimate the expected production of the given water body, from the general relation; and finally compare the observed catches with the expected production and thus determine, to a useful approximation, the state of exploitation.

This appraisal, in the simple form described here, is not species specific. The species composition of different bodies of water varies more than the total production of all species, particularly over wide areas. Within smaller regions the species composition of similar bodies does not vary so much, and if the same species occur in two similar bodies in the same area, the ratio of the abundance (or production) of different species in the two water bodies is likely to be the same. That is, with due caution, the estimate of total production can be broken down to give the expected production of different species by using the percentage species composition of the (known) production in some similar body of water in the same region. Comparisons can be made over a wider area (essentially all bodies of water of similar climatic condition) if made, not in terms of species, but of classes of species with similar trophic and ecological characteristics.

Regulation and management

The appraisal of a fishery is often carried out for important practical reasons, as the first step towards management. While management is not the direct concern of the scientist (or at least of the scientist alone), the scientist needs to have the problems of management in mind in carrying out an appraisal and in presenting the results. This should be done in such a way as to make clear the implications for management, and to facilitate the introduction and acceptance of appropriate measures. Three aspects of management can be considered: the type of *objectives* (what ultimately is to be achieved); choice of the *policies* (what characteristics of the fishery are to be altered and to what values); and the *techniques* (what practical form the regulations should take).

The basic objectives in managing a fishery are very general, and part of the general social and economic objectives—more food, a better living for the individual fisherman, more employment and, especially in richer countries, a more pleasant environment and better fishing as a sport. These diverse objectives are not always wholly compatible, nor are they also easily realized by more narrowly-expressed objectives in relation to a particular stock or fishery. For example, the greatest total supply of food is unlikely to be obtained by attempting to take the maximum possible yield from a given stock but by using appreciably less effort, accepting some reduction in yield from that stock, but using the effort and resources saved to produce a more than equivalent increase in yield from some other, less heavily exploited, fishery, or in some other activity altogether (possibly fish culture) where the marginal productivity is greater. (The marginal productivity of the final unit of input used in taking the maximum sustained yield is virtually zero.)

In practice, therefore, the objectives of management cannot be given a single concise definition, e.g. achieving the maximum sustainable yield, though it is possible, and indeed necessary, to identify the type of objectives to be pursued, and give an indication of priorities, e.g. the first priority in a salmon river may be to ensure adequate sport to anglers; provided that is satisfied, the highest possible commercial catch within that constraint might be aimed at. Given these objectives, and a knowledge of the relation of yield, and other characteristics, to the basic independent fishery parameters of amount of fishing and its selectivity, it is possible to determine a combination of those parameters that best fulfil these objectives.

The desired situation can be brought about by a variety of techniques of regulation, which include:

(a) Closed areas
(b) Closed seasons
(c) Limitation of total catch
(d) Limitation of the total amount of fishing (amount of gear used or length of time it is in use)
(e) Restrictions on the type of gear used
(f) Restrictions on the sizes of fish that may be landed.

Limitation of the total fishing effort will be achieved by (c) and (d), and to some extent by (a), (b) and (e). To the extent that the benefits from limitation of effort often come as much from taking the same catch more cheaply as from increase of total catch, any measure to limit effort should not reduce the efficiency of fishing. Thus restrictions on the use of the most efficient types of gear are an admission of failure to achieve optimum management, at least from the strictly economic point of view, though imposed inefficiency may be desirable in the short run to maintain employment or, also in the long run, for optimizing sports fishing.

Limitation of catch or effort can be applied with an overall quota, with free fishing until the quota is reached, and then a stop; this has effects very similar to a closed season, and if the fishery remains profitable more and more fishermen will enter the fishery so that the quota is reached more quickly, and the season becomes shorter and shorter. Alternatively the total quota of catch and effort can be divided and allocated to particular fishermen or groups of fishermen (limited entry); such licences enable the fishermen to operate more rationally, with probably considerable net economic gain. This gain can accrue to the fishermen or be diverted to other purposes by charging a suitable fee for licences.

Regulation of the size of fish caught can be achieved by methods (e) (e.g. mesh size regulation) and (f), and possibly also by (a) or (b) if the size composition of the catches varies between different areas or different seasons. These measures may not have such drastic effects on the individual fishermen as measures to restrict total fishing, so that the indirect and possibly unexpected effects are likely to be smaller. However, any form of effective regulation is likely to have wider results than merely the simple biological effects on the stock. Therefore, although the need for management and the methods used will depend on biological analysis, the actual techniques, like the ultimate objectives, will involve other considerations.

Acknowledgments

My thanks are due to my colleagues in FAO, especially Robin Welcomme, for developing the ideas expressed in this paper and commenting on the draft.

Appendixes

1

List of Symbols

—   A bar over a symbol indicates a mean value.

$\wedge$ A circumflex over a symbol indicates an estimate.

$\sim$ Approximately equals.

Δ Difference or increment.

a 1. A constant of proportionality in the logistic equation of population growth (Chapter 12)

    2. Y-axis intercept in certain linear regressions.

    3. A sub-space of the population space (Chapter 6).

b Slope in certain linear regressions; regression coefficient.

c 1. A constant used in back-calculation of length (Chapter 5).

    2. Sample of fish examined for marks (Chapter 6).

    3. Average age at which fish reach a fishable size (Chapter 12).

e Mean number of eggs spawned per mature female in a stock (Chapter 6).

e $2\cdot71828\ldots$

f Fishing effort.

i,j Used as subscripts to designate any member of a series of observations, or of a group of parameters.

k 1. Number of samples or subsamples.

    2. A coefficient of proportionality.

    3. Coded age in the Chapman-Robson population estimation method (Chapter 6).

    4. A constant.

l Length of a fish.

l_n Length of a fish at the time an annulus is formed on the scales (Chapter 5).

l_{ts} Average length of survivors to time t.

m 1. Number of fish marked (Chapter 6).

2. Sum of age frequencies.

n 1. Number of individuals in an experimental group or subset.

2. Used for age when t would introduce ambiguity.

p 1. Proportion of one class of fish in the population.

2. Probability of capture, in the Leslie population estimation method (Chapter 6).

q Catchability coefficient relating fishing effort to coefficient of fishing mortality ($q = F/f$).

r 1. Number of recaptured marked fish in a sample (Chapter 6).

2. Daily ration, expressed as a percentage of the body weight of the consumer (Chapter 10).

3. Coefficient of correlation.

4. Average age at first capture (Chapter 12)

r_n Ratio of the total number of individuals in the stock that exceed a specified age or size to the number of mature females in the same stock (Chapter 6).

r_p Ratio of the biomass of the total individuals in a stock that exceed a specified age or size, to the biomass of mature females (Chapter 6).

t 1. A point in time.

2. Age, usually in years.

3. Temperature

Δt An interval of time.

u Total number of unmarked fish (Chapter 6).

v Regression coefficient in functional regression.

var Variance.

w Weight of an individual fish.

x The number of class X fish in a sample (Chapter 6).

z The probability of a fish not being caught (Chapter 6).

A 1. Assimilation (food absorbed by the alimentary canal, less excreta); physiologically useful energy.

2. Mortality rate (fraction dying, of the individuals originally present) ($A = 1 - S$).

3. Anal fin ray number (Chapter 3).

4. The number of area or time units occupied by a fish population (Chapter 6).

5. Absorbed nitrogen (Chapter 10)

$\overline{A}$ Average stomach or gut content.

B   1. Biomass of a population; standing crop.

2. Biocontent (energy content) of a population.

ΔB Increase in biomass or biocontent of an individual or a population. For an individual fish ΔB = growth.

B_{max} Maximum biomass of stock (Chapter 12).

C   1. Consumption (total intake of food by an organism in a specified time interval).

2. Total number of fish in the catch.

D   1. Dorsal fin number (Chapter 3).

2. Duration of egg development (Chapter 7).

3. Defaecation rate.

E   1. Expected value (Chapter 6).

2. Total number of eggs spawned in a reproductive season by the whole stock (Chapter 6).

3. Exploitation rate (Chapter 6).

4. Excreted nitrogen (Chapter 10).

E_{pg} Partial growth conversion efficiency (Chapter 10).

E_{pm} Partial maintenance efficiency (Chapter 10).

E_t Total food conversion efficiency

F   1. Egesta (food not absorbed through the alimentary canal); faeces.

2. Coefficient of mortality caused by fishing, exponential model; instantaneous fishing mortality rate; rate of fishing.

3. Fecundity (number of eggs per female).

4. Faecal nitrogen (Chapter 10).

G   Coefficient of growth in weight, exponential model; instantaneous growth rate of an individual fish.

G_x Instantaneous growth rate in the population.

I   1. Nitrogen intake (Chapter 10).

2. Sexually immature fish (Chapter 6).

K   1. Coefficient of growth in length in the simple von Bertalanffy model (a transformation of the rate at which the asymptotic length is being approached).

2. Ivlev coefficient of utilization of food for growth ($= \Delta B/C$).

3. Coefficient of condition, condition factor.

4. Accumulated catch (Chapter 6).

5. Stomach or gut content turnover coefficient (Chapter 10).

L_∞ Asymptotic length, simple von Bertalanffy growth model.

M   1. Coefficient of mortality due to natural causes, exponential model; instantaneous natural mortality rate.

2. Number of marked fish.

3. Maintenance ration (Chapter 10).

N   Population (size); stock (number).

P   1. Production(1)—For an individual: increase in biomass during Δt, including the weight of any reproductive products released. For a population: the same, plus the weight of fish that died during Δt (recruitment absent).

2. Production(2)—Same as production(1), except that the weight of reproductive products released is not included. For an individual fish, production(2) = growth = ΔB.

3. Probability (Chapter 6).

4. Pectoral fin ray number.

5. $P_{\female}$, $P_{\male}$, P_I, Biomass of sexually mature female, male and immature fish (Chapter 6).

R   1. Respiration: food energy converted to heat or mechanical energy— usually measured by oxygen consumption.

2. Number of fish entering the exploitable phase of a stock; number of recruits.

3. Number of recaptured tagged fish.

4. Retained nitrogen (Chapter 10).

S   1. Survival rate (fraction surviving, of the individuals initially present). In the exponential model, $S = e^{-Z}$.

2. Radius of a fish scale (or otolith, bone, etc.) (Chapter 5).

S_n Radius of a fish scale (otolith, etc) measured to an annulus (Chapter 5).

S.E.   Standard error.

T   1. Turnover ratio, rate of turnover ($=P/B$).

2. A statistic used in the Chapman-Robson population estimation method, based on coded ages (Chapter 6).

U   Excreta. Material released from the body as urine or through the gills or skin.

V   1. Variance.

2. Ventral fin ray number.

W_∞ Asymptotic weight, simple von Bertalanffy growth model (Chapter 12).

Y   Yield from a fish stock, in weight.

Z Coefficient of total mortality, exponential model; instantaneous mortality rate ($Z = F + M$).

Δ Increment, or interval.

ϵ Dynamic ecotrophic coefficient: the ratio of a predator's consumption of a particular prey species to the production of that species (Chapter 1.)

Σ Summation sign.

2

Scientific Names of Fishes mentioned in the Text

albacore	*Thunnus alalunga*
aholehole	*Kuhlia scandevicensis*
alewife	*Alosa pseudoharengus*
Atlantic salmon	*Salmo salar*
bighead	*Aristichthys nobilis*
black bullhead	*Ictalurus melas*
black carp	*Mylopharyngodon piceus*
Blaufelchen	*Coregonus wartmanni*
bleak	*Alburnus alburnus*
bluegill	*Lepomis macrochirus*
bream	*Abramis brama*
brook trout (N. Am.)	*Salvelinus fontinalis*
brown trout	*Salmo trutta*
bullhead (Eur.)	*Cottus gobio*
bullheads (N. Am.)	*Ictalurus nebulosus, melas*, etc.
burbot	*Lota lota*
carp	*Cyprinus carpio*
catfishes	Siluridae, Ictaluridae, Bagridae, etc.
channel catfish	*Ictalurus punctatus*
char (Eur.)	*Salvelinus alpinus*
chinook (salmon)	*Oncorhynchus tshawytscha*
chum (salmon)	*Oncorhynchus keta*
ciscoes	*Coregonus albula, C. artedii*, etc.
cod	*Gadus morhua*
coho (salmon)	*Oncorhynchus kisutch*
crucian carp	*Carassius carassius*
eel (Eur.)	*Anguilla anguilla*
eel (N. Am.)	*Anguilla rostrata*
fathead minnow	*Pimephales promelas*
file fish	*Stephanolepis cirrhifer*

296

goldeye	*Hiodon alosoides*
goldfish	*Carassius auratus*
grass carp	*Ctenopharyngodon idella*
haddock	*Melanogrammus aeglefinus*
halibut	*Hippoglossus* spp.
Hawaiian anchovy	*Stolephorus purpureus*
herring (Atlantic)	*Clupea harengus*
herring (Pacific)	*Clupea pallasi*
horse mackerel	*Trachurus tracurus*
jack mackerel	*Trachurus japonicus*
kokanee	*Oncorhynchus nerka*
lake trout (N. Am.)	*Salvelinus namaycush*
lake whitefish	*Coregonus clupeaformis*
lampreys	Petromyzontidae
largemouth bass	*Micropterus salmoides*
maskinonge	*Esox masquinongy*
milkfish	*Chanos chanos*
minnows	small Cyprinidae
Norway pout	*Trisopterus esmarkii*
Pacific salmon	*Oncorhynchus nerka*
perch (Eur.)	*Perca fluviatilis*
perch (N. Am.)	*Perca flavescens*
pike	*Esox lucius*
pike-perch	*Stizostedion* spp. (= *Lucioperca*)
plaice (Eur.)	*Pleuronectes platessa*
puffer	*Fugi vermicularis*
rainbow trout	*Salmo gairdneri*
redear sunfish	*Lepomis microlophus*
Rio Grande perch	*Cichlasoma cyanoguttatum*
roach	*Rutilus rutilus*
rock bass	*Ambloplites rupestris*
salmon	Salmonidae
salmon (Atlantic)	*Salmo salar*
salmon (Pacific)	*Oncorhynchus* spp.
sandeels	*Ammodytes*
sand goby	*Gobius minutus*
sculpin	*Cottus* spp.

shad, American	*Alosa sapidissima*
shads, European	*Alosa alosa, A. finta*
sheephead	*Aplodinotus grunniens*
silver carp	*Hypophthalmichthys molitrix*
skipjack tuna	*Katsuwonus pelamis*
smelt (Eur.)	*Osmerus eperlanus*
smelt (N. Am.)	*Osmerus mordax*
snakehead	*Ophiocephalus argus*
sockeye (salmon)	*Oncorhynchus nerka*
sole (Eur.)	*Solea vulgaris*
spurdog	*Squalus acanthias*
steelhead (trout)	*Salmo gairdneri*
striped bass	*Roccus saxatilus*
sturgeons	Acipenseridae
suckers	Catostomidae
sunfishes	small Centrarchidae
tench	*Tinca tinca*
threespine stickleback	*Gasterosteus aculeatus*
trout (Eur., brown and sea)	*Salmo trutta*
tunas	*Thunnidae*
walleye	*Stizostedion vitreum*
whitefishes	*Coregonus* (large species)
white perch	*Morone americana*
yellow perch	*Perca flavescens*
zander	*Stizostedion lucioperca*

3

Table of Equivalent Values

In order to be sure of 4-figure accuracy, five significant digits are given; the terminal digit may not be the best one in all cases, but it will not differ from the true value by more than half a unit. A number with less than 5 significant digits is an exact equivalent, usually by definition. A dot over a terminal figure indicates a repeating decimal.

A few important conversions are taken to 6 or 7 digits. However in working at this level it becomes necessary to distinguish between the standards of length used in the United States and the United Kingdom (1 US yard = 0·914402 m; 1 UK yard = 0·914399 m).

The direction of conversion computations is as indicated in this example:

To change feet to metres—multiply by 0·30480 or divide by 3·2808
To change metres to feet—divide by 0·30480 or multiply by 3·2808

Unit	Equivalent		Reciprocal
	LINEAR MEASUREMENTS		
Inch	2·5400	cm	0·39370
	0·083	ft	12·
Foot (ft)	0·30480	metre (m)	3·2808
	12·	inches	0·08$\dot{3}$
Yard (yd)	0·91440	m	1·09361
	3·	ft	0·$\dot{3}$
Fathom	1·82880	m	0·54681
	6·	ft	0·16$\dot{6}$
Rod (or pole)	5·0292	m	0·19884
	16·5	ft	0·060606
Chain (surveyor's)	20·117	m	0·049709
	66·	ft	0·0151515
Furlong	201·17	m	0·0049709
	660·	ft	0·00151515

Table of Equivalent Values

Unit	Equivalent		Reciprocal
LINEAR MEASUREMENTS			
Mile (statute mile)	1·60935	km	0·62137
	5280·	ft	0·000189394
Nautical mile*	1·15078	miles	0·86898
	1852·00	m	0·00053996
	6076·12	feet	0·000164579
AREA			
Square inch	6·4516	cm²	0·15500
Square foot	0·092903	m²	10·764
	144·	inch²	0·00694
Square yard	0·83613	m²	1·1960
	9·	ft²	0·i
Square rod	25·2928	m²	0·039537
	30·25	yd²	0·033058
Acre	4046·9	m²	0·00024711
	0·40469	ha	2·4711
	160·	rod²	0·00625
	4840·	yd²	0·00020661
	43560·	ft²	0·000022957
Square mile	2·59001	km²	0·38610
	640·	acres	0·0015625
Square nautical mile	3·4299	km²	0·29155
	1·3243	mile²	0·75512
Are	100·	m²	0·01
Hectare (ha)	10,000·	m²	0·0001
	0·01	km²	100·
VOLUME			
Cubic inch	16·387	cm³ (cc)	0·061024
Cubic foot	0·028317	m³	35·315
	28·316	litres (l)	0·35315
Cubic yard	0·76455	m³	1·3080
Cubic mile	4·1682	km³	0·23991
Board foot	0·002360	m³	423·78
	0·083	ft³	12·
Cord	3·6245	m³	0·27590
	128·	ft³	0·0078125

*A nautical mile is approximately equal to 1 minute of latitude. It has been variously defined with reference to other units. In 1959 it was officially set at 6076·11549 U.S. feet. by the United States Hydrographic Office, a figure which is very close to the even 1852 m commonly accepted in Europe. Many British and older North American tables give 6080 feet (1853·18 m) as the length of a nautical mile.

Unit	Equivalent		Reciprocal
Acre-foot	1233·5	m³	0·00081072
	43560·	ft³	22·957 × 10⁻⁶
	271330·	Imp gal	3·6855 × 10⁻⁶
	325850·	US gal	3·0689 × 10⁻⁶
Imperial fluid ounce (Imp fl oz)	28·412	ml	0·035197
	0·05	Imp pint	20·

VOLUME

Unit	Equivalent		Reciprocal
Imperial pint (pt)	0·56825	l	1·7598
Imperial quart (qt)	1·13650	l	0·87989
Imperial gallon (gal)	4·545963	l	0·21998
	0·16054	ft³	6·2290
Imp pt, qt, gal	1·200942	US pt, qt, gal	0·83268
US fluid ounce (US fl oz)	29·573	ml	0·033815
	1·04085	Imp fl oz	0·96075
	0·0625	US pint	16·
US pint	0·47317	l	2·1134
US quart	0·94634	l	1·0567
US gallon	3·785332	l	0·26418
	0·13368	ft³	7·4805
Millilitre (ml)	1·000027	cm³	0·999973
Hectolitre (hl)	0·1000027	m³	9·99973

WEIGHT

Unit	Equivalent		Reciprocal
Grain (gr)	0·064799	gram (g)	15·4324
Ounce (oz)	28·350	g	0·035274
Pound (lb)	453·5924	g	0·00220462
	0·4535924	kg	2·20462
	16·	oz	0·0625
	7000·	gr	0·000142857
Stone	6·3503	kg	0·15747
	14·	lb	0·071429
Quarter	12·7006	kg	0·078736
	28·	lb	0·035714
Hundredweight (cwt)	50·802	kg	0·019684
(UK)	112·	lb	0·0089286
Hundredweight (cwt)	45·359	kg	0·0220462
(USA, Canada)	100·	lb	0·01
(Long) ton (UK)	1·0160	m. tons	0·98421
	2240·	lb	0·00044643
(Short) ton	0·90718	m. tons	1·10231
(USA, Canada)	2000·	lb	0·0005
Million pounds	453·59	m. tons	0·0022046
Metric ton (m. ton)	1000·	kg	0·001
	2204·6	lb	0·00045359

Unit	Equivalent		Reciprocal
	WEIGHT (contd)		
Metric quintal or centner	100·	kg	0·01
(USSR tsentner, German	220·46	lb	0·0045359
Doppelzentner)			
Zentner (Germany)	50·	kg	0·02
	110·23	lb	0·0090719
	SPEED		
Foot per second	0·30480	m/sec	3·2808
	0·68182	mile/hr	1·4$\dot{6}$
Mile per hour	0·44704	m/sec	2·2369
	1·4$\dot{6}$	ft/sec	0·68182
Knot (nautical mile per hour)	1·85200	km/hr	0·53996
	1·15078	mile/hr	0·86898
Metre per second	3·6	km/hr	0·2$\dot{7}$
Kilometre per hour	16·$\dot{6}$	m/min	0·06
	27·$\dot{7}$	cm/sec	0·036
	MISCELLANEOUS		
Pound per acre	1·1209	kg/ha	0·89218
	0·11209	g/m^2	8·9218
Metric ton per square kilometre	1·	g/m^2	1·
	10·	kg/ha	0·1
	2·8550	short tons/mi^2	0·35026
Short ton per acre	2·2417	m. tons/ha	0·44609
Long ton per acre	2·5107	m. tons/ha	0·39829
Gram per square metre	10·	kg/ha	0·1
Cubic foot per second	1·6990	m^3/min	0·58857
Grain per US gallon	17·118	mg/l	0·058417
Pound per cubic foot	16·019	kg/m^3	0·062427

General References

Immediately below each reference and on a separate line are given the page number(s) on which the reference is cited in the text.

ACKMAN R.G., EATON C.A., BLIGH E.G. & LANTZ A.W. (1967) Freshwater fish oil: yields and composition of oils from reduction of sheepshead, tullibee, maria, and alewife. *J. Fish. Res. Bd Can.* **24,** 1219–1227.
237

ADAMS L.A. (1940) Some characteristic otoliths of American Ostariophysi. *J. Morph.* **66,** 496–527.
112

AIKAWA H. (1937) Age determination in the chub-mackerel *Scomber japonicus* (Houttyn). *Bull. Jap. Soc. scient. Fish.* **6,** 9–12.
115

ALBRECHTSEN K. (1968) A dyeing technique for otolith reading. *J. Cons. perm. int. Explor. Mer* **32,** 278–280.
114

ALLEN K.R. (1950) The computation of production in fish populations. *N.Z. Sci. Rev.* **8,** 89.
203

ALLEN K.R. (1951) The Horokiwi Stream: a study of a trout population. *Fish. Bull. N.Z.* **10,** 1–238.
178, 182, 200, 211

ALLEN K.R. (1966) A method of fitting growth curves of the von Bertalanffy type to observed data. *J. Fish. Res. Bd Can.* **23,** 163–179.
129

ALLEN K.R. (1969) Application of the Ber-

talanffy growth equation to problems of fishery management: a review. *J. Fish. Res. Bd Can.* **26,** 2267–2281.
134

ALLEN K.R. (1971) Relation between production and biomass. *J. Fish. Res. Bd Can.* **28,** 1573–1581.
208

ALLEN S.E., GRIMSHAW H.M., PARKINSON J.A. & QUARMBY C. (1974) *Chemical Analysis of Ecological Materials.* Blackwell Scientific Publications, Oxford.
236

ALVERSON D.L. & CHENOWITH H.H. (1951) Experimental testing of fish tags on albacore in a water tunnel. *Comml Fish. Rev.* **13,** 1–7.
94

AMLACHER E. (1970) *Textbook of Fish Diseases.* Translated by D.A. Conroy and R.L. Herman. T.F.H. Publications Inc., Neptune, New Jersey, 302pp.
263, 267

ANDERSON B.G. & MITCHUM D.L. (1974) Atlas of trout histology. *Bull. Wyo. Game Fish Dep.* No. **13,** 110 pp.
259

ANDERSON D.R. (1975) Population ecology of the mallard V temporal and geographic estimates of survival, recovery, and harvest rates. *Resour. Publs U.S. Fish Wildl. Serv.* **125,** 110 pp.
161

303

Andrews A.K. (1971) Survival and mark retention of small cyprinid marked with fluorescent pigments. *Trans. Am. Fish. Soc.* **101**, 128–133.
89

ANOKHINA L.E. (1963) Some aspects of the fecundity of the herring in the White Sea. *Rapp. P.-v. Réun. Cons. perm. int. Explor. Mer*, **154**, 123–127.
177

ANON (1968) *Compendium on Registered Uses of Pesticides in Canada* (with annual addenda). Canadian Department of Agriculture, Ottawa. Catalogue Number **A41**–16.
272

ANON (1971) Laser marks in fish. *Agric. Res. Wash.* **19**, 5.
87

ANON (1972a) *Recommended Methods for Water-Data Acquisition.* Preliminary report of the federal interagency work group on designation of standards for water data acquisition. U.S. Geological Survey, Washington, D.C.
262, 271

ANON (1972b) *Water Quality Criteria 1972. A report of the committee on water quality criteria.* U.S. Natn. Acad. Sci. and Natn. Acad. Engng., Washington, D.C., 594 pp.
271

ANON (1972c) *Handbook for Analytical Quality Control in Water and Wastewater Laboratories.* Analytical Quality Control Laboratory, Nat. Environ. Res. Center, Cincinnati, Ohio.
271

ANON (1974a) *Fishes. Guidelines for the Breeding, Care, and Management of Laboratory Animals.* Subcommittee on Fish Standards. Natn. Acad. Sci., Washington D.C., 85 pp.
265, 271

ANON (1974b) *Analytical Methods Manual.* Environment Canada, Inland Waters Directorate, Water Quality Branch, Ottawa.
272

ANON (1975a) Manual of methods in aquatic environment research. Part 1—Methods for detection, measurement and monitoring of water pollution. *F.A.O. Fish. tech. Pap.* No. **137**, 238 pp.
271

ANON (1975b) Suggested procedures for the detection and identification of certain infectious diseases of fishes. *Am. Fish. Soc., Fish Health Section.* (Publ. by U.S. Fish and Wildl. Serv.)
268, 270

ANON (1976) *Standard Methods for the Examination of Water and Waste Water.* American Public Health Association, Washington, D.C., 14th ed., 1193 pp.
260, 261, 262, 271, 272

AOKI T., EGUSA S., KIMURA T. & WATANABE T. (1971) Detection of R factors in naturally occuring *Aeromonas salmonicida* strains. *Appl. Microbiol.* **22**, 716–717.
90

APOSTOLSKI K. (1960) [Electrical fishing on Lake Dojran.] *Izd. Zav. Ribarst. N.R. Maked.* **3**, 165–168.
27

APPLEGATE V.C. & MOFFETT J.W. (1955) The sea lamprey. *Scient. Am.* **192**, 36–41.
27

APPLEGATE V.C., HOWELL J.H., HALL A.E. & SMITH M.A. (1957) Toxicity of 4346 chemicals to larval lampreys and fishes. *Spec. scient. Rep. U.S. Fish Wildl. Serv. Fisheries*, No. **207**, 157 pp.
21

APPLEGATE J. & SMITH L.L. (1951) The determination of age and rate of growth from vertebrae of the channel catfish, *Ictalurus lacustris punctatus. Trans. Am. Fish. Soc.* **80**, 119–139.
115

APSTEIN C. (1909) Die Bestimmung des Alters pelagischlebender Fischeier. *Mitt. dt. SeefischVer.* **25**, 364–373.
188, 189

ARMSTRONG G.C. (1947) Mortality, rate of growth, and fin regeneration of marked and unmarked lake trout fingerlings at the provincial fish hatchery, Port Arthur, Ontario. *Trans. Am. Fish. Soc.* **77**, 129–131.
86

ARNOLD D.E. (1966) Marking fish with dyes and other chemicals. *Tech. Pap. Fish. Wildl. Serv. U.S.* **10**, 44 pp.
89

ASH G.R., CHYMKO N.R. & GALLUP D.N. (1974) Fish kill due to 'cold shock' in Lake Wabamun, Alberta. *J. Fish. Res. Bd Can.* **31**, 1822–1824.
256

ASHLEY L.M. (1972) Nutritional pathology. In *Fish Nutrition*, pp. 439–537. (Ed. J.E. Halver.) Academic Press, New York. 713 pp.
256, 269

ASHLEY L.M. & SMITH C.E. (1963) Advantages of tissue imprints over tissue sections in studies of blood cell formation. *Progve Fish Cult.* **25**, 93–96.
269

ASLANOVA N.E. (1963) Methods of fish tagging in the U.S.S.R. Experiments on using different types of tags and methods of attachment. *Spec. Publs. int. Commn N.W. Atlant. Fish.* **4**, 314–317.
98

ASSOCIATION OF OFFICIAL ANALYTICAL CHEMISTS (1960) *Methods of Analysis.* Ass. Official Anal. Chem., Washington, D.C., 9th ed.
236, 240

ASTAFYEVA A.V. (1964) Concerning the fauna of the breeding mounds of pink salmon in the rivers of the eastern Murmansk region. *Trudy murmansk. morsk. biol. Inst.*, 5 (9), 148–153. Translated from Russian by Fish. Res. Bd Can. Transl Ser. No. 579, 1965.
258

ASTANIN L.P. & PODGORNY M.I. (1968) Osobennosti plodovitosti karasei *Carassius carassius* (L.) i *C. auratus gibelio* (Bloch). [Features of the fertility of *Carassius carassius* (L.) and *C. auratus gibelio* (Bloch).] *Vop. Ikhtiol.* **8**, 266–273. [Translated in *Probl. Ichthyol.* **8**, 209–214.]
172

AVERETT R.C. (1969) Influence of temperature on energy and material utilization by juvenile coho salmon. Ph.D. Thesis, Oregon State University, Cornvallis.
235, 236

AVISE J.C. (1974) Systematic value of electrophoretic data. *Syst. Zool.* **23**, 465–481.
51

BACKIEL T. (1971) Production and food consumption of predatory fish in the Vistula River. *J. Fish Biol.* **3**, 369–405.
215, 216, 217, 249

BAGENAL M. (1955) A note on the relations of certain parameters following a logarithmic transformation. *J. mar. biol. Ass. U.K.* **34**, 289–296.
176

BAGENAL T.B. (1957a) The breeding and fecundity of the long rough dab *Hippoglossoides plattessoides* (Fabr.) and the associated cycle in condition. *J. mar. biol. Ass. U.K.* **36**, 339–373.
126, 170, 176

BAGENAL T.B. (1957b) Annual variations in fish fecundity. *J. mar. biol. Ass. U.K.* **36**, 377–382.
176

BAGENAL T.B. (1966) The ecological and geographical aspects of the fecundity of the plaice. *J. mar. biol. Ass. U.K.* **46**, 161–186.
170, 176, 177

BAGENAL T.B. (1967) A method of marking fish eggs and larvae. *Nature, Lond.* **214**, 113.
89

BAGENAL T.B. (1969a) The relationship between food supply and fecundity in brown trout *Salmo trutta* L. *J. Fish Biol.* **1**, 167–182.
177

BAGENAL T.B. (1969b) Relationship between egg size and fry survival in brown trout *Salmo trutta* L. *J. Fish Biol.* **1**, 349–353.
178

BAGENAL T.B. (1971) The inter-relation of the size of fish eggs, the date of spawning and the production cycle. *J. Fish Biol.* **3**, 207–219.
177

L

BAGENAL T.B. (1972a) The variability in the numbers of perch *Perca fluvialitis* L. caught in traps. *Freshwat. Biol.* **2**, 27–36.
37

BAGENAL T.B. (1972b) The variability of the catch from gill nets set for pike *Esox lucius* L. *Freshwat. Biol.* **2**, 77–82.
36

BAGENAL T.B. (1974) A buoyant net designed to catch freshwater fish larvae quantitatively. *Freshwat. Biol.* **4**, 107–109.
195

BAGENAL T.B. (1978) Aspects of fish fecundity. In *Ecology of Freshwater Fish Production*, pp. 75–101 (Ed. Shelby D. Gerking), Blackwell Scientific Publications, Oxford, 519 pp.
166, 177

BAILEY N.T.J. (1959) *Statistical Methods in Biology*. English Universities Press, London, 200 pp.
122

BAJKOV A.D. (1935) How to estimate the daily food consumption of fish under natural conditions. *Trans. Am. Fish. Soc.* **65**, 288–289.
249

BAKER C. (1963) Fish harvest by wire nets in a stream impoundment. *Publs Div. Wildl. Ohio Dep. nat. Resour.*, No. W-323, 14 pp.
38

BALON E. (1955) Rust plotice (*Rutilus rutilus*) a revise hlavnich metod jeho urcovani. [Wachstum der Plötze und Revision der Haupmethoden seiner Bestimmung.] *Slovenska Akad. Vied., Bratislava.* (German and Russian summaries.)
108

BALON E. (1959) Die Beschuppungsentwicklung der Texas-Cichlide (*Herichthys cyanoguttatus* Baird et Girard). *Zool. Anz.* **163**, 82–89.
108

BALON E.K. (1975) Reproductive guilds in fishes: a proposal and definition. *J. Fish. Res. Bd Can.* **32**, 821–864.
179

BALON E.K. & COCHE A.G. (Ed.) (1974) *Lake Kariba a man-made tropical ecosystem in Central Africa*. Monographiae

Biological, **24**, Junk, The Hague, 767 pp.
31

BANKS J.W. & IRVINE W. (1969) A note on the photography of fish scales, operculas and otoliths using an enlarger. *J. Fish Biol.* **1**, 25–26.
104

BANNISTER R.C.A., HARDING D. & LOCKWOOD S.J. (1974) Larval mortality and subsequent year-class strength in the plaice (*Pleuronectes platessa*). In *The Early Life history of Fish*, 21–37 (Ed. J.H.S. Blaxter), Springer Verlag, Berlin, 765 pp.
178

BARANOV F.I. (1918) K voprosy biologicheskogo osnovaniya rybnogo khozyaistva. [On the question of the biological basis of fisheries.] *Izv. naucho-issled. ikhtiol. Inst.* **1**, 1, 81–128.
129

BARANOV F.I. (1948) *Teoriya i raschet orudii rybolovstva* [Theory and construction of fishing gears]. Pishchepromizdat [Food Industries Press], Moscow, 436 pp.
10

BARDACH J.E. & LE CREN E.D. (1948) A preopercular tag for perch. *Copeia* **1948**, 222–224.
94

BARDACH J.E., RYTHER J.H. & MCLARNEY W.O. (1972) *Aquaculture, the Farming and Husbandry of Freshwater and Marine Organisms*. Wiley-Interscience, New York, 868 pp.
188

BARRACLOUGH W.E. & JOHNSON W.W. (1956) A new mid-water trawl for herring. *Bull. Fish. Res. Bd Can.* **104**, 25 pp.
31, 196

BARRACLOUGH W.E. & JOHNSON W.W. (1960) Further midwater trawl developments in British Columbia. *Bull. Fish. Res. Bd Can.* **123**, 45 pp.
31

BATTLE H.I. (1940) The embryology and larval development of the goldfish (*Carassius auratus* L.) from Lake Erie. *Ohio J. Sci.* **40**, 82–93.
192

BATTLE H.I. & SPRULES W.M. (1960). A

description of the semi-buoyant eggs and early developmental stages of the goldeye, *Hiodon alosoides* (Rafinesque). *J. Fish. Res. Bd Can.* **17**, 245–266.
180

BAU K.-T. (1922) Mikrotechnische Bearbeitung von Knochenfischeiern. *Z. wiss. Mikrosk.* **39**, 165–168.
185

BAXTER I.G. (1959) Fecundities of winter-spring and summer-autumn herring spawners. *J. Cons. perm. int. Explor. Mer*, **154**, 170–174.
171

BAXTER I.G. & HALL W.B. (MS) (1960) The fecundity of Manx herring and a comparison of the fecundities of autumn spawning groups. *Cons. perm. int. Explor. Mer, 1960 meeting, Herring Committee Paper* No. **55**, 8 pp.
174, 176

BAZIGOS G.P. (1974) The design of fisheries statistical surveys—inland waters. *F.A.O. Fish. tech. Pap.* No. **133**, 122 pp.
276

BAZIGOS G.P. (1975) The statistical efficiency of echo surveys with special reference to Lake Tanganyika. *F.A.O. Fish. tech. Pap.* No. **139**, 52 pp.
19

BEAMISH F.W.H. (1974) Apparent specific dynamic action of large-mouth bass, *Micropterus salmoides. J. Fish. Res. Bd Can.* **31**, 1763–1769.
235, 236, 243

BEAMISH F.W.H., NIIMI A.J. & LETT P.K.K.P. (1975) Bioenergetics of teleost fishes: Environmental influences. In *Comparative Physiology—Functional Aspects of Structural Materials*, pp. 187–209 (eds. L. Bolis, H.P. Maddrell & K. Schmidt-Nielsen), North-Holland, Amsterdam.
237

BEATTY R. (1951) When in doubt—troll. *Outboard Boating*, Summer 1951, 4–5, 9.
23

BECKER C.D. (1970) Haematozoa of fishes, with emphasis on North American records. In *A symposium on Diseases of Fishes and Shellfishes*, pp. 82–100 (Ed. S F. Snieszko), *Spec. Publs., Am. Fish. Soc.*, No. 5. Washington D.C., 526 pp.
269

BECKER C.D. & THATCHER T.O. (1973) Toxicity of power plant chemicals to aquatic life. *U.S. Atomic Energy Commission, WASH–1249.*
262

BEDFORD B.C. (1964) Two mechanical aids for otolith reading. *Res. Bull. int. Commn NW Atlant. Fish.* (1), 79–81.
114

BELL G.R. (1967) A guide to the properties, characteristics and uses of some general anaesthetics for fish. *Bull. Fish. Res. Bd Can.*, No. **148**, 2nd ed., 9 pp.
21, 99, 199

BELL G.R. & HOSKINS G.E. (1971) Investigations of wild fish mortalities in B.C. 1969–1970. *Tech. Rep. Fish. Res. Bd Can.*, No. **245**, 17 pp.
256, 262

BELL G.R. & MARGOLIS L. (1976) The fish health program and the occurence of fish diseases in the Pacific Region of Canada. *Fish Path.* **10**, (2), 115–122.
268

BENECH V. (1975) Note sur la préparation des otolithes, plus particulièrement de ceux de l'anguille. *Annls Hydrobiol.* **6**, 173–178
114

BERG L.S., BOGDANOV A.S., KOZHIN N.I. & RASS T.S. (Eds) (1949) *Promyslovye ryby SSSR*. [Commercial Fishes of the USSR.] VNIRO, Moscow. Text, 787 pp. and atlas.
42

BERGMAN P.K., JEFFERTS K.B., FISCUS H.F. & HAGER R.C. (1968) A preliminary evaluation of an implanted coded wire fish tag. *Fish. Res. Pap. St. Wash.* **3**, 1, 63–84.
91

BERNHARDT R.W. (1960) Effect of fyke-net position on fish catch. *N.Y. Fish Game J.* **7**, 83–84.
38

BERST A.H. (1961) Selectivity and efficiency of experimental gill nets in South Bay and

Georgian Bay of Lake Huron. *Trans. Am. Fish. Soc.* **90**, 413–418.
34

BEUKEMA J.J. (1968) Predation by the three-spinal stickleback (*Gasterosteus aculeatus* L.): The influence of hunger and experience. *Behaviour* **31**, 1–126.
231, 232

BEVERTON R.J.H. & BEDFORD B.C. (1963) The effect on the return rate of the condition of fish when tagged. *Spec. Publs. int. Commn NW Atlant. Fish.* No. **4**, 106–116.
98

BEVERTON R.J.H. & HOLT S.J. (1957) On the dynamics of exploited fish populations. *Fishery Invest., Lond.*, Ser. 2, **19**, 533 pp.
129, 134, 278, 283

BEVERTON R.J.H. & HOLT S.J. (1959) A review of the lifespans and mortality rates of fish in nature and their relation to growth and other physiological characteristics. In *The Lifespan of Animals*, pp. 142–180 (Eds. C.E.W. Wolstenholme & M. O'Connor). *CIBA Found. Colloq., Ageing*, Vol. **5**, Churchill, London.
135, 284

BEVERTON R.J.H. & HOLT S.J. (1964) Tables of yield functions for fishery assessment. *F.A.O. Fish. tech. Pap.* **38**, 49 pp.
283

BIGELOW H.B. & SCHROEDER W.C. (1953) Fishes of the Gulf of Maine: First Revision. *Bull. U.S. Fish Wildl. Serv.*, No. **74**, 53, 577 pp.
192

BILTON H.T. (1974) Effects of starvation and feeding on circulus formation on scales of young sockeye salmon of four racial origins, and of one race of kokanee, coho and chinook salmon. In *Ageing of Fish*, pp. 40–70 (Ed. T.B. Bagenal). Unwin Brothers, Old Woking. 234 pp.
102, 111

BILTON H.M. & JENKINSON D.W. (1968) Comparison of the otolith and scale methods for aging sockeye (*Oncorhynchus nerka*) and chum (*O. keta*) salmon. *J. Fish. Res. Bd Can.* **25**, 1067–1069.
111

BIRKET L. (1969) The nitrogen balance in plaice, sole and perch. *J. exp. Biol.* **50**, 375–386.
244

BIRO P. (1969) The spring and summer nutrition of the 300–500 g pikeperch (*Lucioperca lucioperca* L.) in Lake Balaton in 1968. II. The calculation of the consumption, daily and monthly rations. *Annls Inst. biol. Tihany* **36**, 151–162.
249

BIROS F. (1970) Pesticide analytical manual. III. Methods which detect pesticide residues in human and environmental media. *U.S. Dept. of Health, Education and Welfare, Food and Drug Administration.*
272

BIROS F. *et al.* (1970) Pesticide analytical manual. II. Methods for individual pesticide residues. *U.S. Dept. of the Health, Education and Welfare, Food and Drug Administration.*
272

BLACKER R.W. (1964) Electronic flash photography of gadoid otoliths. *Res. Bull. int. Commn NW Atlant. Fish.* **1**, 36–38.
104

BLACKER R.W. (1974) The ICNAF cod otolith exchange scheme. In *Ageing of Fish*, pp. 108–113 (Ed. T.B. Bagenal). Unwin Brothers, Old Woking. 234 pp.
104, 114

BLANCHETEAU M., LAMARQUE P., MOUSSET G. & VIBERT R. (1961) Etude neurophysiologique de la pêche électrique. *Bull. Cent. Étude Rech. scient. Biarritz* **3**, 1–108.
24

BLAXHALL P.C. & DAISLEY K.W. (1973) Routine haematological methods for use with fish blood. *J. Fish Biol.* **5**, 771–781.
258, 263

BLAXTER J.H.S. (1969) Development: Eggs and larvae. In *Fish Physiology*, Vol. 3, 177–252 (Eds. W.S. Hoar and D.J. Randall). Academic Press, New York and London. 485 pp.
189, 193, 197

BLAXTER J.H.S. (Ed.) (1974) *The Early Life*

History of Fish. Springer-Verlag, Berlin. 765 pp.
201

BLAXTER J.H.S. & HEMPEL G. (1963) The influence of egg size on herring larvae (*Clupea harengus* L.). *J. Cons. perm. int. Explor. Mer* **28**, 211–240.
177, 199

BOCCARDY J.A. & COOPER E.L. (1963) The use of roterone and electrofishing in surveying small streams. *Trans. Am. Fish. Soc.* **92**, 307–310.
24

BOIKO E.G. (1951) Metodika opredeleniya vozrasta ryb po spilam plavnikov. [Methods of determining age of fish from finray sections.] *Trudy azov.-chernomorsk. naucho-issled. Inst. ryb. Khoz. Okeanogr.* (AzCher NIRO) 15.
115

BONDE T.J.H. (1965) Comparison of two types of gill nets used for lake survey purposes in Minnesota–Ontario boundary waters. *Dingell-Johnson Project FW-I-R, Investigational Report* No. 285, 11 pp. Minnesota Department of Conservation, Minneapolis.
32

BOUCHARD L.G. & MATTSON C.R. (1961) Immersion staining as a method of marking small salmon. *Progve Fish Cult.* **23**, 34–40.
89

BOWEN S.H. (1976) Feeding ecology of the cichlid fish *Sarotherodon mossambicus* in Lake Sibaya, Kwazulu. Ph.D. dissertation, Rhodes University, Grahamstown, 135 pp.
226, 253

BOYAR H.C. & CLIFFORD R.A. (1967) An automatic device for counting dry fish eggs. *Trans. Am. Fish. Soc.* **96**, 361–363.
169

BRACKEN J.J. & KENNEDY M.P. (1967) A key to the identification of the eggs and young stages of course fish in Irish waters. *Scient. Proc. R. Dubl. Soc.* Ser. B, **2**, 99–108.
186

BRANDER K. (1974) The effect of age reading errors on the statistical reliability of marine fish modelling. In *Ageing of Fish*, pp. 181–191 (Ed. T.B. Bagenal). Unwin Brothers, Old Woking. 234 pp.
117

BRASSINGTON R.A. & FERGUSON A. (1976) Electrophoretic identification of roach (*Rutilus rutilus* L.), rudd (*Scardinius erythrophthalmus* L.), bream (*Abramis brama* L.) and their natural hybrids. *J. Fish Biol.* **9**, 471–477.
51

BRAUHN J.L. & HOGAN J.W. (1972) Use of cold brands on channel catfish. *Progve Fish Cult.* **34**, 112.
87

BRAUM E. (1964) Experimentelle Untersuchungen zur ersten Nahrungsaufnahme und Biologie an Jungfischen von Blaufelchen (*Coregonus wartmanni* Bloch), Weissfelchen (*Coregonus fera* Jurine) und Hechten (*Esox lucius* L.). *Arch. Hydrobiol.* 28, Suppl. **5**, 183–244.
191, 192, 198

BREDER C.M. (1960) Design for a fry trap. *Zoologica, N.Y.* **45**, 155–159.
195

BREDER C.M. & ROSEN D.E. (1966) *Modes of Reproduction in Fishes.* Natural History Press, New York, 941 pp. (Extensive bibliography, pp. 679–901.)
179, 192

BRETT J.R. (1971a) Satiation time, appetite and maximum food intake of sockeye salmon, *Oncorhynchus nerka. J. Fish. Res. Bd Can.* **28**, 409–415.
229, 233

BRETT J.R. (1971b) Growth responses of young sockeye salmon (*Oncorhynchus nerka*) to different diets and planes of nutrition. *J. Fish. Res. Bd Can.* **28**, 1635–1643.
229

BRETT J.R. (1971c) Energetic responses of salmon to temperature. A study of some thermal relations in the physiology and freshwater ecology of the sockeye salmon (*Oncorhynchus nerka*). *Am. Zool.* **11**, 99–113.
232

BRETT J.R. & HIGGS D.A. (1970) Effect of temperature on the rate of gastric digestion

in fingerling sockeye salmon *Oncorhynchus nerka. J. Fish. Res. Bd Can.* **27,** 1767–1779.
249, 250

BRETT J.R., SHELBOURN J.E. & SHOOP C.T. (1969) Growth rate and body composition of fingerling sockeye salmon (*Oncorhynchus nerka*), in relation to temperature and ration size. *J. Fish. Res. Bd Can.* **26,** 2363–2394.
229

BRIDGER I.P. (1961) On the fecundity and larval abundance of Downs herring. *Fishery Invest. Lond.*, Ser. 2, **23,** 3. 30 pp.
171, 172

BRIGGS J.C. (1953) The behaviour and reproduction of salmonid fishes in a small coastal stream. *Fish Bull. Calif.* **94,** 1–62.
183

BRIGHAM R.K. & JENSEN A.C. (1964) Photographing otoliths and scales. *Progve Fish Cult.* **26,** 131–135.
112

BRODY S. (1945) *Bioenergetics and Growth.* Reinhold, New York, 1023 pp.
129, 131, 132, 134

BRONGERSMA-SANDERS M. (1957) Mass mortality in the sea. *Mem. geol. Soc. Am.* **67,** 1, 941–1010.
262

BROTHERS E.B., MATHEWS C.P. & LASKER R. (1976) Daily growth increments in otoliths from larval and adult fishes. *Fishery Bull.*, *Seattle* **74,** 1–8.
113

BROWN D.J.A. & LANGFORD T.E. (1975) An assessment of a tow-net used to sample coarse fish fry in rivers. *J. Fish Biol.* **7,** 533–538.
195

BROWNIE C. & ROBSON D.S. (1976) Models allowing for age-dependent survival rates for band-return data. *Biometrics* **32,** 305–323.
161

BRUEVICH S.W. (1939) [Distribution and Dynamics of Living Matter in the Caspian Sea.] *Dokl. Akad. Nauk SSSR* **25,** 138–141. [In Russian.]
4

BRYUZGIN V.L. (1955) Obchislyuval'nii stolik'—Novyi prilad dlya vivchennya tempu rostu rio po lustsi, kistkakh ta otolitakh. [The computing stage—a new device for calculating the rate of growth of fishes.] *Nauk. Zap. Khersonsk. Pedagogichn. Inst.*, No. 5
124

BRYUZGIN V.L. (1961) Fenomen Li. [Lee's phenomenon.] *Vop. Ikhtiol.* **17,** 140–149.
125

BRYUZGIN V.L. (1963) O metodakh izucheniya rosta ryb po cheshue, kostiam i otolitam. [Methods of studying growth of fish using scales, bones and otoliths.] *Vop. Ikhtiol.* **3,** 347–365 (Old Series No. 27). [FRB Trans. No. 553.]
120, 125

BUCHHOLZ M.M. & CARLANDER K.D. (1963) Failure of yellow bass, *Roccus mississippiensis*, to form annuli. *Trans. Am. Fish. Soc.* **92,** 384–390.
111

BUCKE D. (1972) Some histological techniques applicable to fish tissues. In *Diseases of Fishes*, pp. 153–189 (Ed. L.E. Mawdesley-Thomas), *Symp. zool. Soc. Lond.*, No. 30. Academic Press, London. 380 pp.
264, 266, 269

BÜCKMANN A. (1929) Die Methodik fischereibiologischer Untersuchungen an Meeresfischen. *Handb. biol. Arb. Meth.*, Abt. **9,** 6, 1, 1–194.
41, 46, 101, 112, 114, 115, 181, 182, 185

BULLOCK G.L., CONROY D.A. & SNIESZKO S.F. (1971) Bacterial diseases of fishes. In *Diseases of Fishes*, Book 2A. (Eds. S.F. Snieszko & H.R. Axelrod.) T.F.H. Publications Inc., Neptune, New Jersey. 151 pp.
267, 270

BULLOCK G.L. & SNIESZKO S.F (1969) Bacteria in blood and kidney of apparently healthy hatchery trout. *Trans. Am. Fish. Soc.* **98,** 268–271.
268

BURGNER R.L. (1962) Sampling red salmon fry by lake trap in the Wood River Lakes, Alaska. (Abstract of Article 7.) *Univ. Wash. Publs Fish.*, New Ser. **1,** 315–347.
37

BURNET A.M.R. (1961) An electric fishing machine with pulsatory direct current. *N.Z. Jl Sci.* **4**, 151–161.
26

BURNET A.M.R. (1969) An examination of the use of scales and fin rays for age determination of brown trout (*Salmo trutta* L.). *N.Z. Jl Sci.* **4**, 1, 151–161.
111

BURROWS R.E. (1951) A method for the enumeration of salmon and trout eggs by displacement. *Progve Fish Cult.* **13**, 25–30,
167

BUSS K. (1953) A method of marking trout by branding. *Prog. Rep. Pa Fish. Commn*, Sept. 1953.
87

BYKHOVSKAYA-PAVLOVSKAYA I.E. *et al.* (1962) *Opredelitel parazitov presnovodnykh ryb SSSR.* Izdalel'sl Akademii Nauk SSSR, Moskva-Leningrad. 776 pp. [Translated into English in Bykhovskaya-Pavlovskaya 1964.]
267

BYKHOVSKAYA-PAVLOVSKAYA I.E. *et al.* (1964) *Key to Parasites of Freshwater Fish in the U.S.S.R.* Israel Programme for Scientific Translations, Jerusalem. 919 pp. [Translation of Bykhovskaya-Pavlovskaya 1962.]
267

CALAPRICE J.R. & CUSHING J.E. (1967) A serological analysis of three populations of golden trout, *Salmo aquabonita*, Jordan. *Calif. Fish Game* **53**, 273–281.
96

CAMERON J.N., KOSTORIS J. & PENHALE P.A. (1973) Preliminary energy budget of the ninespine stickleback (*Pungitius pungitius*) in an arctic lake. *J. Fish. Res. Bd Can.* **30**, 1179–1189.
231

CARLANDER K.D. (1953) Use of gillnets in studying fish populations, Clear Lake, Iowa. *Proc. Iowa Acad. Sci.* **60**, 623–625.
36

CARLANDER K.D. (1974) Difficulties in ageing fish in relation to inland fisheries management. In *Ageing of Fish*, pp. 200–205 (Ed. T.B. Bagenal), Unwin Brothers, Old Woking. 234 pp.
117

CARLANDER K.D. & SMITH L.L. (1945) Some factors to consider in the choice between standard, fork, or total lengths in fishery investigations. *Copeia*, 1945, 7–12.
43

CARLIN B. (1955) Tagging of salmon smolts in the River Lagan. *Rep. Inst. Freshwat. Res. Drottningholm* **36**, 57–74.
93

CARLINE R.F. & HALL J.D. (1973) Evaluation of a method for estimating food consumption rates of fish. *J. Fish. Res. Bd Can.* **30**, 623–629.
231

CARLTON W.G. & JACKSON W.B. (1968) The eye lens as an age indicator in carp. *Copeia* **1968**, 633–636.
116

CARROTHERS P.J.G. (1957) The selection and care of nylon gill nets for salmon. *Fish. Res. Bd Can. Industrial Memorandum* No. **19**, 85 pp.
9

CARSCADDEN J.E. & LEGGETT W.C. (1975) Life history variations in populations of American shad, *Alosa sapidissima* (Wilson), spawning in tributaries of the St John River, New Brunswick. *J. Fish Biol.* **7**, 595–610.
171

CARTER E.R. (1954) An evaluation of nine types of commercial fishing gear in Kentucky Lake. *Trans. Ky Acad. Sci.* **15**, 56–80.
38

CASSELMAN J.M. (1974) Analysis of hard tissue of pike *Esox lucius* L. with special reference to age and growth. In *Ageing of Fish*, pp. 13–27 (Ed. T.B. Bagenal). Unwin Brothers, Old Woking. 234 pp.
115

CASSIE R.M. (1954) Some uses of probability papers in the analysis of size frequency distribution. *Aust. J. mar. Freshwat. Res.* **5**, 513–522.
116, 119

CHAMPION A.S. & HILL H.J. (1974) Comparison of pre-migration mortality of

salmon smolts which had been tagged or freeze-branded. *Fish. Mgmt* **5,** 23–24.
87

CHAPMAN D.G. (1952) Inverse, multiple and sequential sample censuses. *Biometrics* **8,** 286–306.
142

CHAPMAN D.G. & ROBSON D.S. (1960) The analysis of a catch curve. *Biometrics* **16,** 354–368.
158

CHAPMAN D.W. (1957a) Use of liquid latex injections to mark juvenile steelhead. *Progve Fish Cult.* **19,** 95–96.
88

CHAPMAN D.W. (1957b) An improved portable tattooing device. *Progve Fish Cult.* **19,** 182–184.
88

CHAPMAN D.W. (1967) Production in fish populations. In *The Biological Basis of Freshwater Fish Production,* pp. 3–29 (Ed. Shelby D. Gerking), Blackwell Scientific Publications, Oxford. 495 pp.
210, 212

CHAPMAN D.W. (1978) Production in fish populations. In *Ecology of Fish Production,* pp. 5–25 (Ed. Shelby D. Gerking), Blackwell Scientific Publications, Oxford. 519 pp.
216

CHEPRAKOVA YU.I. & VASETSKY S.G. (1962) Ostobennosti zreloi ikry vobly (*Rutilus rutilus caspicus* Jak.) v svyazi s kharakterom nerestovogo stada. [Characteristics of the mature eggs of roach (*Rutilus rutilus caspicus* Jak.) in relation to the character of the spawning population.] *Vop. Ikhtiol.* **2,** 262–274.
177

CHILD A.R., BURNELL A.M. & WILKINS N.P. (1976) The existence of two races of Atlantic salmon (*Salmo salar* L.) in the British Isles. *J. Fish Biol.* **8,** 35–43.
51, 96

CHILD A.R. & SOLOMON D.J. (1977) Observations on morphological and biochemical features of some cyprinid hybrids. *J. Fish Biol.* **11,** 125–131.
51

CHISZAR D. & WINDELL J.T. (1973) Predation by bluegill sunfish (*Lepomis macrochirus* R.) upon mealworm larvae (*Tenebrio molitor*). *Anim. Behav.* **21,** 536–543.
232

CHRISTENSEN J.M. (1964) Burning of otoliths, a technique for age determination of soles and other fish. *J. Cons. perm. int. Explor. Mer* **29,** 73–81.
114

CHUGUNOV N.L. (1926) Opredelenie vozrasta i tempa rosta ryb po kostyam. [Determination of age and growth rate of fish from bones.] *Sbornik statei po metodike opredeleniya vozrasta i rosta ryb.* Sibirksaya Ikhtiologicheskaya Laboratoriya, Krasnoyarsk.
115

CHUGUNOVA N.I. (1955) O vosstanovlenie istorii individual' noi zhizni ryby po ee cheschue. [Reconstruction of the life history of an individual fish from its scales.] *Zool. Zh.* **4,** 5.
43

CHUGUNOVA N.I. (1959) *Rukovodstvo po izuchenie vozrasta i rosta ryb.* Akademiya Nauk SSSR, 164 pp., Moscow. [Translated into English in Chugunova, 1963.]
43, 101, 106, 124

CHUGUNOVA N.I. (1963) *Age and Growth Studies in Fish.* National Science Foundation, Washington, 132 pp. [English translation of Chugunova, 1959.]
43, 101, 115

CHURCHILL W.S. (1963) The effect of fin removal on survival, growth and vulnerability to capture on stocked walleye fingerlings. *Trans. Am. Fish. Soc.* **92,** 298–300.
86, 118

CLAIRE, E.W. & PHILLIPS R.W. (1968) The stonefly *Acroneuria pacifica* as a potential predator on salmonid embryos. *Trans. Am. Fish. Soc.* **97,** 50–53.
258

CLEARY R.E. (1957) A comparison of trap net catches and angler success on some Iowa streams. In *Symposium on Evaluation of Fish Populations in Warm Water Streams held at Iowa State College, March 25, 1957,* pp. 28–30, Iowa Cooperative Research Unit, Iowa.
38

CLUTTER R.I. & WHITESEL L.E. (1956) Collection and interpretation of sockeye salmon scales. *Bull. int. Pacif. Salm. Fish. Commn* 9, 159 pp.
109

COBLE D.W. (1967) Effects of fin-clipping on mortality and growth of yellow perch with a review of similar investigations. *J. Wildl. Mgmt* 31, 173–180.
86

COCHRAN W.G. (1963) *Sampling Techniques.* John Wiley & Sons, New York. 413 pp.
155, 212, 276

CONROY D.A. (1972) Studies on the haematology of the Atlantic salmon (*Salmo salar* L.). In *Diseases of Fish*, pp. 101–127 (Ed. L.E. Mawdesley-Thomas). *Symp. zool. Soc. Lond.* No. 30. Academic Press, London. 380 pp.
269

COOPER G.P. & LAGLER K.F. (1956) The measurement of fish population size. *Trans. 21st N. Am. Wildl. Conf.* 281–297.
27

CORMACK R.M. (1968) The statistics of capture-recapture methods. *Oceanogr. mar. Biol.* 6, 455–506.
137

CORNING L.J. (1957) Test netting. *North Dakota Outdoors* 19, 4–5.
8

COUTANT C.C. (1972) Successful cold branding of non-salmonids. *Progve Fish Cult.* 34, 131–132.
87

COWEY C.B. & SARGENT J.R. (1972) Fish Nutrition. In *Advances in Marine Biology*, Vol. 10, pp. 382–492 (Eds. F.S. Russell & C.M. Yonge). Academic Press, New York. 558 pp.
247

CRAIG J.F. (1977) The body composition of adult perch, *Perca fluviatilis* L., in Windermere, with reference to seasonal changes and reproduction. *J. Anim. Ecol.* 46, 617–632.
236, 237

CRAMPTON E.W. & HARRIS L.E. (1969) *Applied Animal Nutrition.* W. H. Freeman, San Francisco.
237

CRICHTON M.J. (1935) Scale-absorption in salmon and sea trout. *Rep. Fishery Bd Scotl.*, Salmon Fish., No. 4.
111

CROSS D.G. (1972) The estimation of the size of freshwater fish populations. *Fish. Mgmt*, 3 (2) 13–17; (3) 12–16; (3) 20–23.
137

CROWE W.R. (1950) Construction and use of small trap nets. *Progve Fish Cult.* 12, 185–192.
38, 40

CUMMINS K.W. & WUYCHECK J.C. (1971) Calorific equivalents for investigations in ecological energetics. *Mitt. int. Verein. theor. angew. Limnol.*, No. 18, 158 pp.
225

CUSHING D.H. (1957) The number of pilchards in the Channel. *Fishery Invest., Lond.*, Ser. 2, 21, 5, 1–27.
151

CUSHING D.H. (1968) *Fisheries Biology. A Study of Population Dynamics.* University of Wisconsin Press, Madison. 200 pp.
137

CUSHING D.H. (1971) The dependence of recruitment on parent stock in different groups of fishes. *J. Cons. perm. int. Explor. Mer* 33, 340–362.
284

CUSHING D.H., DEVOLD F., MARR J.C. & KRISTJONSSON H. (1952) Some modern methods of fish detection—echo sounding, echo ranging and aerial scouting. *Fish. Bull. F.A.O.* 5, 3–4, 1–27.
19

DAGET J. (1952) Mémoires sur la biologie des poissons du Niger Moyen. I. Biologie et croissance des espèces du genre *Alestes*. *Bull. Inst. fr. Afr. noire* 14, 1, 191–225.
103

DAHL K. (1909) The assessment of age and growth in fish. *Int. Revue ges. Hydrobiol. Hydrogr.* 2, 4–5, 758–769.
101

DAVIES C.S. (1955) The injection of latex solution as a fish marking technique. *Invest. Indiana Lakes Streams* 4, 111–116.
88

DAVIES P.M.C. (1964) The energy relations of *Carassius auratus* L. II. The effect of food, crowding and darkness on heat production. *Comp. Biochem. Physiol.* **17**, 893–995.
229

DAVIS A.S. & PAULIK G.J. (1965) The design, operation, and testing of a photo-electric fish egg counter. *Progve Fish Cult.* **27**, 185–192.
169

DAVIS C.C. (1959) A planktonic fish egg from freshwater. *Limnol. Oceanogr.* **4**, 352–355.
180

DAVIS G.E. & WARREN C.E. (1965) Trophic relations of a sculpin in laboratory stream communities. *J. Wildl. Mgmt* **29**, 846–871.
217

DAVIS G.E. & WARREN C.E. (1971) Estimation of food consumption rates. In *Methods for Assessment of Fish Production in Fresh Waters*, pp. 227–248 (Ed. W.E. Ricker), 2nd Ed., Blackwell Scientific Publications, Oxford. 348 pp.
228, 239, 242

DAVIS H.S. (1953) *Culture and Diseases of Game Fishes*. Univ. of California Press, Berkeley. 332 pp.
267

DAVIS J.C. (1975) Minimal dissolved oxygen requirements of aquatic life with emphasis on Canadian species: a review. *J. Fish. Res. Bd Can.* **32**, 2295–2332.
272

DARNELL R.M. & MEIEROTTO R.M. (1962) Determination of feeding chronology in fishes. *Trans. Am. Fish. Soc.* **9**, 313–320.
249

DARROCK J.N. (1958) The multiple-recapture census. I. Estimation of a closed population. *Biometrika* **45**, 343–359.
142, 143

DARROCH J.N. (1959) The multiple-recapture census. II. Estimation when there is immigration or death. *Biometrika* **46**, 336–351.
145

DEACON J.E. (1961) A staining method for marking large numbers of small fish. *Progve Fish Cult.* **23**, 41–42.
89

DE BONT A.F. (1967) Some aspects of age and growth of fish in temperate and tropical waters. In *The Biological Basis of Freshwater Fish Production*, 67–88 (Ed. Shelby D. Gerking). Blackwell Scientific Publications, Oxford. 495 pp.
103

DEELDER C.L. (1976) The problem of the supernumary zones in otoliths of the European eel (*Anguilla anguilla* (Linnaeus, 1758)); a suggestion to cope with it. *Aquaculture* **9**, 373–379.
114

DEELDER C.L. & WILLEMSE J.J. (1973) Age determination of freshwater teleosts based on annular structures in fin rays. *Aquaculture* **1**, 365–371.
115

DELL M.B. (1968) A new fish tag and rapid cartridge-fed applicator. *Trans. Am. Fish. Soc.* **97**, 57–59.
94

DENZER H.W. (1956) Die Electrofischerei. In *Handb. Binnenfisch. Mitteleur.* Suppl. to vol. **5**, 3, 141–233.
25

DE ROCHE S.E. (1963) Slowed growth of lake trout following tagging. *Trans. Am. Fish. Soc.* **92**, 185–186.
118, 121

DE RUITER L. (1963) The physiology of vertebrate feeding behavior: towards a synthesis of the ethological and physiological approaches to problems of behavior. *Z. Tierpsychol.* **20**, 498–516.
232

DE SILVA S.S. (1973) Aspects of the reproductive biology of the sprat, *Sprattus sprattus* (L.) in inshore waters of the west coast of Scotland. *J. Fish Biol.* **5**, 689–706.
169

DICK M.W. (1973) Saprolegniales. In *The fungi, an Advanced Treatise*, Vol. IVB, pp. 113–144 (Eds. G.C. Ainsworth, F.K. Sparrow & A.S. Sussman), Academic Press, New York. 504 pp.
267

DIETRICH G., SAHRHAGE D. & SCHUBERT K. (1959) Locating fish concentrations by thermometric methods. In *Modern Fishing*

Gear of the World, Vol. **1**, pp. 453–461 (Ed. H.K. Kristjonsson), Fishing News (Books) Ltd, London. 640 pp.
20

DOGIEL V.A., PETRUSHEVSKI G.K. & POLYANSKI YU I. (1970) *Parasitology of Fishes*. Translated by Z. Kabata. Oliver & Boyd, Edinburgh. 384 pp.
267

DOUDOROFF D. & SHUMWAY D.L. (1970) Dissolved oxygen requirements of freshwater fishes. *F.A.O. Fish. tech. Pap.*, No. **86**. 291 pp.
272

DUBOS R.J. (1955) Second thoughts on the germ theory. *Scient. Am.* **192**, 31–35.
270

DUNCAN R.N. & DONALDSON I.J. (1968) Tattoo-marking of fingerling salmonids with fluorescent pigments. *J. Fish. Res. Bd Can.* **25**, 2233–2236.
89

DUNN A. & COKER C.M. (1951) Notes on marking fish with biological stains. *Copeia* **1951**, 28–31.
90

DUNSTAN W.A. & BOSTICK W.E. (1956) New tattooing devices for marking juvenile salmon. *Fish. Res. Pap. St. Wash.* **1, 4**, 70–79.
88

DÜRR W. (1957) Untersuchungen über die verschiedene Gestalt der Schuppen beim Karpfen, *Cyprinus carpio* L. *Z. Fisch.* (N.F.) **5**, 325–421.
109

EBEL W.J. (1969) Supersaturation of nitrogen in the Columbia River and its effects on salmon and steelhead trout. *Fishery Bull. Fish Wildl. Serv. U.S.* **68**, 1–11.
256

EBEL W.J. (1974) Marking fishes and invertebrates III. Coded wire tags useful in automatic recovery of chinook salmon and steelhead trout. *Mar. Fish. Rev.* **36**, 10–13.
91

EDMONDSON W.T. (Ed.) (1959) *Freshwater Biology*. 2nd edition. Originally by Ward & Whipple. John Wiley & Sons Inc., New York. 1248 pp.
270

EDWARDS D.J. (1971) Effect of temperature on rate of passage of food through the alimentary canal of plaice *Pleuronectes platessa* L. *J. Fish Biol.* **3**, 433–439.
247

EIFAC (1964) Water quality criteria for European freshwater fisheries. Report on finely divided solids and inland fisheries. *EIFAC tech. Pap.*, No. **1**, 21 pp.
272

EIFAC (1968a) Water quality criteria for European freshwater fish. Report on extreme pH values and inland fisheries. *EIFAC tech. Pap.*, No. **4**, 18 pp.
272

EIFAC (1968b) Water quality criteria for European freshwater fish. Report on water temperature and inland fisheries based mainly on Slavonic literature. *EIFAC tech. Pap.*, No. **6**, 32 pp.
272

EIFAC (1969) Water quality criteria for European freshwater fish. List of literature on the effect of water temperature on fish. *EIFAC tech. Pap.*, No. **8**, 8 pp.
272

EIFAC (1970) Water quality criteria for European freshwater fish. Report on ammonia and inland fisheries. *EIFAC tech. Pap.*, No. **11**, 12 pp.
272

EIFAC (1972) Water quality criteria for European freshwater fish. Report on monohydric phenols and inland fisheries. *EIFAC tech. Pap.*, No. **15**, 18 pp.
272

EIFAC (1973a) Water quality criteria for European freshwater fish. Report on dissolved oxygen and inland fisheries. *EIFAC tech. Pap.*, No. **19**, 10 pp.
262

EIFAC (1973b) Water quality criteria for European freshwater fish. Report on zinc and freshwater fish. *EIFAC tech. Pap.*, No. **21**, 22 pp.
272

EIFAC (1975) Report on fish toxicity testing

procedures. *EIFAC tech. Pap.*, No. **24**, 25 pp.
262

EIFAC (1976) Water quality criteria for European freshwater fish. Report on copper and freshwater fish. *EIFAC tech. Pap.*, No. **27**, 21 pp.
272

EINSELE W. (1943) Über das Wachstum der Coregonen im Voralpengebiet, insbesondere über das Verhältnis von Schuppen- und Längenwachstum. *Z. Fisch.* **41**, 1.
107

EIPPER A.W. & FORNEY J.L. (1965) Evaluation of partial fin-clips for marking largemouth bass, walleyes and rainbow trout. *N.Y. Fish Game J.* **12**, 233–240.
89

ELLIOTT J.M. (1970) Diel changes in invertebrate drift and the food of trout. *Salmo trutta* L. *J. Fish Biol.* **2**, 161–165.
220

ELLIOTT J.M. (1972) Rates of gastric evacuation in brown trout *Salmo trutta* L. *Freshwat. Biol.* **2**, 1–18.
249, 250

ELLIOTT J.M. (1975a) Weight of food and time required to satiate brown trout, *Salmo trutta* L. *Freshwat. Biol.* **5**, 51–64.
229, 232, 233

ELLIOTT J.M. (1975b) Number of meals in a day, maximum weight of food consumed in a day and maximum rate of feeding for brown trout, *Salmo trutta* L. *Freshwat. Biol.* **5**, 287–303.
229, 232, 250

ELLIOTT J.M. (1976) Energy losses in the waste products of brown trout (*Salmo trutta* L.) *J. Anim. Ecol.* **45**, 561–580.
233, 234, 243

ELSON P.F. (1962a) The Pollett apron seine. *J. Fish. Res. Bd Can.* **19**, 93–100.
29

ELSON P.F. (1962b) Predator-prey relationships between fish-eating birds and Atlantic salmon. *Bull. Fish. Res. Bd Can.*, No. **133**, 87 pp.
26

ELSTER H.J. (1933) Eine Schlittendredge.

Int. Revue ges. Hydrobiol. Hydrogr. **27**, 290–292.
184

EMBODY G.C. (1934) Relation of temperature to the incubation period of eggs of four species of trout. *Trans. Am. Fish. Soc.* **64**, 281–292.
192

EL-ZARKA S. EL-DIN (1959) Fluctuations in the population of yellow perch, *Perca flavescens* (Mitchill), in Saginaw Bay, Lake Huron. *Fishery Bull. Fish Wildl. Serv. U.S.* **59**, No. **151**, 136–143.
124

ENGLISH T.S. (1964) A theoretical model for estimating the abundance of planktonic fish eggs. *Rapp. P.-v. Réun. Cons. perm. int. Explor. Mer* **155**, 164–170.
151

ESCHMEYER P.H. (1959) Survival and retention of tags, and growth of tagged lake trout in a rearing pond. *Progve Fish Cult.* **21**, 17–21.
118

ESKILDSEN U.K. & JÖRGENSEN P.V. (1973) On the possible transfer of trout pathogenic viruses by gulls. *Riv. ital. Piscic Ittiopatol. A.* **8** (4), 104–105.
258

EVEREST F.H. & EDMUNDSON E.H. (1967) Cold branding for field use in marking juvenile salmonids. *Progve Fish Cult.* **29**, 175–176.
87

EVERHART W.H., EIPPER A.W. & YOUNGS W.D. (1975) *Principles of Fishery Science.* Cornell University Press, Ithaca. 288 pp.
137

EVERHART W.H. & RUPP R.S. (1960) Barb type plastic fish tag. *Trans. Am. Fish. Soc.* **89**, 241–242.
94

EZZAT A.A., SHABANA M.B. & FARGHALY A.M. (1974) Studies on the blood characteristics of *Tilapia zilli* (Gervais). I. Blood cells. *J. Fish Biol.* **6**, 1–12.
259

FABRICIUS E. (1954) Aquarium observations on the spawning behaviour of the burbot

Lota vulgaris L. *Rep. Inst. Freshwat. Res. Drottningholm.* **35,** 51–57.
180

FABRICIUS E. & GUSTAFSON K.J. (1954) Further aquarium observations on the spawning behaviour of the char *Salvelinus alpinus* L. *Rep. Inst. Freshwat. Res. Drottningholm* **35,** 58–104.
180

FABRICIUS E. & LINDROTH A. (1954) Experimental observations on the spawning of whitefish *Coregonus lavaretus* L. in the stream aquarium of the Hölle laboratory at river Indalsälven. *Rep. Inst. Freshwat. Res. Drottningholm* **35,** 105–112.
180

FABER D. (MS) (1963) Larval fish from the pelagic region of two Wisconsin lakes. Ph.D. thesis, Univ. of Wisconsin, 153 pp., University Microfilms, Ann Arbor, Mich. [*Diss. Abstr.* **24,** 17561].
193

FAGADE S.O. (1971) The food and feeding of *Tilapia* species in the Lagos Lagoon. *J. Fish Biol.* **3,** 151–156.
224

FAGADE S.O. (1974) Age determination in *Tilapia melanotheron* (Ruppell) in the Lagos Lagoon, Nigeria, with a discussion of the environmental and physiological basis of growth markings in the tropics. In *Ageing of Fish*, pp. 71–77 (Ed. T.B. Bagenal). Unwin Brothers, Old Woking. 234 pp.
103

FAGERSTRÖM A., GUSTAFSON K.J. & LINDSTROM T. (1969) Tag shedding, growth and differential mortality in a marking experiment with trout and char. *Rep. Inst. Freshwat. Res. Drottningholm* **49,** 27–43.
118

F.A.O. (1976) Monitoring of fish stock abundance: the use of catch and effort data. A report of the ACMRR Working Party on Fishing Effort and Monitoring of Fish Stock Abundance, Rome, 16–20 December 1975. *F.A.O. Fish. tech. Pap.* **155.**
277

FERGUSON R.G. & REGIER H.A. (1963) Selectivity of four trawl cod ends toward smelt. *Trans. Am. Fish. Soc.* **92,** 125–131.
31

FISHER R.A. & YATES F. (1949) *Statistical Tables.* Hafner Publishing Company Inc., New York. 112 pp.
13

FOERSTER R.E. (1930) An investigation of the life history and propagation of the sockeye salmon (*Oncorhynchus nerka*) at Cultus Lake, British Columbia. No. 3. The down-stream migration of the young in 1926 and 1927. *Contr. Can. Biol. Fish.* **5,** 57–82.
197

FORNEY J.L. (1975) Abundance of larval walleyes (*Stizostedion vitreum*) estimated from the catches in high-speed nets. In *Symposium on the Methodology for the Survey, Monitoring and Appraisal of Fishery Resources in Lakes and Large Rivers.* 581–588 (Ed. Robin L. Welcomme). *EIFAC technical Paper,* No. **23** (Suppl. 1, Vol. 2), 747 pp.
195

FORT R.S. & BRAYSHAW J.D. (1961) *Fishery Management.* Faber and Faber, London. 398 pp.
28, 29

FORTMANN H.R., HAZZARD A.S. & BRADFORD A.D. (1961) The relation of feeding before stocking to catchibility of trout. *J. Wildl. Mgmt* **25,** 391–397.
231

FOX W.W. (1970) An exponential surplus-yield model for optimizing exploited fish populations. *Trans. Am. Fish. Soc.* **99,** 80–88.
280

FRANK T.H. (1968) Telemetering the electrocardiogram of free swimming *Salmo irideus*. *IEEE Trans. biomed. Engng* **15,** 111–114.
95

FRASER C.McL. (1916) Growth of the spring salmon. *Trans. Pacif. Fish. Soc. Seattle,* for 1915, 29–39.
122

FREEMAN K. (1974) Growth, mortality and seasonal cycle of *Mytilis edulis* in two Nova Scotian enbayments. *Tech. Rep. Fish. Res. Bd Can.* **500,** 112 pp.
132, 133

FREIDENFELT T. (1922) Undersökningar över gösens tillväxt särskilt i Hjälmaren. *Meddn K. LantbrStyr.* No. **235**. Stokholm.
115

FROMM P.O. & GILLETTE J.R. (1968) Effect of ambient ammonia on blood ammonia and nitrogen excretion of rainbow trout (*Salmo gairdneri*). *Comp. Biochem. Physiol.* **26**, 887–896.
244

FROST W.E. (1963) The homing of charr (*Salvelinus willughbii*) (Gunther) in Windermere. *Anim. Behav.* **11**, 74–82.
96

FROST W.E. & KIPLING C. (1959) The determination of the age and growth of the pike (*Esox lucius* L.) from the scales and the opercular bones. *J. Cons. perm. int. Explor. Mer* **24**, 314–341.
115

FRY F.E.J. (1943) A method for the calculation of the growth of fishes from scale measurements. *Univ. Toronto Stud. biol. Ser.* **51**, 7–18. Publs Ont. Fish. Res. Lab., No. 61.
123, 124

FRY F.E.J. (1949) Statistics of a lake trout fishery. *Biometrics* **5**, 27–67.
168

FRY F.E.J., CUCIN D., KENNEDY J.C. & PAPSON A. (1960) The use of lead versenate to place a time mark on fish scales. *Trans. Am. Fish. Soc.* **89**, 149–153.
90

FRY D.H. (1931) The ring net, half ring net, or purse lampara in the fisheries of California. *Fish Bull. Calif.* **27**, 65 pp.
29, 31

FRYER G. (1961) Observations on the biology of the cichlid fish *Tilapia variabilis* Boulenger in the northern waters of Lake Victoria (East Africa). *Revue Zool. Bot. afr.* **64**, 1–33.
173, 174

FRYER G. & ILES T.D. (1972) *The Cichlid Fishes of the Great Lakes of Africa.* Oliver & Boyd, Edinburgh. 641 pp.
180

FRYER J.L., PILCHER K.S., SANDERS J.E., ROHOVEC J.S., ZINN J.L., GROBERG W.J. & McCOY R.H. (1976) Temperature, infectious diseases, and the immune response in salmonid fish. *U.S. Environmental Protection Agency, Ecological Research Series. EPA–600/3–76–021.* 72 pp.
256

FUJIHARA M.P. & NAKATANI R.E. (1967) Cold and mild heat marking of fish. *Progve Fish Cult.* **29**, 172–174.
87

FUNK J.L. (1957) Relative efficiency and selectivity of gear used in the study of fish populations in Missouri streams. In *Symposium on Evaluation of Fish Populations in Warm Water Streams held at Iowa State College, March 25, 1957,* pp. 31–44, Iowa Cooperative Research Unit, Iowa.
27, 28, 38

FUNK J.L. (1958) Relative efficiency and selectivity of gear used in the study of stream fish populations. *Trans. 23rd N. Am. Wildl. Conf.* 236–248.
27, 28, 38

FURUKAUA A. & TUSUKAHARA H. (1966) On the acid digestion method for the determination of chronic oxide as an index substance in the study of digestibility in fish feed. *Bull. Jap. Soc. scient. Fish.* **32**, 502–508.
241

GALKIN G.G. (1958) Atlas cheshui presnovodnykh kostistykh ryb. [Atlas of the scales of freshwater bony fishes.] *Izv. vses. naucho-issled. Inst. ozern. rechn. ryb. Khoz.* **46**, 1–105.
109

GARDELLA E.S. & STASKO A.B. (1974) A linear array hydrophone for determining depth of fish fitted with ultrasonic transmitters. *Trans. Fish. Soc.* **103**, 635–637.
95

GARNER J. (1962) *How to Make and Set Nets, or the Technology of Netting.* Fishing News (Books) Ltd, London, 95 pp.
9, 29, 31

GARROD D.J. (1959) The growth of *Tilapia esculenta* Graham in Lake Victoria. *Hydrobiologia* **12**, 268–298.
10, 103

GEBHARDS S.V. (1960) *Net Repair Manual.* Idaho Department of Fish and Game, Moscow, Idaho, 21 pp.
9

GERKING S.D. (1952) The protein metabolism of sunfishes of different ages. *Physiol. Zool.* **25,** 358–372.
244

GERKING S.D. (1955) Influence of rate of feeding on body composition and protein metabolism of bluegill sunfish. *Physiol. Zool.* **28,** 267–282.
236, 244, 248

GERKING S.D. (1958) The survival of fin-clipped and latex injected redear sunfish. *Trans. Am. Fish. Soc.* **87,** 220–228.
88

GERKING S.D. (1962) Production and food utilization in a population of bluegill sunfish. *Ecol. Monogr.* **32,** 31–78.
88, 211, 244

GERKING S.D. (Ed.) (1967) *The Biological Basis of Freshwater Fish Production.* Blackwell Scientific Publications, Oxford. 495 pp.
227, 242

GERKING S.D. (1971) Influence of rate of feeding and body weight on protein metabolism of bluegill sunfish. *Physiol. Zool.* **44,** 9–19.
244

GESAMP (In the press) Report of the 8th Session of Group of Experts on Scientific Aspects of Marine Pollution, F.A.O., Rome, 21 to 27 April 1976.
256

GOLDSPINK C.R. & BANKS J.W. (1971) A readily recognisable tag for marking bream (*Abramis brama* L.). *J. Fish Biol.* **3,** 407–411.
94

GOLTERMAN H.L. (Ed.) (1971) *Methods for Chemical Analysis of Fresh Waters.* I.B.P. Handbook No. **8,** Blackwell Scientifi Publications, Oxford. 180 pp.
271

GOODE G.B. (1884–1887) The Fisheries and Fishery Industries of the United States. *U.S. Comm. Fish and Fisheries,* 5 sects. (bound in 7 vols) Section V, 1887. History and Methods of the Fisheries. (2 vols of text and 1 vol. of 255 pl.)
8

GRAHAM M. (1929) Studies of age-determination in fish. Part II. A survey of the literature. *Fishery Invest. Lond.,* Ser. II, **11,** 2, 50 pp.
101, 125

GRAHAM M. (Ed.) (1956) *Sea fisheries. Their Investigation in the United Kingdom.* Edward Arnold (Publishers) Ltd, London. 487 pp.
181, 185

GRANDE M. (1965) Age determination from scales and otoliths in the brook trout (*Salvelinus fontinalis* Mitchill). *Nytt Mag. Zool.* **12,** 35–37.
111

GRAY J. (1929) The kinetics of growth. *J. exp. Biol.* **6,** 248–274.
135

GREEN G.H. & NORTHCOTE T.G. (1968) Latex injection as a method of marking large catostomids for long-term study. *Trans. Am. Fish. Soc.* **97,** 281–282.
88

GREENLAND D.C. & BRYAN J.D. (1974) Anchor tag loss in channel catfish. *Progve Fish Cult.* **36,** 181–182.
97

GREER WALKER M., MITSON R.B. & STORETON-WEST T. (1971) Trials with a transponding acoustic fish tag tracked with an electronic sonar scanner. *Nature, Lond.* **229,** 196–198.
95

GRIZZLE J.M. & RODGERS W.A. (1976) *Anatomy and Histology of the Channel Catfish.* Auburn University Agricultural Experimental St. Auburn, Alabama. 94 pp.
259

GROVES A.B. & NOVOTNY A.J. (1965) A thermal marking technique for juvenile salmonids. *Trans. Am. Fish. Soc.* **94,** 386–389.
87

GUDGER E.W. (1924) More about spider webs and spider web fish nets. *Bull. N.Y. zool. Soc.* **27,** 94–97.
27

GUDGER E.W. (1950) Fishing with the hand, 'tickling trout' and other fishes in Great Britain, 1602–1943. *Aust. Mus. Mag.* **10**, 61–64.
23

GULLAND J.A. (1958) Age determination of cod by fin rays and otoliths. *Spec. Publs int. Com. NW. Atlant. Fish.* (1), 179–190.
104

GULLAND J.A. (1961) Fishery and the stocks of fish at Iceland. *Fishery Invest. Lond.*, Ser. 2, **23** (4). 52 pp.
281

GULLAND J.A. (1964a) Manual of methods for fish population analysis. *F.A.O. Fish. tech. Pap.* **40**, 1–60.
131

GULLAND J.A. (1964b) Catch by unit as a measure of abundance. *Rapp. P.-v. Réun. Cons. perm. int. Explor. Mer* **155**, 8–14.
277

GULLAND J.A. (1966) Manual of sampling and statistical methods for fisheries biology. Part I—sampling methods. *F.A.O. Manuals in Fisheries Science*, No. **3**. 87 pp.
13

GULLAND J.A. (1974) *The Management of Marine Fisheries*. University of Washington Press, Seattle. 198 pp.
137

GULLAND J.A. & HARDING D. (1961) The selection of *Clarias mossambicus* (Peters) by nylon gillnets. *J. Cons. perm. int. Explor. Mer*, **26**, 215–222.
10

HAGER R. (1975) A technique for the mass recovery of coded wire tags from young salmonids. *Progve Fish Cult.* **37**, 51.
91

HALEY R., DAVIS S.P. & HYDE J.M. (1967) Environmental stress and *Aeromonas liquefaciens* in America and threadfin shad mortalities. *Progve Fish Cult.* **29**, 193.
257

HANSEN D.F. (1944) Rate of escape of fishes from hoopnets. *Trans. Ill. St. Acad. Sci.* **37**, 115–122.
38

HARDING J.P. (1949) The use of probability paper in the graphical analysis of polymodal frequency distributions. *J. mar. biol. Ass. U.K.* **28**, 141–153.
116

HARPER A.E. (1967) Effects of dietary protein content and amino acid pattern on food intake and preference. In *Handbook of Physiology*, Section 6, vol. 1, article 29, pp. 399–410, American Physiological Society, Washington D.C.
225

HARRISON H.M. (1954) An estimation of the population of channel catfish in the Humboldt area with notes on the hoopnet as a sampling instrument. *Q. Biol. Rep. Iowa Fish Game Div.* **6**, 21–25.
38

HARRISON H.M. (1955) Results and discussion of the electrical shocking method of conducting stream surveys in Iowa streams, 1955. *Q. Biol. Rep. Iowa Fish Game Div.* **7**, 16–20.
25

HARRISON H.M. (1959) Preliminary report on the use of a repellant to drive fish in streams. *Q. Biol. Rep. Iowa Fish Game Div.* **11**, 19–23.
35

HARRISON P.G. & MANN K.H. (1975) Chemical changes during seasonal cycle of growth and decay in eelgrass (*Zostra marina*) on the Atlantic coast of Canada. *J. Fish. Res. Bd Can.* **32**, 615–621.
225

HART P.J.B. & PITCHER T.J. (1969) Field trials of fish marking using a jet inoculator. *J. Fish Biol.* **1**, 383–385.
88

HARTT A.C. (1963) Problems in tagging salmon at sea. *Spec. Publs. int. Commn NW. Atlant. Fish.* **4**, 144–155.
97

HASKELL D.C., GUDULDIG D. & SNOEK E. (1955) An electric trawl. *N.Y. Fish Game J.*, **2**, 120–125.
32

HASLER A.D. & FABER W.M. (1941) A tagging method for small fish. *Copeia*, 1941, 161–165.
90

HASS H. (1968) Untersuchungen über die vertikale und horizontale Verteilung der Eier der Finte, *Alosa fallax* (Lacépede 1803), in der Elbe. *Arch. FischWiss.* **19**, 46–55.
182

HAWKINS A.D., MACLENNAN D.N., URQUHART G.G. & ROBB C. (1974) Tracking cod (*Gadus morhua* L.) in a Scottish sea lock. *J. Fish Biol.* **6**, 225–236.
95

HAWKINS R.I. & MAWDESLEY-THOMAS L.E. (1972) Fish haematology—a bibliography. *J. Fish Biol.* **4**, 193–232.
51, 258, 269

HAYES F.R. (1964) The mud-water interface. *Oceanogr. Mar. Biol.* **2**, 121–145.
179

HAZZARD A.S. (1947) Lake trout planting experiment in Lake Michigan. *Mich. Conserv.* **16**, 6–7.
118

HEALEY M.C. (1971) Gonad development and fecundity of the Sand Goby, *Gobius minutus* Pallas. *Trans. Am. Fish. Soc.* **100**, 520–526.
173

HEALEY M.C. (1972) Bioenergetics of a sand goby (*Gobius minutus*) population. *J. Fish. Res. Bd Can.* **29**, 187–194.
228, 230

HEARD W.R. (1964) Phototactic behaviour of emerging sockeye salmon fry. *Anim. Behav.* **12**, 382–388.
196

HANAHAN D.J. (1960) *Lipide Chemistry.* John Wiley & Sons, Inc., New York. 330 pp.
237

HANSON S.W.F. & OLLEY J. (1963) Application of the Bligh and Dyer method of lipid extraction to tissue homogenates. *J. Biochem.* **89**, 101–102.
237

HEDERSTRÖM H. (1959) Observations on the age of fishes. *Rep. Inst. Freshwat. Res., Drottningholm* **40**, 161–164.
101

HEMMINGSEN A.M. (1960) Energy metabolism as related to body size and respiratory surfaces and its evolution. *Rep. Steno meml Hosp.* (Copenhagen), **9**, 3–110.
135

HENDERSON H.F., RYDER R.A. & KUDHONGANIA A.W. (1973) Assessing fishery potential of lakes and reservoirs. *J. Fish. Res. Bd Can.* **30**, 2000–2009.
285

HENDERSON H.F. & WELCOMME R.L. (1974) The relationship of yield to Morpho-Edaphic Index and numbers of fishermen in African inland fisheries. *Committee for Inland Fish. Afr.* **1**, 19 pp.
285

HENSEN V. (1887) Über die Bestimmung des Planktons oder des in Meere freilebenden Materials an Pflanzen und Tieren. *Wiss. Meeresunters.* **5**, 1–108.
170

HICKLING C.F. (1940) The fecundity of herring of the southern North Sea. *J. mar. biol. Ass. U.K.* **24**, 619–632.
172

HICKLING C.F. (1971) *Fish Culture.* Faber & Faber, London. 317 pp.
188

HILE R. (1936) Age and growth of the ciscoe, *Leucichthys artedi* (Le Sueur), in the lakes of the northeastern highlands, Wisconsin. *Bull. Bur. Fish. U.S.* **48**, 19, 211–317.
125

HILE R. (1941) Age and growth of the rock bass, *Ambloplites rupestris* (Rafinesque), in Nebish Lake, Wisconsin. *Trans. Wis. Acad. Sci. Arts Lett.* **33**, 189–337.
123, 124

HILE R. (1948) Standardization of methods of expressing lengths and weights of fish. *Trans. Am. Fish. Soc.* **75**, 157–164.
43

HILE R. (1950) A monograph for the computation of the growth of fish from scale measurements. *Trans. Am. Fish. Soc.* **78**, 156–162.
106

HILE R. (1970) Body-scale relation and calculation of growth in fishes. *Trans. Am. Fish. Soc.* **99**, 468–474.
120

HILE R. & JOBES F.W. (1941) Age, growth and production of the yellow perch, *Perca flavescens* (Mitchill), of Saginaw

Bay. *Trans. Am. Fish. Soc.* **70,** 102–122.
124

HINTON, D.E., KENDALL M.W. & SILVER B.B. (1973) Use of histologic and histochemical assessments in the prognosis of the effects of aquatic pollutants. In *Biological Methods for the Assessment of Water Quality*, pp. 194–208. American Society for Testing Materials, ASTM STP 528.
269

HIYAMA Y. & ICHIKAWA R. (1952) A method to mark the time in the scale and other hard tissues of fishes to see their growth. *Jap. J. Ichthyol.* **2,** 156–157.
90

HJORT J., JAHN G. & OTTESTAD P. (1933) The optimum catch. *Hvalråd Skr.* **7,** 92–127.
129

HOBBS D.F. (1937) Natural reproduction of quinnat salmon, brown and rainbow trout in certain New Zealand waters. *Fish. Bull. N.Z.* **6.** 104 pp.
182

HOBBS D.F. (1948) Trout fisheries in New Zealand. Their development and management. *Fish. Bull. N.Z.* **9.** 175 pp.
182, 183, 200

HODDER V.M. (1963) Fecundity of Grand Bank haddock. *J. Fish. Res. Bd Can.* **20,** 1465–1488.
176

HOFFMAN G.L. (1976) *Parasites of North American Freshwater Fishes.* University of California Press, Berkeley. 486 pp.
267

HOFFMAN G.L. (1970) Intercontinental and transcontinental dissemination and transfaunation of fish parasites with emphasis on whirling disease (*Myxosoma cerebralis*). In *A Symposium on Diseases of Fishes and Shellfishes*, pp. 69–81 (Ed. S.F. Snieszko), *Spec. Publs. Am. Fish. Soc.*, No. **5,** Washington D.C. 526 pp.
256

HOFFMAN G.L. (1975) Lesions due to internal helminths of freshwater fishes. In *The Pathology of Fishes*, pp. 151–187 (Eds

W.E. Ribelin and G. Migaki), University of Wisconsin Press, Madison. 1004 pp.
269

HOFFMAN G.L., PRESCOTT G.W. & THOMPSON C.R. (1965) *Chlorella* parasitic in bluegills. *Progve Fish Cult.* **27,** 175.
256

HOGMAN W.J. (1968) Annulus formation on scales of four species of coregonids reared under artificial conditions. *J. Fish. Res. Bd Can.* **25,** 2111–2172.
Fig. 5.9

HOLDEN M.J. (1955) Ring formation in the scales of *Tilapia variabilis* Boulenger and *T. esculenta* Graham from Lake Victoria. *Rep. E. Afr. Freshwat. Fish. Res. Org.* 1954/55, Appendix C, 36–40.
103

HOLDEN M.J. & MEADOWS P.S. (1964) The fecundity of the spurdog (*Squalus acanthias* L.) *J. Cons. perm. int. Explor. Mer* **28,** 418–424.
169

HOLDEN M.J. & VINCE M.R. (1973) Age validation studies on the centra of *Raja clavata* using tetracycline. *J. Cons. perm. int. Explor. Mer* **35,** 13–17.
105

HOLT S.J. (1957) Method of determining gear selectivity and its application. MS of paper presented to the Joint Scientific Meeting ICNAF, ICES and FAO, Lisbon (No. **5,** 15).
10

HOLT S.J. (1964) Computer programs for fishery problems. *F.A.O. Fish. Circ.*, No. **7,** Revision 4. 9 pp.
15

HOPSON A.J. (1965). Winter scale rings in *Lates niloticus* (Pisces: Centropomidae) from Lake Chad. *Nature, Lond.* **208,** 1013–1014.
103

HORAK D.L. (1969) The effects of fin removal on the stamina of hatchery reared rainbow trout. *Progve Fish Cult.* **31,** 217–220.
86

HORAK D.L. & TANNER H.A. (1964) The use of vertical gillnets in studying fish depth distribution, Horsetooth Reservoir,

Colorado. *Trans. Am. Fish. Soc.* **93,** 137–145.
35

Hösl A. (1959) Dangers and precautions in the electrical fishery. In *Modern Fishing Gear of the World,* Vol. 1, pp. 589–591 (Ed. H. Kristjonsson), Fishing News (Books) Ltd, London. 640 pp.
25

Hubbs C.L. & Lagler K.F. (1947) Fishes of the Great Lakes region. *Bull. Cranbrook Inst. Sci.* **26.** 186 pp.
62

Hubbs C.L. & Rechnitzer A.B. (1952) Report on experiments designed to determine effects of underwater explosions on fish life. *Calif. Fish Game* **38,** 333–366.
24

Huebner G.L. (1975) The marine environment. In *Manual of Remote Sensing,* 1553–1622, The American Society of Photogrammetry, Falls Church, Virginia, U.S.A.
19

Huet M. (1970) *Textbook of Fish Culture. Breeding and Cultivation of Fish.* Fishing News (Books) Ltd, London. 436 pp.
188

Hunt B.P. (1960) Digestion rate and food consumption of Florida gar, warmouth, and large mouth bass. *Trans. Am. Fish. Soc.* **89,** 206–210.
247

Hunt R.L. (1966) Production and angler harvest of wild brook trout in Lawrence Creek, Wisconsin. *Tech. Bull. Wis. Conserv. Dept.,* No. **35.** 52 pp.
211

Hunter J.G. (1954) A weir for adult and fry salmon effective under conditions of extremely variable runoff. *Can. Fish Cult.* **16,** 27–33.
37

Huntsman A.G. (1919) The scale method of calculating the rate of growth in fishes. *Trans. R. Soc. Can.* (IV), **12,** 47–52.
124

Hynes H.B.N. (1950) The food of freshwater sticklebacks (*Gasterosteus aculeatus* and *Pygosteus pungitius*), with a review of methods used in studies of the food of fishes. *J. Anim. Ecol.* **19,** 36–58.
223

Ichikawa R. & Hiyama Y. (1954) Scale growth of the common goby assured by the lead acetate injection method. *Jap. J. Ichthyol.* **3,** 49–52.
90

Igarashi S. (1963) Studies on air screen in water. (1) Applications for fishing gear; (2) On intercepting effect upon fishes. *Bull. Fac. Fish. Hokkaido Univ.* **14,** 23–29.
36

Ishida T. (1963) Mesh selective biases on the gillnet caught sockeye and chub salmon. *Bull. Hokkaido reg. Fish. Res. hab.* **27,** 7–12.
34

Ishida T. (1964) Gillnet mesh selectivity curves for sardine and herring. *Bull. Hokkaido reg. Fish. Res. Lab.* **28,** 56–60.
34

Ishiwata N. (1968a) Ecological studies on the feeding of fishes. I. Satiation amount as indicator of amount consumed. *Bull. Jap. Soc. scient. Fish.* **34,** 495–497.
232, 233

Ishiwata N. (1968b) Ecological studies on the feeding of fishes. II. Acclimatization of a school of fish and satiation amount. *Bull. Jap. Soc. scient. Fish.* **34,** 498–502.
232

Ishiwata N. (1968c) Ecological studies on the feeding of fishes. III. Degree of hunger and satiation amount. *Bull. Jap. Soc. scient. Fish.* **34,** 604–607.
232

Ishiwata N. (1968d) Ecological studies of the feeding of fishes. IV. Satiation curve. *Bull. Jap. Soc. scient. Fish.* **34,** 691–694.
232

Ishiwata N. (1968e) Ecological studies on the feeding of fishes. V. Size of fish and satiation amount. *Bull. Jap. Soc. scient. Fish.* **34,** 781–784.
232

Ishiwata N. (1968f) Ecological studies on the feeding of fishes. VI. External factors

affecting satiation amount (1). *Bull. Jap. Soc. scient. Fish.* **34**, 785–791.
232

IVLEV V.S. (1939a) The energy balance of the growing larva of *Silurus glanis. Dokl. Akad. Nauk SSSR*, New Ser. **25**, 87–89. [In Russian.]
228, 244

IVLEV V.S. (1939b) Energy balance in the carp. *Zool. Zh* **18**, 303–318. [In Russian.]
228

IVLEV V.S. (1945) Biologischeskaya produktivnost' vodoemov. *Usp. sovrem. Biol.* **19**, 1, 98–120. [Translated into English in Ivlev 1966.]
4, 6, 202, 228, 237

IVLEV V.S. (1955) *Eksperimental'naya ekologiya pitaniya ryb.* Pishchepromizdat, Moskva. 252 pp. [Translated into English in Ivlev 1961.]
200

IVLEV V.S. (1960) On the utilization of food by planktophage fishes. *Bull. Math. Biophys.* **22**, 371–389.
235

IVLEV V.S. (1961) *Experimental Ecology of the Feeding of Fishes.* Yale University Press, New Haven. 302 pp. [English translation of Ivlev, 1955.]
200

IVLEV V.S. (1966) The biological productivity of waters. *J. Fish. Res. Bd Can.* **23**, 1727–1759. [Translation of Ivlev 1945, with annotations.]
4, 202, 228

IWATA K. (1970) Relationship between food and growth in young crucian carps, *Carassius auratus cavieri*, as determined by nitrogen balance. *Jap. J. Limnol.* **31**, 129–151.
244

JAKOBSSON J. (1970) On fish tags and tagging. *Oceanogr. Mar. Biol.* **8**, 457–499.
91

JEFFERTS K.B., BERGMAN P.K. & FISCUS H.F. (1963) A coded wire identification for macro organisms. *Nature, Lond.* **198**, 460–462.
91

JENKINS I.T. (1901) The methods and results of the German plankton investigations with special reference to plankton nets. *Proc. Trans. Lpool biol. Soc.* **15**, 279–341.
170

JENKINS T.M. (1969) Social structure, position choice and microdistribution of two trout species (*Salmo trutta* and *Salmo gairdneri*) resident in mountain streams. *Anim. Behav. Monogr.* **2**, 57–123.
248

JENKINS R.M. (1967) The influence of some environmental factors on standing crop and harvest of fishes in U.S. reservoirs. In *Reservoir Fishery Resources Symposium*, pp. 298–321. American Fisheries Society, Southern Division, Athens.
285

JENSEN A.C. (1967) Effects of tagging on the growth of cod. *Trans. Am. Fish. Soc.* **96**, 37–41.
119

JESSOP B.M. (1973) Marking alewife fry with biological stains. *Progve Fish Cult.* **35**, 90–93.
89

JOHNELS A.G. (1952) Notes on scale rings and growth of tropical fishes from the Gambia River. *Ark. Zool.*, Ser. **2**, 3, **28**, 363–366.
103

JOHNSON E.E. & FIELDS P.E. (1959) The effectiveness of an electric hot wire branding technique for marking fingerling steelhead trout. *Tech. Rep. Sch. Fish. Univ. Wash.*, No. **47**. 5 pp.
87

JOHNSON W.E. (1956) On the distribution of young sockeye salmon (*Oncorhynchus nerka*) in Babine and Nilkitkwa Lakes, B.C. *J. Fish. Res. Bd Can.* **13**, 695–708.
32, 197

JOLLY G.M. (1965) Explicit estimates from capture-recapture data with both death and immigration-stockastic mode. *Biometrika* **52**, 225–248.
145

JONES J.R.E. (1964) *Fish and River Pollution.* Butterworths, London. 203 pp.
256, 257

JONES J.W. & BALL J.N. (1954) The spawn-

ing behaviour of brown trout and salmon. *Behaviour* **2**, 103–114.
180

JONES R. (1958) Lee's phenomenon of 'apparent change in growth-rate' with particular reference to haddock and plaice. *Spec. Publs int. Commn NW. Atlant. Fish.* **1**, 229–242.
125, 136

JONES R. (1960) Mesh selection and apparent growth in haddock. *J. Cons. int. Explor. Mer* **25**, 177–184.
125

JONES R. (1973) Stock and recruitment with special reference to cod and haddock. *Rapp. P.-v. Réun. Cons. perm. int. Explor. Mer* **164**, 156–173.
136

JONES R. (1977) Tagging: Theoretical methods and practical difficulties. In *Fish Population Dynamics*, 46–66 (Ed. J.A. Gulland), John Wiley & Sons, London. 372 pp.
91

JORDAN F.P. & SMITH H.D. (1968) An aluminium staple tag for population estimates of salmon smolts. *Progve Fish Cult.* **30**, 230–234.
93

JUDAY C. (1940) The annual energy budget of an inland lake. *Ecology* **21**, 438–450.
4, 216

JUNGE C.O. & LIBOSVARSKY J. (1965) Effects of size selectivity on population estimates based on successive removals with electrical fishing gear. *Zool Listy* **14**, 171–178. (Czech summary.)
27

KABATA Z. (1963) Parasites as biological tags. *Spec. Publs int. Commn NW. Atlant. Fish.* **4**, 31–37.
96

KABATA Z. (1970) Crustacea as enemies of fishes. In *Diseases of Fishes*, Book 1. (Eds S.F. Snieszko and H.R. Axelrod), T.F.H. Publications Inc., Neptune, New Jersey. 171 pp.
267

KÄNDLER R. & PIRWITZ W. (1957). Über die Fruchtbarkeit der Plattfische im Nordsee–Ostsee–Raum. *Kieler Meeresforsch.*, **13**, **1**, 11–34.
170

KANWISHER S., LAWSON K. & SUNDNES G. (1974) Acoustic telemetry of fish. *Fishery Bull. Fish. Wildl. Serv. U.S.* **72**, 251–255.
20

KARZINKIN G.S. & KRIVOBOK M.N. (1962) Metodika postanovki balansovykh opytov po izucheniyu obmena azota u ryb. In *Rukovodstro po metodike issledovanni fiziologii ryb.*, pp. 108–126, Akademiya Nauk SSSR, Ikhtiologicheskaya Kommissiya, Moscow. 375 pp. [Original version of 1964.]
244

KARZINKIN G.S. & KRIVOBOK M.N. (1964) Balance sheet experiments on nitrogen metabolism of fish. In *Techniques for the Investigation of Fish physiology*, pp. 91–105. Office of Technical Services, Washington, No. 64–11001. 313 pp. [English translation of, 1963.]
244, 245

KASK J.L. & HIYAMA Y. (1943) Japanese fishing gear. *Fishery Leafl. Fish Wildl. Serv. U.S.*, No. **234**. 107 pp.
8

KAUSHIK N.K. & HYNES H.B.N. (1968) Experimental study on the role of autumnshed leaves in aquatic environments. *J. Ecol.* **56**, 229–243.
225

KAVANAGH A.J. & RICHARDS O.W. (1934) The autocatalytic growth curve. *Am. Nat.* **68**, 54–59.
135

KAWAMOTO N.Y. (1956) Experiments with the fish gathering lamp. *Proc. Indo-Pacif. Fish. Coun.*, 6th Session, Tokyo, Japan, 1955, Sections II and III, 278–280.
36

KEAST A. & WELSH L. (1968) Daily feeding periodicities, food uptake rates, and dietary changes with hour of the day in some lake fishes. *J. Fish. Res. Bd Can.* **25**, 1133–1144.
220, 249

KEETON D. (1965) Application of Stoeltzner's method to determine growth of fish

scales. *Trans. Am. Fish. Soc.* **94,** 93–94.
111

KELLER W.T. (1971) Floy tag retention by small brook trout. *N.Y. Fish Game J.* **18,** 142–143.
97

KELLY W.H. (1967a) Marking freshwater and marine fish by injected dyes. *Trans. Am. Fish. Soc.* **96,** 163–175.
88

KELLY W.H. (1967b) Relation of fish growth to the durability of two dyes in jaw-injected trout. *N.Y. Fish Game J.* **14,** 199–205.
88

KENNEDY C.R. (1969) Tubificid oligochaetes as food of dace *Leuciscus leuciscus* (L.) *J. Fish Biol.* **1,** 11–15.
219

KENNEDY W.A. (1951) The relationship of fishing effort by gillnets to the interval between lifts. *J. Fish. Res. Bd Can.* **8,** 264–234.
35

KERR S.R. (1971a) Analysis of laboratory experiments on growth efficiency of fishes. *J. Fish. Res. Bd Can.* **28,** 801–808.
243

KERR S.R. (1971b) Prediction of fish growth efficiency in nature. *J. Fish. Res. Bd Can.* **28,** 809–814.
135, 243

KERR S.R. (1971c) A simulation model of lake trout growth. *J. Fish. Res. Bd Can.* **28,** 815–819.
135, 243

KESTEVEN G.L. (Ed.) (1960) Manual of field methods in fisheries biology. *F.A.O. Manuals in Fisheries Sciences,* No. **1,** F.A.O. Rome. 152 pp.
45, 46

KETCHEN K.S. (1950) Stratified subsampling for determining age distributions. *Trans. Am. Fish Soc.* **79,** 205–212.
12, 14

KEVERN N.R. (1966) Feeding rate of carp estimated by a radioisotopic method. *Trans. Am. Fish. Soc.* **95,** 363–371.
245, 246, 247

KIONKA B.C. (1972) A bioenergetic study of artificial and natural food transformation

in a cold water vertebrate. Ph.D. thesis, University of Colorado, Boulder.
236

KIONKA B.C. & WINDELL J.T. (1972) Differential movement of digestible and indigestible food fractions in rainbow trout *Salmo gairdneri. Trans. Am. Fish. Soc.* **101,** 112–115.
252

KIPLING C. & FROST W.E.F. (1969) Variations in the fecundity of pike *Esox lucius* L. in Windermere. *J. Fish Biol.* **1,** 221–237.
168

KITCHELL J.F. (1970) The daily ration for a population of bluegill sunfish (*Lepomis macrochirus* Raf.). Ph.D. thesis, University of Colorado, Boulder.
249, 250

KITCHELL J.F., KOONCE J., O'NEILL R., SHAGART H., MAGNUSON J. & BOOTH R. (1972) Implementation of a predator-prey biomass model for fishes. *Eastern Deciduous Forest Biome Memo Report* No. 72–118.
250, 252

KITCHELL J.F. & WINDELL J.T. (1968) Rate of gastric digestion in pumpkin seed sunfish, *Lepomis gibbosus. Trans. Am. Fish. Soc.* **97,** 489–492.
250

KLEIBER M. (1961) *The Fire of Life—An Introduction to Animal Energetics.* John Wiley & Sons, New York.
229, 237, 239

KLONTZ G.W. (1973) Syllabus of Fish Health Management. Texas A & M University, Sea Grant Program, Document TAMU–SG–74–401. 165 pp.
267, 268

KLONTZ G.W. (1972) Haematological techniques and the immune response in rainbow trout. In *Diseases of Fish,* pp. 89–99 (Ed. L.E. Mawdesley-Thomas). *Symp. zool. Soc. Lond.,* No. 30, Academic Press, London. 380 pp.
269

KNAKE B.O. (1947) Methods of net mending —New England. *Fishery leafl. Fish Wildl. Serv. U.S.,* No. **241.** 7 pp.
9

KNAKE B.O. (1956) Assembly methods for

otter-trawl nets. *Fishery leafl. Fish and Wildl. Serv. U.S.*, No. **437**. 29 pp.
31

KNIGHT W. (1969) A formulation of the von Bertalanffy growth curve when the growth rate is roughly constant. *J. Fish. Res. Bd Can.* **26**, 3069–3072.
129

KNUDSEN J.W. (1966) *Biological Techniques —Collecting, Preserving, and Illustrating Plants and Animals.* Harper and Row, New York. 525 pp.
9

KOBAYASHI K. & IOUE N. (1960) New type otter-boards for midwater trawl. *Bull. Fac. Fish. Hokkaido Univ.* **11**, 20–22.
31

KOBAYASHI S. YUKI R., FURUI T. & KOSUGI-YAMA T. (1964) Calcification in fish and shellfish. I. Tetracycline labelling patterns on scale, centrum and otolith in young goldfish. *Bull. Jap. Soc. scient. Fish.* **30**, 6–13.
105

KOHLER A.C. (1963) Use of tagging data in Subarea 4 cod growth investigations. *Spec. Publs int. Commn N.W. Atlant. Fish.* **4**, 66–70.
119

KOLEHMAINEN S.E. (1974) Daily feeding rates of bluegill (*Lepomis macrochirus*) determined by a refined radioisotope method. *J. Fish. Res. Bd Can.* **31**, 67–74.
245

KOLEHMAINEN S.E., HÄSÄNEN E. & MIETTINEN J.K. (1967) ^{137}Cs in fish, plankton and plants in Finnish lakes during 1964–1965. In *Radioecological Concentration Processes*, pp. 913–919 (Eds. B. Aberg & F.P. Hungate). Pergamon Press, New York.
246

KOLGANOV D. (1959) [*Catching Fish by Spinning.*] Moscow. 182 pp. (in Russian).
22, 23

KOO T.S.Y. (1962) *Age Designation in Salmon. Studies of Alaska Red Salmon.* University of Washington Press, Seattle, Wash., pp. 37–48.
106

KOOPS H. (1959) Der Quappenbestand der Elbe. Untersuchungen über die Biologie und die fischereiliche Bedentung der Aalquappe (*Lota lota* L.) im Hinblink auf die Auswerkungen des im Bau befindlichen Elbstaues bei Gasthacht. *Kurze Mitt. Inst. Fisch. Biol. Univ. Hamb.* **9**, 1–60.
120

KOSHINSKY G.D. (1972) An evaluation of two tags with northern pike (*Esox lucius*). *J. Fish. Res. Bd Can.* **29**, 469–476.
93, 97, 98

KOTTHAUS A. (1963) Tagging experiments with North Sea sole (*Solea solea*) in 1959 and 1960. *Spec. Publs int. Commn N.W. Atlant. Fish.* **4**, 123–129.
98

KRASON W.S. (1949) Floating trawls. *Fishery Leafl. Fish. Wildl. Serv. U.S.*, No. **343**. 5 pp.
32

KRISTJONSSON H. (Ed.) (1959, 1964, 1972) *Modern Fishing Gear of the World*, Vol. **1**, 1959, 640 pp.; Vol. **2**, 1964, 600 pp.; Vol. **3**, 1972, 550 pp. Fishing News (Books) Ltd, London.
8, 9

KROGER R.L., GUTHRIE J.F. & MAYO J.H. (1974) Growth and first annulus formation of tagged and untagged Atlantic menhaden. *Trans. Am. Fish. Soc.* **103**, 292–297.
91

KROGH A. (1916) *Respiratory Exchanges of Animals and Man.* Longmans, Green & Co., London. 173 pp.
243

KRYZHANOVSKY S.G. (1949) [Ecological-morphological principles in the development of cyprinid, cobitid and silurid fishes.] *Trudy Inst. Morf. Zhiv.* **1**, 5–332.
179, 185, 200

KRYZHANOVSKY S.G., SMIRNOV A.I. & SOIN S.G. (1951) Materialy po razvitiyu ryb reki Amura. [Information concerning the development of Amur River fishes.] *Trudy Amurskoi Ikhtiologicheskoi Ekspeditsii,* 1945–1949, **2**, 5–222.
180

KUROKI T., NAKAYAMA H. & UENO K.

(1964) Studies on the fluorescent color-lamp for attracting fish (II). *Bull. Fac. Fish. Hokkaido Univ.* **14,** 215–235.
36

KUZNETSOV V.V. (1957) O tak nazyvaemom fenomene Li [On the so-called 'Lee's phenomenon'.] *Vop. Ikhtiol.* **8,** 141–154.
125

LAEVASTU T. (Ed.) (1965) Manual of methods in fisheries biology. *FAO Manuals in Fisheries Science,* No. **1,** FAO, Rome. 10 fasc.
14

LAGLER K.F. (1947). Lepidological studies. 1. Scale characters of the families of Great Lakes fishes. *Trans. Am. microsc. Soc.* **66,** 2, 149–171.
109

LAGLER K.F. (1956) *Freshwater Fishery Biology.* Wm. C. Brown Company, Dubuque, Iowa. 421 pp.
15, 28, 40, 42, 44, 101, 109, 219

LAGLER K.F. & DE ROTH G.C. (1953) Populations and yield to anglers in a fishery for largemouth bass. *Pap. Mich. Acad. Sci.* **38,** 235–253.
23

LAGLER K.F. & RICKER W.E. (1943) Biological fisheries investigations of Foots Pond, Gibson County, Indiana. *Invest. Indiana Lakes Streams* **2,** 47–72.
38

LAIRD L.M. & OSWALD R.L. (1975) A note on the use of benzocaine (Ethyl P-Aminobenzoate) as a fish anaesthetic. *Fish. Mgmt* **6,** 92–94.
99

LAIRD L.M., ROBERTS R.J., SHEARER W.M. & MCARDLE J.F. (1975) Freeze branding of juvenile salmon. *J. Fish Biol.* **7,** 167–171.
87

LALANNE J.J. & SAFSTEN G. (1969) Age determination from scales of chum salmon (*Oncorhynchus keta*). *J. Fish. Res. Bd Can.* **26,** 671–681.
Figs. 5.5 and 5.6

LAMBOU V.W. (1963) Application of distribution pattern of fishes in Lake Bistineau

to design of sampling programs. *Progve Fish Cult.* **25,** 79–86.
152, 154

LAMBOU V.W. & STERN H. (1958) An evaluation of some of the factors affecting the validity of rotenone sampling data. *Proc. 11th Conf. SE. Ass. Game & Fish Commissioners for 1957,* 91–98.
154

LAPIN YU. E. (1969) O 'kompensationnom roste' i 'fenomene Li' kak otrazhenii protseesa prostranstvennoi different-sirovki raznorazmernykh ryb. [Compensatory growth' and 'Lee's phenomenon' as reflections of the process of spacial differentiation of fish of different sizes.] *Zool. Zh.* **48,** 469–484.
125

LARRAÑETA M.G. (1964) A criterion to locate rings in ctenoid scales. *Proc. tech. Pap. gen. Fish. Coun. Mediterr.* **7,** 57–61.
111

LATTA W.C. (1959) Significance of trap-net selectivity in estimating fish population statistics. *Pap. Mich. Acad. Sci.* **44** (1958), 123–138.
40

LATTA W.C. (1963) The history of the small-mouth bass *Micropterus d. dolomieu*, at Waugoshance Point, Lake Michigan. *Bull. Mich. Inst. Fish. Res.,* No. **5.** 56 pp.
124

LAWLER G.H. (1963a) Using the trammel net in Canadian waters. *Can. Fisherm.* **50,** (8), 1–3.
36

LAWLER G.H. (1963b) Spring stainless steel anchor tag. *J. Fish. Res. Bd Can.* **20,** 1553.
94

LAWRENCE J.M. (1956) Preliminary results on the use of potassium permanganate to counteract the effects of rotenone on fish. *Progve Fish Cult.* **18,** 15–21; also in *Proc. Conf. S East. Ass. Game Fish Commn.,* 1955, 87–92.
22

LEA E. (1910) On the methods used in herring investigations. *Publs Circonst. Cons. perm. int. Explor. Mer,* No. **53.**
120

LEARY D.F. & MURPHY G.I. (1975) A successful method for tagging the small fragile engraulid *Stolophorus purpureus*. *Trans. Am. Fish. Soc.* **105**, 53–55.
91

LEBEDEV E.A. (1959) O rabote trala v vode. [Behaviour of a trawl in water.] *Ryb. Khoz.* **35**, 39–42.
32

LE CREN E.D. (1947) The determination of the age and growth of the perch (*Perca fluviatilis*) from the opercular bone. *J. Anim. Ecol.* **16**, 188–204.
115, 120, 124

LE CREN E.D. (1951) The length-weight relationship and seasonal cycle in gonad weight and condition in the perch (*Perca fluviatilis*). *J. Anim. Ecol.* **20**, 201–219.
126, 129

LE CREN E.D. (1954) A subcutaneous tag for fish. *J. Cons. perm. int. Explor. Mer* **20**, 72–82.
91

LE CREN E.D. (1962) The efficiency of reproduction and recruitment in freshwater fish. In *The Exploitation of Natural animal Populations*, pp. 283–296 (Eds E.D. Le Cren & M.W. Holdgate). Blackwell Scientific Publications, Oxford. 399 pp.
178, 215

LE CREN E.D. (1965) Some factors regulating the size of populations of freshwater fish. *Mitt. int. Verein. theor. angew. Limnol.* **13**, 88–105.
200

LE CREN E.D. (1974) The effects of errors in ageing in production studies. In *Ageing of Fish*, pp. 221–224 (Ed. T.B. Bagenal). Unwin Brothers, Old Woking. 234 pp.
117

LE CREN E.D. & KIPLING C. (1963) Some marking experiments on spawning populations of char. *Spec. Publs int. Commn NW. Atlant. Fish.* **4**, 130–139.
86

LEE R.M. (1920) A review of the methods of age and growth determination by means of scales. *Fishery Invest., Lond.*, Ser. II, **4**, 2. 32 pp.
122

LEHMANN J. & STÜRENBERG F.-J. (1974) Haematologisch-serologische substratuntersuchungen an de regenbogenforelle (*Salmo gairdneri* Richardson). I. Methodik zur blutentnahme und blutuntersuchung bei fischen. *Gewäss. Abwäss* **53/54**, 114–132.
259, 263

LEHMANN J. & STÜRENBERG F.-J. (1975) Haematologisch-serologische substratuntersuchungen an de regenbogenforelle (*Salmo gairdneri* Richardson). II. Beschreibung und darstellung der wichtigsten zellen in der blutbildungsstätte und im peripheren blutgefässsystem. *Gewäss. Abwäss.* **55/56**, 1–123.
259, 269

LENNON R.E. (1959) The electrical resistivity meter in fishery investigations. *Spec. scient. Rep. U.S. Fish Wildl. Serv.* Fisheries No. 287. 13 pp.
25

LENNON R.E. (1966) Antimycin—a new fishery tool. *Wis. Conserv. Bull.* **31**, 2, 4–5.
21

LESLIE P.H. & DAVIS D.H.S. (1939) An attempt to determine the absolute number of rats on a given area. *J. Anim. Ecol.* **8**, 94–113.
152

LIBOSVARSKY J. & LELEK A. (1965) Über die Artselektivität beim elektrischen Fischfang. *Z. Fisch.* **13**, 291–302.
24

LIGNY W. DE (Ed.) (1971) Proceedings of the special meeting on the biochemical and serological identification of fish stocks. *Rapp. P.-v. Réun. Cons. perm. int. Explor. Mer*, 161.
51

LIEDER U. (1959) Über Jahresmarken und Störungszonen auf den Schuppen von Teichsypriniden. *Z. Fisch.* **8**, 67–86.
111, Fig. 5.8

LILLELUND K. (1961) Untersuchungen über die Biologie und Populationsdynamik des Stintes (*Osmerus eperlanus eperlanus* L.) der Elbe. *Arch. FischWiss.* **12**, 1–128.
192

LILLELUND K. (1967) Versuche zur Erbrütung der Eier vom Hecht, *Esox lucius* L., in Abhängigkeit von Temperatur und

Licht. *Arch. FischWiss.* **17,** 95–113.
192

LINDEMAN R.L. (1942) The trophic-dynamic aspect of ecology. *Ecology* **23,** 399–418.
4

LINDROTH A. (1946) Zur Biologie der Befruchtung und Entwicklung beim Hecht. *Meddn St. Unders.-o. FörsAnst. SotvattFisk.*, No. **24,** 1–173.
191

LINDROTH A. (1955) Internal tagging salmon smolts. II. Method of recapture. Returns 1954. *Rep. Inst. Freshwat. Res. Drottningholm* **36,** 120–125.
91

LINDROTH A. (1956) Salmon stripper, egg counter and incubator. *Progve Fish Cult.* **18,** 165–170.
167

LOCKARD D.V. (1968) An opercular streamer tag. *Progve Fish Cult.* **30,** 175–177.
94

LOEB H.A. (1955) An electrical surface device for carp control and fish collection in lakes. *N.Y. Fish Game J.* **2,** 220–231.
32

LOEB H.A. (1957) Night collection of fish with electricity. *N.Y. Fish Game J.* **4,** 109–118.
26

LOEB H.A. (1966) Marking brown trout fry with the dye Sudan Black B. *N.Y. Fish Game J.* **13,** 232–233.
89

LOTRICH V.A. & MEREDITH W.H. (1934) A technique and the effectiveness of various acrylic colours for subcutaneous marking of fish. *Trans. Am. Fish. Soc.* **103,** 140–142.
88

LOWE R.H. (1952) Report on the *Tilapia* and other fish and fisheries of Lake Nyasa, 1945–47. *Fishery Publs colon. Off.* **1,** 2. 126 pp.
103

LOWE R.H. (1955) The fecundity of *Tilapia* species. *E. Afr. agric. J.* **21,** 45–52.
173

LOWE R.H. (1956) Observations on the biology of *Tilapia* (Pisces-Cichlidae) in Lake Victoria, East Africa. *Suppl. Publs E. Afr. Fish. Res. Org.* **1,** 1–72.
46

LOWE MCCONNELL R.H. (1964) The fishes of the Rupununi savanna district of British Guiana, South America. *J. Linn. Soc. Zool.* **45,** 304, 103–144 (pp. 124–128 on growth).
103

LUDGATE H.T. (1948) *Popular Netcraft.* The Netcraft Co., Toledo, Ohio, 7th edition. 72 pp.
9

LUDGATE H.T. (1950) *Trot Line Fishing for Pleasure and Profit.* The Netcraft Co. Toledo, Ohio. 48 pp.
23

LUKE D.McG., PINCOCK D.G. & STASKO A.B. (1973) Pressure-sensing ultrasonic transmitter for tracking aquatic animals. *J. Fish. Res. Bd Can.* **30,** 1402–1404.
95

LYTHGOE J.N. (1975) Problems of seeing colours underwater. In *Vision in Fishes: New Approaches to Research*, pp. 619–634 (Ed. M.A. Ali). Plenum Press, New York and London. 836 pp.
98

MACER C.T. (1974) The reproductive biology of the horse mackerel *Trachurus trachurus* (L.) in the North Sea and English Channel. *J. Fish Biol.* **6,** 415–438.
173, 176

MACFADYEN A. (1948) The meaning of productivity in biological systems. *J. Anim. Ecol.* **17,** 75–80.
4

MACIOLEK J.A. (1962) Limnological organic analysis by quantitative dichromate oxidation. *Res. Rep. U.S. Fish Wildl. Serv.* **60,** 1–61.
234, 236

MACKAY H.H. (1950) A novel method of catching sea lampreys. *Can. Fish Cult.* **7,** 28–34.
37

MACKAY I. & MANN K.H. (1969) Fecundity of two cyprinid fishes in the River Thames,

Reading, England. *J. Fish. Res. Bd Can.* **26**, 2795–2105.
172, 173

MACKENTHUN K.M. (1969) *The Practice of Water Pollution Biology*. U.S. Department of the Interior Federal Water Pollution Control Administration, Division of Technical Support. 281 pp.
260

MAGNUSON J.J. (1969) Digestion and food consumption by skipjack tuna (*Katsuwonus pelamis*). *Trans. Am. Fish. Soc.* **98**, 99–113.
233, 247, 250

MANN K.H. (1964) The pattern of energy flow in the fish and invertebrate fauna of the River Thames. *Verh. int. Verein. theor. angew. Limnol.* **15**, 485–495.
227, 242

MANN K.H. (1965) Energy transformation by a population of fish in the River Thames. *J. Anim. Ecol.* **34**, 253–275.
215, 227, 242

MANN K.H. (1967) The cropping of the food supply. In *The Biological Basis of Freshwater Fish Production*, pp. 243–257 (Ed. Shelby D. Gerking). Blackwell Scientific Publications, Oxford. 495 pp.
235

MANN K. (1969) The dynamics of aquatic ecosystems. In *Advances in Ecological Research*, Vol. 6, pp. 1–81 (Ed. J. Cragg). Academic Press, London. 236 pp.
228, 233, 242, 243

MANN R.H.K. (1973) Observations on the age, growth, reproduction and food of the roach *Rutilus rutilus* (L.) in two rivers in southern England. *J. Fish Biol.* **5**, 707–736.
124, 170

MANN R.H.K. (1974) Observations on the age, growth, reproduction and food of the dace, *Leuciscus leuciscus* (L.) in two rivers in southern England. *J. Fish Biol.* **6**, 237–253.
124

MANN R.H.K. & ORR D.R.O. (1969) A preliminary study of the feeding relationships of fish in a hard-water and a soft-water stream in Southern England. *J. Fish Biol.* **1**, 31–44.
219

MARGOLIS L. (1963) Parasites as indicators of the geographical origin of sockeye salmon *Oncorhynchus nerka* (Walbaum) occuring in the North Pacific Ocean and adjacent seas. *Bull. int. N. Pacif. Fish. Commn* **11**, 101–156.
96

MARKERT C.L. (Ed.) (1975) *Isozymes*, Vol. **1**, 856 pp.; Vol. **2**, 890 pp.; Vol. **3**, 1034 pp; Vol. **4**, 965 pp. Academic Press, London.
51

MARR D.H.A. (1966) Influence of temperature on the efficiency of growth of salmonid embryos. *Nature, Lond.* **212**, 957–959.
198

MARR J.C. (1956) The 'critical period' in the early life history of marine fishes. *J. Cons. perm. int. Explor. Mer* **21**, 160–170.
200

MARR J.C. & SPRAGUE L. (1963) The use of blood group characteristics in studying subpopulations of fishes. *Spec. Publs int. Commn NW. Atlant. Fish.* **4**, 308–313.
96

MATHEWS C.P. (1970) Immersion staining of coarse fish in the Thames. *J. Fish Biol.* **2**, 57–58.
89

MATHEWS C.P. (1970) Estimates of production with reference to general surveys. *Oikos* **21**, 129–133.
211, 217

MATHEWS C.P. (1974) An account of some methods of overcoming errors in ageing tropical and subtropical fish populations when hard tissue growth markings are unreliable and the data sparse. In *Ageing of Fish*, pp. 158–166 (Ed. T.B. Bagenal). Unwin Brothers, Old Woking. 234 pp.
103, 116

MATHEWS J.E. (MS) (1972) Interpretation and use of data. In *Investigation of Fish Kills*, pp. 83–86. Collection of papers presented at the Fish Kill Investigation Seminar, sponsored jointly by Environmental Protection Agency and Oklahoma Cooperative Fishery Unit. 134 pp.
272

MATIDA Y., KIMURA S., YOSHIMUTA C., KUMADA H. & TOKUNAGA E. (1967) A

toxic fresh-water algae, *Glenodinium gymnodinium* Penard, caused fish kills in artificially impounded Lake Sagami. *Bull. Freshwat. Fish. Res. Lab. Tokyo* 17, 73–77.
256

MATSON C. & BAILEY J.E. (1969) A frame for holding juvenile salmon during spray marking. *Progve Fish Cult.* 2, 118–120.
90

MAYNARD L.A. & LOOSLI J.K. (1969) *Animal Nutrition.* McGraw-Hill, New York. 500 pp.
240

MAYR E., LINSLEY E.G. & USINGER R.L. (1953) *Methods and Principles of Systematic Zoology.* McGraw-Hill, New York. 328 pp.
48

MCCARTHY D.H., STEVENSON J.P. & ROBERTS M.S. (1973) Some blood parameters of the rainbow trout (*Salmo gairdneri* Richardson). I. The Kamloops variety. *J. Fish Biol.* 5, 1–8.
258

MCCARTHY D.H., STEVENSON J.P. & ROBERTS M.S. (1975) Some blood parameters of the rainbow trout (*Salmo gairdneri* Richardson). II. The Shasta variety. *J. Fish Biol.* 7, 215–219.
258

MCCLEAVE J.D. & STRED J.A. (1975) Effect of dummy telemetry transmitters on stamina of Atlantic salmon (*Salmo salar*) smolts. *J. Fish. Res. Bd Can.* 32, 559–563.
95

MCCOMBIE A.M. & FRY F.E.J. (1960) Selectivity of gillnets for lake whitefish *Coregonus clupeaformis. Trans. Am. Fish. Soc.* 89, 176–184.
10, 34

MCCOMISH T. (1970) Laboratory experiments on growth and food conversion by the bluegill. Ph.D. thesis, University of Missouri, Springfield. 185 pp.
251

MCCRACKEN F.D. (1963) Comparison of tags and techniques from recoveries of sub-area 4 cod tags. *Spec. Publs int. Commn NW. Atlant. Fish.* 4, 89–100.
98

MCDONALD J.G. (1969) Distribution,

growth, and survival of sockeye fry (*Oncorhynchus nerka*) produced in natural and artificial stream environments. *J. Fish. Res. Bd Can.* 26, 229–267.
31

MCEVLAIN A.J. & KENNEDY J.S. (1968) Comparison of some anaesthetic properties of benzocaine and MS 222. *Trans. Am. Fish. Soc.* 97, 496–498.
99

MCFADDEN J.T. & COOPER E.L. (1964) Population dynamics of brown trout in different environments. *Physiol. Zool.* 37, 355–363.
169

MCGREGOR E.A. (1922) Observations on the egg yield of Klamath River king salmon. *Calif. Fish Game,* 8, 160–164.
171

MCKEE J.E. & WOLF H.W. (Eds) (1963) *Water Quality Criteria.* 2nd Ed. The Resources Agency of California, State Water Resources Control Board. Publication 3-A. 548 pp.
262, 271

MCKERN J.L., HORTON H.F. & KOSKI K.V. (1974) Development of the steelhead trout (*Salmo gairdneri*) otoliths and their use for age analysis and for separating summer from winter races and wild from hatchery stocks. *J. Fish. Res. Bd Can.* 31, 1420–1426.
104

MCKINNON J.C. (1973) Analysis of energy flow and production in an unexploited marine flatfish population. *J. Fish. Res. Bd Can.* 30, 1717–1728.
231

MCLEOD H.A. & RITCEY W.R. (Eds) (1973) Analytical Methods for Pesticide Residues in Foods. Health Protection Branch, Department of National Health and Welfare, Information Canada, Cat. No. H44–2869–REV.
272

MCMAHON B.M. *et al.* (1975) Pesticide analytical manual. I. (revised.) Methods which detect multiple residues. U.S. Dept. of Health, Education and Welfare, Food and Drug Administration.
272

MᴄNᴇᴇʟʏ R.L. (1961) The purse seine revolution in tuna fishing. *Pacif. Fisherm.* June **1961**, 27–58.
31

Mᴇᴅᴀᴡᴀʀ P.B. (1945) Shape, size and age. In *Essays on Growth and Form Presented to D'Arcy Wentworth Thompson*, pp. 157–187 (Eds W.E. Le Gros Clark & P.B. Medawar). Clarendon Press, Oxford.
135

Mᴇɪᴇɴ V.A., Kᴀʀᴢɪɴᴋɪɴ G.S., Iᴠʟᴇᴠ V.S., Lɪᴘɪɴ A.N. & Sʜᴇɪɴᴀ M.P. (1937) Utilization by two-year-old carp of the natural food supply of a pond. [In Russian.] *Zool. Zh.* **16**, 209–223.
244

Mᴇɴᴅᴇʟ B., Kᴇᴍᴘ A. & Mʏᴇʀs D.K. (1954) A calimetric micro-method for the determination of glucose. *Biochem. J.* **56**, 639–646.
237

Mᴇɴᴏɴ M.D. (1950) The use of bones, other than otoliths, in determining the age and growth-rate of fishes. *J. Cons. perm. int. Explor. Mer* **16**, 311–340.
103, 115

Mᴇɴᴏɴ M.D. (1953) The determination of age and growth of fishes of tropical and subtropical waters. *J. Bombay nat. Hist. Soc.* **51**, 3.
103

Mᴇɴᴢᴇʟ D.W. (1959) Utilization of algae for growth by the angelfish, *Holacanthus bermudensis*. *J. Cons. perm. int. Explor. Mer* **24**, 308–313.
244

Mᴇɴᴢᴇʟ D.W. (1960) Utilization of food by a Bermuda reef fish, *Epinephelus grettatus*. *J. Cons. perm. int. Explor. Mer* **25**, 216–222.
244

Mᴇɴᴢɪᴇ C.M. (1966) Metabolism of pesticides. *Spec. scient. Rep. U.S. Fish Wildl. Serv.*, No. **96**. 274 pp.
272

Mᴇsᴋᴇ C. (1973) *Aquakultur von Warmwassernutzfische*. Verlag Eugen Umer, Stuttgart. 163 pp.
188

Mᴇssɪᴇʜ S.N. (1972) Use of otoliths in identifying herring stocks in the Southern Gulf of St. Lawrence and adjacent waters. *J. Fish. Res. Bd Can.* **29**, 1113–1118.
96

Mᴇssɪᴇʜ S.N. & Tɪʙʙᴏ S.N. (1970) A critique on the use of otoliths for ageing Gulf of St. Lawrence herring (*Clupea harengus* L.). *J. Cons. perm. int. Explor. Mer* **33**, 181–191.
104

Mᴇʏᴇʀ F.P. (MS) (1972) The roll of diseases in fish kills. In *Investigation of Fish Kills*, pp. 46–60. Collection of papers presented at the Fish Kill Investigation Seminar, sponsored jointly by Environmental Protection Agency and Oklahoma Cooperative Fishery Unit. 134 pp.
268

Mᴇʏᴇʀ V. (Ed.) (1975) *Atlas zur anatomie und morphologie der nutzfische für den praktischen gebrauch in wissenschaft und wirtschaft*. Vol. **3**. *Salmo gairdneri* Richardson, 1836. Regenbogenforelle: rainbow trout. Paul Parey, Hamburg. 15 pp.
259

Mᴇʏᴇʀ-Wᴀᴀʀᴅᴇɴ P.F., Hᴀʟsʙᴀɴᴅ E. & Hᴀʟsʙᴀɴᴅ I. (1960) Bibliographie über die Electrofischerei und ihre Grundlagen. *Arch. FischWiss.* **11**, 1–104.
25

Mᴇʏᴇʀ-Wᴀᴀʀᴅᴇɴ P.F., Hᴀʟsʙᴀɴᴅ I. & Hᴀʟsʙᴀɴᴅ E. (1965) *Einführung in die Electrofischerei*. Berlin, Westliche Berliner Verlagsgesellschaft Heenemann K.G. 292 pp.
25, 26

Mɪɢʜᴇʟʟ J.L. (1969) Rapid cold-branding of salmon and trout with liquid nitrogen. *J. Fish. Res. Bd Can.* **26**, 2765–2769.
87

Mɪʟʟᴇʀ A.B. (1961) A modification of the small Hardy plankton sampler for simultaneous high-speed plankton hauls. *Bull. mar. Ecol.* **5**, 165–172.
193, 194

Mɪʟʟᴇʀ J.M. (1973) A quantitative push-net system for transect studies of larval fish and macrozooplankton. *Limnol. Oceanogr.* **18**, 175–178.
193, 194

Mɪʟʟᴇʀ N.E. (1959) Liberalization of basic

S–R concepts: extensions to conflict behavior, motivation, and social learning. In *Psychology: A study of a Science.* Study I, Vol. 2, pp. 196–242 (Ed. S. Koch). McGraw-Hill, New York.
232

MINA M.V. (1965) On the development of a method of objective estimation of otolith zone structure. [In Russian.] *Vop. Ikhtiol.* 5, 732–735.
104

MING A. (1964) Contributions to a bibliography on the construction, development, use and effects of electrofishing devices. *Semi-a Rep. Okla. Fish Res. Lab.,* Jan.–June 1964, 33–46.
25

MITCHELL A.M. (1913) On the egg production of certain fishes. *Rep. N. Sea Fish. Invest. Comm.* 5th Report (Northern Area), pp. 191–204.
168, 172

MITSON R.B. & STORETON-WEST T.J. (1971) A transponding acoustic fish tag. *Radio electron. Engng* 41, 483–489.
95

MITSON R.B. & YOUNG A.H. (1975) A survey of the engineering problems of developing small acoustic fish tags. In *Proc. Conf. Instrumn Oceanogr. Univ. N. Wales, Bangor,* 163–174.
95

MOEN T.E. (1958) Notes on the use of a sixteen-foot otter trawl for sampling bull head populations. *Q. Biol. Rep. Iowa Fish Game Div.* 10, 13–17.
31

MOHR E.W. (1927, 1930, 1934) Bibliographie der Alters- und Wachstumbestimmung bei Fischen. *J. Cons. perm. int. Explor. Mer* 2, 236–258; 5, 88–100; 9, 377–391.
101

MØLLER-CHRISTENSEN J. (MS) (1961) Survey of the Danish sole tagging experiments with notes on the growth rate. *Cons. perm. int. Explor. Mer, 1961 meeting, Northern Seas Committee Paper,* No. 126. 14 pp.
118

MOLNÁR G. & TÖLG I. (1960) Röntgenologic investigation of the duration of gastric digestion in the pike perch (*Lucioperca lucioperca*). *Acta biol. Hung.* 11, 103–108.
247

MOLNÁR G. & TÖLG I. (1962a) Experiments concerning gastric digestion of pike perch (*Lucioperca lucioperca* L.) in relation to water temperature. *Acta biol. Hung.* 13, 231–239.
247

MOLNÁR G. & TÖLG I. (1962b) Relation between water temperature and gastric digestion of largemouth bass (*Micropterus salmoides* Lacépède). *J. Fish. Res. Bd Can.* 19, 1005–1012.
247

MONASTYRSKY G.N. (1930) O metodakh opredeleniya lineinogo rosta po cheshue ryb. [Methods of determining the growth in length of fish by their scales.] *Trudy nauch. Inst. ryb. Khoz.* 5, 4.
123

MONASTYRSKY G.N. (1934) *Instruktsiya dlya rabot po tempu rosta na schetnom pribore sistemy Monastyrskogo.* [*Instructions for growth rate studies with the Monastyrsky calculating device.*] Vsesoyuznyi nauchno-issledovatel'skii institut morskogo rybnogo khozyaistva i okeanografi, Moscow.
124

MOORE W.H. & MORTIMER C.H. (1954) A portable instrument for the location of subcutaneous fish tags. *J. Cons. perm. int. Explor. Mer* 20, 83–86.
91

MOOSE P.H. & EHRENBERG J.E. (1971) An expression for the variance of abundance using a fish echo integrator. *J. Fish. Res. Bd Can.* 28, 1293–1301.
19

MORAN P.A.P. (1951) A mathematical theory of animal trapping. *Biometrika*, 38, 307–311.
152

MORGAN R.I.G. (1974) The energy requirements of trout and perch populations in Loch Leven, Kinross. *Proc. R. Soc. Edinb.* B74, 33–345.
243

MORGAN R.I.G. & ROBERTS R.J. (1976) The histopathology of salmon tagging. IV. The effect of severe exercise on the induced

tagging lesion in salmon parr at two temperatures. *J. Fish Biol.* **8**, 289–292.
98

MORGAN R.P. (1973) Marking fish eggs with biological stains. *Chesapeake Sci.* **14**, 303–305.
89

MORIARTY C. (1973) A technique for examining eel otoliths. *J. Fish Biol.* **5**, 183–184.
114

MORIARTY C.M. & MORIARTY D.J.W. (1973) Quantitative estimation of the daily ingestion of phytoplankton by *Tilapia nilotica* and *Haplochromis nigripinnus* in Lake George, Uganda. *J. Zool.*, **171**, 15–23.
252

MORIARTY D.J.W. (1973) The physiology of digestion of bluegreen algae in the cichlid fish *Tilapia nilotica*. *J. Zool.* **171**, 25–39.
226

MOROZ V.N. (1968) Biologiya linya *Tinca tinca* (L.) Kiliiskoi del'ty Dynaya. [Biology of the tench *Tinca tinca* (L.) in the Kiliya Channel, Danube Delta.] *Vop. Ikhtiol.* **8**, 1, 106–115. [Translated in *Probl. Ichthyol.* **8**, 81–89.]
172

MOYLE J.B. (1950) Gillnets for sampling fish populations in Minnesota waters. *Trans. Am. Fish. Soc.* **79**, 195–204.
36

MUIR B.S. & NÜMI A.J. (1972) Oxygen consumption of the euryhaline fish Aholehole (*Kuhlia sanduicensis*) with reference to salinity, swimming and food consumption. *J. Fish. Res. Bd Can.* **29**, 67–77.
235, 243

MÜLLER K. (1953) Das otolithengewicht als Ergänzung der. Altersbestimmung bei Fischen. *Ber. limnol. Flusstn Freudenthal* **5**, 63–66.
116

MUNCY R.J. (1957) Factors affecting hoop net and trap net catches of channel catfish. In *Symposium on Evaluation of Fish Populations in Warm Water Streams held at Iowa State College, March 25, 1957*, pp. 23–27. Iowa Cooperative Research Unit, Iowa.
38

MUNRO J.L. (1967) The food of a community of freshwater fishes. *J. Zool.* **151**, 389–415.
224

MUZINIĆ R. (1964) Comparative study of scales and otoliths in sardine (*Sardina pilchardus* Walb.). *Proc. tech. Pap. gen. Fish. Coun. Mediterr.* **7**, 171–189.
111

NAGIEĆ M. (1961) Wzrost sandacza (*Lucioperca lucioperca* L.) w jeziorach polnocnej Polski. [Growth of zander in north Polish lakes.] *Roczn. Nauk roln.* 77–B (2), 549–580. [Russian and English summaries.]
123

NASSIF C. & ZAKI S. (1960) The effect of mesh size on the catch of lizard fish in the Gulf of Suez. *Notes Mem. hydrobiol. Dep. U.A.R.*, No. **45**. 8 pp.
32

NÉDÉLEC C. (1975) *FAO Catalogue of Small Scale Fishing Gear*. Fishing News (Books) Ltd, London. 191 pp.
8

NEEDHAM A.E. (1964) *The Growth Processes in Animals*. Pitman, London. 522 pp.
229

NELLEN W. & SCHNACK D. (1974) Sampling problems and methods of fish eggs and larvae investigations with special reference to inland waters. In *Symposium on the Methodology for the Survey, Monitoring and Appraisal of Fishery Resources in Lakes and Large Rivers*, 538–551 (Ed. Robin L. Welcomme). *EIFAC tech. Pap.* 23 (Suppl. 1, Vol. 2). 747 pp.
182

NESBIT R.A. (1934) A convenient method for preparing celluloid impressions of fish scales. *J. Cons. perm. int. Explor. Mer* **9**, 373–376.
109

NEW D.A.T. (1966) *The Culture of Vertebrate Embryos*. Logos Press and Elek Books, London. 245 pp.
188

NEWELL R. (1965) The role of detritus in the nutrition of two marine deposit feeders, the prosobranch *Hydro-*

bia ulvae and the bivalve *Malcoma balthica. Proc. Zool. Soc. Lond.* **144,** 25–45.
226

NIIMI A.J. (1972) Changes in the proximate body composition of largemouth bass (*Micropterus salmoides*) with starvation. *Can. J. Zool.* **50,** 815–819.
236

NIKOLSKY G.V. (1963a) *Ekologiya ryb.* Vysshaya Shkola Press, Moscow. 368 pp. [Translated into English in Nikolsky, 1963b.]
45, 46, 179, 186

NIKOLSKY G.V. (1963b) *The Ecology of Fishes.* Academic Press, London and New York. 352 pp. [Translation of Nikolsky, 1963a.]
46, 179, 186

NIKOLSKY G.V. (1965) *Teoriya dinamiki stada ryb kak biologicheskaya osnova ratsional'noi ekspluatapii i vosproizvodstva rybnykh resursov.* Nauka Press, Moscow. [Translated into English in Nikolsky, 1969.]
177

NIKOLSKY G.V. (1969) *Theory of Fish Population Dynamics as the Biological Background for Rational Exploitation and Management of Fishery Resources.* Oliver & Boyd, Edinburgh. 323 pp. (Translation of Nikolsky 1965.]
177, 178, 179

NITSCHE M., HEIN W. & ROHLER E. (1932) *Die Süsswasserfische Deutschlands.* Berlin. 89 pp.
109

NOBLE R.L. (1970) Evaluation of the Miller high-speed sampler for sampling yellow perch and walleye fry. *J. Fish. Res. Bd Can.* **27,** 1033–1044.
193, 195

NOMURA M. (1962) Stick-held dip net fishery in Japan. *Protok. FischTech.* **7,** 34, 330–348.
27

NOMURA S., IBARAKI T., HIROSE H. & SHIRAHATA S. (1972) Applications of backpack cardiotelemeter for fishes. I. Heart rate and cardiac reflex in fishes during unrestrained swimming. *Bull. Jap. Soc.*

scient. Fish. **38,** 1105–1117. Eng. trans. *Fish. Res. Bd Can. Transl. Ser.* 2438. 28 pp.
95

NORDEN C.R. (1967) Age, growth and fecundity of the alewife, *Alosa pseudoharengus* (Wilson), in Lake Michigan. *Trans. Am. Fish. Soc.* **96,** 387–393.
126

NORRIS J.S., NORRIS D.O. & WINDELL J.T. (1973) Effects of simulated meal size on gastric acid and pepsin secretory rates in bluegill (*Lepomis macrochirus*). *J. Fish. Res. Bd Can.* **30,** 201–204.
250

NOSE T. (1967) Recent advances in the study of fish digestion in Japan. In F.A.O. Symposium on *Feeding in Trout and Salmon Culture*, pp. 83–94 (Ed. J.L. Gaudet). *EIFAC tech. Pap.*, No. **3.** 94 pp.
240

NOVOTNY D.W. & PRIEGE G.R. (1974) Electrofishing boats improved designs and operational guidelines to increase the effectiveness of boom shockers. *Tech. Bull. Wis. Dep. nat. Resour.* **73.** 48 pp.
25, 26

NUNNALLEE E.P. (1974) *A hydroacoustic data acquisition and digital analysis system for the assessment of fish stock abundance.* Univ. Wash., Division of Mar. Resources, Seattle, WSG–74–2. 48 pp.
19

NYMAN L. (1965a) Species specific proteins in freshwater fishes and their suitability for a 'protein taxonomy'. *Hereditas* **53,** 117–126.
50, 51

NYMAN L. (1965b) Inter- and intraspecific variations of porteins in fishes. *K. svenska VetenskAkad. Årsb.* **9,** 1–18.
51

NYMAN L. (1975) Behaviour of fish influenced by hot water effluents as observed by ultrasonic tracking. *Rep. Inst. Freshwat. Res. Drottningholm* **54,** 63–74.
95

OLSEN S. (1959) Mesh selection in herring gill nets. *J. Fish. Res. Bd Can.* **16,** 339–349.
10, 11

OUCHI K. (1969) Effects of water temperature on the scale growth and width of the ridge distance in goldfish. *Bull. Jap. Soc. scient. Fish.* **35,** 25–31.
111

PALING J.E. (1971) Causes of mortality. In *Methods for Assessment of Fish Production in Fresh Waters*, pp. 249–258 (Ed. W.E. Ricker), IBP Handbook No. **3,** 2nd ed. Blackwell Scientific Publications, Oxford. 348 pp.
255

PALOHEIMO J.E. & DICKIE L.M. (1965) Food and growth of fishes. I. A growth curve derived from experimental data. *J. Fish. Res. Bd Can.* **22,** 521–542.
135, 243

PALOHEIMO J.E. & DICKIE L.M. (1966a) Food and growth of fishes. II. Effects of food and temperature on the relation between metabolism and body weight. *J. Fish. Res. Bd Can.* **23,** 869–908.
135, 243

PALOHEIMO J.E. & DICKIE L.M. (1966b) Food and growth of fishes. III. Relations among food, body size, and growth efficiency. *J. Fish. Res. Bd Can.* **23,** 1209–1248.
135, 243

PALOUMPIS A.A. (1958) Measurement of some factors affecting the catch in a minnow seine. *Proc. Iowa Acad. Sci.* **65,** 580–586.
28, 29

PANDIAN T.J. (1967a) Intake, digestion, absorption and conversion of food in the fishes *Megalops cyprinoides* and *Ophiocephalus striatus*. *Mar. Biol.* **1,** 16–32.
244

PANDIAN T.J. (1967b) Transformation of food in fish *Megalops cyprinoides*. I. Influence of quality of food. *Mar. Biol.* **1,** 60–64.
237, 244

PANNELLA G. (1974) Otolith growth patterns: an aid in age determination in temperate and tropical fishes. In *Ageing of Fish*, pp. 28–39 (Ed. T.B. Bagenal). Unwin Brothers, Old Woking. 234 pp.
113

PANTULU R.V. (1963) Studies on the age and growth, fecundity and spawning of *Osteogeneiosus militaris* (Linn.). *J. Cons. perm. int. Explor. Mer* **28,** 295–315.
176

PAPPAS C.J., TIEMEIER O.W. & DEYOE C.W. (1973) Chromix sesquioxide as an indicator in digestion studies on channel catfish. *Progve Fish Cult.* **35,** 97–98.
247

PARK Y.J. (1963) Illustrated review of Korean fishing gear. *Protok. FischTech.* **8,** 36, 85–130.
8

PARKER R.R. & LARKIN P.A. (1959) A concept of growth in fishes. *J. Fish. Res. Bd Can.* **16,** 721–745.
129, 135

PARR M.J., GASKELL T.J. & GEORGE B.J. (1968) Capture-recapture methods of estimating animal numbers. *J. Biol. Educ.* **2,** 95–117.
137

PARRISH B.B. (1956) The cod, haddock and hake. In *Sea Fisheries, their Investigation in the United Kingdom*, 251–331 (Ed. M. Graham). Edward Arnold (Publishers) Ltd, London. 487 pp.
101

PARRISH B.B. (Ed.) (1973) Fish stocks and recruitment. Proceedings of a symposium held in Aarhus, 7–10 July 1970. *Rapp. P.-v Réun. Cons. int. perm. Explor. Mer* **164.** 372 pp.
284

PARRISH B.B., BAXTER I.G. & MOWAT M.I.D. (1960) An automatic fish egg counter. *Nature, Lond.* **185,** 777.
169

PAULIK G.J. & ROBSON D.S. (1969) Statistical calculations for change-in-ratio estimators of population parameters. *J. Wildl. Mgmt* **33,** (1), 1–27.
139, 148, 149

PAYNE R.H., CHILD A.R. & FORREST A. (1971) Geographic variation in the Atlantic salmon. *Nature, Lond.* **231,** 250–252.
96

M

PELLA J.J. & TOMLINSON P.K. (1969) A generalised stock production model. *Bull. inter-Am. trop. Tuna Commn* **13**, (3), 421–496.
279

PEÑÁZ M. & TESCH F.W. (1970) Geschlechtsverhältnis und Wachstum beim Aal (*Anguilla anguilla*) an verschiedenen Lokalitäten von Nordsee und Elbe. *Ber. dt. wiss. Kommn Meeresforsch.* **21**, 290–310.
114, 120

PERKINS F.O. (1974) Phylogenetic considerations of the problematic thraustochytriaceous–labyrinthulid–Dermocystidium complex based on observations of fine structure. *Veröff. Inst. Meeresforsch. Bremerh.*, Suppl., **5**, 45–63.
267

PETTERS D.S. & HOSS D.E. (1974) A radioisotopic method of measuring food evacuation time in fish. *Trans. Am. Fish. Soc.* **103**, 626–629.
247, 249

PETERSEN C.G.J. (1896) The yearly immigration of young plaice into the Limfjord from the German Sea. *Rep. Dan. biol. Stn* **6**, 1–48.
86

PHILLIPS J.B. (1951) Lampara net-pulling gurdies. *Calif. Fish Game* **37**, 121–123.
29

PHILLIPSON J. (1964) A miniature bomb calorimeter for small biological samples. *Oikos* **15**, 130–139.
236

PHILLIPSON J. (1970) *Methods of Study in Soil Ecology*. UNESCO, Paris. 303 pp.
225

PHINNEY D.E. (1974) Growth and survival of fluorescent pigment-marked and fin-clipped salmon. *J. Wildl. Mgmt* **38**, 132–137.
86

PHINNEY D.E. & MATHEWS S.B. (1969) Field test of fluorescent pigment-marking and fin-clipping of coho salmon. *J. Fish. Res. Bd Can.* **26**, 1619–1624.
89

PHINNEY D.E. & MATHEWS S.B. (1973) Retention of fluorescent pigment by coho salmon (*Oncorhynchus kisutch*) after two years. *Progve Fish Cult.* **35**, 161–163.
89

PHINNEY D.E., MILLER D.M. & DAHLEBERG M.L. (1967) Mass marking of young salmonids with fluorescent pigment. *Trans. Am. Fish. Soc.* **96**, 157–162.
89

PIGGINS D.J. (1972) Cold branding as a smolt marking technique. *Fish. Mgmt* **3**, 9–11.
87

PILLAY T.V.R. (Ed.) (1973) *Coastal Aquaculture in the Indo-Pacific Region*. Fishing News (Books), London. 497 pp.
188

PIRIE N.W. (1955) Proteins. In *Modern Methods of Plant Analysis*, Vol. **4**, pp. 23–68 (Eds K. Paech & M.V. Tracy), Springer-Verlag, Berlin.
225

PITCHER T.J. & McDONALD P.D.M.A. (1973) A numerical integration method for fish population fecundity. *J. Fish Biol.* **5**, 549–554.
176

PITT T.K. (1964) Fecundity of the American plaice *Hippoglossoides platessoides* (Fabr.) from the Grand Bank and Newfoundland areas. *J. Fish. Res. Bd Can.* **25**, 2237–2240.
170, 176

PLETCHER F.T. (1968) A subcutaneous dart tag for fish. *J. Fish. Res. Bd Can.* **25**, 2237–2240.
94

PODDUBNYI A.G., SPEKTOR YU I. & KIDUN S.M. (1966) Results of the first experiments in tracking sturgeon carrying electronic tags. *J. Ichthyol.* **6**, 725–734.
95

POPE I.A., MILLS D.H. & SHEARER W.M. (1961) The fecundity of the Atlantic salmon (*Salmo salar* Linn.). *Freshwat. Salm. Fish Res.* **26**. 12 pp.
167, 174, 175, 176

POPE J.A. (1966) Manual of methods for fish stock assessment. Part III. Selectivity of fishing gear. *F.A.O. Fish. tech. Pap.*, No. **41**. 9 pp.
9, 11

Popova O.A. (1967) The 'predator-prey' relationship among fishes (a survey of soviet papers). In *The Biological Basis of Freshwater fish Production*, pp. 359–376 (Ed. Shelby D. Gerking). Blackwell Scientific Publications, Oxford. 495 pp.
222, 249

Potapova T.L., Lebedeva T.V. & Shatunovsky M.I. (1968) O raznokachestvennosti samok i ikry trekhigloi kolyushki—*Gasterosteus aculeatus* L. [Differences in the condition of females and eggs of the three-spined stickleback—*Gasterosteus aculeatus* L.] *Vop. Ikhtiol.* **8**, 184–187. [Translated in *Probl. Ichthyol.* **8**, 143–146.]
177

Poy A. (1970) Über das Verhalten der Larven von Knochenfischen beim Ausschlupfen aus dem Ei. *Ber. dt. wiss. Kommn Meeresforsch.* **21**, 377–392.
193

Prat J. & Giraud A. (1964) *The Pollution of Water by Detergents*. Organisation for Economic Co-operation and Development, Directorate of Scientific Affairs, Publ. No. **16601**. 86 pp.
272

Price C.A. (1965) A membrane procedure for the determination of the total protein in dilute algal suspensions. *Analyt. Biochem.* **12**, 213–218.
225

Price J.W. (1940) Time-temperature relations in the incubation of the whitefish, *Coregonus clupeaformis* (Mitchill). *J. gen. Physiol.* **23**, 449–468.
191, 192

Priede I.G. & Young A.H. (1977) The ultrasonic telemetry of cardiac rhythms of wild free-living brown trout (*Salmo trutta* L.), as an indicator of bioenergetics and behaviour. *J. Fish Biol.* **10**, 299–318.
95

Priegel G.R. (1964) Early scale development in the walleye. *Trans. Am. Fish. Soc.* **93**, 199–200.
108

Prokês M. (1975) Hand-stripping and embryonic development of *Coregonus peled* (G melin, 1788). *Zool. Listy* **24**, 185–196.
187

Radovich J. & Gibbs E.D. (1954) The use of a blanket net in sampling fish populations. *Calif. Fish Game* **40**, 353–365.
27

Raitt D.F.S. (1968) The population dynamics of the Norway Pout in the North Sea. *Mar. Res.*, 1968, No. **5**. 24 pp.
170, 175, 176

Raitt D.S. (1933) The fecundity of the haddock. *Scient. Invest. Fishery Bd Scotl.*, No. **1**, 1–42.
176

Rasalan S.B. & Datingaling B. (1956) Observations on fishing with light in the Philippines. (Abstract.) *Proc. Indo-Pacif. Fish. Coun.*, 6th Session, Tokyo, Japan, 1955, Sections II and III, 275.
36

Rauck G. (1975) A new technique of sawing otoliths. *Cons. perm. int. Explor. Mer Demersal Fish (Northern) Comm.*, C.M. F: 23.
114

Rauck G. (1976) A technique of sawing thin slices out of otoliths. *Ber. dt. wiss. Kommn Meeresforsch* **24**, 339–341.
114

Raymond H.L. (1974) State of the art of fish branding. *Mar. Fish. Rev.* **36**, 1–6.
87

Reay P.J. (1972) The seasonal pattern of otolith growth and its application to back-calculation studies in *Ammodytes tobianus* L. *J. Cons. perm. int. Explor. Mer* **34**, 485–504.
120, 124

Redkozubov Yu.N. (1966) Press dlya polucheniya otpechatkov cheshui ryb. [A press for obtaining impressions of fish scales.] *Ryb. Khoz.* **42**, 3, 23.
109

Regier H.A. (1962) Validation of the scale method for estimating age and growth of bluegill. *Trans. Am. Fish. Soc.* **91**, 362–374.
111, 214

Regier H.A., Cordone A.J. & Ryder R.A. (1971) Total fish landings from fresh waters as a function of limnological variables with special reference to lakes of East Central Africa. Fish stock assessment on African inland waters. *F.A.O. Working Paper* No. 3, FI: SF/GHA 10 Rome. 285

REGIER H.A. & ROBSON D.S. (1966) Selectivity of gill nets, especially to lake whitefish. *J. Fish. Res. Bd Can.* **23**, 423–454. 10

REGIER H.A. & ROBSON D.S. (1967) Estimating population number and mortality rates. In *The Biological Basis of Freshwater Fish Production*, 31–36 (Ed. Shelby D. Gerking). Blackwell Scientific Publications, Oxford. 495 pp. 12, 138

REIBISCH I. (1899) Über die Eizahl bei *Pleuronectes platessa* und die Altersbestimmung dieser Form aus den Otolithen. *Wiss. Meeresunters.* **4**, 231–248. 168

REICHENBACH-KLINKE H.H. (1973) *Fish Pathology*. T.F.H. Publications Inc., Neptune, New Jersey. 512 pp. 267

REID G.K. (1955) The pound-net fishery in Virginia. Part 1. History, gear description, and catch. *Comml Fish. Rev.* **17**, 5, 1–15. 36

RIBELIN W.E. & MIGAKI G. (Eds) (1973) *The Pathology of Fishes*. University of Wisconsin Press, Madison. 1004 pp. 269

RICHARDS F.J. (1959) A flexible growth function for empirical use. *J. exp. Bot.* **10**, 290–300. 135

RICKER W.E. (1946) Production and utilization of fish populations. *Ecol. Monogr.* **16**, 373–391. 203, 237

RICKER W.E. (1949) Mortality rates in some little-exploited populations of freshwater fishes. *Trans. Am. Fish Soc.* **77**, 114–128. 12, 26

RICKER W.E. (1954) Stock and recruitment. *J. Fish. Res. Bd Can.* **11**, 559–623. 165, 257, 284

RICKER W.E. (1958) Handbook of computations for biological statistics of fish populations. *Bull. Fish. Res. Bd Can.*, No. **119**. 300 pp. 137, 207, 278

RICKER W.E. (1969) Effects of size-selective mortality and sampling bias on estimates of growth, mortality, production and yield. *J. Fish. Res. Bd Can.* **26**, 479–541. 125, 136

RICKER W.E. (1973) Linear regressions in fishery research. *J. Fish. Res. Bd Can.* **30**, 409–434. 122, 127, 176, 234

RICKER W.E. (1975) Computation and interpretation of biological statistics of fish populations. *Bull. Fish. Res. Bd Can.* **191**. 382 pp. 101, 122, 127, 129, 131, 134, 135, 137, 140, 156, 161, 275

RICKER W.E. & FOERSTER R.E. (1948) Computation of fish production. *Bull. Bingham Oceanogr. Coll.* **11**, 4, 173–211. 178, 200, 211

RICKER W.E. & LAGLER K.F. (1942) The growth of spiny-rayed fishes in Foots Pond, Indiana. *Invest. Indiana Lakes Streams* **2**, 85–97. 123

RICKER W.E. & MERRIMAN D. (1945) On the methods of measuring fish. *Copeia*, **1945**, 184–191. 43

RIEDEL D. (1965) Some remarks on the fecundity of *Tilapia* (*T. mossambica* Peters) and its introduction into Middle Central America (Nicaragua) together with a contribution towards limnology of Nicaragua. *Hydrobiologia* **25**, 357–388. 173

RIETHMILLER R.H. (1948) Efficiency of the fyke test net in determining fish populations of Mt. Gilead Lake. Paper presented to *Tenth Midwest Wildlife Conference*, Ann Arbor, Mich, Dec. 9–11. 7 pp. 38

RILEY G.A. (1970) Particulate organic matter in sea water. *Adv. mar. Biol.* **8**, 1–118. 225

RILEY J.D. (1966) Liquid latex marking technique for small fish. *J. Cons. perm. int. Explor. Mer* **30**, 354–357. 88, 89

RINNE J.N. (1976) Coded spine clipping to identify individuals of spiny-rayed Tilapia.

J. Fish. Res. Bd Can. **33**, 2626–2629. 86

ROBSON D.S. (1971) Statistical methods for a tag-recapture experiment on a population closed to recruitment. Preliminary report. *Biometrics Unit, Cornell University, Ithaca, N.Y.*, BU–374–M. 11 pp. 156

ROBSON D.S. & CHAPMAN D.G. (1961) Catch curves and mortality rates. *Trans. Am. Fish. Soc.* **91**, 181–189. 158, 159, 161

ROBSON D.S. & REGIER H.A. (1964) Sample size in Petersen mark-recapture experiments. *Trans. Am. Fish. Soc.* **93**, 215–226. 140

ROBSON D.S. & REGIER H.A. (1968) Estimation of population number and mortality rates. In *Methods for Assessment of Fish Production in Fresh Waters*, 2nd edition, pp. 131–165 (Ed. W.E. Ricker), IBP Handbook No. 3, Blackwell, Oxford. 348 pp. 140, 143, 144

ROBSON D.S. & YOUNGS W.D. (1971) Statistical analysis of reported tag recaptures in the harvest from an exploited population. *Biometrics Unit, Cornell University, Ithaca, N.Y.*, BU–369–M. 15 pp. 161

ROLLEFSEN G. (1954) Observations on the cod and cod fisheries of Lofoten. *Rapp. P.-v. Réun. Cons. perm. int. Explor. Mer* **136**, 40–47. 116

ROTH H. & GEIGER W. (1961) Die Fortpflanzung der Forelle im Bach und in der Brutanstalt. *Schweiz. FischZtg.* **69**, 60. 183, 192

ROTHSCHILD B.J. (1961) Production and survival of eggs of American smelt, *Osmerus mordax* (Mitchill), in Maine. *Trans. Am. Fish. Soc.* **90**, 42–48. 152, 184, 200

ROTHSCHILD B.J. (1963) Graphic comparisons of meristic data. *Copeia*, **1963**, 601–603. 62

ROUNSEFELL G.A. & EVERHART W.H. (1953) *Fishery Science: its Methods and Applica-*

tions. J. Wiley and Sons, New York. 444 pp. 101, 112, 154

ROYCE W.F. (1942) Standard length versus total length. *Trans. Am. Fish. Soc.* **71**, 270–274. 43

ROYCE W.F. (1954) Preliminary report on a comparison of the stocks of yellow fin tuna. *Proc. Indo-Pacif. Fish. Coun.* **4**, 130–145. 63

ROYCE W.F. (1972) *Introduction to the Fishery Sciences.* Academic Press, New York. 351 pp. 137, 258

ROZIN P. & MAYER J. (1964) Some factors influencing short-term food intake of the goldfish. *Am. J. Physiol.* **206**, 1430–1436. 232

RUSSELL-HUNTER W.D. (1970) *Aquatic Productivity: An Introduction to some Basic Aspects of Biological Oceanography and Limnology.* Collier-MacMillan, London. 306 pp. 225

RUSTAD J.T., *et al.* (1961) *A Report Concerning Electronic Aids to Navigation for the Fisheries and Other Users.* Norway, Ministry of Fisheries and Ministry of Defence, Committee to Investigate the Demands for Electronic Navigational Aids for the Fisheries and other Users. 80 pp. 8

RYDER R.A. (1965) A method for estimating the fish production of north-temperate lakes. *Trans. Am. Fish. Soc.* **94**, 214–218. 285

SAROKON J.A. (1975) Feeding frequency, evacuation, absorption, growth and energy balance in rainbow trout, *Salmo gairdneri.* Ph.D. thesis, University of Colorado, Boulder. 236

SAUNDERS R.L. (1968) An evaluation of two methods of attaching tags to Atlantic

salmon smolts. *Progve Fish Cult.* **30**, 104–109.
93

SAUNDERS R.L. & ALLEN K.R. (1967) Effects of tagging and fin clipping on the survival and growth of Atlantic salmon between smolt and adult stages. *J. Fish. Res. Bd Can.* **24**, 2595–2611.
98, 118

SAVILLE A. (1964) Estimation of the abundance of a fish stock from egg and larval surveys. *Rapp. P.-v. Réun. Cons. perm. int. Explor. Mer* **155**, 164–170.
151

SAVITZ J. (1969) Effect of temperature and body weight on endogenous nitrogen excretion in the bluegill sunfish (*Lepomis macrochirus*). *J. Fish. Res. Bd Can.* **26**, 1813–1821.
244

SAVITZ J. (1971a) Nitrogen excretion and protein consumption of the bluegill sunfish (*Lepomis macrochirus*). *J. Fish. Res. Bd Can.* **28**, 449–451.
244

SAVITZ J. (1971b) Effects of starvation on body protein utilization of bluegill sunfish (*Lepomis macrochirus* Rafinesque) with a calculation of calorific requirements. *Trans. Am. Fish. Soc.* **100**, 18–21.
244

SCARRATT J. & ELSON P.F. (1965) Preliminary trials of a tag for salmon and lobsters. *J. Fish. Res. Bd Can.* **22**, 421–423.
94

SCHAEFER M.B. (1954) Some aspects of the dynamics of populations important to the management of commercial marine fisheries. *Bull. inter-Am. trop. Tuna Commn* **1**, (2), 26–56.
278, 279

SCHAEFER M.B. (1957) A study of the dynamics of the fishery for yellow fin tuna on the eastern tropical Pacific Ocean. *Bull. inter-Am. trop. Tuna Commn* **2**, (6), 247–283.
278, 279

SCHÄPERCLAUS W. (1954) *Fischkrankheiten* (3rd Edition). Berlin, Akademie Verlag. 708 pp.
267

SCHÄPERCLAUS W. (1961) *Lehrbuch der Teichwirtschaft*. P. Parey, Berlin. 582 pp.
192

SCHARFE J. (1972) *FAO Catalogue of Fishing Gear Designs*. Fishing News (Books) Ltd, London. 155 pp. Revision of 1965 ed.
8

SCHIEMENZ F. (1943) Fischfang durch Sprengung. *Fischereizeitung, Neudamn* **46**, 14–15, 1–8.
24

SCHIEMENZ F. (1953) Das Verhalten der Fische, insbesondere die Konkurrenz von reflektorischen und psychischen Reaktionen, bei der Elektrofischerei. *Z. Fisch.* **1**, 369–372.
24

SCHIEMENZ F. & SCHÖNFELDER A. (1927) Fischfang mit Elektrizität. *Z. Fisch.* **25**, 161–187.
24

SCHINDOWSKI E. & TESCH F.W. (1957) Methodisches zur Wachstumsrückberechnung, erläutert am Beispiel von *Lucioperca sandra* Cuv. u. Val., *Perca fluviatilis* L. und *Salmo trutta fario* L. *Z. Fisch.* (N.F.), **5**, 247–267.
122

SCHLIEPER C. (1968) *Methoden der Meeresbiologischen Forschung*. VEB G. Fischer, Jena. 322 pp.
182

SCHMIDT W. (1968) Vergleichend-morphologische Studie über die otolithen mariner Knockenfische. *Arch. FischWiss.* **19** (1 Beiheft), 1–96.
112

SCHNABEL Z.E. (1938) The estimation of the total fish population of a lake. *Am. math. Mon.* **45**, 348–352.
142

SCHOFFMAN R.J. (1954) Age and growth of the channel catfish in Reelfoot Lake, Tennessee. *J. Tenn. Acad. Sci.* **29**, 1.
115

SCHOTT J.W. (1965) A visual aid for age determination of immersed otoliths. *Calif. Fish Game* **51**, 56.
114

SCHUCK H.A. (1942) The effect of jaw-tagging on the condition of trout. *Copeia*, **1942**, 33–49.
95

SCHULZ H. (1965) Der Photowiderstand ORP 63 in der Mikrophotographie. *Mikrokosmos* **54**, 2, 57–62.
114

SCHWOERBEL J. (1966) *Methoden der Hydrobiologie*. Kosmos Franckh, Stuttgart. 207 pp.
182

SCIDMORE W.J. & OLSON D.F. (1969) Marking walleye fingerlings with oxytetracycline antibiotic. *Progve Fish Cult.* **31**, 213–216.
90

SCOFIELD W.L. (1951a) An outline of California fishing gear. *Calif. Fish Game* **37**, 361–370.
8, 22

SCOFIELD W.L. (1951b) Purse seines and other roundhaul nets in California. *Fishery Bull. Calif.*, No. **81**. 83 pp.
29

SCOTT D.B.C. (1974) The reproductive cycle of *Mormyrus kannume* Forsk. (Osteoglossomorpha, Mormyriformes) on Lake Victoria, Uganda. *J. Fish Biol.* **6**, 447–454.
46

SCOTT D.P. (1962) Effect of food quantity on fecundity of rainbow trout *Salmo gairdneri*. *J. Fish. Res. Bd Can.* **19**, 715–731.
168, 177

SCOTT W.W. (1964) Fungi associated with fish diseases. *Devs ind. Microbiol.* **5**, 109–123.
267

SEABURG K.G. & MOYLE J.B. (1964) Feeding habits, digestion rates, and growth of some Minnesota warmwater fishes. *Trans. Am. Fish. Soc.* **93**, 269–285.
249

SEBER G.A.F. (1965) A note on the multiple-recapture census. *Biometrika* **42**, 249–259.
145

SEBER G.A.F. (1970) Estimating time-specific survival and reporting rates for adult birds from band returns. *Biometrika* **57**, 313–318.
161

SEBER G.A.F. (1973) *The Estimation of Animal Abundance and Related Parameters*. Griffin, London. 506 pp.
137, 140, 143, 145, 149, 152, 153, 155, 156, 161

SEBER G.A.F. & LE CREN E.D. (1967) Estimating population parameters from catches large relative to the population. *J. Anim. Ecol.* **36**, 631–643.
154

SEGERSTRÅLE C. (1933) Über scalimetrische Methoden zur Bestimmung des linearen Wachstums bei Fischen insbesondere bei *Leuciscus idus* L., *Abramis brama* L. und *Perca fluviatilis* L. *Acta. zool. fenn.* **15**, 1–169.
123

SETTE O.E. & AHLSTROM E.H. (1948) Estimations of abundance of the eggs of the Pacific pilchard (*Sardinops caerulea*) off southern California during 1940 and 1941. *J. mar. Res.* **7**, 511–542.
181

SHAKESPEARE H. (1962) *Secrets of Successful Fishing*. Dell Publishing Co. Inc., New York. 200 pp.
22, 23

SHARPE F.P. (1964) An electrofishing boat with a variable voltage pulsator for lake and reservoir studies. *Circ. Bur. Sport Fish Wildl.*, No. **195**, 6 pp.
25, 26

SHETTER D.S. (1938) A two-way fish trap for use in studying stream-fish migrations. *Trans. 3rd N. Am. Wildl. Conf.*, 331–338.
197

SHETTER D.S. (1967) Effects of jaw tags and fin exision upon growth, survival and exploitation of hatchery rainbow trout fingerlings in Michigan. *Trans. Am. Fish. Soc.* **96**, 394–399.
118

SHIRAHATA S. (1966) Note on the feeding of rainbow trout in relation to forced culture. In F.A.O. Symposium on *Feeding in Trout and Salmon Culture*, pp. 73–82 (Ed.

J.L. Gaudet). *EIFAC tech. Pap.*, No. 3. 94 pp.
250

SHIRAISHI Y. & FURUTA Y. (1963) Estimation of the distribution and stock number of fishes in Lake Ashinoko, Kanagawa Prefecture from the records of the fish-finder. *Bull. Freshwat. Fish. Res. Lab. Tokyo* **13**, 57–76.
19

SICK K. (1961) Haemoglobin polymorphism in fishes. *Nature, Lond.* **192**, 894–896.
51, 96

SILLIMAN R.P. (1969) Comparison between Gompertz and von Bertalanffy curves for expressing growth in weight of fishes. *J. Fish. Res. Bd Can.* **26**, 161–165.
129

SIMKISS K. (1974) Calcium metabolism of fish in relation to ageing. In *Ageing of Fish*, pp. 1–12 (Ed. T.B. Bagenal). Unwin Brothers, Old Woking. 234 pp.
102

SIMPSON A.C. (1951) The fecundity of the plaice. *Fishery Invest. Lond.*, Ser. 2, **17**, 5. 27 pp.
168, 169, 170, 171, 176

SIMPSON A.C. (1959a) Method used for separating and counting the eggs in fecundity studies on the plaice (*Pleuronectes platessa*) and herring (*Clupea herengus*). *Occ. Pap. F.A.O. Indo-Pacif. Fish. Coun.*, No. 59/12.
169, 171

SIMPSON A.C. (1959b) The spawning of the plaice in the North Sea. *Fishery Invest. Lond.*, Ser. 2, **22**, 7. 111 pp.
166

SINDERMANN C.J. (1961) Parasite tags for marine fish. *J. Wildl. Mgmt* **25**, 41–47.
96

SINGH C. & NOSE T. (1967) Digestibility of carbohydrates in young rainbow trout. *Bull. Freshwat. Fish. Res. Lab.*, *Tokyo* **17**, 831–835.
241

SINHA V.R.P. & JONES J.W. (1967) On the age and growth of the freshwater eel (*Anguilla anguilla*). *J. Zool.* **153**, 99–117.
114

'SINKER' (1952) Line fishing gear and methods. *Wld Fishg* **1**, 120–126.
22

SMITH B.W. & LOVELL R.T. (1971) Digestibility of nutrients in semi-purified rations by channel catfish in stainless steel troughs. *Proc. 25th a. Conf. SEast. Ass. Game Fish. Commn.*
241

SMITH B.W. & LOVELL R.T. (1973) Determination of apparent protein digestibility in feeds for channel catfish. *Trans. Am. Fish. Soc.* **102**, 831–835.
241

SMITH L.L., FRANKLIN D.R. & KRAMER R.H. (1959) Electro-fishing for small fish in lakes. *Trans. Am. Fish. Soc.* **88**, 141–146.
26

SMITH L.S. & BELL G.R. (1975) A practical guide to the anatomy and physiology of Pacific salmon. *Misc. spec. Publs Fish. Mar. Serv. Can.* **27**. 14 pp.
259, 263

SMITH O.R. & AHLSTROM E.H. (1948) Echo-ranging for fish schools and observations on temperature and plankton in waters off central California in the spring of 1946. *Spec. scient. Rep. U.S. Fish Wildl. Serv. Fisheries*, No. 44. 31 pp.
19

SMITH S.H. (1954) Method of producing plastic impressions of fish scales without using heat. *Progve Fish Cult.* **16**, 75–78.
109

SMITH S.H. (1956) Life history of lake herring of Green Bay, Lake Michigan. *Fishery Bull. Fish. Wildl. Serv. U.S.* **57**, 87–138.
125

SMYLY W.J.P. (1957) The life history of the bullhead or Miller's thumb (*Cottus gobio* L.). *Proc. zool. Soc. Lond.* **128**, 431–453.
169

SNEDECOR G.W. & COCHRAN W.G. (1967) *Statistical Methods*. Iowa State University Press, Ames, Iowa. 593 pp. (6th Edition.)
13, 122

SNIESZKO S.F. (1972) Nutritional fish diseases. In *Fish Nutrition*, pp. 403–437

(Ed. J.E. Halver). Academic Press, New York.
256

SNIESZKO S.F. (1974) The effects of environmental stress on outbreaks of infectious diseases of fishes. *J. Fish Biol.* **6,** 197–208.
257

SOKAL R.R. & ROHLF F.J. (1967) *Biometry.* W.H. Freeman and Company, San Francisco. 776 pp.
224

SOKAL R.R. & SNEATH P.H.A. (1963) *Principles of Numerical Taxonomy.* W.H. Freeman, San Francisco and London. 359 pp.
63

SOLOMON D.J. & BRAFIELD A.E. (1972) The energetics of feeding, metabolism and growth of perch (*Perca fluviatilis* L.). *J. Anim. Ecol.* **41,** 699–718.
228, 234

SPENCER E.Y. (1973) Guide to the chemicals used in crop protection. *Research Branch, Canada Dept. of Agriculture.* Publication 1093, 6th edition. 543 pp.
272

STAINTON M.P., CAPEL M.J. & ARMSTRONG F.A.J. (1977) The chemical analysis of fresh water. *Misc. spec. Publs Fish. Mar. Serv. Can.*, 2nd Ed., No. **25.** 166 pp.
271

STARRETT W.C. & BARNICKOL P.G. (1955) Efficiency and selectivity of commercial fishing devices used on the Mississippi River. *Bull. Ill. St. nat. Hist. Surv.* **26,** 325–366.
23

STASKO A.B. (1975) Annotated bibliography of underwater biotelemetry. *Tech. Rep. Fish. mar. Serv. Can.* **534.** 31 pp.
95

STAUFFER T.M. & HENSEN M.J. (1969) Mark retention, survival and growth of jaw-tagged and fin-clipped rainbow trout. *Trans. Am. Fish. Soc.* **98,** 225–229.
118

STUART T.A. (1953) Spawning migration, reproduction and young stages of loch trout. *Freshwat. Salm. Fish. Res.* **5,** 1–39.
182

STUART T.A. (1958) Marking and regeneration of fins. *Freshwat. Salm. Fish. Res.* **22,** 1–14.
85

STEEL R.G.D. & TORRIE J.H. (1960) *Principles and Procedures of Statistics.* McGraw-Hill, New York. 481 pp.
62

SUNSHINE I. (Ed.) (1969) *Handbook of Toxicology.* The Chemical Rubber Co., Cleveland, Ohio. 1081 pp.
271

STRUHSAKER P. & UCHIYAMA J.H. (1976) Age and growth of the nehu, *Stolephorus purpureus* (Pisces: Engraulidae), from the Hawaiian Islands as indicated by daily growth increments of sagittae. *Fishery Bull. Seattle* **74,** 9–17.
113

SULLIVAN J.L. & ROBERTS R.J. (1975) Expert witnesses and environmental legislation. *J. Air Pollut. Control Ass.* **25,** 353–361.
261

SUVOROV E.K. (1948) *Osnovy ikhtiologii* [*Foundations of ichthyology.*] Sovetskaya Nauka Press, Moscow. [For German version see Suworow, 1959.]
101

SUWOROW E.K. (1959) *Allgemeine Fischkunde.* Deutscher Verlag der Wissenschaften. 581 pp.
101

SUZUKI K. (1967) Age and growth of *Limanda yokohamae* (Günther) in Ise Bay. *Rep. Fac. Fish. Univ. Mie* **6,** 17–27.
Fig. 5.13

SVÄRDSON G. (1949) Natural selection and egg number in fish. *Meddn. St. Unders.-o. ForsAnst SotvattFisk.* **29,** 115–122.
166

SWAIN A. (1974) The efficiency of certain types of smolt tags and tagging techniques adopted by the Ministry of Agriculture, Fisheries and Food. *Fish. Mgmt* **5,** 67–71.
93, 98

SWENSON W.A. & SMITH L.L. (1973) Gastric digestion, food consumption, feeding periodicity, and food conversion efficiency in walleye (*Stizostedion vitreum vitreum*).

J. Fish. Res. Bd Can. **30**, 1327–1336.
253

SYCH R. (1970) Elements of the theory of age determination of fish according to scales. The problem of validity. *Papers of the 6th Session of EIFAC*, No. 70/SC I–3. 67 pp. [Polish version in *Roczn. Nauk. roln.* (H)], **93**, 7–73.
111

SYCH R. (1974) The sources of errors in ageing fish and considerations of the proofs of reliability. In *Ageing of Fish*, pp. 78–86 (Ed. T.B. Bagenal). Unwin Brothers, Old Woking. 234 pp.
111

TAKAYAMA S. (1956) Fishing with light in Japan. *Proc. Indo-Pacif. Fish. Coun.*, 6th Session, Tokyo, Japan, 1955, Sections II and III, 276–277.
36

TANAKA S. (1962) A method of analysing a polymodel frequency distribution and its application to the length distribution of the porgy, *Taius tumifrons* (T. and S.). *J. Fish. Res. Bd Can.* **19**, 1143–1159.
116

TÅNING A.V. (1938) Method for cutting sections of otoliths of cod and other fish. *J. Cons. perm. int. Explor. Mer* **13**, 213–216.
114

TAYLOR C.C. (1958) A note on Lee's phenomenon in Georges Bank haddock. *Spec. Publ. int. Commn NW. Atlant. Fish.* **1**, 243–251.
125, 136

TARZWELL C.M. (Ed.) (1965) Biological problems in water pollution. *3rd Seminar*, *U.S. Public Health Service, Publ.* 999–WP–25. 424 pp.
257

TEMPLEMAN W. & FLEMING A.M. (1963) Distribution of *Lernaeocera branchialis* L. on cod as an indicator of cod movements in the Newfoundland area. *Spec. Publs int. Commn NW. Atlant. Fish.* **4**, 318–322.
96

TESCH F.W. (1955) Das Wachstum des Barsches (*Perca fluviatilis* L.) in verschiedenen Gewässern. *Z. Fisch.* (N.F.) **4**, 321–420.
110, 111

TESCH F.W. (1956a) Percidenwachstum in eutrophen norddeutschen Flachseen. *Z. Fisch.* (N.F.) **4**, 321–420.
117

TESCH F.W. (1956b) Über Unterschiede in der Häufigkeit des Auftretens von regenerierten Schuppen bei der Bachforelle (*Salmo trutta fario* L.) unter verschiedenen unweltverhältnissen. *Biol. Zbl.* **75**, 625–631.
107

TESCH F.W. (1962) Witterungsabhängigkeit der Brutentwicklungs und Nachwuchsförderung bei *Lucioperca lucioperca* L. *Kurze Mitt. Inst. FischBiol. Univ. Hamburg.* **12**, 37–44.
117

TESCH F.W. (1977) *The Eel.* Chapman & Hall, London. (English translation from the German edition.)
120

TESTER A.L. (1941) A modified scale projector. *Trans. Am. Fish. Soc.* **70**, 98–101.
109

THOMAS A.E. (1975) Marking channel catfish with silver nitrate. *Progve Fish Cult.* **37**, 250–252.
87

THOMPSON H. (1923) Problems in haddock biology with special reference to the validity and utilization of the scale theory. *Rep. Fishery Bd Scotl.*, 1922, No. 5. 78 pp.
124, 125

THORPE J.E. (1975) Monel versus silver wire for the attachment of disc tags to trout. *Fish. Mgmt* **6**, 42–43.
93

THORSEN K.N. (1967) A new high speed tagging device. *Calif. Fish Game* **53**, 289–292.
94

THREINEN C.W. (1956) The success of a seine in the sampling of a largemouth bass population. *Progve Fish Cult.* **18**, 81–87.
28, 29

TIBBO S.N., SCARRATT D.J. & McMULLON P.W.G. (1963) An investigation of herring

(*Clupea harengus* L.) spawning using free-diving techniques. *J. Fish. Res. Bd Can.* **20**, 1067–1079.
184

TOMPKINS W.A. & BRIDGES C. (1958) The use of copper sulfate to increase fyke-net catches. *Progve Fish Cult.* **20**, 16–20.
35, 38

TRACY H.B. & BERNHARDT J.C. (1973) Guidelines for evaluating fish kill damages and computing fish kill damage claims in Washington State. *State of Washington, Department of Ecology, Tech. Rep.*, No. **72-10**.
260

TRAVERSY W.J. (1971) *Methods for Chemical Analysis of Waters and Waste Waters.* Environment Canada, Inland Waters Directorate, Water Quality Branch, Ottawa. 169 pp.
261

TREFETHEN P.S. (1956) Sonic equipment for tracking individual fish. *Spec. scient. Rep. U.S. Fish Wildl. Serv.* **179**. 11 pp.
95

TROJNAR J.R. (1973) Marking rainbow trout fry with tetracycline. *Progve Fish Cult.* **35**, 52–54.
90

TSUYUKI H. & ROBERTS E. (1965) Zone electrophonetic comparison of muscle myogens and blood proteins of artificial hybrids of salmonidae with their parental species. *J. Fish. Res. Bd Can.* **22**, 767–773.
51

TSUYUKI H. & ROBERTS E. (1966) Interspecific relationships within the genus *Oncorhynchus* based on biochemical systematics. *J. Fish Res. Bd Can.* **23**, 101–107.
50, 51

TSUYKI H., ROBERTS E. & VANSTONE W.E. (1965) Comparative zone electrophoresis of muscle myogens and blood haemoglobins of marine and freshwater vertebrates and their applications to biochemical systematics. *J. Fish. Res. Bd Can.* **22**, 203–213.
51

TULLY J.P. (1954) Conditions for troll fishing. *Prog. Rep. Pacif. Cst Stns* **101**, 12–16.
23

TUNNISON A., BROCKWAY D., MAXWELL J., DORR A. & MCCOY C. (1942) Protein utilization by brook trout. *Fish. Res. Bull. N.Y.*, No. 4, The Nutrition of Trout. Cortland Hatchery Rep. No. **11**, 24–42.
240

TURNER S.E., PROCTOR G.W. & PARKER R.L. (1974) Rapid marking of rainbow trout. *Progve Fish Cult.* **36**, 172–174.
87

TYLER A.V. (1970) Rates of gastric emptying in young cod. *J. Fish. Res. Bd Can.* **27**, 1177–1189.
250

UMALI A.F. (1950) Guide to the classification of fishing gear in the Philippines. *Res. Rep. U.S. Fish. Wildl. Serv.* **17**. 165 pp.
8

UNESCO (1968) Zooplankton sampling. *UNESCO Monogr. Oceanogr. Methodol.* **2**. 174 pp.
182

UTTER F.M., HODGINS H.O. & ALLENDORF F.W. (1974) Biochemical genetic studies of fishes: Potentialities and limitations, pp. 213–238. In *Biochemical and Biophysical Perspectives in Marine Biology* (Eds D.C. Malins & J.R. Sargeant), Vol. **1**. Academic Press, New York.
51

VAN COILLIE R. (1967) Etude à l'aide de tetracyclines de la croissance periodique des écailles de téléostéens. *Naturatiste can.* **94**, 29–58.
111

VAN LEEUWEN P.I. (1972) A new method for treating plaice (*Pleuronectes platessa*) gonads in order to facilitate the estimation of egg production. *Aquaculture* **1**, 135.
168

VAN OOSTEN J. (1929) Life history of the lake herring (*Leucichthys artedii* LeSueur) of Lake Huron, as revealed by its scales, with a critique of the scale method. *Bull.*

Bur. Fish., Wash. **44**, 265–448.
125

VAN OOSTEN J. (1936) Logically justified deductions concerning the Great Lakes fisheries exploded by scientific research. *Trans. Am. Fish. Soc.* **65**, 71–75.
35

VAN OOSTEN J. (1953) A modification in the technique of computing average lengths from the scales of fishes. *Progve Fish Cult.* **15**, 85–86.
124

VAN OOSTEN J.H., DEASON J. & JOBES F.W. (1934) A microprojector machine designed for the study of fish scales. *J. Cons. perm. int. Explor. Mer* **9**, 241–248.
109

VAN SOMEREN V.D. & WHITEHEAD P.J. (1959) Methods of marking *Tilapia* spp. (Pisces: Cichlidae). *Nature, Lond.* **183**, 1747–1748.
86

VAN UTRECHT W.L. & SCHENKKAN E.J. (1972) On the analysis of the periodicity in the growth of scales, vertebrae and other hard structures in a teleost. *Aquaculture* **1**, 299–316.
114

VASNETSOV V.V. (1953a) Etapy razvitiya kostistykh ryb. [Developmental Stages of Young Fishes.] Pp. 207–217 in *Ocherki po obshchim voprosam ikhtiologii*. Akademiya Nauk Press, Moscow. 320 pp.
125

VIBERT R. (Ed.) (1967) *Fishing with Electricity. Its Application to Biology and Management*. Fishing News (Books) Ltd, London. 276 pp.
24, 25

VLADIMIROV V.I. (Ed.) (1965) *Vliyanie kachestva proizvoditelei na potomstvo u ryb*. [*Influence of Quality of Parents on their Progeny among Fishes*.] Akademiya Nauk Ukrainskoi SSR. 143 pp. Naukova Dumka Press, Kiev.
177

VLADIMIROV V.I. (1970) Raznokachestvennost' ontogeneza kak odin iz faktorov dinamiki chislennosti stada ryb. [Quality differences during ontogenesis as one of the factors in the dynamics of abundance

of fish stocks.] *Gidrobiol. Zh.* **6**, 2, 14–27.
177

VON BERTALANFFY L. (1938) A quantitative theory of organic growth. *Hum. Biol.* **10**, 181–243.
129

VON BRANDT A. (1962) Midwater Trawling. *Fishing News International*, January 1962, 1–3.
32

VON BRANDT A. (1964) *Fish Catching Methods of the World*. Fishing News (Books) Ltd, London. 191 pp.
8

VOVK F.I. (1956) [Methods for reconstructing a fish's growth from its scales.] *Trudy biol. Sta. Borok* **2**.
124, 125

WAGNER C.C. & COOPER E.L. (1963) Population density, growth and fecundity of the creek chubsucker *Erimyzon oblongus*. *Copeia*, 1963, 350–357.
168

WALLIN O. (1957) On the growth structure and development physiology of the scale of fishes. *Rep. Inst. Freshwat. Res. Drottningholm* **38**, 385–477.
111

WARD F.J. & VERHOEVEN L.A. (1963) Two biological stains as markers for sockeye salmon. *Trans. Am. Fish. Soc.* **92**, 379–383.
89

WARE D.M. (1975a) Growth, metabolism, and optimal swimming speed of a pelagic fish. *J. Fish. Res. Bd Can.* **32**, 33–41.
235, 243

WARE D.M. (1975b) Relation between egg size, growth, and natural mortality of larval fish. *J. Fish. Res. Bd Can.* **32**, 2503–2512.
136

WARNER K. (1971) Effects of jaw tagging on growth and scale characteristics of landlocked Atlantic salmon, *Salmo salar*. *J. Fish. Res. Bd Can.* **28**, 537–542.
95

WARREN C.E. & DAVIS G.E. (1967) Laboratory studies on the feeding, bioenergetics,

and growth of fish. In *The Biological Basis of Freshwater Fish Production*, pp. 175–214 (Ed. Shelby D. Gerking). Blackwell Scientific Publications, Oxford. 495 pp.
228, 229, 235, 236, 243

WATERS T.F. (1969) The turnover ratio in production ecology of freshwater invertebrates. *Am. Nat.*, 103, 930, 173–185.
216, 217

WATSON M.E., GUENTHER R.W. & ROYCE R.D. (1956) Hematology of healthy and virus-diseased sockeye salmon, *Oncorhynchus nerka. Zoologica, N.Y.* 41, 27–38.
269

WEATHERLY A.H. (1972) *Growth and Ecology of Fish Populations*. Academic Press, London. 293 pp.
129, 228, 242, 257

WEATHERLY A.H. (1976) Factors affecting maximization of fish growth. *J. Fish. Res. Bd Can.* 33, 1046–1058.
242

WEBER D. & RIDGWAY G.J. (1962) The deposition of tetracyline drugs in bones and scales of fish and its possible use for marking. *Progve Fish Cult.* 24, 150–155.
90, 105

WEBER D. & RIDGWAY G.J. (1967) Marking Pacific salmon with tetracycline antibiotics. *J. Fish. Res. Bd Can.* 24, 849–865.
90

WEBER D. & WAHLE R.J. (1969) Effect of fin clipping on survival of sockeye salmon (*Oncorhynchus nerka*). *J. Fish. Res. Bd Can.* 26, 1263–1271.
86, 90

WEDERMEYER G. (1970) Stress of anaesthesia with MS–222 and benzocaine in rainbow trout (*Salmo gairdneri*). *J. Fish. Res. Bd Can.* 27, 909–914.
99

WEDEMEYER G., MEYER F.P. & SMITH L. (1976) Environmental stress and fish disease. In *Diseases of Fishes* (Eds S.F. Snieszko & H.R. Axelrod), Book 5. T.F.H. Publications Inc., New Jersey. 192 pp.
257

WELCOMME R.L. (1967) The relationship between fecundity and fertility in the mouth-brooding cichlid fish *Tilapia leucosticta. J. Zool.* 151, 453–468.
173

WELCOMME R.L. (Ed.) (1975) Symposium on the methodology for the survey, monitoring and appraisal of fishery resources in lakes and large rivers. Panel reviews and relevant papers. *EIFAC tech. Pap.*, No. 23, Suppl. 1, in 2 vols. 747 pp.
278

WELCOMME R.L. (1976) Some general and theoretical considerations on the fish yield of African rivers. *J. Fish. Biol.* 8, 351–364.
285

WENNER C.A. & MUSICK J.A. (1974) Fecundity and gonad observations of the American eel, *Anguilla rostrata*, migrating from Chesapeake Bay, Virginia. *J. Fish. Res. Bd Can.* 31, 1387–1391.
169

WEYMOUTH F.W. & MCMILLIN H.C. (1931) The relative growth and mortality of the Pacific razor clam (*Siliqua patula* Dixon), and their bearing on the commercial fishery. *Bull. Bur. Fish., Wash.* 46, 543–567.
129

WHALLS M.J., PROSHEK K.E. & SHETTER D.S. (1955) A new two-way fish trap for streams. *Progve Fish Cult.* 17, 103–109.
37

WHITLEATHER R.T. & BROWN H.H. (1945) *An Experimental Fishery Survey in Trinidad, Tobago and British Guiana with Recommended Improvements in Methods and Gear*. Anglo-American Caribbean Commission, Washington D.C. 130 pp.
8

WIBORG K.F. (1951) The whirling vessel. *Rep. Norw. Fishery mar. Invest.* 9, 1–16.
170

WICKETT W.P. (1954) The oxygen supply to salmon eggs in spawning beds. *J. Fish. Res. Bd Can.* 11, 933–953.
179

WIGLEY R.L. (1952) A method of marking larval lampreys. *Copeia* 1952, 203–204.
88

WILIMOVSKY N.Y. (1963) A radioactive internal tag for herring. *Spec. Publs int. Commn NW. Atlant. Fish.* **4**, 359–361.
91

WILLIAMS T. (1967) A method of measuring headless fish. *J. Cons. perm. int. Explor. Mer* **31**, 279–283.
41

WILLIAMS T. & BEDFORD B.C. (1974) The use of otoliths for age determination. In *Ageing of Fish*, pp. 114–123 (Ed. T.B. Bagenal). Unwin Brothers, Old Woking. 234 pp.
104, 114

WILSON J.G.M. (1976) Immunological aspects of fungal disease in fish. In *Recent Advances in Aquatic Mycology* (Ed. E.B. Gareth-Jones). Paul Elek (Scientific Books) Ltd, London. 749 pp.
267

WILSON R.C. (1953) Tuna marking, a progress report. *Calif. Fish Game* **39**, 429–442.
94

WINBERG G.G. (1956) *Rate of Metabolism and Food Requirements of Fishes*. Belorussian State University, Minsk. (Translated from Russian by Fish. Res. Bd Can. Transl. Ser. No. **194**, 1960.)
233, 235, 242

WINBERG G.G. (1971) *Methods for the Estimation of Production of Aquatic Animals*. Academic Press, London. 174 pp.
237

WINDELL J.T. (1966) Rate of digestion in the bluegill sunfish. *Invest. Indiana Lake Streams* **7**, 185–214.
248

WINDELL J.T. (1967) Rates of digestion in fishes. In *The Biological Basis of Freshwater Fish Production*, pp. 151–173. (Ed. Shelby D. Gerking.) Blackwell Scientific Publications, Oxford. 495 pp.
231, 249, 250, 252

WINDELL J.T. (1968) Food analysis and rate of digestion. In *Methods for Assessment of Fish Production in Fresh Waters*, pp. 197–203, 1st ed. (Ed. W.E. Ricker). Blackwell Scientific Publications, Oxford. 313 pp.
248

WINDELL J T. (1971) Food analysis and rate of digestion. In *Methods for Assessment of Fish Production in Fresh Waters*, pp. 215–226. 2nd ed. (Ed. W.E. Ricker). Blackwell Scientific Publications, Oxford. 348 pp.
248

WINDELL J.T., NORRIS D.O., KITCHELL J.F. & NORRIS J.S. (1969) Digestive response of rainbow trout, *Salmo gairdneri*, to pellet diets. *J. Fish. Res. Bd Can.* **26**, 1801–1812.
248

WINSOR C.P. (1932a) The gompertz curve as a growth curve. *Proc. natn Acad. Sci. U.S.A.* **18**, 1–8.
129

WINSOR C.P. (1932b) A comparison of certain symmetrical growth curves. *J. Wash. Acad. Sci.* **22**, 73–84.
129

WINTERS G.H. (1971) Fecundity of the left and right ovaries of the Grand Bank capelin (*Mallotus villosus*). *J. Fish. Res. Bd Can.* **28**, 1029–1033.
170

WOLF K. (1970) Guidelines for virological examination of fishes. In *A Symposium on Diseases of Fishes and Shellfishes* (Ed. S.F. Snieszko). *Spec. Publs Am. Fish Soc.*, No. **5**, Washington D.C. 526 pp.
265, 270, 271

WOLF K. (1972) Advances in fish virology: a review 1966–1971. In *Diseases of Fish*, pp. 305–331 (Ed. L.E. Mawdesley-Thomas). *Symp. Zool. Soc. Lond.*, No. **30**. Academic Press, London. 380 pp.
267

WOLF P. (1951) A trap for the capture of fish and other organisms moving downstream. *Trans. Am. Fish. Soc.* **80**, 41–45.
20, 37, 197

WOLFERT D.R. (1969) Maturity and fecundity of walleyes from the eastern and western basins of Lake Erie. *J. Fish. Res. Bd Can.* **26**, 1877–1888.
172, 176

WOLKE R.E. (1975) Pathology of bacterial and fungal diseases affecting fish. In *The Pathology of Fishes*, pp. 33–116 (Ed. W.E. Ribelin & G. Migaki). University of Wisconsin Press, Madison. 1004 pp.
267

WOOD J.W. (1974) *Diseases of Pacific Salmon their Prevention and Treatment.* 2nd edition. State of Washington, Dept. of Fisheries. 82 pp.
267

WOOLAND J.V. & JONES J.W. (1975) Studies on the grayling *Thymallus thymallus* (L.) in Llyn Tegid and the upper River Dee, North Wales. I. Age and growth. *J. Fish Biol.* **7**, 749–773.
120

WOYNARÓWITCH E. (1955) Neuere Methoden der künstlichen Vermehrung von Süswassernutzfischen in Ungarn. *Dt. FischZtg, Radebeul* 1955, 311–316, 335–336, 357–367.
187

WOYNARÓWITCH E. (1961) Ausreifen von Karpfenlaich in Zuger-Gläsern und Aufzucht der Jungfische bis rum Alter von 10 Tagen. *Allg. FischZtg*, **86**, 680–682.
187

YASUTAKE W.T. (1975) Fish viral diseases: clinical, histopathological and comparative aspects. In *The pathology of Fishes*, pp. 247–271 (Ed. W.E. Ribelin & G. Migaki). University of Wisconsin Press, Madison. 1004 pp.
270

YOUNG A.H., TYTLER P., HOLLIDAY F.G.T. & MACFARLANE A. (1972) A small sonic tag for measurement of locomotor behaviour in fish. *J. Fish Biol.* **4**, 57–65.
95

YOUNG P.H. (1950) Netting bait and cannery fish with the aid of lights. *Calif. Fish Game* **36**, 380–381
35

YOUNGS W.D. (1974) Estimation of the fraction of anglers returning tags. *Trans. Am. Fish. Soc.* **103**, 616–618.
162

YOUNGS W.D. & ROBSON D.S. (1975). Estimating survival rate from tag returns. Model tests and sample size determination. *J. Fish. Res. Bd Can.* **32**, 2365–2371.
161

ZAMACHAEV D.F. (1941) K metodike rastshisslenia roste treski po otolitam. [A method for calculation of the growth of cod.] *Zool. Zh.* **20**, 258–266.
120

ZIPPIN C. (1956) An evaluation of the removal method of estimating animal populations. *Biometrics* **12**, 163–189.
152, 154

ZIPPIN C. (1958) The removal method of population estimation. *J. Wildl. Mgmt* **22**, 82–90.
152

ZITKO V. & CHOI P.M.K. (1971) PCB and other industrial halogenated hydrocarbons in the environment. *Tech. Rep. Fish. Res. Bd Can.*, No. **272**. 55 pp.
272

ZUROMSKA H. (1961) Wzrost okonia (*Perca fluviatilis* L.) w jeziorach okolic Węgorzewa. [Growth of perch in lakes of the Węgorzewo district.] *Rocz. Nauk roln*, 77–B(2), 603–639. (English and Russian summaries.)
123

ZUROMSKA H. (1966) A method of marking hatched roach (*Rutilus rutilus* L.) with biological stain. *Ekol. pol.*, Ser. B, **12**, 73–76.
89

Index